Theo-
logy
&
Life

In Pursuit of Love

Catholic Morality
and
Human Sexuality

by

Vincent J. Genovesi, S.J.

A Michael Glazier Book
THE LITURGICAL PRESS
Collegeville, Minnesota

About the Author

Vincent J. Genovesi, S.J., received his Ph.D. in Christian Ethics from Emory University. He is currently Professor of Theology at St. Joseph's College in Philadelphia. His articles have appeared in such scholarly journals as *Theological Studies, The Thomist, The Way,* and *The American Ecclesiastical Review.* His books include *The Dynamism of Christian Hope: A Liberating and Shaping Element in Ethical Reflection;* and *Expectant Creativity: The Action of Hope in Christian Ethics.*

A Michael Glazier Book
published by
THE LITURGICAL PRESS

Scriptural quotations are from *The Jerusalem Bible,* copyright 1966, 1967 and 1968 by Darton, Longman & Todd Ltd, and Doubleday & Company, Inc.

Typography by Connie Runkel. Cover design by Lillian Brulc.

5	6	7	8	9

Library of Congress Cataloging-in-Publication Data

Genovesi, Vincent J.
    In Pursuit of love : Catholic morality and human sexuality / by Vincent J. Genovesi.
        p.   cm.
    "A Michael Glazier book."
    Reprint. Originally published: Wilmington, Del. : M. Glazier, 1986. (Theology and life series ; v. 18).
    Includes bibliographical references.
    ISBN 0-8146-5590-4
    1. Sex—Religious aspects—Catholic Church. 2. Christian ethics—Catholic authors. 3. Catholic Church—Doctrines. I. Title.
    II. Series: Theology and life series ; v. 18.
    BX1795.S48G46 1991
    241'.66—dc20   91-3384
                                                                        CIP

Contents

To My Students,
Past and Present,
At
Saint Joseph's University

Preface

This book has grown out of my experience as a professional educator working mainly with Catholic university students and with Catholic adults interested in furthering their understanding of what impact their Christian faith might and should have upon their efforts at living morally. Clearly, then, the book is meant for non-specialists in the area of theology. It is not presented, however, as a textbook on Catholic moral principles or teaching, but rather as an aid to provoking analysis, discussion and further investigation. Throughout the book, my intention is to chart some of the details of the moral course being drawn by a number of theologians who have been influential in shaping Roman Catholic thinking about the meaning and implications of Christian ethics. Obviously and necessarily, however, Catholic authors today are in dialogue with representatives of other Christian traditions whose insights we will also have to attend to in our own reflections.

As this book took shape I found myself further strengthened in my conviction that the ethical study of Christian living reaches out in two directions: its spirit and vitality are rooted in biblical theology; and in the articulation of its conclusions it touches closely upon both the comfort and the challenge associated with ascetical or spiritual theology and the guidance this provides for a person's growth in the life of God. Too often, I think, writings in Christian ethics have attempted to shape people's external behavior without enflaming their hearts. I regard such attempts as somewhat misconceived and inevitably incomplete.

When speaking either of theory or of practice, this book tries to address both the human mind and heart. Regarding theory, my plan is to develop in some detail the ideas presented in the following scenario describing the movement of a person who is intent upon living morally as a Christian. We will first look at the meaning of morality and then seek to uncover the spirit which gives spark to the special character and shape of Christian morality. If it makes sense to suggest that our Christian lives should take shape around the biblical command that we are to love God with all our being and our neighbor as ourselves (Mt. 22:34-40), then we should also acknowledge the fact that our calling to love comes to us from a God who already loves us deeply. In a real sense, then, the love with which we live as Christians is an expression of gratitude for the love we have been shown by God.

Our lives, moreover, are marvelously blessed by God, for it is precisely through the faithful observance of our call to love that we are empowered to work with Christ in the establishment of our Father's kingdom. While we engage in this work well aware of the reality and power of human sinfulness with which we must struggle, we are at the same time also deeply moved by God's invitation to us to live no longer simply as servants but as friends, as people, in other words, who no longer feel the need to grasp at salvation in fear and trembling, but rather can enjoy the liberty which is the expression and fruit of God's life within us, and which enables us to labor out of love.

In the freedom which we experience as sons and daughters of God, Christians are called to live prophetically and thus to challenge those worldly values which stand in opposition to the message of Christ. To live as prophets, however, is no easy task and pseudo-prophecy is no stranger to history. For this reason, we must seriously involve ourselves in the development of a well-informed conscience which will serve as an indispensable aid in our effort to lead authentic Christian lives. It happens, however, that the dictates of personal conscience will not infrequently cast our lives into some turmoil because of the tensions stirred up by disagreements among well-intentioned and even well-informed individuals and groups. For Roman Catholics, the state of tension may be further heightened when, as sometimes happens, a well-developed conscience beckons an individual to move in one direction, while the very articulate and very insistent hierarchical voice of the magisterium is engaged in its official teaching capacity and summons that same individual to move in another. Disconcerting as this experience undoubtedly is, it is also often unavoidable, given the state of theological thinking today.

In the book's later chapters where the practical concerns of some specific moral issues are addressed, the topics of discussion center, for the most part, around personal sexual morality. An analysis of the meaning of human sexuality provides the setting for an investigation into the moral questions surrounding premarital sex, marital sexuality and contraception, homosexuality and masturbation. The book's final chapter moves somewhat beyond the realm of sexual concerns and addresses the life-and-death issue of abortion.

The selection of these particular topics for moral discussion deserves some explanation. The reader should realize, first of all, that my choice of these specific issues as subject matter for ethical analysis in no way reflects a judgment on my part that these matters are, or should be, the only, or even the most important, moral questions of concern to Christians today. Not for a moment do I believe such to be the case. As Christians we are undeniably confronted with other major moral problems and dilemmas as we labor to live responsibly as citizens of a society and inhabitants of a world which appear either to ignore totally the gospel of Christ or to heed it only haphazardly and selectively.

Any Christian who is unconcerned about the establishment of social justice by means of a persistent struggle against the varied forms of political, military, economic, racial and sexual oppression in the world has failed, I fear, to unravel the meaning and mystery of Christ's new and radical command that we are to love one another as he has first loved us

(Jn. 15:12). My selection, therefore, of the specific moral issues treated in this book is not meant to dichotomize the realms of personal and social morality; both God's expectation that we live as lovers and our accountability in meeting that expectation necessarily transcend such a dichotomy. My choice of topics simply reflects my conviction that the moral issues presented here are quite pertinent. Many Christians remain puzzled and in doubt about them. These doubts and questions they give rise to, I deem worthy of attention.

I write as a Roman Catholic, and yet the tone of this book may perhaps be different from that at times reflected in the official moral documents of the Church. Whatever the form of moral teaching undertaken, it seems to me imperative that the faithful must clearly sense that their difficulties and life-struggles are understood and appreciated; only then are they likely to retain their basic good will and be more inclined to hear what is said as possibly an echo of the gospel. I must acknowledge here that on specific points of moral teaching I present and discuss views different from the traditional position of the Roman Catholic Church; the reader should understand, however, that the questioning expressed by theologians does not in itself invalidate the official teaching of the Church; clearly, the magisterium, as the authentic teaching body in Roman Catholicism, enjoys the presumption of truth in its pronouncements so that if ever a Catholic undertakes to differ with an official Church teaching, this may never be done lightly or facilely, but only cautiously, conscientiously, prayerfully and respectfully.

In discussing the specific moral issues every attempt is made to distinguish between what the Roman Catholic Church presents as official moral teaching and what theologians offer as personal opinion or theological speculation. Not to acknowledge this distinction would surely be misleading; but to try somehow to deny that there is such a distinction by presenting only the Church's authoritative moral doctrine, would be a disservice to the reader whom I envision as someone interested enough and intelligent enough to comprehend some of the major complexities to be faced in any attempt to live not only morally as a Christian, but also faithfully as a member of the Roman Catholic community.

Any book on Christian ethics must remain sensitive to the truth that Christianity fundamentally is a way of living, a way of love; the spirit of Christ and of Christians can never be understood, and indeed is distorted, when any attempt is made to compress it into a static ethical code. This fact seems to have been forgotten by those generations of textbook manuals of moral theology which did little or nothing to impress the faithful with this foundational truth: that even the Old Testament's Law of Moses came to light only within the living context of a personal dialogue that was initiated by Yahweh out of concern for those whom he loved.

My hope is that through this book the reader will be encouraged to look beyond the window dressings of Christianity, for there is nothing in a window but well-attired, yet lifeless, mannequins. The music, the drama, the life and treasury of Christianity lie elsewhere. Just as we never spend money while looking in a window, so too we will never spend ourselves or get others to spend themselves on a lifeless law. But to live out of love — well, this is another motivation, another struggle, and a whole other story, one that begins with our Father's eternal love for us. As Christians, we believe that this story took on flesh in Jesus Christ who walked among us so that we might come to know the touch of our Father's love. The tale is still being told, and if it is to be brought to a happy conclusion, we must surely be careful not to alter the story line, for we have "only one Teacher, the Christ" (Mt. 23:10), who by God's doing, "has become our wisdom, and our virtue, and our holiness, and our freedom" (1 Cor. 1:30).

In the preparation of this book I realize not only that I have consciously borrowed from some writers, but also that I have been unconsciously influenced by others. My appreciation extends to all, even as I seek forgiveness from those who may be slighted or neglected in my acknowledgments. Let me also express my gratitude to all those who have through the years shared with me both their knowledge and their faith. In so many instances, far more than their words, their very lives have given testimony to their realization that as Christians we must, above all else, stand tall but humbly before the gospel of Christ. It is from this vantage point that the faithful are most encouraged not only to love truth, but also to struggle in its pursuit, and to dare to contemplate its implications.

I offer some words of special thanks to my former students at Saint Joseph's University. They probably little realize how important a role they have played for more than a decade in the shaping and refinement of these reflections on Christian morality. It is not enough to say simply that I have learned from my students, for while it is true that their questions have frequently challenged me, so also have their interest and vitality often thrilled me, their goodness humbled me and their faith inspired me. In all these ways, they have kept me mindful of both the privilege and the responsibility involved in teaching. And, quite simply, thanks to these students, teaching remains a joy.

As my work on this book draws to a close, I gladly acknowledge my indebtedness to those who have helped make its completion possible. I offer my thanks to James J. Neville, S.J., the Acting Chairman of the Theology Department at Saint Joseph's University, who graciously managed the arrangements for my leave of absence from teaching during the spring semester of 1986. Also, I am most grateful to Joseph L. Lombardi, S.J., Richard A. McCormick, S.J., Ladislas Örsy, S.J., William C. Spohn, S.J., Martin R. Tripole, S.J., and Edward C. Vacek, S.J., who so kindly agreed to read all or parts of the manuscript and who offered me the invaluable benefit of their pastoral sensitivity and their philosophical and theological insight and learning. Many others of my Jesuit brothers and superiors have my gratitude for their untiring encouragement and support. Finally, for their patience and fine work, I sincerely thank Mrs. Ruth Malinowski, Catherine McSherry and Janet Jackson who typed various parts of the manuscript.

I

The Meaning and Spirit of Christian Living

I. Introduction

Over the years I have perhaps taken a bit too much delight in the confused and somewhat incredulous expressions which often appear on the faces of students in my Christian ethics course when, on the first day of class, I ask them whether their interest in living morally as good Christians ever costs them any sleep. Once they have recovered from the obvious impertinence of the question, most students, of course, usually lose no time in professing their earnest desire both to be ethical and to live good Christian lives. In the ensuing discussions, however, it quickly becomes apparent that if any meaningful dialogue is to occur, some agreement on a definition or explanation of terms is imperative.

For this reason, then, we will attempt to do several things in this chapter. To begin with, an effort must be made to arrive at some reasonable understanding of what is generally meant by "ethics" or "morality." Once this is done, we will try to indicate how the broad notion of "ethics" or "morality" is further specified when considered from the perspective of Christianity. And yet, while a basic and obvious concern of this chapter is to establish and deepen our appreciation of the meaning and spirit of Christian ethics, we hope to show that as an academic endeavor, Christian ethics is scarcely more than sustained and systematic reflection upon the meaning of Christianity with a view to indicating what expectations and practical implications any serious commitment to Christian living entails. To the extent that the authenticity of Christian ethics would seem, then, to be derived from the accuracy of its understanding of the Christian life itself, our aim and intention must be to identify and explore some of the data provided by faith and by theological investigation, which seem best able to explain not only the meaning of Christian living, but also its vitality and motivating dynamism.

Without supposing that it is possible to capture or express the spirit of Christian living in all its richness, I suggest, nonetheless, that a good deal of insight into its beauty and spark might be gained from looking at the Christian life in the following ways: as an acknowledgment of, and affirmative response to, God's calling us to love; as a eucharistic endeavor manifesting our gratitude for all that we are in God and for all that we have received from him; as an eschatological involvement in the building up of God's kingdom; as a life of faith which is active in love; and, finally, as a responsible exercise of the freedom offered us by Christ through participation in the life of the Holy Spirit. Overall, what I trust will become clear in the course of this chapter is that, for us as Christians, there is a definite, even unavoidable, connection between the attempt to live ethically or as morally good people, and the struggle for holiness, personal spiritual growth or growth in the Spirit of God.

II. *Understanding Morality: General and Christian*

THE MEANING OF ETHICS

Although the words "morality" and "ethics" are often used interchangeably, they may also be employed in a more nuanced way to indicate a distinction between the activity of "lived" experience and the intellectual reflection associated with an academic enterprise. In the context of this distinction, it might be said in general that "morality" is what we live, whereas "ethics" is what we study. Thus, as human beings we may be engaged in the ongoing effort to live good lives, which is to say that we are striving to live in a "morally" appropriate way. If however, we hope to stay on course in this endeavor, it is frequently necessary that we carefully direct our attention to specific questions like "how ought I to act in such a situation," or "what is the right thing to do in such circumstances." Insofar as we are caught up in a systematic consideration of such questions, we may be said to be involved with ethics; we are engaged, in other words, in the study of ethics.

Precisely as an area of academic interest, ethics may be defined as the study of morality, a reflective investigation into what is the morally proper thing to do. But then, of course, we must immediately ask what is meant by "morality," or what makes a course of action "morally" proper. In response to such questions, we might suggest that morality or the practice of morally good and appropriate actions is the routine which embodies our efforts to become ever more truly and fully human, and to live accordingly. In other words, living morally, or the practice of morality, is the expression of our desire to live as full and authentic human beings. The struggle to be moral is, in effect, nothing other than the ongoing pursuit of our true human destiny.

The necessity of describing morality as a striving for "true" or "authentic" humanity, or as an attempt to realize our "true" human destiny, arises from the fact that, given our freedom as human beings, it is quite possible for us to live out our humanity in a false or inauthentic way. Any of us can freely take it upon ourselves to live our lives in ways which we simply ought to avoid. Here, then, is the sad paradox: human beings can live in falsely human ways, in ways, even, that must be seen as inhuman, at least in the sense that they contradict the meaning of true humanity. Hence we must insist that it is the fostering of our "true" or "authentic" humanity which serves as the reference point or criterion in trying to determine what is right or wrong from the viewpoint of morality. The same point might also be expressed as follows: the effort to be moral is simply an attempt to be true to our authentic nature as human beings, whereas the decision to live in an immoral way constitutes a betrayal of our authentic human nature and a denial of the true selves which we are called to be. In an unavoidable sense, to live immorally, then, is to be engaged in a process of true self-violation, self-frustration and, ultimately, self-destruction.

Whatever is immoral is such only insofar as it expresses our free decisions to live in ways which are inhuman or falsely human. The fact that we can say no to our real nature and destiny as human beings reveals perhaps the most serious implication of the truth that each of us individually can indeed be our own worst enemy. Whatever our other achievements and successes in the eyes of the world, to the extent that any of us can destroy ourselves by failing precisely as human beings, we have no need of other foes. If our privileged status as human beings is linked to the fact that we have the ability to consciously and freely pursue our true destiny, we must immediately acknowledge that such a status is easily jeopardized, for it is not enough to say simply that as human beings we can be actively and freely involved in the realization of our true calling; rather, note should be made of the fact that we also must be so involved. And yet the truth remains: because we are not forced or interiorly programmed to pursue our true destiny as human beings, because, in other words, we have been granted the gift of personal freedom, and because this prized possession can be misused, as human beings we are empowered to live in ways that betray the true meaning and purpose of our humanity. As human beings, then, we have, quite simply, the capacity not only to ruin ourselves but also to perpetrate "man's inhumanity to man."

Up to this point, we have suggested that, as a field of study, ethics tries to guide us in our efforts to live good moral lives, lives, that is, which reflect the true meaning of humanity and hence are directed toward the realization of our true destiny. One further observation seems pertinent here: the realization of our true destiny or the fulfillment of our authentic human nature is also the only experience that ultimately brings us lasting joy as human beings. It is sensible, therefore, to suggest that in making the effort to be moral, we are at the same time walking the pathway not only to real human fulfillment, but also to true happiness.[1] Of course, saying simply that ethics tries to guide us in our movement toward the fulfillment of our true human nature, reveals absolutely nothing of the real meaning of humanity or of the destiny to which we are called. It is to this issue, therefore, that we now turn our attention. Our specific concern is to arrive at a fuller understanding and appreciation of the true meaning and destiny of humanity as perceived in the Christian tradition.

LOCATING CHRISTIAN ETHICS

To speak rather generally, we might say that Christian ethics is an attempt to articulate in a rather systematic and consistent way the structure and characteristics of a lifestyle that is in keeping with the basic insights and values of the Judeo-Christian tradition. Of course, both Christian ethics itself and those who profess to be Christians seem fully convinced of the fact that in striving to be good Christians, people are at the same time living in a manner which is indeed conducive to their development as true human beings and hence to the realization of their human destiny. But what is the reason for this fundamental conviction? The explanation is rooted, it seems to me, in what are some of the essential affirmations of the Christian faith.

While specific formulations may vary, I think it is fair to say that in professing to be Christians, we owe allegiance to some basic assertions. We confess that there is a God known to us as Father, who so loves and cares for us that he literally enfleshed himself in humanity in the person of his Son, Jesus Christ. What is simply remarkable about this Christ, this God our brother, is his complete responsiveness to the Father, who, as creator of all things, knows fully the meaning of our humanity, and offers this knowledge to all who will listen. Christ does

[1] Vincent E. Rush, *The Responsible Christian. A Popular Guide for Moral Decision Making According to Classical Tradition* (Chicago: Loyola University Press, 1984), p.88.

indeed listen and he learns so well that he uniquely embodies the rich truth and fulness of human existence. In full filial openness, Christ is moved by his Father's interests, his concerns, his values and the universal extent of his love. And thus, just as the Father is Father of all, so Christ, as the first-born of a new order of creation, is no less expansive; he is the redeemer and lover of all, the one through whom all of us are ultimately empowered to enjoy the company of our God forever.

For us as Christians, Jesus Christ is obviously unique. We know and affirm no one else to be both fully divine and really human. Because of his divinity, Christ could indeed fully and deeply learn the true meaning of humanity; at the same time, however, because of his real humanness, Christ's struggle to incarnate the full richness of humanity was undeniable. Were Christ not fully divine, we might indeed question the validity of his understanding of the true meaning of humanity; likewise, however, were Christ not really human, we could scarcely be inclined to regard him as a model, for in no way could he inspire in us the courage needed to meet the challenges which are invariably involved in any effort to grow as human beings.

Here, then, is the state of affairs: because Christ is really divine and really human, because he learned well the meaning of humanity and embodied that meaning in a uniquely rich way, we, as Christians, are fully confident that in following the life and teaching of Jesus Christ, we are not only maturing as Christians but are also developing as true human beings. Our understanding and appreciation of our true human destiny are invariably linked, then, to the person and life of Jesus Christ, the divine-human person who "has been tempted in every way that we are, though he is without sin" (Heb. 4:15). The temptations experienced by Jesus Christ merit our attention because they are revelatory not only of the character of this unique individual, but also of the very nature of temptation itself.

As recounted in the Gospels of Matthew (4:1-11), Mark (1:12-13) and Luke (4:1-13), shortly after Jesus' baptism when a heavenly voice was heard to say of him, "You are my Son, the Beloved; my favor rests on you" (Lk. 3:22), Jesus retreated into the wilderness where the devil tried to persuade him to live in a manner other than that desired and intended by his heavenly Father. In various ways Christ was brought face to face with the temptation to be not the kind of Messiah and Savior the Father called him to be, but rather, one more in keeping with the expectations and ways of the world. Thus in place of the prospect of spending himself selflessly in the love and service of others, Jesus was tempted through the devil's urgings to focus attention on himself by assuming the manner and methods of earthly rulers—the accumulation of material possessions, the achievement of social and political prestige, the exercise of military might.

In a very fundamental way, by rejecting the devil's suggestions and choosing to remain in compliance with his Father's will, Jesus reveals his appreciation of the fact that both moral goodness of character and the realization of our destiny are discovered only by positive reference to the intention and design which God our Father has for us. Jesus' experience with the temptations in the wilderness also illustrates an important point about the very nature of all the temptations which we face as human beings: every temptation, every inclination to the evil which is sin, is nothing more than our attraction to being other than our Father intends us to be (cf. Mt. 16:23). When we yield to temptation and sin, we are immoral; and this is to say, quite simply, that we are taking a stand against our true humanity, and are acting in a way that is unresponsive to our human calling and destiny as determined by God.

Given the fact that as Christians we acknowledge no ultimate disparity or present conflict between the effort to be truly human and the desire to be good Christians, we naturally expect that as a way of realizing our God-given destiny, we can do no more and no better than to pattern our lives according to the life and teachings of Jesus Christ. In listening to Jesus articulate his understanding of the purpose and meaning of his own life, we, therefore, learn something that is obviously and profoundly revelatory of the meaning and purpose of our own lives, both as human beings and as Christians.

Clearly, Jesus does not refrain from testifying about the purpose of his life. He tells us, for example, that he has come from heaven, not to do his own will, but to do the will of the Father who sent him (Jn. 6:38); indeed, in doing his Father's will and in thus completing the work assigned to him, Jesus claims to find his strength and vitality (Jn. 4:34). Going further, Jesus indicates just what his Father's will for him entails when he says that he has come among us not to be served but to serve, "and to give his life as a ransom for many" (Mk. 10:45). Jesus, of course, realizes that it is only by his life of service in keeping with the Father's will that he can accomplish what both the Father and he desire and intend, namely, that we "may have life and have it to the full" (Jn. 10:10).

However Christ voiced his own understanding of himself and his life, we know that, at root, his presence among us was a labor of love; his life was not only an expression of his own love for us, but also a manifestation of the love our Father bears for us. It was precisely by his love, his life of caring service, his complete "being for others," that Jesus succeeded both in showing us the way, and in making it possible for us, to be what God our Father has called us to be. And this means, quite simply, that it is through love that we have been redeemed. If there is any truth, then, to the idea that as Christians we are expected to be actively involved in the ongoing mission of Christ, it seems clear that we can meet this expectation only by choosing to let our own lives be formed in the spirit of Christ's love. If love, indeed, finally explains the life of the divine-human being, Jesus Christ, it also embodies the challenge of Christian living and reveals the secret of humanity in light of which all our attempts to be moral must take shape.

The revelation of Jesus' life and love serves effectively to uncover our roots and to remind us that our true destiny is born in our beginnings, since as Christians we affirm not only that all human beings are formed in the image of God (Gen. 1:26-7), but also that God is love (1 Jn. 4:8). Made in the likeness of God, we are meant to be reflections of his love; created out of love, we are called to love. We grow, then, in moral goodness and in true humanity only by our striving to be God-like lovers. And as Christians, we believe, of course, that we have been infinitely gifted in our efforts to love as God does, because we are guided by Jesus Christ in whom we find the truly human face and form of God.

III. Christian Life: Recognizing Our Call to Love

Our discussion of Christian living up to this point has indicated that the way in which we lead good moral lives and hence express the true meaning of our humanity is by remaining constant in our efforts to embody the kind of love which God expects of us and which we see reflected in the life of Christ. Bernard Häring affirms the essence of this idea in his suggestion that Christian morality or the practice of the Christian life is simply "fidelity to the human vocation to love."[2] As human beings, our destiny lies in loving; called to be lovers, then, we can only conclude that all of our specifically human attributes—our intelligence, our freedom, our emotions—are to be put into the service of love. Mindful not only of our own personal destiny, but also of the fact that this destiny is shared in company with others, as Christians, we meet the challenge of living as moral human beings only by faithfully pursuing the ways of love and by enabling and encouraging others to do the same.

Because we are created for love, nothing else can fulfill us ultimately, and lacking fulfillment, we cannot be truly happy. In light of our destiny, our only chance for lasting happiness is our persistent willingness to love. At the same time, however, the thought might also be suggested that to whatever extent we have learned the art and secret of loving, the practice of moral living becomes, as it were, natural to us, for we are now doing nothing other than what we have been made to do.[3]

In affirming, as we have, that we are created in the image of God and thus are called to be lovers, we also acknowledge the fact that as human beings, it is not we who determine what it is or means to be truly human. Rather, God does, and it is he who initiates our destiny by inscribing in our hearts the only law which reveals the true meaning and purpose of humanity and draws us toward the fulfillment of our nature. The law referred to here is, of course, the law of love; it is this law which is the most fundamental law of our human nature. As such, the law of

[2]Bernard Häring, *Morality Is for Persons. The Ethics of Christian Personalism* (New York: Farrar, Straus and Giroux, 1971), p.125.

[3]Rush, *op.cit.*, pp. 86-7.

love is never cast aside with impunity, for in refusing to love, we deny our true humanity, and this takes its toll in terms of our own self-frustration and ultimate self-destruction.

We might better appreciate the significance of this point by considering it in the context of the laws of physical nature which govern the well-being of our bodies. At times, we may try to deny the physical laws of our nature by acting in ways which seem either to pretend that such laws do not exist, or to claim that while others may indeed need to concern themselves with these laws, we, at least, are certainly not bound by them. Usually, however, it is not long before we are confronted with the error of our ways. Should I, for example, decide to take a walk out of a second-storey window, I am immediately brought face-to-face with the demands made upon me by the law of gravity. Likewise, my physical system is not immune to the effects of ingested poison, nor can I blithely disregard my body's need for proper nutrition, sleep and hygiene. Ignoring the physical laws of nature to which my body is subject is nothing less than a form of self-violation which ends, sooner or later, in self-destruction.[4]

The point to be emphasized, however, is that just as there is more to us as human beings than our physical nature, so also are we bound by more than simply the laws of this nature; because we are not simply bodies, but also spirits, and because we are expected to flourish in the life of the spirit, we need to concern ourselves with the law that governs our spirits' growth—the law, that is, of love. Just as our bodies are directed and ruled by the physical laws of nature, so are our spirits directed and ruled by the law of love. The law of love is just as real and just as binding upon us as are the laws of physical nature; thus, in ignoring the law of love, no less than in ignoring the laws of physical nature, we are engaged in a process of serious self-frustration which runs its course finally in self-destruction.

The unfortunate truth of the matter, however, is that we seem able to live more easily with our refusal to love because evidence of the harm we thus inflict upon ourselves is often less

[4]Edward Stevens, *The Morals Game* (New York: Paulist Press, 1974), pp. 186-87.

immediately apparent and accumulates much more slowly than is the case when we violate the laws of our physical nature. Of course, our wanderings from love, no matter how far-ranging, do nothing to change the fact that love is the reason for our being; for this, we are made, and to this, we are called. But if we are to understand our vocation as lovers, and perhaps even be inspired to respond to it positively, it will be helpful for us as Christians to hear how this calling has been articulated by Christ.

JESUS AND THE COMMANDS TO LOVE

To any questioners inquiring about the first or the greatest of all the commandments, Jesus' response is always the same: "This is the first: 'Listen, Israel, the Lord our God is the one Lord, and you must love the Lord your God with all your heart, with all your soul, with all your mind and with all your strength.' The second is this: 'You must love your neighbor as yourself.' There is no commandment greater than these" (Mk.12:29-31; Mt.22:37-40). In answering as he does, Jesus draws together two texts of the Hebrew scriptures (Dt.6:4-5 and Lv.19:18) to establish the point that there is an indissoluble bond between our love for God and the love of our neighbor, and thus there can be no ultimate separation between our service of God and our social behavior. This, indeed, is the truth indicated by the prophet Micah when he reminds us that what the Lord God asks of us is only this: "to act justly, to love tenderly and to walk humbly with...[our] God" (6:8).

Jesus' insistence on the essential link between our love for God and our love for one another is exemplified further in the judgment scene presented in Matthew's gospel (25:31-46). Here Jesus clearly indicates that our relationship to God is manifested in our relationships with other human beings. And so, as Charles Curran points out, in the mind of Jesus, there is no way for us to claim that we love God if we neglect our neighbor "who is hungry, thirsty, naked, alone, or in prison."[5]

[5]Charles E. Curran, *A New Look at Christian Morality* (Notre Dame, Ind.: Fides Publ., 1968), p. 3.

John himself has no doubts about the crucial significance of the bond between our love for God and our love for others. Thus he warns us that if we profess to love God while failing to love our neighbor, we are liars, since it is impossible to love God whom we have never seen, if we do not love the neighbor whom we do see (1 Jn. 4:20).

Unquestionably, then, Jesus recognizes an unavoidable connection between the two commandments of love, the effect of which upon the Christian life might be expressed as follows: our love for God is realized and specified in the challenge to meet our neighbor with love; at the same time, however, the reality of our love for God facilitates and inspires our love for others, especially when the call to love reaches us where we least want to hear it, or when it directs our attention toward those whom we are not at all fond of or whom we clearly dislike.

This last point—our being called to love, no matter what our feelings for the people involved—serves to highlight an element of critical importance in the Christian life: Jesus Christ expects us to be distinguished by a love that is universal. We are to have no pre-conceived ideas about anyone, and hence no one is to be automatically excluded from the concept of "neighbor"; our neighbor is, in fact, anyone and everyone in need. Thus, as followers of Christ, we cannot be satisfied simply with loving those who love us (Mt. 5:43-7; Lk. 6:27-35); instead, as Jesus' parable of the Good Samaritan illustrates (Lk. 10:29-37), we are to love as neighbors even our known enemies.

As followers of Christ, we now know that loving God and our neighbor is the only way, but also a sure way, for us to enjoy the eternal life for which we have been created (Lk.10:25-8). And yet, however closely love for God and love for our neighbor may be bound together, they remain different forms of love. At root, our love for God is an expression of worship and gratitude in recognition of all that he is and all that he has done for us;[6] no matter how great our love for God, moreover, we can never love him as much as he deserves. But perhaps the hardest and strangest truth we have to face as Christians is that

---

[6] *Ibid.*, p. 4.

we can love God at all only to the extent that we learn to love others—and this, whether they deserve to be loved or not.

We need to reflect deeply upon the fact that the first item of the good news of Christianity is "that God loves the unworthy, that he does not need us to be worthy in order to love us."[7] This, indeed, is the heart of the lesson which Jesus lived to teach us. His whole life puts flesh upon the Father's love for us, and what we can least fail to notice is his consistent care for those most in need of love. As James Gaffney notes, however, ". . . needing love has little to do with what is normally meant by deserving love. Thus it is the sinner who most needs God's love, though it is also the sinner who least deserves it. And so it is the sinner whom the Gospel most emphatically assures of God's love."[8] Indeed, in answering his critics, Jesus explains his frequent association with known sinners by saying simply: "It is not those who are well who need the doctor, but the sick. I have not come to call the virtuous, but sinners to repentance" (Lk. 5:31-2). In thus drawing close to sinners, Jesus reveals love's power to find as lovable even those most unworthy of his love.

Because the proper love of our neighbor cannot be divorced from the love which unites us with our heavenly Father, Jesus spares no effort in showing us the way to true love of others. Thus, he is not content to remind us simply to obey the golden rule: "Treat others as you would like them to treat you" (Lk. 6:31; Mt .7:12); nor does he think it sufficient only to exhort us once again to love our neighbors as we love ourselves. Rather, at his Last Supper with the disciples, on the night before his death, Jesus offers a final clarification regarding the love which is expected of his followers. He tells us: "As the Father has loved me, so I have loved you" (Jn. 15:9). "I give you a new commandment: love one another; just as I have loved you, you must love one another. By this love you have for one another, everyone will know that you are my disciples" (Jn. 13:34-5).

[7]Louis Evely, *Our Prayer. A New Approach to Everyday Prayer* (Garden City, N.Y.: Doubleday Image Books, 1974), p. 31.

[8]James Gaffney, *Moral Questions* (New York: Paulist Press, 1974), pp. 66-7.

To love one another as Christ has first loved us is no simple task, of course, and even our most sincere attempts to do so must be futile, when we are left to our own resources. But it is never Christ's expectation or intention that we struggle with love on our own. He knows, rather, that we can love as he loves only to the extent that we first live with his own life within us—a point that will be made more fully later in this chapter.

For now, however, let us look more carefully at the love which Christ, as God, has revealed for us. Known as *agape,* this love is a self-sacrificing and unconditional love, which leads Christ to live and die for us without waiting for us to prove that we are deserving or worthy of his love. Recognizing the quality of Christ's love for us, Paul himself can only marvel, for he realizes that it is never easy to die for anyone, even for someone who is good—though a person might be prepared to die for someone who is really worthy; as Paul notes, however, "what proves that God loves us is that Christ died for us while we were still sinners"(cf. Rom. 5:6-10). In his living and dying for us, the character of Christ's love is further revealed as both a redemptive forgiving and a creative giving in that this love opens the door to our reconciliation with our Father, and enables us to live no longer as his enemies, but as friends. Thus, while always respecting our freedom, Christ, nonetheless, has done both everything within his power, and also all that is necessary, to make it possible for us to realize our potential and calling as lovers. We can only wonder, then, with Paul, that if Christ was willing to spend himself in life and death for us as sinners, how much more can and must he love us as friends? Paul's hope is simply that we will be inspired by the life and love of Christ to live accordingly, and thus he encourages us: "Be friends with one another, and kind, forgiving each other as readily as God forgave you in Christ. Try, then, to imitate God, as children of his that he loves, and follow Christ by loving as he loved you, giving himself up in our place 'as a fragrant offering and a sacrifice to God'" (Eph. 4:32-5:2).

THE EXPERIENCE OF TRUE LOVE:
CREATIVELY LIVING FOR OTHERS

Since love is so essential to our lives both as human beings and as Christians, it is important that we try to gain as much insight into it as possible. In addition to the fact that there are many impersonations of love which are often mistaken for the real thing, it is also true that there is a valid richness to love which enables us to relate lovingly in many different ways with many different people. It is precisely because love can wear so many faces that we must focus our attention on what best identifies and explains the kind of love which constitutes our human calling. The revelation of Christ's life suggests, I think, that the heart of true human love is found in the desire and willingness to live creatively in the service of others' fulfillment, and it is this suggestion that I would like to explore at some length.[9]

All love, it seems, is rooted in the experience where we become aware of being drawn beyond ourselves toward others in a way that says quite clearly "I want to live and be *for* you." In many instances, of course, we also want to live and be *with* the people whom we love, but this is not essential to the experience of true love which enables us to be *for* others even when we are unable or unwilling to be *with* them. It is important that we understand why our desire to live or be *with* certain others is not, in and of itself, any indication that we love them.

Often, we want to be *with* people simply because we find them attractive for any number of reasons—they have pleasing personalities, physical charm, intelligence and wit. And yet, wanting to be *with* others simply, or even mainly, because we find their company enjoyable, stimulating and personally fulfilling, does not testify to the presence of love, the reason being, that in relationships characterized by the expression "I want to be *with* you," we are still very much preoccupied with

---

[9]In the following reflections on love I have been influenced by the work of Gabriel Marcel whose phenomenology of love is nicely presented by William A. Luijpen, O.S.A., *Existential Phenomenology* (Pittsburgh: Duquesne Univ. Press, 1963), pp. 214-31.

the effects that "you," the others, have upon us. We are, in other words, more aware of, and responsive to, *what* these others *have,* not *who* they *are,* and so we relate to them more in terms of their real or imagined contribution to our own lives, while failing to recognize or appreciate them for their own unique being. In short, when we only want to be *with* others, it is probably because we have been mesmerized by the effects upon us of their pleasing and attractive qualities, but we have not at all been captivated by the heart of these people's existence. For this reason, the experience of wanting simply to be *with* others—while, indeed, an expression of our social nature—would seem to have much more to do with infatuation than with human love.

True love, to be sure, is much more than a longing to have certain others as a part of our lives. Although the desire to be *with* certain people may indeed serve as an occasion and catalyst for our growth into loving, I believe that the love which specifically marks our lives as human beings is that which embodies our desire and willingness to live creatively *for* others. Thus, we live as lovers primarily when we are inspired and motivated to move beyond ourselves in order to support and strengthen, as best we can, the lives and existence of others. Nor is this a matter merely of pious desires and wishful thinking. On the contrary, love proves itself in action (1 Jn. 3:18), and thus is expressed in the work that we undertake to create an atmosphere or situation in which those whom we love can become all that they are called to be. In theological terms, love means more than simply wishing others well; rather, what love does, is move us to desire and seek on behalf of others simply what God wishes for them, namely, that they be friends of His and members of His people who are courageous and free enough not only to accept His love for them but also to love Him in return, and to offer love to others.

To the extent that we basically want for others only what God wants for them—and this, of course, is what is best for them—real love stands quite apart from any sentimental indulgence. Thus answering the call to love in no way obliges us to comply with the arbitrary desires and requests expressed by those we love, and little good is served by our affirming, "Your wish is my command." Love, in fact, must refuse to be a part of any enterprise that is seen as impeding or destroying the potential which those whom we love have for responding positively to their God-given calling or destiny.

It should be noted that to speak, as we have, of love as laboring on behalf of others' fulfillment, suggests not only that we know what such fulfillment entails, but also that we have some sense of the various ways in which others are being directed to pursue their destiny. Such suggestions seem terribly presumptuous, of course, and they certainly contain the potential for abuse by inciting an attempt on our part to manage the lives of those we claim to love. Undoubtedly, abuse—however much unintended—is still abuse, and thus love must take and endure great pains in order to avoid it.

At least this much can and must be said, however. Because love recognizes and desires to respect the dignity and freedom which belong to human beings, it finds no joy and takes no satisfaction in whatever power it may have to dominate the lives of others. Should it happen, then, that some of those whom we love have begun a course of action which we clearly and sincerely perceive as threatening and harmful to their fulfillment, we will indeed struggle to bring them to the same perception; cautiously, for sure, and perhaps even reluctantly, yet willing to risk the pain of being misunderstood, we will even try to draw these loved ones into walking a different path. Failing to accomplish this, however, and unwilling to be a part of what we see as a ruinous decision taken by those we love, we may finally have no other honest choice but to allow them to walk their course alone. Should this be our decision, however, we can only and fully expect to share deeply in an agony of hurt.

Pain, of course, can find its way into the experience of love from many different directions. It is simply unavoidable that we face the possibility of pain in any serious human relationship; in fact, striving to love while at the same time refusing to take the risk of being hurt is an exercise in futility. If love consists in living for others, it necessarily involves a lowering of our self-defense, and in the vulnerability which ensues, we face the possibility of pain. Love knows no other way, however, as C.S. Lewis so wisely reminds us:

> To love at all is to be vulnerable. Love anything and your heart will certainly be wrung and possibly be broken. If you want to make sure of keeping it intact, you must give your heart to no one, not even to an animal. Wrap it carefully round with hobbies and little luxuries; avoid all entanglements; lock it up safe in the casket or coffin of your selfishness. But in that casket—safe, dark, motionless, airless—it will change. It will not be broken; it will become unbreakable, impenetrable, irredeemable. The alternative to tragedy, or at least to the risk of tragedy, is damnation. The only place outside Heaven where you can be perfectly safe from all the dangers and per-turbations of love is Hell.[10]

Despite—or perhaps precisely because of—the pain that love's vulnerability so often gives rise to, no involvement of ours in real love is ever wasted, provided we maintain a proper attitude toward it, for in truly loving we are only doing what we are called to do, and being as we are called to be. Not only does true love come to birth only in our daily willingness to die a bit to our selfishness and self-indulgence, but it also works an amazing transformation within us since it is only by loving that we are made freer and stronger to love those still in need of love.[11]

If not always immediately, at least ultimately, love fulfills us, and in truly loving, we are truly human. Both as human beings and as Christians, we express our truest selves when we move beyond ourselves in love for others; true self-fulfillment, then, demands self-transcendence and this is possible only through the sort of self-forgetfulness that allows us to put others at the center of our attention. But in the process of moving beyond ourselves something marvelous occurs, for we are interiorly enriched; we are made rich, in fact, by what we give of ourselves to others. In this way, the gospel paradox is verified: in giving, we receive, and in dying to self, we come into new life (Lk. 6:38;

---

[10]C.S. Lewis, *The Four Loves* (New York: Harcourt Brace Jovanovich, Inc., 1960), p. 169.

[11]Dom Aelred Watkin, *The Enemies of Love* (New York: Paulist Press Deus Books, 1965), p. 25.

Jn. 12:24-5). Because we are called to be lovers, loving is our true life and "to love is to learn to live."[12]

In light of the self-fulfillment that is realized through our loving, a question is often raised: if it is true that in loving—no matter how deep the accompanying pain may be—we are ourselves blessed with growth and new life, can we really be said to be unselfish in our giving of self to others? Or are we ever really forgetting ourselves when we love, since we know that, at least in the end, love brings us happiness and fulfillment? At root, what I think is being questioned here is the very possibility that as human beings we can love in a Christ-like and unselfish way, valuing others, not because it suits our purposes, but simply for themselves.

In responding, I would suggest that the key to keeping human love authentic is a balanced perspective: in loving, it may well be that we never fully forget ourselves, but our own satisfaction and fulfillment can never be our motive for loving if we hope to live as true lovers; nor, of course, can we ever love in order to be loved, for loving "*in order* to be loved is not love . . . if we love *in order* to be loved we are not loving God or a human being for themselves but for ourselves. Our motive is not another but ourself. This does not mean that we may not hope for our love to be returned or that we may not long for reciprocation, but it does mean that our love precedes and exists beyond the hope of return."[13] It seems fair to say, then, that while gratitude obviously remains our appropriate response for the love shown us by others, our own willingness and ability to love are never truly tested until we persevere in loving even though our love remains unnoticed, seems unappreciated or is clearly unrequited.

Emerging from this analysis of love is the realization that in any truly loving relationships, the focus of our attention must be on the people whom we are called to love, and whenever this ceases to be the case, love loses its authenticity or is destroyed. Keeping those whom we love at the center of our attention is

[12] *Ibid.*, p. 25.
[13] *Ibid.*, p. 22.

not always easy, of course, but we are immensely aided in our striving to do so by the very reality of love which gifts us with a clear-sightedness that not only offers us insight into the people we love, but also inspires us to the kind of creative involvement in the world that encourages and assists those whom we love in their own quests for true human fulfillment. What is being suggested here is an idea that stands in opposition to the popular notion that "love is blind," and proposes, rather, that in going beyond ourselves, in relating lovingly to others and in thus deciding to live for them, we actually begin to see these people in a new and better light.

Love, of course, never denies the faults of others, but it does refuse to reduce people to, or equate them with, their failings. Love, likewise, has no inclination to minimize the beauty and virtues of others in whom it finds much joy, but love still believes that people transcend their measurable or objectifiable qualities, both good and bad. And so, while never prescinding from these qualities, love certainly sees and goes beyond them in an effort to support and enhance the personal subjectivity and uniqueness of others. Thus it can be said of love that it blesses us with a privileged vision in light of which we are not only empowered to keep the failings and virtues of others in proper perspective, but also inspired to work creatively in assisting others to appreciate and realize their God-given beauty and potential.

LOVE'S DEMANDS FOR CHRISTIAN SOCIAL LIVING

The description of love as the desire and willingness to work to foster the fulfillment of others so that they can become all that they are called to be leads to the sobering realization that much that tries to pass for love is indeed not love at all. To illustrate this point, we might reflect on those activities like clothing-drives and canned-food drives which are popularly referred to as "works of charity." Such activities, and others like them, are basically short-term emergency responses to the needs of people; and yet, while essential in the present situation, these activities in themselves acknowledge and embody no attempt at the long-term solutions to the problems of the needy which demand an opening up of our nation's economic structures in order to permit greater social mobility. Our present social structures, in fact, can scarcely be judged as less than sinful in light of the way in which they allow so many people to be abused, neglected or forgotten while others of us remain content to capitalize upon these structures, and thus continue to grow in profits, power, prestige and pleasure. In a real and undeniable way, we allow the structures of our society to do to some among us what we, as good people, would never think of doing to another face to face.[14]

It is not being suggested here that we should simply abandon our "works of charity," but there is no escaping the fact that while these activities may indeed go a long way in soothing our consciences and thus in making us feel good, they are, nonetheless, in themselves attending only to the symptoms, not to the root causes, of society's moral disorder. The inadequacy of "works of charity" alone is reflected in the fact that, for the most part, they require of us only that we give of our surplus and not of our substance;[15] even more importantly, however, our "works of charity" leave much to be desired because, as short-term responses, they are also shortsighted and frequently

[14]Some of these ideas were suggested by Fr. Michael Czerny, S.J., in a lecture at St. Joseph's University (Philadelphia) in June, 1984. It should be noted, further, that in the same year the Food and Agriculture Organization estimated that there were 500 million malnourished people throughout the world; moreover, according to *Unicef,* 40,000 children die every day from hunger-related diseases that we know how to cure. In America alone, 33.7 million people—including 20% of all children—are trapped in poverty. In 1984, to be "officially" poor in the U.S. meant that an individual earned less than $5,278, while a family of four had a cash income of less than $10,610. Statistics further indicate that the poorest 40% of Americans receive only 15.7% of the national income, while the richest 40% take in 67.3% of the income. (Confer the editorial, "A Ghost Haunts U.S. Feast," *The Philadelphia Inquirer,* Sunday, Dec. 1, 1985.)

[15]Vatican II's *Pastoral Constitution on the Church in the Modern World (Gaudium et Spes)* speaks strongly to this point: "The Fathers and Doctors of the Church held ... that men are obliged to come to the relief of the poor, and to do so not merely out of their superfluous goods. If a person is in extreme necessity, he has the right to take from the riches of others what he himself needs. Since there are so many people in this world afflicted with hunger, this Sacred Council urges all, both individuals and governments, to remember the saying of the Fathers: 'Feed the man dying of hunger, because if you have not fed him you have killed him'" (#69).

distract us from involvement in the planning needed to change the social and economic status quo which is wreaking havoc upon the lives of the poor. Left to themselves, unaccompanied by any attempts at societal restructuring, our "works of charity" appear as largely unresponsive to the human rights and needs of the poor; there is also something almost insulting about them insofar as they often amount to little more than the offer of band-aids in situations calling for radical surgery.

It is understandable, therefore, that in various ways the poor among us are more and more voicing both their pain and their impatience with their cry "Damn your 'charity,' give us justice." This plea is indeed instructive and warrants our attention and response, for in demanding that justice be shown them, the needy are asking simply that they be given, not what is due them in recognition of their function in, or contribution to, society, but rather what they are owed purely and simply as human beings. Of course, what they are owed as human beings is everything that they need in order to live with decency and dignity. In the area of socio-economics, this means that everyone possesses rights to such things as nourishing food, suitable clothing, decent housing, standard medical care, and employment that offers fair wages and safe working conditions. In issuing their call for justice, it might be noted that the poor are, in effect, only challenging us to live up to our human and Christian vocation to love, for justice is really love's minimum expectation, and thus there is simply no way for us to face the responsibilities of love unless we begin to meet the demands of justice; without justice, love is just a word. Thus we are masters of self-deception if we see ourselves as lovers while making no attempt to resist or correct the injustices which oppress our neighbors.

There is, I suggest, much truth in the observation that as Christians, and perhaps especially as Roman Catholics, we do not have a particularly well-developed or acute sense of the social responsibility we necessarily face as a result of our moral calling to be lovers. Lacking much understanding of our social responsibility, it follows that we have a difficult time acknowledging the presence, or even the possibility, of "social sin" in our lives since our social failings are found quite often in the area of our omissions, while our consciences seem trained to reproach us more for things that we have done than for what we have left undone. The truth is, however, that people are hurt, and sin can occur, as much through our failure to do good as through our perpetration of evil. Thus our moral sensitivity needs further honing in order to recognize the fact that we fail in justice, and hence in love, not only by the outright abuse or conscious oppression of others, but also by being mindlessly ravenous or self-centeredly incautious in our expenditures and material acquisitions.

Even when we do affirm the presence of the social responsibility facing us as Christians, we seem able to survive rather peacefully with our failures to live up to it because, as James Gaffney points out, we tend to identify this social responsibility as a common one that is shared by many; thus each of us carries only a diminished portion of this responsibility and any blame we may bear in failing to meet it, is clearly infinitesimal. Thus, notes Gaffney, "if we think of ourselves simply as one of the many who share a common responsibility, our sense of obligation is inevitably lessened, and with it our readiness to make any active response." Moreover, our prevailing attitude that "we are willing to accept our fair share of social responsibility" generally means in effect that when we are reminded of the pain and suffering of others, we are inclined to make our escape into the whole crowd of other potential benefactors who, while being in a position to offer assistance to those needing it, rarely do.[16]

As Gaffney maintains, however, Christianity's perception of our moral obligations in and toward society is never reflected simply in our willingness to accept a fair share of social responsibility, but rather only in our determination to love our neighbors as we love ourselves; to do this, however, we must put ourselves in our neighbors' place so that we can begin to view our social responsibility from their perspective, the perspective, that is, of the suffering, the poor, and the marginalized victims of society. Instead, then, of trying to extricate ourselves from

[16]Gaffney, *op.cit.,* pp. 109-12.

the hook of moral responsibility by identifying with all those others around us who make no effort to assist the people in need, we must identify rather with the suffering and deprived themselves;[17] to the extent that we can do this, we quickly come to appreciate how much they want and need to be helped to the point, at least, of being able to help themselves. Furthermore, in attempting to identify with the poor and suffering, we are only responding to Christ's command that his love for us is to be the model of our love for one another. As we have seen, Christian love, like Christ's love, is to be directed toward the people most in need of it, and in light of Christ's life, we know that it is not just sinners who especially need love's attention, but also the people most often ignored and neglected by the structures of society.

To the extent that love succeeds in moving us to work for greater flexibility in society's economic structures so that they might allow for more mobility among the deprived of our nation, we need not fear excessively for our own well-being; although success in our venture will change not only society's, but also our own, status quo, we can take some courage and comfort in the realization that while not everyone's greed can be satisfied, there are riches enough to meet everyone's needs. Quite independently of this realization, however, as Christians who can find our way to love only by meeting the requirements of justice, we have no other option but to be especially concerned for the poor and suffering among us. Sensitivity to the needs of the poor has been a constant teaching in our Judeo-Christian tradition. Thus the notice served by Proverbs 14:31, "If you oppress poor people, you insult the God who made them, but kindness shown to the poor is an act of worship," only focuses attention on what was a prevailing and more comprehensive Jewish sentiment, namely, that justice among them was to be measured by their treatment of the powerless in society—the orphan, the widow, the poor and the refugee from foreign oppression.

Furthermore, in keeping with Christianity's centuries-long encouragement that we attend carefully to the needy, Pope

[17] *Ibid.,* pp. 111-13.

John Paul II has urged that we see our special obligation to the poor as a calling that involves a particular openness to "the small and the weak, those that suffer and weep, those that are humiliated and left on the margin of society, so as to help them win their dignity as human persons and children of God."[18] This same call to careful attention to the poor is presently being echoed by the American Catholic bishops who are preparing a major pastoral letter in which they offer their reflections on the United States economy in light of Catholic social teaching. The final version of the document is due to be completed by November of 1986, but in the letter's second draft which appeared in the autumn of 1985, the bishops have already made their starting point quite clear by insisting that all decisions about America's economic future must be ethically evaluated and judged "in light of what they do *for* the poor, what they do *to* the poor, and what they enable the poor to do *for themselves.* The fundamental moral criterion for all economic decisions, policies, and institutions is this: They must be at the *service of all people, especially the poor.*"[19]

Pertinent to the claim that all economic decisions must be morally judged in terms of their contribution to everyone's well-being, but especially the poor's, is the fact that the bishops see themselves as loyal proponents of a position long affirmed by Christianity, namely, "*that misuse of the world's resources or appropriation of them by a minority of the world's population betrays the gift of creation since 'whatever belongs to God belongs to all.'*"[20] As their creator, God is indeed the owner of the earth's resources, but as Vatican II reminds us, "God intended the earth and all that it contains for the use of every human being and people" (*Church in the Modern World,* #69). Thus, no nation, no class of people, no individual has exclusive

---

[18] Pope John Paul II, Address to Bishops of Brazil, #6.9, *Origins,* 10,9 (July 31, 1980), 135.

[19] Second Draft of the American Catholic Bishops' Pastoral Letter on Catholic Social Teaching and the U.S. Economy (Washington, D.C.: USCC, 1985), p. 8, #28, underscoring in original.

[20] *Ibid.,* p. 12, #40, underscoring in original.

rights to the goods of the earth; on the contrary, all of us, nations and individuals alike, are confronted with the duty of not acting at all as owners of the earth's resources, but rather as stewards or managers of God's gifts so that they will be used, as he intends, for the good of everyone.

Because the poor are greatly deprived of the benefits of God's creation, and because they are often powerless to speak and act on their own behalf, they hold a special place in the heart of Christ who calls us, in turn, to be particularly responsive to their needs and rights. It is within this context that the bishops urge us to see to it that all our economic decisions reflect a special care or "option for the poor." Their intention in the use of this phrase is not, of course, to pit "one group or class against another," but rather to indicate both that "the deprivation and powerlessness of the poor wounds the whole community," and that the extent of the poor's suffering "is a measure of how far we are from being a true community of persons."[21] The bishops are well aware, moreover, that if we clearly focus on the dignity and rights of all people, the poor are not the sole beneficiaries, for we quickly come to appreciate that just as "the needs of the poor take priority over the desires of the rich," so also do "the rights of workers over the maximization of profits; the preservation of the environment over uncontrolled industrial expansion; production to meet social needs over production for military purposes."[22]

As we bring these reflections on Christian social responsibility to a conclusion, several cautionary remarks are appropriate. Clearly, of course, any profession of our concern and love for the poor is ungodly, senseless and deceitful if it is unaccompanied by any effort to win release for the poor from the economic, political and social chains that keep them imprisoned both in body and in spirit.[23] At the same time,

---

[21] *Ibid.,* p. 27, #90.

[22] *Ibid.,* p. 28, #95. The Bishops here are quoting Pope John Paul II's "Address on Christian Unity in a Technological Age," Toronto, September 14, 1984, *Origins,* 14, 16 (October 4, 1984), 248.

[23] In this and the following paragraphs I am presenting, with some variations and re-arrangements, material from my article, "Christian Poverty: Sign of Faith and Redemptive Force," *The Way,* Supplement 32 (Autumn, 1977), 78-82 at 80-2.

however, it is certainly misrepresentative of Christianity to suggest that, in itself, liberating others from economic deprivation or oppression either fully reveals or finally exhausts the riches promised by our Father. Christian love demands, rather, that the poor be drawn to the realization that their liberation from the multiple forms of human oppression is ultimately significant only insofar as it helps them to arrive at that interior and spiritual freedom by means of which they can live as children of God, gratefully receiving his love and heartfully returning it.

However much, then, we are obliged to struggle for the increased economic well-being of the poor, we must also encourage them not to be blinded into seeing and desiring nothing beyond the enjoyment of material riches. The simple truth is that all Christians alike—poor, middle-class and rich—live under the warning of Christ: "How hard it is for those who have riches to enter the kingdom of God!.... It is easier for a camel to pass through the eye of a needle than for a rich man to enter the kingdom of God"(Mk. 10:23, 25). There is, of course, neither vice nor virtue in the mere possession of wealth, but what Christ calls our attention to is the fact that as we come to share more richly in "the good life" of this earth, we can easily develop a distorted sense of personal accomplishment, independence and self-sufficiency. Thus we are led to close our hearts to God and to presume that just as we are providing for our present well-being in this world, so also can we independently achieve our future fulfillment in the world to come. All of us, then,—whether we be poor, middle-class or wealthy—must allow our lives to be tempered by God's perspectives lest this earth's happiness be the only one we ever come to know.

The temptations associated with the accumulation of material possessions can be resisted, of course, and their presence alone is no excuse for our failure to enable the poor to share more fully in the comforts offered by this world. Neither must we forget, however, that the gospel of Christ is not for the poor alone. The rich also need its life-offering, and God himself desires the salvation of all. Thus there is always the danger that in our attempting to enhance the material welfare of the poor, we will become myopic and unchristian by wresting wealth and power from their possessors, forcing indeed the hands of the rich, but all the while leaving their hearts untouched, unnoticed and even uncared for, so that they are, in short, left ill-disposed for receiving the Father's life. This, of course, is a most unsatisfactory situation, and one with which no follower of Christ can be complacent.

We must conclude, then, that while the Christian life does indeed involve laboring to relieve the burden of the poor, it also entails a commitment to communicate to all who need redemption a knowledge of, and a yearning for, the best and the most that our Father offers us: his life and his love. If as Christians we must not betray the poor, neither must we abandon the rich; if the rich do not take the gospel to heart, we may wonder why, but we must also increase our efforts and our pleadings that their hearts may be opened to the message of Christ. Moreover, should the rich respond, not only will there be rejoicing in heaven but also on earth, for the poor cannot help but be materially benefited by the entrance of the wealthy into the spirit of the gospel which calls us to love not only our Father but also one another. Enlightened by the life and message of Christ, we know that if any return of love is made to God, it is necessarily made to those whose fullest dignity lies in being sons and daughters of our Father who provides the riches of the earth and wants them to be shared by all. Thus if the gospel moves the rich to lose their hearts to the Father, it must also move their hands to refashion the earth and to make way for the poor so that they can come more easily to know and enjoy the goodness of our Father's love.

IV. Christian Life As Eucharistic

As we have seen so far, our personal identity, both as Christians and as human beings, is fundamentally shaped by the fact that God loves us and calls us to be lovers, in turn, not only of himself but also of one another. To the extent that we make a positive response to this calling, our lives may be seen as eucharistic, which is to say that they become expressions of our gratitude and thanksgiving to God. Grateful for all that he has done for us and for being who we are—people deeply loved by God—we try to live in a loving way. Thus we are sparked by the true spirit of Christianity when our attempts to live morally embody or reflect the following attitude: "Recognizing with gratitude the love that God already has for us, we are trying to lead lives of love as he wishes us to do."

This mentality, indeed, stands a world apart from, and is far differently inspired than, the much more anxiety-prone one which is so often suggested by the statement: "If we live good lives, then God will love us." The attitude reflected in this latter proposition seems clearly inadequate in that it makes God's love for us conditional upon our good behavior; thus, according to this view, we must somehow win or earn God's love, whereas, by contrast, the truth of Christianity begins with the fact that God already loves us and will love us forever. Our lives as Christians, then, are not meant to be characterized basically and primarily by fear-and-trembling efforts to gain God's love, but rather by the grateful or eucharistic return of love for the love already shown us (1 Jn. 4:19).

Something very central to an understanding of the proper Christian mentality is being highlighted here, namely this, that the moral challenges we face as human beings and as Christians are derived precisely from our being who we *are;* who we *are* points to how we *ought to be*; our "indicative" gives rise to our "imperative." Both our dignity and our destiny are rooted in the God who created us in his image, and out of our dignity as people loved by God is born our destiny to be lovers.

We can perhaps come to a fuller appreciation both of our dignity and of our destiny when we view them in terms of the special personal relationship or covenant which God initiated with the people of Israel. Over and over, the Hebrew scriptures remind the Israelites of the Lord Yahweh's promise: "I will be your God and you will be my people" (cf. Gen.17:3-8; Ezek. 36:29; Jer. 31:34). As Christians, we believe that Christ, as the enfleshed Word of God, has made us and all others heirs to this promise given originally to Israel. It is a promise, moreover, which is profoundly stirring because it contains elements both of gospel or good news and of challenge. In light of Christ's revelation, the eminently good news presented us is this: "I,

God, love you—all you people of the earth." At the same time, however, we are confronted with this challenge: "I, God, call all you people of the earth to love me and one another, even as you first have been shown love. Let me love you into life forever, and we will be together in my kingdom."

To say that our life of love as Christians is meant to be eucharistic is to acknowledge only one of its characteristics; much more may be learned of Christian living by viewing it in a somewhat broader theological context. To begin with, the reference to God's kingdom directs our attention to a whole new dimension of our lives as Christians, and it will be helpful for us to explore what significance our commitment to love has when made as a response to God's invitation into his kingdom.

V. Christian Life as Eschatological

In calling us to be members of his kingdom, God, of course, is not primarily giving us a lesson in geography; he is not, in other words, so much telling us *where* he wishes us to abide, but rather *how* he intends us to live. God has a new quality of life in mind for us if only we will allow him into our lives; indeed, he promises us that his reign and power and presence are enough to change our existence forever. We should note, however, that just as God's promise to make us his covenantal people involves, as we have seen, both the gospel of his love for us and the challenge that we are to be lovers in turn, so also does his promise to make his kingdom available to us contain elements both of gospel and of challenge: the good news is that God's kingdom is already among us, but we are challenged by the fact that the establishment of this kingdom is not yet completed and the power and majesty of God's rule are still to be fully manifested.

Jesus himself seems quite aware of the fact that God's power and presence already belong to history. Thus at the start of his public life, he announces that "The time has come and the kingdom of God is close at hand. Repent, and believe the Good News" (Mk. 1:15). Only a short while later, Jesus goes further and does not hesitate to identify himself as the presence of

God's power in history. In Nazareth's synagogue, after reading the prophet Isaiah's words: "The spirit of the Lord has been given to me, for he has anointed me. He has sent me to bring the good news to the poor, to proclaim liberty to captives and to the blind new sight, to set the downtrodden free, to proclaim the Lord's year of favor," Jesus then astonishes the congregation by proclaiming: "This text is being fulfilled today even as you listen" (cf. Lk. 4:16-22).

Regardless of our acceptance of Jesus' affirmation that in him and in his activity the kingdom of God has indeed entered into history, the fact remains that God's kingdom is still not yet fully realized. It is this fact, moreover, which gives rise to the challenge we face today. For just as John the Baptist was called to "prepare a way for the Lord" in anticipation of the public appearance of Jesus (Mt. 3:3), so are we called to be actively involved somehow in preparing for the Second Coming of Christ when the kingdom of God will be finally completed and his power fully manifested.

Mindful of God's covenant with us, we are to live with our eyes on the promised kingdom, fully committed to walking the path which will lead us to the future being prepared for us by God. It can be said, further, that because we ourselves are directed to assist in building up God's kingdom, our lives as Christians have a basic eschatological thrust; this means that while we undeniably and unavoidably live in this world and are to make the best of it for everyone, ultimately we are not of this world and so our lives must be shaped by the *eschaton* or end-time. Still unaddressed, however, is the question of how and to what degree we as human beings may contribute to the preparation of God's kingdom, or what is the nature of the role which we are expected to play in order that God's reign may be fully realized. It is to this issue that we now turn.

THREE THEORIES OF ESCHATOLOGY

There is no surprise, I suppose, in the fact that Christianity offers no uniform response to the question asked. Rather three theories or forms of eschatology may be identified and each describes the human contribution to God's kingdom differently.[24] To begin with, teleological eschatology reflects the view that since there is a basic continuity between earth and heaven, this world and the kingdom of God, heaven on earth is a distinct possibility by means of a gradual or progressive transformation and elimination of this world's evils. Spurred on by their utopian expectations, proponents of teleological eschatology reflect a "no holds barred" mentality in their attempt to improve the human condition. They believe strongly in the primacy and efficacy of human action for the establishment of God's kingdom, but they appear too insensitive to the consummate pride which can accompany their views.

In stark contrast to the teleological version of eschatology, apocalyptic eschatology is convinced that at the end of time there is a catastrophic break with history, and thus a fundamental discontinuity exists between this world and the kingdom of God. There is no final or complete earthly success, and any hope for a heaven on earth is illusory. Since this world cannot be radically changed and since God's kingdom is of a totally new and different age, some advocates of this apocalyptic version of eschatology congregate in sects and withdraw from active involvement in society. Overall, great emphasis is put on the primacy of God's action in history and it is he who builds his kingdom. In order to counteract the human sloth which this view might encourage, its proponents maintain that as human beings we must indeed be involved in the performance of good, but such effort on our part manifests simply our yearning and desire for the arrival of God's kingdom. Nonetheless, it is still God who must bring his kingdom to full realization, and in the end our labors remain somehow alien to his accomplishments.

Mediating between the two preceding views of eschatology is a third one known as prophetic eschatology; its basic assertion is that God and human beings labor together in building up God's coming kingdom. Our human cooperation with the

---

[24]The following theories of eschatology are discussed in Harvey Cox's *On Not Leaving It to the Snake* (New York: Macmillan Paperbacks, 1969), pp. 29-43.

divine initiative means that we always work in response to God's continuing action in history. What is perhaps most striking about prophetic eschatology is its insistence that the positive results of human labor are not ultimately annihilated, but rather are permanently transformed for inclusion within God's kingdom. Thus in building up the earth, human beings are at the same time laying down the real foundations of the kingdom of God. In this way, the point is made that our human involvement in history is indispensable and eternally significant, and not because we wish it to be so, but rather because God does and thus he graces our activities with this importance.

One way of expressing the insight offered by prophetic eschatology is to suggest that the positive achievements of our involvement in history constitute a kind of "rough draft" or "preliminary sketch" of the kingdom which Christ finally transfigures at the time of his return when the kingdom will be established in all its glory. As artists and artisans of the earth, we are called to work continually under the guidance and inspiration of Christ, the creative genius, whose masterful touch is always needed and is graciously given in order that our human creation may be permanently transformed into the kingdom of God. We always remain incapable of bringing about God's kingdom on our own; and yet, however insufficient in itself, our work still remains necessary for the kingdom's appearance. Such is God's design. Thus we hear the call to be real co-creators, together with God, of the kingdom still to come.[25]

In reflecting upon the three models of eschatology, it might be said that while there is a definite straightforwardness about the teleological and apocalyptic views, they are perhaps too facile in maintaining that all responsibility for the appearance of God's kingdom lies, respectively, either with human beings or with God. By contrast, prophetic eschatology adopts what may be regarded as a more nuanced position and prefers to view

[25]The imagery of human labor as a "preliminary sketch" for God's kingdom has been used by Pierre Teilhard de Chardin, S.J., whose views are presented more fully in my book, *Expectant Creativity: The Action of Hope in Christian Ethics* (Lanham, Md.: University Press of America, 1982).

the coming kingdom as the co-responsibility of God and human beings. Once this stance is taken, we as human beings are then confronted with the difficulty of trying to determine both the extent and limit of our responsibility, and this is a task whose only chance of success lies with our participation in an ongoing dialogue of prayer. And yet, however hard, and even unsettling, the challenge posed by prophetic eschatology may be, I believe that it is this view which is the most adequate and richest indication of what is expected of us as Christians.

We involve ourselves actively in the preparation of God's kingdom by patterning our lives on the life and teaching of Jesus Christ. In doing this, we are effectively announcing, anticipating and even approximating the quality of life which we hope to enjoy fully in the glory of God's kingdom.[26] It is true, of course, that this glorious kingdom is something of which we presently have only glimmerings; as Paul reminds us, our eyes have not seen, our ears have not heard and our minds can scarcely comprehend all the joy God is preparing for those who love him (cf. 1 Cor.2:9). We do know at least this much, however: that the final realization of God's kingdom means indeed freedom from all forms of oppression, and the establishment of humanity in justice and love, truth and peace.

This suggests that even though we have no fully detailed knowledge of God's coming kingdom, we can nonetheless prepare positively for its arrival by negating the present negatives that surround us. What this means, in other words, is that although we have not yet experienced full humanity, we can still recognize and resist what is inhuman about us; likewise, while perfect justice may remain a distant and even vague ideal, present injustices are clear enough, and these must be fought and rejected as being simply incompatible with the kingdom of God.

While there is no doubt that as Christians we are to be actively engaged in the building up of God's kingdom, prophetic eschatology would have us remember that we are not called

---

[26]Carl E. Braaten, *Eschatology and Ethics. Essays on the Theology and Ethics of the Kingdom of God* (Minneapolis: Augsburg Publishing House, 1974). pp. 110-11.

to do as much good as is possible, but rather only as much good as is *morally* possible. Since the fundamental principle of the moral life is that we are to "do good and avoid evil," we are not allowed to do what is morally evil in order to achieve good; our efforts to accomplish what is good are necessarily restricted by the charge to avoid moral evil. Here, then, we are confronted with a basic question of faith: do we really believe that God is involved in our history and cares enough about us to make a difference, that he appreciates our frustration, pain and impatience in the face of evil and thus intervenes against it in his own way? Only if we can answer this question affirmatively are we likely to accept with grace not only the limitations of our power to overcome all present evils, but also the restrictions upon our responsibility for the establishment of God's kingdom.

All that is expected of us—and it is much—is that we are to live as signs of the coming kingdom. The call to live prophetically, as "the salt of the earth," "the light of the world," "the leaven of society" (Mt. 5:13,14; 13:33), reveals both our duty and our dignity. Like the prophets of old who dared to challenge the world to a way of living that was in keeping with the perspective and expectations of God, we too are called to speak out against all that stands in contradiction to God and his kingdom. But more than talk is required of us; our lives are to be expressions of *eschatopraxis* which means, simply, that we are to busy ourselves with "doing the future now ahead of time"; we are to live in the present in a way that not only embodies our faith and hope in the future promised us by God, but also encourages and facilitates its arrival.[27] We do, indeed, have an effective ability to work for the kingdom of God, but we have it only because, in and through Christ, this kingdom has already begun and is present among us, calling and empowering us to the kind of love which alone makes us true co-creators with God of the kingdom still to be realized.

As Christians, then, we live peacefully with the realization that by ourselves we cannot produce God's kingdom because

[27] *Ibid.*, pp. 121-22.

we know that this, in fact, is not expected of us. God calls us, nonetheless, to make a real contribution to his kingdom, and we succeed in doing so only insofar as we live and labor with the vision, strength and vitality of Jesus Christ within us; it is in the same way, moreover, that we ourselves come to share personally in the glory of the kingdom, for in working on behalf of God's kingdom, we are at the same time interiorly preparing ourselves to be part of it. In the next section of this chapter we will attend more fully to the issue of personal salvation and our place in the kingdom of God. For now, however, I simply offer this reflection: just as we can never bring about God's kingdom on our own, and yet must continue to contribute positively to its establishment, so also, we can never save ourselves, and yet we will never be saved against our will, or without our own effort and cooperation with God.

VI. Salvation: The Fulfillment of Faith Working in Love

Having considered the different answers which the three forms of eschatological thinking propose to the question of how we as human beings may contribute to the building up or preparation of God's kingdom, we will now apply these same three theories to a related question, namely, how might we best explain the way in which we as individuals come to share personally in the full joys of life in the kingdom of God. This question has deep roots in the history of Christianity, although most often the query has been posed in somewhat different terms, perhaps the most familiar of which are those that framed the bitter sixteenth-century Reformation debate on the theories of personal justification and the means by which we arrive at salvation.

There is, I suggest, a certain compatibility and consistency between teleological eschatology's view that as human beings we have the capacity to build God's kingdom on our own, and the notion that by ourselves we can do what is necessary to gain our personal salvation. Indeed, such an assessment of our innate ability as human beings was given by a fourth-century British monk called Pelagius, who maintained that we are quite self-sufficient to achieve salvation by our own free efforts, for in his view, salvation is nothing more than God's reward to us which we truly earn or merit through the performance of good works.

Although Pelagius' view was rejected as heretical, it nonetheless continued to influence Christian thinking for centuries and sparked, in fact, one of the great debates of the Reformation era. By way of offering some background to this debate, it might be said that by the sixteenth century authentic Christian tradition seemed firmly committed to the idea that just as we human beings cannot, by ourselves, establish the kingdom of God, so neither can we save ourselves. Thus salvation must be seen not as a reward earned by the human performance of good deeds, but rather as a gift freely given by God to those who have faith in him.

This was clearly the view of Martin Luther who, as a leader of the Reformation, argued strongly for the idea that a definite separation exists between the kingdom of God and the kingdom of this world. Greatly influenced by the apocalyptic tradition of eschatology and deeply committed to the view that as human beings we are saved only by the grace of God which we receive as a gift in faith, Luther was convinced that the Church of Rome, despite its professed rejection of the teaching of Pelagius, was nonetheless still showing too many signs of Pelagian influence, and thus was responsible for the lingering perception of salvation as a reward which is merited through the performance of good deeds. Luther accused the Roman Catholic Church of thus fostering a mentality of "good-works righteousness"—a view which claims that it is the activity of doing good deeds which makes us good and righteous or justified people in the eyes of God. While Luther had no sympathy for this position, he nonetheless expected that as good and righteous people we would certainly do good works, but we would do them, not in order to gain justification, but rather in recognition and appreciation of the justification that is already ours because of God's grace and our own faith.

In this way the stage came to be set for the debate between Luther and the Roman Church on whether we as Christians are saved by faith or by good works. For our purposes, there is no need of an extended analysis of the different positions advanced by the two major parties to this debate, but I do think that it will be helpful for us to look briefly at some of the scriptural data on this question and then to indicate how this information was interpreted by the Council of Trent in its attempt to clarify and articulate Roman Catholicism's understanding of the way in which we come to be saved.

SCRIPTURAL DATA ON FAITH AND GOOD WORKS

Although there are any number of scriptural texts[28] which affirm that it is indeed by faith that we are saved, perhaps the clearest and most emphatic statement of this position appears in Paul's letter to the Ephesians where he says: "... God loved us with so much love that he was generous with his mercy: when we were dead through our sins, he brought us to life with Christ—it is through grace that you have been saved—and raised us up with him and gave us a place with him in heaven, in Christ Jesus... it is by grace that you have been saved, through faith; not by anything of your own, but by a gift from God; not by anything that you have done, so that nobody can claim the credit" (2:4-6,8-9).

Had texts such as this been the only ones available for consideration, the debate over the question of what is expected of us in order that we might enter into the joys of salvation would have been quickly ended—if, indeed, it had ever gotten started. But such is not the case. Thus James, for example, does not hesitate to warn us that faith alone, that is, faith which is unaccompanied by good works, will never save us, for faith, "if good works do not go with it, ... is quite dead" and "useless" (Jas. 2:17,21). James presses his point by insisting that we are to prove our faith in the performance of good deeds; otherwise, just as "a body dies when it is separated from the spirit," so also is our faith dead "if it is separated from good deeds" (Jas. 2:18,26). James then reaches the unavoidable conclusion that we are saved "by doing something good, and not only by

---

[28]See, for example, Rom. 3:28, Rom. 5:1-2, Titus 3:4-8.

believing" (2:24). In taking this position, James is effectively reminding us as Christians of our need for what may be called a "living faith," a faith, in other words, which performs good deeds. And precisely on this point, the thinking of James converges with that of St. Paul who is firmly convinced that our righteousness as Christians is characterized by an active faith, a faith, that is, which works and "expresses itself in love" (Gal. 5:6).

What emerges from the scriptural data, then, is a position that is articulated in the following synthesis: as Christians we are saved neither by faith alone—a faith, that is, without deeds—nor by good works alone; rather, we are saved by a living faith which is engaged in the labor of love. Since we are also told both that salvation is a gift and that it comes to us through faith, we may legitimately conclude that salvation is ours through the gift of living faith. But then we need to ask further what is meant by faith and what is the sense of calling it a gift.

THE GIFT OF LIVING FAITH

Turning to these questions, we move directly to the heart of the matter when we say that faith is the free and personal response of love which we make to God in recognition of his love for us. Through our positive response of love which faith is, we enter into a personal relationship with God that involves our whole being. Of course, as the very designation of faith as "a response of love" indicates, it is not we who are initially responsible for any personal relationship we may come to enjoy with God. Rather, it is God who initiates the relationship by first coming out of himself and offering us the gift of himself in love. It is, in fact, God's generous offering of himself, his grace and love, his very life, which makes our own return of love in the relationship of faith possible.

By being so graciously disposed toward us, God literally surrounds and supports us with his presence and thus creates an atmosphere which both reveals his love and invites and empowers us to love him in return. While it is true, of course, that we always retain the freedom to refuse or reject God's love for us, it is also true that whatever power we have to enter into the faith-relationship through our free response of love is itself an expression of God's enlivening goodness toward us. We can say, then, that in a real sense we are doubly blessed by God, for not only does he gift us by loving us first, but also his very love inspires, encourages and frees us to love him in return. God's love, in short, gifts us with the ability to enter into faith, and yet our entrance into faith can never be forced, for the only true love is love that is freely given. This means that while our faith-response is indeed born out of God's prior gift of love for us, it is also an expression of our free decision to receive or accept this gift and to use it as God intends.

Through our free cooperation with the gracious action of God's love in our lives, we enter into the response of faith and in this way the personal relationship of mutual love to which God calls us is finally begun. As we have seen earlier, however, love is a matter, not of words, but of deeds, and thus we must see to it that our faith comes alive in the works of love, for so long as our faith remains inactive or dead, it makes a lie of any profession of our love for God. For us as Christians, any true love of God means that we put on the mind and heart of Christ (1 Cor. 2:16; Ph. 2:5), and just as his love for the Father led him to spend himself for us, so also does our love for God turn us toward our neighbor. Thus when James and Paul remind us that we are called to a living faith that expresses itself in love, what they are effectively telling us is simply this: that our love and service of God is manifested, tested and verified only in the love and service of our neighbor. When our faith-response of love for God is alive, then indeed God becomes "a life [we] live with, a love [we] love with, a current going through [us], a gale blowing [us] towards others."[29]

This analysis of living faith reveals not only that our love for God is proven and proclaimed through our love of neighbor, but also that our love for neighbor is rooted in our love of God, and from there it draws its vitality and power. Thus as

[29]Evely, *op. cit.,* p. 36.

Christians, our love of neighbor is a faith-rooted or faith-inspired love which means that it embodies both our gratitude for God's love of us and our desire to love him in return. Of course, if we truly love God and our neighbor, then they must remain the focus of our attention so that our response of living faith does not become the expression of an egocentric concern on our part about working out our salvation.

Perhaps we need reminding that we love neither God nor our neighbor properly if all we do is view and use others as "tickets" or "stepping-stones" to heaven; we have, in fact, little choice but to seek corrective lenses if our vision of Christianity has us believing that the reason why we should struggle to live as lovers is just so that God will look kindly upon us and one day reward us with a place in the kingdom of heaven. The truth is, that we have a much clearer and better insight into Christianity when our realization of God's present love for us frees us from the crippling effects of anxious preoccupation with the requirements for salvation; indeed, having an interior sense of God's abiding love for us encourages us to be less defensive and more forgetful of self. Deeply aware of God's love, we come to see ourselves in a new and better light and this, in turn, helps to open our eyes and hearts to a caring love for others.

THE VIEWS OF TRENT

Against the background of this analysis of the response of living faith or faith that expresses itself in love, we will now look at how the Council of Trent (1545-63) came to provide the basis for Roman Catholicism's present understanding of the role which we as human beings are to play in our own salvation. We should note, first of all, that the Council takes a strong stand against Pelagius by denying that human beings can do anything to gain salvation on their own, that is, without the grace of Jesus Christ. At the same time, however, the Council argues against Luther by insisting that our salvation as human beings cannot be achieved without our free cooperation with God.

In developing its position, Trent avoids both the mentality of teleological eschatology which regards salvation simply as an earned reward for good deeds, as well as the attitude of apocalyptic eschatology which sees salvation solely as a gift of God's gracious generosity given to us in recognition of our entrance into a relationship of living faith. Not being satisfied with either of these views, the Council Fathers adopt a position that reflects the perspective of prophetic eschatology by claiming that personal salvation is best seen as coming to us primarily as a gift of God, but also as a true reward for our lives of love.

To explain their position, the Council Fathers remind us that in any personal relationship we come to enjoy with God, the initiative is always God's; he is the one who freely and graciously—without our meriting it in any way—makes a gift of himself to us in love and frees us to accept him into our lives. But to the extent that we freely cooperate with this gracious offer and allow God into our lives through our response of active faith, we are indeed interiorly transformed, for we now begin to live and love with the life and love and grace of God-in-Christ within us (Gal. 2:20). Precisely insofar as Christ takes form within us and we start to live and move and have our very being in him (Acts 17:28), we become "new creatures" (2 Cor. 5:17), who are now gifted, most remarkably, with the ability truly to merit salvation as a reward through our continuing labors of love that express our faith-relationship with God.

In adopting this position, the Council of Trent is advocating what has come to be called the theory of "intrinsic justification," which means simply that the free gift of God's life or grace within us so radically transforms us that it enables us to merit the reward of salvation. On this point, the Council distances itself from Luther who proposes a view now known as the theory of "extrinsic or imputed justification" according to which we as human beings can simply never earn salvation; for Luther, the good works, which are expected of us as an expression of our gratitude for God's love, in themselves gain us no merit or reward; we are saved, rather, by the pure gift of Christ's merits which are freely imputed or externally applied to us through our continued acceptance of God in a relationship of living faith.

While Trent clearly differs with Luther by asserting that as human beings we can effectively merit the reward of salvation through our works of faith-inspired love, it nonetheless makes every effort to affirm the fundamental character of salvation as a gift of God. Thus as human beings we have the capacity to merit salvation, but this power is ours only insofar as we cooperate with Christ's grace within us and thus are filled, like branches on the vine (Jn. 15: 1-5), with the life of God that has been freely given us as a gift. Trent knows very well that Christ is the only Savior and that we do not save ourselves, but at the same time the Council is convinced that God fully expects and enables us to participate effectively in the work of our own salvation. It is in an attempt to preserve both these insights that the Council Fathers adopt as their own the view of Augustine who sees the goodness of God as being so great that "He wishes his gifts to become our merits"; and, indeed, if the truth be told, "in crowning our merits, God is [really] crowning his gifts" (*Epist.* 194).[30]

A CALL TO LOVE, TO FAITH, TO CONVERSION

Before moving on to the last section of this chapter, it might be helpful if we noted the connection that exists between two ideas that are central to our understanding of the Christian life, namely, the call to love and the response of faith. The point to be made is simply this: if we understand that our lives as human beings and as Christians take shape around God's calling us to be lovers, then it is reasonable to say that we answer this calling precisely through our response of living faith by means of which we gratefully acknowledge God's love for us by loving him in turn and our neighbors as well. The call to love is indeed nothing other than the call to living faith or the faith that is active in love, and through our entrance into the relationship of faith is born not only our love of God but also our love for others.

---

[30] In my treatment of the Council of Trent I am indebted to Robert W. Gleason, S.J., *Grace* (New York: Sheed & Ward, 1962), pp. 212-22, especially 215, 218-19.

Now, however, we may go a step further to suggest that the call to love or to living faith must in fact be identified with the call to conversion or repentance which Jesus issues at the beginning of his public life (Mt. 4:17, Mk. 1:15). Here Jesus confronts us with the hard truth that the only way for us to enter into a relationship of faith and love is by undergoing a radical or deep-rooted re-orientation of our lives, which means that we must be willing to cease living only for ourselves and begin to live for God and others. The experience of conversion or repentance is marked, then, both by our turning away from the selfishness which is the essence of sin, and by our commitment to the loving service of God and our neighbor.[31]

Several things may be noted about the experience of conversion. First of all, there is something joyful about any authentic conversion insofar as it expresses our grateful acceptance of the good news that God is here and now offering us his love. Secondly, in answering the call to conversion, we undergo a profound interior change of heart, and as a result of this internal change we begin to live and act differently; in other words, our personal response of faith (love for God) gives birth to the social works of love. Thirdly, like any true relationship of love, our conversion must be marked by the kind of continued growth that flows from renewed commitment for, without nurturing, love stagnates and is apt to die. Unless love is lived, all we have is talk of love, and it is not long before such talk is reduced to idle chatter.

There is, finally, a sense of urgency surrounding the call to conversion, but it is an urgency best understood as arising out of our appreciation of the greatness of God's gift of love which is being offered to us. Thus our conversion to faith and love is inspired much more by gratitude than by any fear of punishment. In fact, it might be suggested that if the motive of fear of punishment has any legitimacy at all in the Christian life, we first have to redirect our attention away from God as the source or author of our punishment and look rather to ourselves, since

---

[31]The following analysis of the call to conversion is derived from Curran, *op. cit.*, pp. 26-31.

God desires and works only to save us and it is we who bring about our own punishment when we exercise our power to sin. The point here is that the connection or relationship between our sinning and the punishment that results is not arbitrarily determined and imposed. Thus we are not punished for our sinfulness in the way a child who misbehaves might be deprived of TV by disapproving parents. There is no unavoidable connection, for example, between a child's refusal to eat dinner and the parents' subsequent decision to forbid the child to watch TV.

The situation resulting from our decision to sin is quite otherwise, however, for here punishment comes to us as the logical and necessary or intrinsic consequence of our decision to separate ourselves from God by our refusal to love. In thus asserting our independence from God who is the author of life, it is we who bring the punishment of spiritual death upon ourselves for, by cutting ourselves off from God, it is simply impossible for us to live (Jn. 15:6). To accuse God, then, of punishing us for our sinfulness is somewhat like blaming the electric company when an appliance is not working because it is not plugged in; there is simply not much sense in either reaction.

VII. Christian Living As Freedom In Christ

It is time now to draw attention to one final facet of the Christian life. To our description of this life as one that is focused on a call to love, which is really a call to be converted to the living faith that expresses itself in love, we must add the detail that the Christian life is also fundamentally a call to liberty (Gal. 5:13). This is, in fact, an insight of such great significance in Paul's understanding of our life in Christ that it has won him recognition as the apostle of Christian liberty. Paul seems unable to contain the enthusiasm that springs from his realization that through our response of faith in which we take God's love for us to heart, we ourselves are interiorly transformed and strengthened by the life and love of God within us. It is this life of God inside us which both frees us to greater love and loves us into freedom.[32]

There are, of course, other ways of referring to God's life within us. We may speak, for example, of living with the grace of Christ, or of living in the Holy Spirit, but for Paul, whatever the expression used, the basic truth is simply this: that to whatever extent we open ourselves up to God's love in faith and let his Spirit of love come alive within us, to this same extent we are freed from the restrictions of the Law of Moses, and indeed from the restrictions of any written law which tries to exert external pressure or force upon us. As Paul himself sees it, "if . . . [we] are led by the Spirit, no law can touch . . . [us]" (Gal. 5:18). What we never escape, however, are the responsibilities and demands of the law of love which is the law of God's Spirit within us and the law of our true nature as lovers. Real as the demands of love are, however, the force by which they oblige us is not externally imposed upon us, but rather arises from within ourselves and thus is far different from the pressure exerted upon us by the numerous written laws surrounding us, including the Law of Moses.

Paul's idea of the liberty which we enjoy in Christ is one of great sophistication; thus if we hope to get a better understanding of his teaching, we will have to examine it more carefully. We can best begin by noting that the Christian liberty of which Paul speaks has two aspects: by living in the Holy Spirit who is the life of God, we are interiorly freed *for* relating in love with God and our neighbor; but precisely to the extent that we exercise our freedom *for* loving, we are at the same time freed *from* the coercion and constraints of the written prescriptions, not only of the Mosaic Law, but also of all laws that are external to ourselves. For Paul, then, it is obvious that the primary or more basic aspect of Christian liberty is the freedom we are given for loving, and it is only by properly living in love,

---

[32]In reflecting on St. Paul's notion of Christian liberty I am most indebted to the work of Stanislas Lyonnet, S.J., "St. Paul: Liberty and Law," which is found in C. Luke Salm, F.S.C. (ed.), *Readings in Biblical Morality* (Englewood Cliffs, N.J.: Prentice-Hall, Inc., 1967), 61-83. Also helpful is Jerome Murphy-O'Connor, O.P., *Becoming Human Together. The Pastoral Anthropology of St. Paul* (Wilmington: Michael Glazier, Inc., 1984), pp. 111-22; 199-207.

that we come to enjoy freedom from the constraints of written or external laws. Having thus stated Paul's fundamental thesis on this point, we must now articulate it in more detail, first, by explaining how Paul views both the written or external law and the new law of love given us by Christ, and then, by illustrating how the two laws are related. We begin with the written Law of Moses, but we should note that what Paul says about freedom from this Law is applicable, as well, to any external law.

PAUL'S VIEW OF THE MOSAIC LAW

Any discussion of Paul's view of the written Law of Moses should begin by noting that Paul was himself a Jew, well-trained in the Judaic teachings by one of the most famous rabbis of the time, a Pharisee named Gamaliel. Given his background and heritage, Paul's perception of the Mosaic Law would naturally shock the Jews for whom this Law was indeed the very word of God and, as such, revealed treasures of wisdom and knowledge. Paul's training notwithstanding, however, once he becomes a follower of Christ, his vision of the Law of Moses is radically recast and he begins to remind us that as Christians we live no longer under the Law but under grace (Rom. 6:14). It is, however, only because we have joined ourselves to Christ through faith and have come alive with his life and grace within us, that Paul can say to us that "now we are rid of the Law, freed by death [i.e., Christ's and our own dying to selfishness] from our imprisonment, free to serve in the new spiritual way and not the old way of a written law" (Rom. 7:6). Paul is here telling us that Christ has delivered us from the restrictions of the written Law, and to explain his point, he refers to this Law as playing two roles in our lives: it functions both as a pedagogue and as a curse.

Looking first at the notion of pedagogue, the point must be made that while this word is sometimes used today to refer to a teacher, Paul's use of the word suggests something quite different, for in his day a pedagogue (a leader of children) was a household slave who had the task of leading the master's children to the schoolhouse where they would meet the teacher.

It was not the function of the pedagogue to teach, but only to serve in a temporary and provisional role as a guardian and guide for the children until the teacher began working with them. It is in this context that Paul calls the Mosaic Law a pedagogue or guardian when he writes to the Galatians: "Before faith came, we were allowed no freedom by the Law; we were being looked after till faith was revealed. The Law was to be our guardian until the Christ came and we could be justified by faith. Now that that time has come we are no longer under that guardian, and you are, all of you, sons [and daughters] of God through faith in Christ Jesus" (3:23-26).

Paul's realization of the freedom from the Law which is given us in and by Christ excites him so much that he tells us over and over "now we hold that faith in Christ rather than fidelity to the Law is what justifies us, and that 'no one can be justified' by keeping the Law" (Gal. 2:16; 3:11-12; Rom. 3:28). Indeed, for Paul, the Law's inability to make us good and righteous people is so obvious that it leads him to declare that "if the Law can justify us, there is no point in the death of Christ" (Gal. 2:21). The fact is, of course, that Paul recognizes that it is precisely by Christ's submission, for our sake, to the curse of a death on a cross that he "redeemed us from the curse of the Law. . ." (Gal. 3:13).

Turning now to Paul's reference to the Law as a curse, we must try to understand the context which gives meaning to such a description of the Law. Paul himself says: "What I mean is that I should not have known what sin was except for the Law. I should not for instance have known what it means to covet if the Law had not said 'You shall not covet.' But it was this commandment that sin took advantage of to produce all kinds of covetousness in me, for when there is no Law, sin is dead" (Rom. 7:7-8). What Paul is suggesting here is that he had been able to live a rather carefree life of "ignorant bliss" so long as he remained uninformed about the requirements of the Law, but once the stipulations of the Law were made known, Paul became unsettled by the awarenesss of how imperfect and misdirected his life really was. Thus it is the Law which reveals our transgressions and makes it possible for us to sin; the Law places us under the "curse" of responsibility in the sense that once our transgressions and imperfections are unmasked and brought to our attention, we are challenged to do something about them. For Paul, then, the Law can indeed tell us what is sinful, but that is all it can do; and Paul never passes up an opportunity to remind us that we can never be justified in the sight of God simply by keeping the Law or by doing what it tells us to do (Rom. 3:20, 38).

THE NEW LAW OF LOVE

As we have seen earlier, Paul's constant refrain is that we are justified by the response of living faith which we are empowered to make by God's life and love within us. Paul now tells us, however, that insofar as we are in fact people of faith and are living with the love of God inside us, we are no longer under the Law but rather under grace (Rom. 6:14). For Paul, this means that there is a new law in our lives; it is the law of love or "the law of the spirit of life in Christ Jesus" (Rom. 8:2), and it is utterly unlike any other law. Because of its uniqueness, this new law deserves our careful attention.

The first thing to be noted about the new law of love is that it is not at all a law which is external to ourselves. Rather it comes to life within us and is, in fact, the same law which Yahweh promised in the writings of the prophets. Thus in the book of Jeremiah, Yahweh says: "Deep within them I will plant my Law, writing it on their hearts" (31:33); and Yahweh sends the same message through the prophet Ezekiel: "I shall give you a new heart, and put a new spirit in you; I shall remove the heart of stone from your bodies and give you a heart of flesh instead. I shall put my spirit in you, and make you keep my laws and sincerely respect my observances" (36:26-7).

Centuries later, Thomas Aquinas takes very seriously Yahweh's promises to plant His law within us and to put His spirit in us. Thus it is that in his commentaries on the letters of Paul, Thomas can reach the marvelous conclusion that the new law of love or "the law of the spirit of life in Christ Jesus," which is so dear to Paul, must in fact be "identified either with the person of the Holy Spirit or with the activity of that same Spirit in us." Thomas presses his point further by saying that, unlike any other law, including the Mosaic Law, this new law which governs the believer is not just a code, not even if we were to consider it a code "given by the Holy Spirit"; neither is this new law any kind of external norm for our activity; rather, the law of love is one that is "produced in us by the Holy Spirit" and thus serves as our new inner source of spiritual energy. As Christians, then, we find ourselves in this situation: by entering into the relationship of faith through our cooperation with the gift of God's grace, we are actually welcoming the Holy Spirit into our lives with the result that we are further inspired and empowered by the life of this same Spirit which is love. Thus the law which motivates and directs us now is the inner force of love which is the very life of God himself.[33]

THE LAW OF MOSES AND THE LAW OF THE SPIRIT

We are now in a position to consider the relationship existing between the Mosaic Law and the new law of love. What we discover is that when we receive the Holy Spirit and begin to live with his life of love within us, we are actually living and acting in accordance with what the Law of Moses has wanted of us all along, namely, that we live as lovers. Thus Paul writes: "Avoid getting into debt, except the debt of mutual love. If you love your fellow men [and women] you have carried out your obligations. All the commandments . . . are summed up in this single command: 'You must love your neighbor as yourself.' Love is the one thing that cannot hurt your neighbor; that is why it is the answer to every one of the commandments" (Rom. 13:8-10; also see Gal. 5:13-14).

Here, Paul is telling us in effect that we have been called to the freedom of living out of love, but in no way is this freedom to be interpreted as the permission or license to do whatever we desire or please. On the contrary, a life of love, or life in the

---

[33]cf. Lyonnet, pp. 71-2 with references to St. Thomas' *In Hebr.,* cap. 8, lect. 2 and *In 2 Cor.,* cap. 3, lect. 2. In his *Summa Theol. I-II,* q. 106, a. 1,c, Thomas says: ". . . the New Law is chiefly the grace itself of the Holy Spirit, which is given to those who believe in Christ."

Spirit of God, stands in contradiction to a life of selfishness or self-indulgence which we must struggle to avoid; when we fail to do so, the results are obvious and our lives are marked by such things as: "fornication, gross indecency and sexual irresponsibility; idolatry and sorcery; feuds and wrangling, jealousy, bad temper and quarrels; disagreements, factions, envy; drunkenness, orgies and similar things" (cf. Gal. 5:16-21). What the Spirit of God brings into our lives is very different, however: "love, joy, peace, patience, kindness, goodness, trustfulness, gentleness and self-control." Paul is left to conclude that the only way for us to belong to Christ Jesus is by crucifying all our "self-indulgent passions and desires." Moreover, he says, "since the Spirit is our life, let us be directed by the Spirit. We must stop being conceited, provocative and envious" (Gal. 5:22-26).

THE MEANING OF CHRISTIAN LIBERTY

Having looked both at Paul's understanding of the Mosaic Law and the law of the Spirit, as well as at the relationship that exists between them, we are perhaps now ready to appreciate what he means by Christian liberty. I believe that the essence of Paul's insight into this reality is revealed in his comment that if we are led by the Spirit, no law can touch us (Gal. 5:18). I offer the diagram below as one way of illustrating the significance of Paul's remark here.

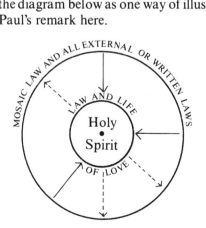

The area enclosed by the large circle represents the Christian life at the very center of which is the Holy Spirit whose life of love is meant to enliven, not only the whole Christian community, but also its individual members.

According to Paul, insofar as we open ourselves up to the life of the Holy Spirit within us and thus fulfill every requirement of the Law out of love, we are freed from the external pressure of any written laws, including that of Moses. In terms of the diagram presented, this means that as we let the life of God's Holy Spirit, which is love, take hold of us, we are drawn more and more to the center of the circle which represents the heart of the Christian life. With our lives energized by, and focused on, love, we find ourselves well removed from, and free of, the external forces and pressures exerted by the requirements of the Mosaic Law and other written laws as represented by the circle's circumference. Moreover, living, as we are, at the center of the Christian life, not only are we doing exactly what is expected of us, namely, loving, but we are also fulfilling the precepts of the Law superabundantly; we do so, however, without even adverting to this fact, and we also do it freely, for indeed "where the Spirit of the Lord is, there is freedom" (2 Cor. 3:17).

Should our love grow cold, however, and begin to weaken, we then start to drift away from the center of the Christian life and sooner or later we run head-on into the many and varied stipulations of written laws. Without the interior flame of love to inspire and motivate us, our lives as Christians are reduced to the struggle of going through the motions of external conformity to the written laws which are all around us, and whose requirements now feel like chains which constrict and constrain us. We are obviously at a point which calls for a decision on our part: we can either violate the stipulations of the law (and break through the circle's circumference), or we can turn around, "be converted," and move with rekindled love back to the center of the Christian life.

Given this scheme of things, I would describe Christian liberty or freedom in Christ as follows: Christian freedom is the experience that comes from being so filled with the life of God's love (the Holy Spirit) within us that we are empowered to love in return and to do what God expects of us freely out of love, not out of fear or because of external coercion. Of course, when we live in a way that is truly loving, we are at the same time fulfilling the basic purpose of the Mosaic Law itself. Now, however, instead of being slaves to the stipulations of the written Law, we are servants of love; the demands of the Law which exert external pressure upon us yield now to the demands of love which arise from within us because of the personal bonds uniting us with God and our neighbor.

There is no question, of course, but that love involves obligations and responsibilities. Even on the psychological level, in real love we experience both the need and the desire to express that love. We both have to, and want to, manifest our love. But whatever the demands of love, given the inner life that inspires us to meet these demands, when we love, we ultimately are doing what we ourselves want to do and thus we are free. This is a far different experience from that which results when we are compelled to act due to the external pressure put upon us by another person or by the stipulations of any written law.

Thomas himself contributes to our understanding of Christian liberty when he reminds us that we are free when we do what we should, namely, refrain from evil, precisely because it is evil, and not because some precept of God forbids it; we are not free, however, when we avoid evil simply because God's precept forbids our doing otherwise.[34] Thomas also discusses our liberty as Christians in a way that is more directly derived from Paul when he says quite simply that we are free whenever the inner dynamism of love, which is the life of the Holy Spirit within us, motivates and empowers us to do what is expected of us. Thus our freedom in Christ consists not at all in our being outside the boundaries of the divine law, but rather in our being so far inside them, where it is neither fear nor any external force which moves us to do what this law requires, but only love.[35]

In light of Paul's belief in the centrality of love and the liberty that is born of it, there is much sense in his view that laws are not made for good and righteous people but rather for those who are unjust (1 Tim. 1:9). If, in fact, all Christians were just and loving, there would be no need for the restraints imposed by the Law; Paul recognizes, however, that we can misuse our

[34] *Ibid.*, p. 79 with reference to Thomas' *Summa Contra Gentiles, III,* c. 122.
[35] *Ibid.*, with reference to Thomas' *In 2 Cor.,* cap. 3, lect. 3.

freedom and thus move away from love, in which case, since we are no longer willing to accept the inner light and strength offered us by the Holy Spirit, the written stipulations of the Law can serve both to highlight the present misdirection of our lives and to remind us of our need for reconsideration and conversion.

Even when we struggle faithfully to live in love, the fact is that since we now possess only "the first-fruits of the Spirit" of God (Rom. 8:23), we always remain imperfect and incomplete lovers. Given the precariousness of our decision to live as lovers, it should not surprise us that the liberty we enjoy in Christ is not immune to peril, for when our love cools, we do not always see what it requires and expects of us. In this instance, we may indeed be well served once again by the guiding provocation of the written Law.

IMPLICATIONS FOR CHRISTIAN MORALITY

On the basis of what we have seen so far regarding the freedom we have in Christ, I want to suggest some implications which Paul's thinking has for our understanding of our moral lives as Christians. As indicated earlier, our life in the Holy Spirit which frees us to love does not give us license to do anything and everything we please. Thus, while it is true that we always retain the freedom to allow our love to die, if our desire is, rather, that our love continue to grow, then we must resist the obvious threats to love that are born of selfishness; beyond this, however, we also need to realize that love may never be taken for granted, for it can be killed just as surely by complacency and neglect as by self-centeredness. For love to grow, then, it needs not only to be protected but also nurtured.

Since, as we have already indicated, love does not exist in a vacuum and is not a matter merely of words but must prove itself in action, it is necessary to discover how we go about protecting and nurturing love. In order to do this, we need to look more closely at the relationship between the demands of love and the commands of the written Law; or, to put the matter in different terms, we need to examine the connection that exists between the spirit of the Law which is love and the letter of the Law as articulated in its various precepts and prohibitions.

Paul has told us (Rom. 3:20,28) that we cannot be justified simply by keeping the Law or by doing what it tells us to do; what Paul means by this is that if all we do is externally observe or obey the letter of the Law (its written precepts or commands), but we do so without any love in our lives, then our actions lack any true moral significance, because all we are doing is going through the exterior motions of Christian living without, as it were, any heart and Spirit. As Paul makes clear, this is not how we are justified; what is needed for our justification is the faith (our response of love for God) which gives birth to our loving care for others. But now another question surfaces: granted that our exterior observance of the letter of the Law does not justify us, what should be said about our external violation of the letter of the Law? Is every violation of the Law's letter (its commands and prohibitions) also a sin? Does disobeying the letter of the Law necessarily mean that we are no longer justified or righteous?

Before answering this question, let us establish a context for our response. As an expression of love, the Christian life involves our personal commitment to God and the service of our neighbor, and as with any serious commitment, the Christian life thus engages our heart and will. As a refusal to love, sin is the breaking of our basic commitment to God and others, and thus it too must engage our heart and will. To put it differently, if love is a gift that is freely given, then sin must be the free retraction of our gift of love; this means, of course, that we never sin involuntarily or by accident, any more than we accidentally "fall" in love. We decide to sin just as we decide to love.

Having said all this, what about the question posed above: is every violation of the letter of the Law a sin? The answer is no. Because sin is a free and conscious refusal to love, a violation of the letter of the Law is a sin only if that violation of the written Law is also a rejection of the Law's spirit which is love; if, however, our violation of the Law's letter is not also a rejection of the spirit of the Law, then the violation of the letter of the Law is not a sin. Sin is more properly understood, then, not as a violation of the written Law but as a conscious and free rejection of the Law's spirit of love. Thus, to whatever extent we may violate the letter of the Law without violating its spirit, to that same extent, there is no sin. But some cautions are in order.

Nothing of what we have just said is meant to imply that as Christians we should be occupied with finding loopholes in the written Law that allow us to disobey its precepts with impunity; neither does it speak well of the vitality of our Christian love if our major concern is to discover how far we may wander from the letter of the Law without sinning. In addition, the point should be made that we seriously distort the reality of Christian living if we reduce it to an expression of subjectivism which says that particular actions are morally good or bad simply because we judge them to be so, and that in the end it really does not matter what we do so long as we mean well and have good intentions and a loving disposition.[36] What subjectivism fails to realize is that in the real or objective world, there is a lot of harm inflicted by people claiming to be well-intentioned, and that the pain thus caused is often no less devastating just because it is unintended. Furthermore, there is no justification or validity in the claim to be "well-meaning" when we make neither the time nor the effort to consider the individual effects and social implications of our actions.

But subjectivism, or the idea that thinking lovingly and having good intentions are enough to make us moral people, is not the only distortion of Christian living which should cause us concern. Just as perverted, of course, is the view known as legalism which claims that we are morally good people if only we obey the letter of the Law. For legalism, the Law is raised to the level of a deity and the argument is made that this Law has the power to save us if we live according to its written precepts. Our external observance of moral laws is thus regarded not only as necessary, but also as *sufficient,* for our being good or moral people; from legalism's perspective, moreover, our

[36]Timothy E. O'Connell, *Principles for a Catholic Morality* (New York: Seabury Press, 1978), p. 145.

salvation ultimately hinges exclusively upon our obedience and conformity to the letter of the Law.

This legalistic mentality stands in stark contradiction to both Paul's teaching and the authentic tradition of Christianity, for, in fact, as one author puts it, "the Christian life is not, ultimately, a matter of following the law; it is not an exercise in obedience. Instead the Christian life is a matter of doing the good, an exercise in love."[37] We must, of course, avoid the mistake of establishing a false dichotomy between the letter and the spirit of the Law, between the written Law and the new Law, or between acts of obedience and faithful loving. What I would maintain, therefore, is that we live as true Christians and as morally good people only when the material or physical conformity of our actions to the requirements of the written Law reflects or expresses a much fuller or deeper conformity, namely, a conformity of our heart and will to the heart and will of God. Moreover, although the conformity of our actions to the written Law may be understood as the usual way in which we embody the conformity of our heart and will to the heart and will of God, it is only this latter conformity which makes us truly moral.[38] This is why it is so true that Christian morality cannot be legislated. There is simply no written law that can touch our hearts or change us into lovers; all that written laws may succeed in doing is to frighten us into holding our selfishness or heartlessness sufficiently at bay so that we do not externally victimize others.[39]

Two things may be said, then, about our observance of the written Law: first, we must obey its commands and prohibitions, and thus act or refrain from acting in certain ways, when

---

[37] *Ibid.*

[38] Leslie Dewart, "Some Early Historical Development of New Testament Morality," in William Dunphy (ed.). *The New Morality: Continuity and Discontinuity* (New York: Herder & Herder, 1967), pp. 83-4, 102-3.

[39] A similar view was expressed by Martin Luther King, Jr. in May, 1961 at Ralph Abernathy's First Baptist Church in Montgomery: "We hear the familiar cry that morals cannot be legislated. This may be true, but behavior can be regulated. The law may not be able to make a man love me, but it can keep him from lynching me." See Flip Schulke (ed.), *Martin L. King, Jr. A Documentary . . . Montgomery to Memphis* (New York: W.W. Norton & Co., 1976), p. 42.

this is necessary for the preservation and nurturing of the spirit of love; secondly, if we are ever really to obey the written Law, we must do so out of love, for it seems that the only true Christian obedience is an obedience of love. If we merely go through the external motions of obedience to the Law without love, then we are not really obeying the Law; rather, we are circumventing it, since the written Law's sole aim is to protect and foster the inner spirit and dynamism of Christian love. Even when we appreciate the written Law as having been authored by God, the fact remains that this Law is created not as an end in itself, but rather as a guide to love.[40] This means that we are really faithful to the written Law only when our external conformity to its requirements embodies our desire to answer our true calling to be lovers. We can say, finally, that the whole value of the letter of the Law is derived from its relationship to the spirit of the Law, and our observance of the written Law is morally necessary and good only insofar as it is needed in order to meet the real demands of a vitalized Christian love.

In speaking to this question of the relationship between the letter of the Law and the Law's spirit of love, or between the commands of the Law and the demands of love, Häring makes the point that "between love and law, as such, there is no incompatibility. Law protects love .... Properly formulated, interpreted, and administered, law defines and guards the outer boundaries of the order of love, beyond which lie arbitrariness, injustice, and self-serving utilitarianism ...."[41] It is with these latter realities, of course, that love is incompatible. But within this context of Häring's understanding of the relationship that exists between love and law, it makes sense to say that were we ever morally convinced that our observance of some precept of the written Law would constitute a violation of justice or love, then obviously we would be bound not to obey the Law's command. Since, however, the Law is authored by God, we must honestly wonder how likely it is that we would often, if ever, find ourselves in such a situation.

[40]Lyonnet, *op. cit.,* pp. 77-8.
[41]Häring, *op. cit.,* p. 125.

I would suggest that in trying to understand and explain Christian morality, we do best to say that as Christians we ultimately find our integrity both as human and as moral beings, not in conformity to laws, but in conformity to the person of Jesus Christ. But Jesus, we recall, is the one who tells us: "Do not imagine that I have come to abolish the Law or the Prophets. I have come not to abolish but to complete them" (Mt. 5:17). What Jesus' completion or fulfillment of the Law amounts to, however, is really a total transformation or radical metamorphosis, such that the connection or relationship between the written Law and the law of the Spirit of love might never be appreciated or realized apart from the example and teaching of Christ himself. The relationship between the Old Law and the New Law might, in fact, be compared to the relationship between a caterpillar and a butterfly. The caterpillar's earth-bound existence differs so much from the butterfly's freedom of flight that we would never identify the relationship which connects them unless someone had told us about it, or we had witnessed the transformation ourselves.

So it is with Jesus' completion of the Law. Through his life and teaching, the hidden meaning and dynamism of the written Law are revealed; but more than this, we are invited and empowered by Christ and his Spirit to live a qualitatively new and different style of life, which consists in moving beyond the minimal commands of the Law's negative prohibitions so as to meet the maximal challenges of the positive commands to love. Perhaps the new kind of life to which Christ calls us is best portrayed in the scene from the gospels of Matthew (19:16-22), Mark (10:17-22) and Luke (18:18-23) where, in answer to a rich young man's inquiry concerning what he must do in order to have eternal life, Jesus responds by telling him to keep the commandments of the Law. But when the man replies that he has indeed obeyed the Law from the days of his youth, Jesus then calls him to the perfection of a life of personal discipleship: "Come, follow me."

Insofar as Christ calls all of us to enter into a personal relationship with him and to follow him wherever he leads, the static and minimal commands and prohibitions of the written

Law are transformed into the dynamic and maximal demands of loving living persons—Christ and our neighbors. In all living relationships, the predictability of always knowing exactly what is required of us by the written Law yields to the unpredictability of having and wanting to meet the true, but changing, corporal and spiritual needs of others. No longer can we be satisfied, it seems, with the security of a life lived in obedience to the stipulations of the written Law when Christ calls us to follow him in a personal relationship that necessarily implies risks and the need for vulnerability and trust.

The written Law does indeed reveal the minimum moral standards whose observance usually guarantees that we will not harm others or infringe upon their human rights. Thus, for example, we should neither kill nor steal, but it is only love which is likely to enlighten and inspire us to find effective alternatives to war, or to create a society in which all people have what is necessary to live with decency and dignity and thus are freed from the desperate need to steal.[42]

VIII. Conclusion

There is perhaps no better way for us to conclude our discussion of the meaning and spirit of Christian living than to say simply that we truly live as Christians when we live in a personal relationship with Jesus Christ, whose gracious life within us enables us to continue growing in our faithful response to our God-given vocation to be lovers. That our Christian lives are focused, primarily and fundamentally, on the call we have received to love as we have first been loved by God, is undeniable. And yet, I suggest that we gain a fuller understanding and a deeper appreciation of the implications and expectations of this call to love, not only when we listen to it prayerfully, but also when we allow it to pass under the review of theological reflection, as we have done in this chapter, in an attempt to uncover its various elements or components.

[42]See Albert R. Jonsen, *Christian Decision and Action* (New York: The Bruce Publishing Company, 1970), pp. 77-96, 53.

Just as the colors of the spectrum are revealed when light passes through a prism, so does theological analysis make clear that our calling to God-like love may be variously articulated. Thus our vocation to live as lovers is at one and the same time: 1) a call to live eucharistically, or in grateful recognition of the love already shown us by God; 2) a call to live eschatologically as active co-creators with God of his coming kingdom; 3) a call to live prophetically or as prophets who are willing to subject the values of this world to the scrutiny of God's perspective; 4) a call to living faith by means of which our love for God is embodied in our caring service of others; 5) a call to salvation which is the promise of our full enjoyment of the gift of God's life in which we already share through faith; 6) a call to the continual conversion that allows Christ to be more fully alive within us as we grow more forgetful of self and more mindful of others; 7) a call to freedom in Christ because of whom we can live in the Holy Spirit of love and thus no longer be subjected to the coercion of the external Law.

At this point, there is little more to be said except that in the final analysis our call to be lovers is a call to be perfect and compassionate as is our Father in heaven (Mt. 5:48; Lk. 6:36); our response to this call, needless to say, is the labor of a lifetime, but it is a labor which we are empowered and expected to undertake in cooperation with the grace of Christ in whom the presence and power of God's kingdom have come among us. In the person of Christ, the kingdom of God does indeed make present claims upon us; we have only to think, for example, of the radical demands and high ideals revealed in Jesus' Sermon on the Mount (Mt. 5-7).

It would, of course, be a terrible mistake for us to view all of Christ's teachings as universal norms of conduct which must always be observed under pain of sin, but what the life and teachings of Jesus do indicate, is that the basic direction in which our lives as Christians must move is toward the realization of God's kingdom. We know that the establishment of this kingdom is a work of love—God's and our own—so we will never be able to say that we have loved enough. At times, moreover, our desire and intention to love may have to make conscious accommodations or concessions to the realities of an imperfect and sinful world, with the result that we find ourselves doing what we do not desire to do and would never choose to do were the world and our situation in it other than they are.[43]

Thus, for example, should it prove necessary for us to resort to violence and the taking of human life in order to defend innocent people, we would find no joy in such activity. Rather, to the extent that this action embodies a compromising of the Christian ideal to hold all human life as sacred and worthy of respect, it would serve as a poignant reminder to us of how much more creative we must learn to be in trying to resolve the tensions and conflicts which mark our presence in this time between the beginning of God's kingdom and its desired completion.

[43]See Curran, *op. cit.*, pp. 11-21 for a fuller discussion of these ideas.

II

Listening to Moral Authority: The Magisterium and the Role of Conscience

Rooted in faith, alive with hope, and active in love, we Christians can find joy in our efforts to be moral, for in so living we are also bearing witness to the spirit of Christ within us. No less are we continuing the work of Christ as we struggle to build up the kingdom of God by responding to the deepest human and spiritual needs of others. But in carrying on the mission of Christ and in preparing the way for his return, we are often reminded of the fact that we remain "a pilgrim people who move slowly and not always directly toward the beckoning God of truth."[1] It should not surprise us, then, that we are in need of guidance and direction as we attempt to live faithfully in response to our call to be lovers. It is in acknowledgment of this need that we now turn to a consideration of the two voices, namely, of the magisterium and of personal conscience, which

---

[1]Daniel C. Maguire, "Moral Absolutes and the Magisterium," *Absolutes in Moral Theology?*, ed. Charles Curran (Washington: Corpus Books, 1968), 57-107 at 84.

Roman Catholics recognize not only as interpreters and mediators of God's word but also as legitimate bearers of moral authority within their lives.

I. The Official Teaching Authority within the Catholic Community

In light of Vatican II, Roman Catholics have come to appreciate the fact that the Church is a community of believers united in and by the Holy Spirit. As members of this gathering of faith, all of us share in the being of Christ as prophet, king and priest. So also, does each of us share in some way in the function of teacher, in that everyone bears some responsibility for handing on the heritage of our faith. Some among us, however, have the specific responsibility not only to live and preach the gospel of Christ, but also to protect, encourage and oversee its transmission. Those charged with this task are the bishops collectively, with the pope as their head. In other words, it is the college of bishops or the hierarchy (pope, archbishops, bishops) which is entrusted with the responsibility of serving as the official teaching body of the Church. Perceived in their function as teachers, the members of the hierarchy are referred to as "the magisterium," and only they are the proponents of what we call the Church's "official" teaching.[2] Thus, while each

---

[2]In developing the ideas pertaining to the teaching office of the Church, I found the following works to be most helpful: Francis A. Sullivan, S.J., *Magisterium. Teaching Authority in The Catholic Church* (New York: Paulist Press, 1983); Avery Dulles, S.J., *A Church To Believe In. Discipleship and the Dynamics of Freedom* (New York: The Crossroad Publ, Co., 1982); see especially chapters 7–9. It should be noted that Dulles presents a fine brief history of the term "magisterium" and shows, as well, that there are solid grounds for speaking of two magisteria (the hierarchical one and a theological one made up of professional theologians of acknowledged competence as indicated by "the possession of a theological degree, a distinguished career of teaching, noteworthy publications, and esteem by one's colleagues" [p. 122]). Thomas Aquinas also spoke of two types of magisteria, but Sullivan has reservations about the pastoral wisdom of emphasizing this notion (pp. 28–9). See also Charles E. Curran and Richard A. McCormick, S.J. (eds.) *Readings in Moral Thoelogy, No. 3: The Magisterium and Morality* (New York: Paulist Press, 1982).

of us has a mission to announce the kingdom of God and proclaim the gospel by word and example, the exercise of this mission varies, so that not all of us are involved in proposing the Church's magisterial or "authentic" teaching.

Vatican II's *Dogmatic Constitution on the Church* (*Lumen Gentium*) refers to bishops as the Church's "authentic teachers, that is, teachers endowed with the authority of Christ" (#25), and in its *Dogmatic Constitution on Divine Revelation* (*Dei Verbum*), the Council notes that "the task of authentically interpreting the word of God, whether written or handed on, has been entrusted exclusively to the living teaching office of the Church, whose authority is exercised in the name of Jesus Christ" (#10). We must mention immediately that it is unfortunate that the Latin words, *authenticum* and *authentice,* have been translated in these passages as "authentic" and "authentically," because in the context the correct translation for the intended meaning is rather "authoritative" and "authoritatively." In other words, the teaching put forth by the magisterium is seen as having special significance and weight precisely because it is proposed by the bishops who, in their official functioning as teachers, are "endowed with the authority of Christ" and thus exercise their authority to teach "in the name of Jesus Christ."[3] To speak, then, of "authentic" teachings of the Church does not mean that such teachings are necessarily true or accurate. Rather, the "authentic" teachings of the Church are those which are "official" or "authoritative" because they are proposed by the hierarchical magisterium.

THE EXTRAORDINARY AND ORDINARY EXERCISES OF TEACHING AUTHORITY

As the authoritative teaching body of the Church, the magisterium performs its teaching role in two basic ways, one that is "extraordinary" or "solemn," and one that is "ordinary." A "solemn" or "extraordinary" exercise of teaching authority occurs only when a doctrine is defined either by the bishops of

[3]Sullivan, *op. cit.,* pp. 26-8..

the world gathered together in an ecumenical council (the extraordinary universal magisterium), or by a pope speaking *ex cathedra* (this expression meaning "from the throne or chair" is used to indicate that the pope is exercising his teaching authority in an infallible way; more will be said about this extraordinary papal magisterium later).

All other exercises of the Church's teaching authority are called "ordinary." Thus, for example, we have the ordinary papal magisterium which appears in a pope's letters, speeches and encyclicals, or in the declarations of various Vatican congregations that are issued with a pope's approval; another instance of the Church's ordinary magisterium is the teaching presented by bishops in their own dioceses, in regional synods or in national conferences; finally, there is the exercise of the Church's ordinary universal magisterium which occurs when all the bishops dispersed throughout the world (not in an ecumenical council) are in conscious and deliberate agreement with one another and with the pope about a particular teaching. In the context of these distinctions, Francis A. Sullivan's reminder regarding the teachings presented by Vatican II is pertinent: "Although the Second Vatican Council was an extraordinary event, its documents represent what we mean here by 'ordinary' teaching, since this Council chose not to use the authority it had to define any new dogma of Catholic faith."[4] The decision of Vatican II to avoid any new solemn definitions indicates that all the teachings put forth by this Council alone are fallibly proposed. We shall now look at what is meant by the notions of teaching fallibly and infallibly.

TEACHING INFALLIBLY AND FALLIBLY

If we are to have an adequate understanding of the way in which the magisterium exercises its teaching authority, another distinction must be considered. For the most part, the authentic or authoritative teaching of the Church is fallible or open to the possibility of error; by its very nature, this kind of teaching can

[4]*Ibid.*, p. 121; also pp. 60, 62, 123.

be reformed or changed.[5] On occasion, however, the magisterium teaches in an infallible manner, which means that the very possibility of error is precluded and thus the teaching is not subject to reform or change. Since the notion of infallibility is so often misunderstood, something more must be said of it.

To begin with, although the words "infallible" and "infallibility" are popularly used most often in reference to the pope ("the pope is infallible," "the pope's infallibility"), the terms are applied originally and primarily to the Church as understood in broader terms. Thus scholars note that as far back as the ninth century, there is evidence of the Church's explicit belief in the capacity of ecumenical councils to teach infallibly. The matter is otherwise, however, with respect to the issue of papal infallibility; although some biblical citations (Mt. 16:18, Lk. 22:32) have often been given in support of the idea of the pope's ability to teach infallibly, these texts themselves do not directly assert any such idea. In fact, the doctrine of papal infallibility was not formally taught until the last quarter of the thirteenth century and it remained a matter of much controversy and debate until 1870 when the First Vatican Council solemnly defined the teaching as a dogma of faith.[6]

As Vatican I made clear, however, the infallibility which the pope enjoys under certain conditions is that same infallibility "with which the divine Redeemer willed his Church to be endowed in defining doctrine concerning faith or morals."[7] The same point is made in Vatican II's *Lumen Gentium* (#25). In essence, then, what is being affirmed is this: under certain conditions, the Church's ability to teach infallibly is concentrated or crystallized in the office of the papacy. What exactly are the conditions to be met in order for a pope to teach infallibly or, to pose the question differently, when is a pope said to be teaching or speaking "*ex cathedra*"?

[5] For examples of teachings which have changed, see Maguire, *art. cit.*, p. 83.

[6] This is the thesis of B. Tierney, *Origins of Papal Infallibility* (Leiden: Brill, 1972) as quoted in *Theological Studies*, 40 (1979), 125, 146–47; also see Sullivan *op. cit.*, p. 82.

[7] Denzinger-Schönmetzer, *Enchiridion Symbolorum, Definitionum, Declarationum*, #3074. Future references will be to D-S.

Theologians agree that four conditions must be fulfilled if a pope is to exercise his teaching authority in an infallible manner. Avery Dulles lists the four conditions nicely: (1) "The pope must be speaking not as a private person but as a public person and more specifically as supreme pastor and teacher of all Christians"; (2) he "must appeal to his supreme apostolic authority, i.e., that which pertains to him as successor of Peter"; (3) he "must be teaching within the sphere of 'faith and morals'"; and (4) finally, the pope "must be proposing the doctrine as something to be held by the whole Church, that is to say, as a doctrine having universal obligatory force."[8]

In addition to its embodiment in the solemn definitions of a pope speaking "*ex cathedra*," the Church's infallibility may also be exercised in two other ways: (1) in the solemn definitions authored by the college of bishops meeting in an ecumenical council, and (2) in its ordinary universal magisterium when all the bishops, even while dispersed throughout the world, are united among themselves and with the pope in maintaining that a particular teaching in the area of faith or morals must be held conclusively or definitively (*Lumen Gentium,* #25).[9] What should be clear from what has been said so far but must be mentioned, nonetheless, is this: neither the pope nor the magisterium as a whole is always or habitually infallible; rather the magisterium can teach infallibly "only at certain times and under certain limiting conditions."[10]

The only possible explanation for the magisterium's ability to teach infallibly is to say that this power is available simply as a result of a charism, gift or grace offered by God. In other words, when the pope and the hierarchy teach infallibly, they can do so only because of the assistance of the Holy Spirit;

---

[8]Dulles, *op. cit.,* pp. 137–38; internal quotes are of Vatican I's definition; also see John Jay Hughes, "Hans Küng and the Magisterium," *Theological Studies,* 41 (1980), 368-89 at 383.

[9]Sullivan, *op. cit.,* pp. 56-7, gives an example of the ordinary universal magisterium teaching in an infallible manner: "The Church has never defined that 'Jesus is Lord, and that God raised him from the dead,' but these are far more basic articles of our faith than many dogmas that have been solemnly defined."

[10]Peter Chirico, S.S., *Infallibility: The Crossroads of Doctrine* (Kansas City: Sheed, Andrews & McMeel, 1977), p. 231.

moreover, at such times as these, the Church is confident that God does not allow a pope, an ecumenical council, or the ordinary universal magisterium to bind the faithful to any teaching which is contrary to the truth contained at the heart of Christ's message of salvation. This talk, both of infallibility as a charism and of the assistance of the Holy Spirit which is given to the magisterium, ought not to mislead us, however, into thinking that the Church's teaching function is somehow magically executed. Such is not the case at all, for the Church has never claimed that the pope or the other members of the hierarchy are the recipients of special private revelations, either as a result of visions or through any kind of direct infusion of knowledge by God.[11]

Clearly, then, if the magisterium is to fulfill in a responsible manner its role as the authoritative teacher within the community of faith, it succeeds in doing so only by continually reminding itself that God's assistance is not received without human cooperation; in the words of the Council of Trent (1545-1563), divine assistance and grace are given to human beings as God wishes, and according to each person's "own proper disposition and cooperation."[12] Thus the responsible exercise of the Church's teaching authority involves not only the gift or charism offered by the Holy Spirit, but also a task which this same Spirit imposes. This means that if the magisterium is going to teach well, whether fallibly or infallibly, it must also learn well; if it is going to speak effectively, it must also listen effectively. There is much sense, therefore, in the caution expressed by Dan Maguire: "the teaching office is not just a gift; it is a task" at which the magisterium can fail.[13] This task is acknowledged in *Lumen Gentium* itself. We read there that while the pope and bishops operate "under the guiding light of the Spirit of truth" in their attempt to preserve and explain God's revelation, it is expected, nonetheless, that they "strive painstakingly and by appropriate means to inquire

---

[11]Richard P. McBrien, *Who Is A Catholic?* (Denville, N.J.: Dimension Books, 1971), pp. 115-16; Hughes, *art, cit.,* p. 383.

[12]D-S #1529.

[13]Maguire, *op, cit.,* pp. 90-1.

properly into that revelation and to give apt expression to its contents" (#25).[14]

In concluding this brief discussion of infallibility, one final thing should be noted. It is expected that just as the Holy Spirit on occasion absolutely preserves the magisterium from error, thereby enabling it to teach infallibly, so also will this same Spirit inspire the community of believers to submit in faith to whatever doctrine is infallibly proposed (*Lumen Gentium,* #25). Should it happen, however, that a seemingly infallible teaching not be received or accepted as such by the body of the faithful, we are given some indication that the magisterium has failed to fulfill the necessary conditions for teaching infallibly and thus has exceeded its competence to do so.

This is not to say, of course, that either the pope's or the entire magisterium's authority, power or ability to teach infallibly depends upon the consent of the faithful; this idea was explicitly denied by both the First and Second Vatican Councils (D-S 3074 and *Lumen Gentium,* #25). What can be maintained, however, is this: while it is not the faithful's acceptance or reception in faith that makes a particular teaching of the magisterium infallible, nonetheless, such acceptance by the believing community does certify or notarize that the teaching is in fact infallible. This role of the faithful in the life of the Church seems unavoidable, for if the same Spirit of God is at work throughout the Church in both the magisterium and the people, we can do no less than assert that "the assent of the Church can never be wanting" to what is infallibly taught (*Lumen Gentium,* #25); as Dulles notes in commenting on Vatican II's view, "the infallibility of popes and councils in teaching" is matched "by the infallibility of the entire people of God in believing."[15]

---

[14]This point is also made clearly in the 1973 Declaration of the Congregation for the Doctrine of the Faith, *Mysterium Ecclesiae,* #3.

[15]Dulles, *op. cit.,* pp. 116, 109, 139; also see *Lumen Gentium,* #12 and #25; Sullivan also treats the notion of "reception," *op. cit.,* pp. 108-11; Chirico, *op. cit.,* pp. 239-42.

THE MAGISTERIUM'S TEACHINGS IN MORALITY

In modern times, the magisterium has rarely used its extraordinary ability to teach infallibly: it is generally acknowledged that in the last century and a half, there have been only two solemn papal definitions, one concerning the Virgin Mary's Immaculate Conception (1854), the other, her Assumption (1950); in addition, Vatican I (1870) solemnly defined the doctrine of papal infallibility. The new Code of Canon Law reminds us, moreover, that "no doctrine is understood to be infallibly defined unless this is manifestly demonstrated" (Canon 749,3).[16] It should be noted that neither in recent years nor beyond has there ever been an infallible definition by a pope or an ecumenical council concerning specific moral issues; as a matter of fact, there is a broad consensus among Roman Catholic theologians today that even in the exercise of its ordinary universal magisterium, the Church has never taught infallibly in the area of concrete moral norms.[17]

Later in this book in our discussion of contraception we will indeed consider the case which some theologians have made for viewing the Church's prohibition of artificial contraceptives as an instance of infallible teaching by the ordinary universal magisterium. For now, I propose that we listen to some of the theological voices in the consensus which denies that there can be any infallible teaching when dealing with specific moral norms and questions. According to Karl Rahner, S.J., "apart from wholly universal moral norms of an abstract kind,... there are hardly any particular or individual norms of Christian morality which could be proclaimed by the ordinary or extraordinary teaching authority of the Church in such a way that they could be unequivocally and certainly declared to have

[16]In the infallible teachings regarding Mary's Immaculate Conception and Assumption, and the pope's infallibility, the language used follows some such course as this: "We declare, pronounce and define that... [this teaching] is a doctrine divinely revealed by God... Anyone saying otherwise has departed from union with the Church." Confer D-S #2803-04; 3903-04; 3074-75.

[17]Richard A. McCormick, S.J., "Authority and Morality," *America,* 142 (1980), 169-71 at 169.

the force of dogmas."[18] A similar, but perhaps slightly stronger, position is taken by Charles Curran: "There has never been an infallible pronouncement or teaching on a specific moral matter; the very nature of specific moral actions makes it impossible, in my judgment, to have any infallible pronouncements in this area."[19]

In light of the fact that the Church's official teachings on specific moral issues are not infallibly proposed, they are rightly regarded as authoritative but fallible expressions of the magisterium. As such, these moral teachings do not require that the faithful simply respond to them in an attitude of divine faith. In response to such teachings, what is called for, rather, is an internal religious assent. As *Lumen Gentium* (#25) puts it: "In matters of faith and morals, the bishops speak in the name of Christ and the faithful are to accept their teaching and adhere to it with a religious assent of soul. This religious submission of will and mind must be shown in a special way to the authentic teaching authority of the Roman Pontiff, even when he is not speaking *ex cathedra*."

In calling for a "religious" assent or submission of mind and will, the document's intention is to indicate that the faithful's acceptance of an authoritative fallible teaching does not flow primarily from the intellectual force of the reasons given in defense of that teaching; rather, the motive for the community's assent is a religious one: God has given the magisterium authority to teach and in the responsible exercise of this authority, the pope and bishops enjoy the enlightening assistance of the Holy Spirit. We should note, however, that the faithful's obligation to give an internal religious assent to noninfallible teachings was never explicitly stated in Church documents until the middle of the nineteenth century; furthermore, this obligation of "internal religious assent" to fallible Church teachings has never been proposed in an infallible manner and therefore the community of believers is not bound

[18]*Ibid.*, quoting Rahner's *Theological Investigations*, v. 14.

[19]Charles E. Curran, *Contemporary Problems in Moral Theology* (Notre Dame: Fides Publishers, 1970), p. 257.

to accept this teaching with the submission of faith.[20] Thus, in the presence of the Church's authoritative fallible teachings, the situation of the faithful might fairly be described as follows: we are called at root to responsible assent and obedience, but we are permitted responsible dissent and disobedience. Obviously, the conditions for such dissent need to be carefully articulated.

RELIGIOUS DOCILITY AND RESPONSIBLE DISSENT

Richard McCormick has suggested that in the presence of the Church's authoritative fallible teachings, two extreme reactions are to be avoided. On the one hand, we ought not to adopt the attitude that such teaching is only as good as the arguments or reasons which support it. This mentality in effect perceives the pope and bishops simply as theologians among theologians, because it fails to acknowledge the special charism of the Holy Spirit which is given to those who hold the office of teachers in the Church; in this way, the magisterium is stripped of its truly authoritative character.

The second extreme reaction, on the other hand, would be to maintain that any authoritative fallible teaching is totally independent of its supporting line of argumentation; this notion opens the magisterium to the charge of arbitrarily issuing decrees and edicts; instead of really teaching, the magisterium simply dictates or legislates. This is a crucial point, for as McCormick says, "If a teaching is considered valid independently of the reasons and arguments, then the possibility of objectively founded dissent is eliminated on principle."[21] When this happens, that is, when the very possibility of dissent is withdrawn, we must wonder what sense remains in referring to any teaching as noninfallible since, in effect, we would find ourselves constrained "to live with a notion of noninfallible

[20]Joseph A. Komonchak, "Ordinary Papal Magisterium and Religious Assent," in *Contraception: Authority and Dissent,* ed. Charles E. Curran (New York: Herder & Herder, 1969), pp. 101-26 at 115-16, 107.

[21]Richard A. McCormick, S.J., "Notes in Moral Theology," *Theological Studies,* 29 (1968), 731.

teaching which demands that it be treated as practically infallible."[22]

Between these two extremes, McCormick lays the ground-work for a mediating position. Because the hierarchical magisterium enjoys "an eminence not conceded to any other religious teacher," its official teachings are seen as generating "a presumption not enjoyed by other teaching authorities." And the presumption generated is simply this: that the Church's authoritative fallible teachings are correct. Thus we stand before these teachings with the knowledge that as a rule they are true, even though we realize that by way of exception they may be false. Within the context of this presumption of truth, McCormick suggests that responsible people need not immedi-ately respond to authoritative fallible teachings with internal assent; their appropriate response, rather, is to adopt an attitude of "religious docility and deference" which expresses itself in a sort of "connatural eagerness to accept and adhere to" the Church's proposed teachings.[23]

In speaking of docility, Francis Sullivan describes it as "a willingness to be taught, a willingness to prefer another's judgment to one's own when it is reasonable to do so." As such, "docility calls for an open attitude toward the official teaching, giving it a fair hearing, doing one's best to appreciate the reasons in its favor, so as to convince oneself of its truth, and thus facilitate one's intellectual assent to it."[24] For McCormick, the attitude of religious docility is concretized in a number of ways: (1) it means that we retain a reverent respect for the person and office of those in the magisterium, and that we remain open to their teaching; (2) we maintain a readiness to reassess our own views in light of the magisterium's teaching; (3) because of the magisterium's charism to teach, we prefer to say that a particular fallible teaching is doubtful rather than erroneous; (4) finally, our demeanor is such that it encourages support for the magisterium and its authority to teach.[25]

[22]*Ibid.*, p. 732.

[23]*Ibid.*, pp. 715-16.

[24]Sullivan, *op. cit.*, p. 164.

[25]McCormick, *Theological Studies*, 29 (1968), 716.

If this is in fact the nature of our response to the magisterium's noninfallible teachings, then we are acting appropriately and responsibly in light of the Church's authority to teach. Beyond this, the ethical teaching of the magisterium can impose no further binding obligation on the Catholic conscience.[26] Nonetheless, we might reasonably expect that when the attitude of docility is present, it will generally lead us to receive the Church's authentic fallible teaching in a spirit of religious assent. Should it happen, however, that dissent does occur, McCormick proposes that it can do so "only after the passage of a certain amount of time, since time is needed for the arduous reflection suggested here." [27]

On this matter of responsible dissent, McCormick makes it clear that the presumption in favor of the truth of the Church's teaching prevails "until a sufficient number of mature and well-informed members of the community" of faith are agreed that the teaching warrants dissent.[28] Far from being in a rush to dissent, we must make this decision carefully; moreover, should we decide to act on our dissent, prudence would seem to dictate, as Sullivan observes, that we first consider the degree to which our dissent is shared by other Catholics, especially by those whose judgment is worthy of special consideration "by reason of their exemplary Christian lives, or their theological expertise."[29]

Dissent from the authoritative moral teachings of the Church is often regarded with suspicion because the faithful, we are told, are expected to form their consciences and make moral judgments under the direction of the magisterium. This expectation is well founded, but not without limits. In Vatican II's *Declaration on Religious Freedom* (*Dignitatis Humanae*), we read: "In the formation of their consciences, the Christian faithful ought carefully to attend to the sacred and certain doctrine of the Church" (#14). When this document was debated

[26]McCormick, "Personal Conscience," in *An American Catholic Catechism* (New York: Seabury Press, 1978), p. 185, or see *Chicago Studies,* 13, 3 (Fall, 1974), 244-45.

[27]McCormick, *Theological Studies,* 29 (1968), 716.

[28]*Ibid.,* p. 732.

[29]Sullivan, *op. cit.,* p. 171.

by the Council, an attempt was made to change the text so that instead of saying that in forming their consciences, the faithful "ought carefully to attend to" the Church's teaching, it would read that the faithful "ought to form their consciences according to" the Church's sacred teaching. This emendation was rejected, however, as being too restrictive. In light of this text, Sullivan suggests that when Catholics have carefully attended to the Church's official teaching but have honestly been unable to form their consciences according to it, "despite serious and sustained effort to do so," they cannot be accused of moral fault or of "a lack of religious submission to the teaching authority of the Church."[30]

To affirm that there is a legitimate place for responsible and loyal dissent in the Church is to acknowledge at the same time that limits exist in the magisterium's authority to teach. John L. McKenzie has noted some of the obvious boundaries encountered: "The teaching office is not empowered to control either the world of learning or the world of morality. The teaching office is not commissioned to tell people what to do, but to make it possible for people to decide what to do.... The Church does best what Jesus Christ empowered it to do, and he did not empower the Church to be every man's schoolmaster and every man's conscience. By attempting the impossible the officers of the Church sometimes lose the possible."[31]

No less than others in the Church, the magisterium is subject to the word of God (*Dei Verbum* #10), and only to the extent that the magisterium faithfully serves the message of Christ, is it also of true service to God's people. The magisterium is called to communicate God's truth, and in doing so it is promised the assistance of the Holy Spirit. But the magisterium is not empowered to create truth or to find certainty where none is possible. Thus Vatican II's *Gaudium et Spes* notes that "the Church guards the heritage of God's word and draws from it religious and moral principles, without always having at hand

---

[30] *Ibid.*, pp. 169-70.

[31] John L. McKenzie, *Authority in the Church* (New York: Sheed & Ward, 1966), p. 135.

the solution to particular problems" (#33). The document goes on to remind the laity that "it is generally the function of their well-formed Christian conscience to see that the divine law is inscribed in the life of the earthly city." Moreover, the laity are advised not to think that their pastors "are always such experts" that they can readily provide a concrete solution "to every problem which arises, however complicated." Such, indeed, is not the mission of pastors (#43). Finally, *Gaudium et Spes* affirms that "all the faithful, clerical and lay, possess a lawful freedom of inquiry and of thought, and the freedom to express their minds humbly and courageously about those matters in which they enjoy competence" (#62).

Clearly, then, unquestioning, uncritical obedience is an unacceptable interpretation of the religious assent which Vatican II asks of the faithful when presented with the magisterium's noninfallible teachings. This fact, along with the realization that the presumption of truth enjoyed by the Church's authoritative moral teachings can be overridden by contrary evidence, explains why, "with sufficient reason and solid evidence, a Catholic can take a stand that disagrees with certain aspects of an authoritative teaching in moral matters."[32] In a similar vein, McCormick judges that dissent from an official Church teaching is permitted, perhaps even required, when "it is reasonably clear that the magisterium has inadequately formulated its teaching or even positively erred." Such reasonable clarity will emerge, moreover, "when a competent individual, after arduous study, prayer and consultation, arrives at genuinely persuasive reasons and arguments against the teaching. This conclusion would be strengthened if other competent individuals arrived independently at the same conclusion."[33]

All that has been said here indicates the tension that can and sometimes does exist between the magisterium's authority to teach and the rights of individual conscience. At some point,

---

[32]Richard M. Gula, S.S., *To Walk Together Again, The Sacrament of Reconciliation* (New York: Paulist Press, 1984), p. 177.

[33]McCormick, *Chicago Studies,* 13 (1974), 245.

such tension may well be inevitable given two facts: the Church's authority can never supplant or suppress the human conscience, but neither can the Catholic's conscience ever be properly formed in isolation from the Church's accumulated wisdom. In the life of the Catholic community, both the magisterium and the individual's conscience have established and essential roles. Thus, as Richard Gula points out, "both authority and conscience are complementary aspects of the search for what is true and good. Authority may continue to insist on conformity, but conscience will continue to cry out for its own dignity and freedom."[34] It is obvious, then, that the proper and responsible functioning of the community of faith demands not only that the voice of authority always be heard, but also that the voice of conscience never be silenced. It is to this latter voice that we now turn our attention.

II. Personal Conscience: Its Dignity and Inviolability

There is perhaps no better way to acknowledge and affirm the dignity of human beings than to encourage and facilitate their growth in responsibility. In its *Declaration on Christian Education,* Vatican II has urged the point that children and young people:

> ...should be helped to acquire gradually a more mature sense of responsibility toward ennobling their own lives through constant effort, and toward pursuing authentic freedom... [The young likewise] have a right to be encouraged to weigh moral values with an upright conscience, and to embrace them by personal choice, and to know and love God more adequately. Hence...all who exercise government over peoples or preside over the work of education...[should] see that youth is never deprived of this sacred right (#1).[35]

---

[34]Gula, *op. cit.,* p. 178.

[35]A similar view is presented in the Council's *Declaration on Religious Freedom, #8.*

In keeping with its desire to highlight the dignity which is inherent in human beings, Vatican II on several occasions thought it necessary to remind us that a person's conscience has an indispensable, even inviolable, role to play in explaining and expressing that dignity. Thus *Gaudium et Spes* (#16) tells us:

> In the depths of his conscience, man detects a law which he does not impose upon himself, but which holds him to obedience. Always summoning him to love good and avoid evil, the voice of conscience can when necessary speak to his heart more specifically: do this, shun that. For man has in his heart a law written by God. To obey it is the very dignity of man; according to it he will be judged (cf. Rom. 2:15-16).
>
> Conscience is the most secret core and sanctuary of a man. There he is alone with God, whose voice echoes in his depths. In a wonderful manner conscience reveals that law which is fulfilled by love of God and neighbor (cf. Mt 22:37–40; Gal. 5:14).

With the beauty and meaning of conscience thus established, the Council, in its *Declaration on Religious Freedom* (#3), goes on to insist that a person must be faithful to his or her conscience:

> ...man perceives and acknowledges the imperatives of the divine law through the mediation of conscience. In all his activity a man is bound to follow his conscience faithfully, in order that he may come to God, for whom he was created. It follows that he is not to be forced to act in a manner contrary to his conscience. Nor, on the other hand, is he to be restrained from acting in accordance with his conscience, especially in matters religious.

The Church's emphasis on conscience should not be viewed as a recent development. Thomas Aquinas described conscience as "the practical judgment or dictate of reason, by which we judge what here and now is to be done as being good, or to be avoided as evil."[36] Thomas was of the clear opinion that an individual's conscience is to be taken most seriously. Thus he wrote: "Anyone upon whom the ecclesiastical authority, in ignorance of the true facts, imposes a demand that offends against his clear conscience, should perish in excommunication rather than violate his conscience."[37] As a practical judgment of reason which is to be followed faithfully, a person's conscience plays a crucial role in his or her life. Thus if conscience is to be our ultimate personal guide, and if we are supposed to hand our lives over to it, then we must be certain that it is reliable. It is imperative, therefore, that we discover what true conscience is, lest we allow ourselves to be misled by any imposter or counterfeit conscience.

FROM SUPEREGO TO CONSCIENCE

A good deal of confusion appears in the discussion concerning conscience, due in large part to the fact that theologians and psychologists often use the term to refer to different realities. Whereas theologians in general think of conscience as a free function of the human person who is involved in the evaluation of moral good and evil, many psychologists are likely to use the word "conscience" in such a way that it is clear that what they are really referring to is that element of our personality which Freud called the *superego*.

In the Freudian school of psychology, the *superego*, along with the *ego* and the *id*, exists as one of the essential components of our personality. As Gula remarks, the superego is best understood as "the ego of another superimposed on our own to serve as an internal censor to regulate our conduct by using guilt as its powerful weapon." In other words, in our early years we are easily and simply molded according to the norms and values of those who have authority over us; we react initially to the influence of our parents and later to that of

---

[36]This description is given by the American Bishops in their 1968 pastoral letter, *Human Life in Our Day* (Washington: USCC), p. 14.

[37]Thomas Aquinas, *IV Sent.*, dist. 38, art. 4.

various teachers, and civil and religious leaders. This external influence, which is seen in our uncritical acceptance of other people's values, is mediated through the agency of the superego. Again and again, "the superego tells us we are good when we do what we are told to do, and it tells us we are bad and makes us feel guilty when we do not do what the authority over us tells us to."[38]

In a fine treatment of the distinction between conscience and the superego, John Glaser has urged that what should be noted most about the superego is that its commands and prohibitions "do not arise from any kind of perception of the intrinsic goodness or objectionableness of the action contemplated. The source of such commands and prohibitions can be described positively as the desire to be approved and loved or negatively as the fear of loss of such love and approval."[39] Glaser makes much of the fact that there are really two quite distinct dynamisms explaining the functioning of the conscience and the superego. On the one hand, the motivating force of the true moral conscience arises from a person's desire to respond to God's call to be loving. The conscience, in other words, impels and inspires a person to the extroverted action of loving others. By contrast, on the other hand, the dynamism of the superego "springs from a frantic compulsion to experience oneself as lovable"; under the influence of the superego, then, what motivates a person is the introverted concern to be accepted and loved.[40]

In psychological terms, the functioning of the superego makes eminent sense, for in children and young people especially, the need and desire to be approved and loved are primary and fundamental. Gula notes that as children we fear punishment "not for its physical pain only, but more because it represents a withdrawal of love. So we regulate our behavior so

---

[38]Gula, *op. cit.,* pp. 146-47.

[39]John W. Glaser, S.J., "Conscience and Superego: A Key Distinction," *Theological Studies,* 32 (1971), 30-47 at 32-3.

[40]*Ibid.,* p. 32; also see p. 38 for a listing of major contrasts between conscience and superego; also Gula, *op. cit.,* p. 150.

as not to lose love and approval."[41] Freud himself has suggested that in the early years of personal development, our original experience of guilt is associated primarily with the fear that we will be punished by our parents through the withdrawal of their love. Thus the guilt feelings stirred up by the superego create in us a sense of isolation. For example, when a child disobeys or does something wrong in the eyes of parents, he or she has a feeling of being isolated from them, because from past experience the child knows that "being bad" means being separated from the parents and others who are good: "Go to your room!," the child is told. Understandably, the child wants to rejoin those who are good; he or she wants to be accepted and loved again; only in this way does the child develop and preserve a sense of belonging.[42]

As should be obvious from this analysis, the superego serves well the process of socialization; children become well versed in the conventional "do's and don't's" of a particular culture, but the motivating dynamism of the superego is basically inadequate to the task of inspiring Christian living. Merely to have the acceptance and love of others is no sign that a person is living responsibly as a Christian.[43] Rather, as we saw earlier, true Christianity is marked by a loving movement toward the kingdom of God. And on this journey, it can easily happen that Christians enjoy little company and less understanding as they resist the social status quo precisely because it stands between them and the future promised by God. Answering the call to prophetic life involves Christians in the attempt to take seriously God's perspective on the world. This attempt in itself often proves to be a sure cure for popularity.

Ideally, of course, what happens during a person's maturation process is that the work of the superego, which is in some ways like a primitive precursor of true conscience, is gradually taken over by the individual's ego or self. In this way a person's life comes to be directed not so much by external authority

---

[41]Gula, *op. cit.*, p. 147.

[42]Glaser, *art. cit.*, pp. 33-5.

[43]*Ibid.*, p. 36.

figures, but rather by one's own perceptions of facts and values which serve as the bases for decisions made under the name of true moral conscience. Thus when we are mature people acting in a responsible manner, our moral life is no longer shaped so much either by the conventionalities of society or by the external influences of others who simply tell us what to do; instead, our decisions are more internalized and self-directed, which means that they reflect our own appreciation of what is right and wrong.[44] For us as Christians, moreover, to be directed by a true moral conscience means that we are giving honest expression to our desire to live in the manner that we think best embodies the kind of love revealed in and by Christ for our imitation.

Many of us, to be sure, never completely transcend the influence of our superego. Then again, even when we are largely able to identify, isolate and suppress the proddings of an insistent superego, we may not be at all sure of the practical meaning and profound implications contained in our duty "to follow our conscience." Thus if we are to fulfill this duty successfully, we must seek a fuller understanding of the positive meaning of conscience. To this end, we now turn to Timothy O'Connell's masterful analysis of conscience.[45]

CONSCIENCE AND ITS LEVELS OF MEANING

Before developing the positive understanding of conscience, O'Connell offers some introductory remarks about the place of human feelings in our lives. It is essential, he believes, that we not immediately equate these feelings with the promptings of our moral conscience. Thus, for example, the statement, "I feel

[44]The movement from superego to conscience seems to reflect the stages of moral development as identified by psychologist Lawrence Kohlberg who speaks of pre-conventional, conventional and post-conventional levels of morality. For a brief presentation of Kohlberg's views see Edward Stevens, *The Morals Game* (New York: Paulist Press, 1974), pp. 21-34 or Frank J. McNulty and Edward Wakin, *Should You Ever Feel Guilty?* (New York: Paulist Press, 1978), pp. 33-7.

[45]Timothy E. O'Connell, *Principles for A Catholic Morality* (New York: The Seabury Press, 1978), pp. 83-97.

guilty," is not automatically to be translated into "my conscience is bothering me" or "I have a guilty conscience."
Sometimes we simply feel guilty when in fact we have done
nothing which requires or demands repentance; at other times,
of course, our actions may be morally reprehensible and yet we
"feel" no guilt at all. In these latter situations we may even say "I
feel good about what I did; I have a clear conscience." Such
statements may indeed indicate the presence of moral virtue in
our lives, but they may just as well reflect the fact that we have
no conscience at all, or a very undeveloped one, or one that is
lazy or deceived.

In all of this, the point to be remembered is simply that the
origin of our feelings is often clouded in mystery, and to a great
extent, feelings themselves "stand apart from human freedom
and human rationality." It is for this very reason that feelings as
such are morally neutral, and feeling or not feeling guilty is
simply not a reliable measure for taking moral stock of
ourselves. Thus O'Connell concludes: "If and when such
feelings coincide with the actual moral facts of the case, that is
purely an accident. It is just as likely that they will not."[46] The
truth of the matter may be simply put: "feeling good" or "feeling
guilty" often has much more to do with the external proddings
of a superego than with the internal promptings of a true
conscience.

With these cautions in place, let it now be said that the
experience of guilt is often an appropriate response to the
situation in which we find ourselves, and in this sense the
experience can be positive and conducive to moral growth. But
whether or not it will be such, depends upon whether we are in
fact experiencing authentic or neurotic guilt, and this can best
be determined by the outcome of the experience. Thus neurotic
guilt, for example, is largely disproportionate to our perceived
wrongdoing; we simply make more of our transgression than it
deserves. Most often, moreover, neurotic guilt leads us to a
sense of despair or desperation; we become so pre-occupied
with our evil-doing that we isolate ourselves in a circle of

[46]*Ibid.*, pp. 83-5.

self-accusation and self-condemnation. Left unchallenged or unchecked, neurotic guilt gives birth to self-hatred; when it pushes us to this extreme, the full harmfulness of neurotic guilt is unmasked, for it deceives us into accepting a view of ourselves which is simply unacceptable to God: God does not hate us and we have neither reason nor right to hate ourselves.

In contrast to neurotic guilt, authentic guilt is our proportionate response to any real evil we have done; even as we accept responsibility for our wrongdoing, we express sorrow for our sinful failings and we ask forgiveness. Far from reveling in self-recrimination, however, we move beyond ourselves in the process of conversion or repentance, and thus seek reconciliation with those whom we have offended, with the God who deserves better, and the neighbor who needs more, from us.

Clearly, the experiences of neurotic and authentic guilt turn our attention in opposite directions. Neurotic guilt captivates and immobilizes us in self-contemplation; not liking what we see, we despair of being loved either by ourselves or by God. Authentic guilt, however, is the prelude to action, the challenge to growth; we stand reminded of who we are and how we are to live; the call to love is heard anew. Beyond this, it may further be said that neurotic guilt is simply not in touch with reality, especially with the reality of God and his infinite capacity for love; authentic guilt, however, knows this reality and is grateful for it. Neurotic guilt, finally, appears as the unconscious reflection of human pride: we imagine ourselves to be so good at doing evil, so successful at it, that we outdistance God's capacity and desire to forgive us; authentic guilt fashions a far different perspective; it enables us to stand tall but humbly before the God who has loved us into life and now is once again beckoning us toward forgiveness.

Once it is established that the stirrings of our conscience cannot simply be equated or identified with subjective feelings of guilt or innocence, what may be said of the positive meaning of conscience? O'Connell suggests that there are three senses in which conscience can be understood; or we might say that conscience operates on three different levels in a person's life. The three senses in which conscience is used are these: (1) we speak of the "habit of conscience" or "the basic sense of responsibility that characterizes the human person"; (2) conscience also operates in "the exercise of moral reasoning" as a person searches for objective moral values; (3) and finally, we can identify a decision of conscience as "the judgment by which we evaluate a particular action." As we probe these meanings more deeply, we will, for simplicity's sake, follow O'Connell's lead and refer to the three senses of conscience as conscience/1, conscience/2 and conscience/3.[47]

Conscience/1 refers to the overall sense of value which characterizes what it means to be a human being; in general, we have an awareness of our personal responsibility; we sense that we are accountable for what we do, and precisely because we have a capacity for self-direction, we also sense that we should attempt to move in the right direction. Apart from psychopaths and sociopaths who are regarded as sick because they are devoid of any sense of right and wrong, people agree that good is to be done and evil avoided. Of course, we often have different opinions about what is good or evil, right or wrong, but, as O'Connell observes, any discussion about these matters can only occur "because we agree that there is such a thing as good and bad, and that we ought to do the good and avoid the bad." It is highly unlikely, moreover, that the debate about *what* is right or wrong would be so vigorous or prolonged, were it not for the fact that we are deeply convinced that it matters greatly *whether* some action or lack of action is right or wrong.[48]

Given the complexities of human living, we often find ourselves in situations which are so confusing that we are uncertain as to what is morally expected of us; it is then that conscience/2 comes into play as we seek "to find and understand the concrete moral values" which are at stake in the present circumstances of our lives. We want to discover what is the right and proper thing to do; in our desire to do what is good, we look for assistance and guidance; in the process of seeking information that will enable us to direct our lives

[47] *Ibid.*, pp. 88-93; also Gula, *op. cit.*, pp. 139-45.
[48] *Ibid.*, p. 90.

properly, we are engaged in what is known as the "formation of conscience," which is simply the honest and humble pursuit of truth.

In its search for the truth that it so desires, conscience/2 is open to every available source of wisdom: we study, we dialogue with friends, we consult with theologians and ethicists, and we especially pay attention to the magisterium's teachings. As Catholics, we should be particularly sensitive to the official teachings of the Church for several reasons: we know, for one thing, that as a cross-cultural institution, the Church "is perhaps more likely to overcome the biases and blindnesses that can afflict the consciences of people within a particular cultural context"; in many ways, moreover, the Church's official teachings express the accumulated wisdom of the ages; we know, finally, that in the exercise of its teaching role, the magisterium enjoys the assistance of the Holy Spirit. And so our respectful attention to the insights of the Church is both "a dictate of common sense and a consequence of deeply held faith"; listening to the magisterium, however, is not supposed to deafen us to other voices.[49]

What is most essential to the search for truth is that our investigation be carried out in a prayerful manner. I mean by this only one thing: that if we are prayerful, if we really desire to know God's will and not simply to do our own, then our minds will be illuminated and sensitized to the truth; we will then be able to see and interpret data with greater freedom from prejudice or self-interested motivation. Apart from the attentiveness to God which prayer is, our search for moral truth can hardly be seen as either honest or full.

While the pursuit of truth lasts a lifetime, we obviously spend our lives making decisions and acting upon them. Often we find ourselves at the point where we must say: "I have honestly tried to find out what is the right thing to do; I know that it is still theoretically possible that I may be wrong, but I really think now that I ought to do this." This decision or judgment upon which we then act is an exercise of conscience/3. It is possible,

---

[49] *Ibid.*, pp. 94-5.

of course, that in following the dictates of conscience/3, we may wind up doing something that is *objectively* wrong, but should we later discover that this is indeed the case, we cannot be said to have acted in a *morally* sinful way. Quite simply, human morality demands that we do what we honestly think is right and avoid what we honestly think is wrong. Provided we fulfill this demand as best we can, whatever objective wrong may be attributable to us does not carry with it the malice of sin.

We are now in a position to understand the real meaning of the maxim: "I must always follow my conscience." Clearly, what the statement requires is that I must always follow my *informed* conscience (level 3); I must, in other words, always do what I discover to be right after having prayerfully and honestly formed my conscience (level 2) in the pursuit of truth.[50] This means that even if the judgment made by conscience/3 is mistaken or erroneous and I am unaware of this fact, I am still bound to follow conscience/3. If my mistake is an honest one and my error unavoidable, then I am not morally responsible for any objective wrong I may do, that is, I am not guilty of any moral transgression. If, however, the erroneous judgment of conscience/3 is made as a result of a lazy, half-hearted or dishonest pursuit of truth, or if my decision springs solely from my own instincts, intuitions or feelings, then I am responsible for the error of my ways, because, as far as possible, I am morally expected to think and to seek the truth before I act.

III. Conclusion

What main points may be drawn from our consideration of the magisterium and personal conscience? Several observations seem warranted:

1. As Catholics, we are to attend carefully to official Church teachings; we expect to learn from the magisterium and hence we approach its teachings with openness and docility; and yet

[50]*Ibid.*, pp. 91-2.

we are not absolutely bound to obey the authoritative fallible teachings of the Church.

2. Responsible dissent from the Church's moral teaching can occur as the result of a dictate of an honest and well-informed conscience. This means, of course, that we are never justified in dissenting from a teaching of the magisterium simply because we do not like the teaching or find it difficult to follow. There is, moreover, no room for haste in coming to a disagreement with official Church teaching, as we are warned by Cardinal John Henry Newman: "...when I speak of conscience, I mean conscience truly so called....If in a particular case it is to be taken as a sacred and sovereign monitor, its dictate, in order to prevail against the voice of the pope, must follow upon serious thought, prayer, and all available means of arriving at a right judgment on the matter in question."[51] The presumption of truth enjoyed by authoritative Church teachings yields slowly, but yield it must if evidence so dictates. It may well happen, of course, that some people, after having conscientiously concluded to the possibility of responsible dissent on a particular moral issue, will nonetheless remain hesitant at the prospect of acting on this possibility, and thus opt for continued observance of the magisterium's authoritative fallible teaching. Such a decision is understandable and is to be respected, but it does not present itself as the only moral course of action that is available to responsible members of the Catholic community.

3. To live responsibly, we must make moral decisions *for ourselves,* but in no way does this mean that we make these decisions *on our own.* Recognizing the social nature of human existence and the real dangers of rationalization, vested self-interest and self-deception, we must seek counsel before reaching decisions of conscience. Ultimately, it is we who decide, however, and in the end we have to explain these decisions only to God.

4. As a practical judgment or dictate of reason, my conscientious decision binds only me. My well-informed conscience (conscience/3) tells only me what I must or must not

---

[51]Quoted by the American bishops in *Human Life in Our Day,* pp. 14-5.

do; it does not morally oblige anyone else because, as the American bishops remind us, an individual's conscience is "not a teacher of doctrine."[52]

5. It is good to remember, also, that individual judgments of conscience are not to be isolated from our overriding responsibility to love. Paul makes this clear in his advice to the Christians in Rome. In trying to settle a dispute they are having over whether or not some types of food are unclean and thus should not be eaten, Paul maintains that "no food is unclean in itself; however, if someone thinks that a particular food is unclean, then it is unclean for him." But Paul immediately reminds those who share his view that all food is clean, that they "are hardly being guided by charity" if this view of theirs is upsetting others in the community of faith. Paul concludes by telling the Christians: "You are certainly not free to eat what you like if that means the downfall of someone for whom Christ died" (cf. Rom. 14:13–21; also 1 Cor. 10:23–30). The situation, then, is this: Paul is convinced that that judgment of conscience is objectively correct which says "all food is clean"; he, nonetheless, maintains that a Christian's love for others requires that scandal be avoided. Thus Christian responsibility calls for abstinence from the food in question unless or until the erroneous consciences of those in the community who view the food as unclean become better informed or can in some way be more sensitively accommodated.

Regarding our obligation to be sensitive to the dictates of conscience which shape the lives of others in our community of faith, one caution seems appropriate: we must be careful not to confuse the requirements of Christian love with the constraints of any false charity which would allow the judgments of an erroneous conscience to go unchallenged. In the scriptural passages referred to above, Paul, so well known as the apostle of Christian liberty, is surely neither condoning nor encouraging a situation where Christians must be complacently and permanently indifferent to any infringement upon the freedom gained for them by Christ. On the contrary, as Christians we have every right to struggle to preserve or to regain the freedom

[52]*Ibid.,* p. 14.

promised us in the gospel. Furthermore, it is incumbent upon us to invite and encourage one another to share in the joys of this freedom, and one sure way in which growth in Christian liberty may be facilitated is by our mutually assisting one another in the correct formation or re-formation of our consciences according to the truth of Christ which alone has the power to make us free (Jn. 8:32).

6. It needs to be said, finally, that in acting upon an honestly mistaken or erroneous judgment of conscience/3, we are not immoral; yet every reasonable effort should be made to ensure that our moral judgments are not only honest and sincere, but also correct. As we shall see in the following chapter, objectively wrong decisions, if made despite our best attempts at finding the truth, are not sinful, but neither are they helpful to our personal growth and happiness. On the contrary, in fact, mistaken decisions of conscience most often prove frustrative of the human potential not only of ourselves, but also of those others whom our decisions affect. Mistakes can and should be corrected; so, too, must we learn from them.

III

The Death of Love:
A Radical Theology of Sin

I. Stating the Problem: Sins versus Sinfulness

In these days of revolutionaries, reactionaries, and counter-culturists it is not inappropriate, perhaps, to suggest that sinfulness, not money, is the root of all sins. This statement is meant to be neither facile nor facetious, and it is certainly not tautological. Sinfulness and sins are quite distinct realities. Yet moral theology for too long has stressed sins, rather than sinfulness. This emphasis is seen in traditional theology's attempt to sort out human acts according to their external appearances. Thus we have the Church's insistence that for the integrity of sacramental confession, the penitent must recite the species and number of mortal sins committed, along with any of their special characteristics. Too many moralists have apparently forgotten that the sins we see are in effect only the signs and symptoms of a diseased and fragmented heart. It is what proceeds from the heart of a person that makes him unclean: "For it is from within, from men's hearts, that evil intentions emerge: fornication, theft, murder, adultery, avarice, malice, deceit, indecency, envy, slander, pride, folly. All these evil things come from within and make a man unclean" (Mk. 7:21-23; also Mt. 15:17-20). Moral theology's need today is for less emphasis on an analysis of individual actions, with more attention being paid to the formation of human hearts in goodness, for "a good man draws good things from his store of goodness; a bad man draws bad things from his store of badness" (Mt. 12:35).

This is hardly the time, of course, to minimize the destructive reality of human sin, as Karl Menninger has so forcefully reminded us.[1] And yet our concern must be with more than the mere acknowledgment of sin; we want also to resist it, and this will demand that we try to uncover the secret hiding-place of sin through an analysis of the human situation in which sin is rooted. An example may help us to locate the problem. We are often asked these days: "Is it still considered a mortal sin to miss Mass on Sunday?" There is no simple and direct answer to the question as posed. I would like to indicate briefly why this is the case and then to consider the question of sin in somewhat broader terms. The issue of Sunday Mass may be looked at from two perspectives: it may be seen as an instance of the broader question of external church discipline, and it may also be viewed on its own merits, with consideration being given to the very meaning of the eucharistic celebration.

Both dimensions of the question have been treated by Bernard Häring. He first locates the issue of compulsory attendance at Sunday Mass under the general rubric of the larger question, "Can human laws be imposed under pain of mortal sin?," such that any transgression of the law is intended to imply punishment by eternal condemnation.[2] Häring is of

[1]Karl Menninger, M.D., *Whatever Became of Sin?* (New York: Hawthorn Books, Inc., 1973).

[2]Bernard Häring, *Sin in the Secular Age* (Garden City, N.Y.: Doubleday, 1974), pp. 198-206; 209-11.

the opinion that the Church should not impose under pain of mortal sin any obligation that is not demanded by Christ's gospel or by our own nature as beings created in the image and likeness of God. Häring's reasoning on this point is direct: he cannot imagine any positive law, which is neither part of the gospel nor of the natural law in the human heart, and yet which at the same time "could be so important as to be proportionate to the threat of eternal punishment."[3]

On the precise question of the obligation pertaining to attendance at Sunday Mass, Häring suggests that since absolute regularity in the Sunday observance is not a divine law, it seems inappropriate to lay the threat of eternal punishment upon anyone who occasionally, and by way of exception, neglects Mass. The suggestion that missing Mass embodies an individual's eternal rejection of God and provokes in turn God's eternal rejection of that individual definitely appears excessive where "it is not a case of obstinate bad will or contempt, but only an expression of human weakness or superficiality." The disproportion of the threatened punishment is even more frightening, as Häring remarks, when the eucharistic celebration is unattractively and hastily conducted "without joy, without communication of the gladdening news, without a minimum of authentic experience that it is a visible celebration of unity and solidarity for the people of God."[4] This imperfection in the celebration of the Eucharist, as well as its inadequate pedagogical presentation, and the general lack of evangelization, are important factors to be considered in any discussion of the gravity pertaining to the obligation of Sunday Mass.[5]

Häring's conclusion is that it is reasonable to speak of grave obligation in the matter of attending Mass, but he understands the designation of "grave obligation" not as implying mortal sin, but rather "as a warning about grave danger."[6] The matter,

[3] *Ibid.*, pp.206, 204.
[4] *Ibid.*, pp. 210-11, 209.
[5] *Ibid.*, p. 210.
[6] *Ibid.*, pp. 210; 211 n. 6.

then, is a serious one and should be seen as such by all. I take this to mean that, given the theological significance of the Mass as a prayerful act in which the community of faith is invited by Christ to join together with him in the praise of the Father and in the service of others, the question of whether or not an individual chooses to respond to this invitation is a serious and important one. But the mere physical presence at Sunday Mass is no more an indication that a person has done something morally good than is physical absence from Mass an indictment that a person has done something morally evil.

Such moral determinations are dependent upon what meaning the Mass really has for a person in terms of his or her relationship to God and neighbor.[7] For example, if, on the one hand, a person realizes the theological significance of the Mass and appreciates the need to share in the life of the community to which he has committed himself by belief, then missing Mass without a serious reason, to the extent that this indicates a turning away from a relationship with God and one's neighbor, would seem to be sinful. On the other hand, however, if an individual has no such understanding of the Mass as an effective expression of his relationship with God and others through Jesus Christ, his failure to attend Mass would appear in itself not to be sinful. But this latter situation can hardly be seen as one with which a person who is sincere in his faith-commitment will be satisfied indefinitely.

There is an obligation both for him to learn and for his co-believers to teach. More specifically, it is incumbent upon Christian educators on every level to provide an atmosphere in which growth in knowledge of both the theory and practice of faith is facilitated and encouraged. It is quite right, then, to say that the question of Sunday Mass is a serious and important one, even if, unfortunately, its significance is not always immediately obvious. It is quite another thing, however, to say that the omission of Sunday Mass is seriously sinful, for this implies that a person knows the meaning and serious implica-

---

[7] I am relying here on some ideas of Gregory Kenny, "Sex and the Young Catholic," *U.S. Catholic/Jubilee* XXXVI, 10 (October, 1971), p. 12.

tions of his omission and freely accepts them. In point of fact, however, whether or not a person is guilty of really refusing the praise and worship of God, and of infidelity to his commitment to the community of faith, will be known only to God and to the individual himself. The point of all this, then, is simply to suggest that personal sins are not properly proclaimed from outside the individual. They arise, rather, from the heart of anyone who pretends that all will be well if only he can succeed in silencing the demands of an annoying God.

What we learn from Scripture, however, as Franz Böckle reminds us, is that sin is not simply a transgression of some law. Sin lives more deeply within us; "all deeds of sin are preceded by a state of sin that affects man at the core of his existence." When we speak of sins in the plural we are talking of the concrete shapes that our lives can take on as a result of our interior sinfulness, our fundamental sinful dispositions or tendencies. The actions which appear as sins on the surface of our lives are indeed such only insofar as they are signs and symptoms of what is happening deep inside us.

In further distinguishing between sinfulness, the fundamental choice of sin, and specific "sins" in the plural, Böckle makes the helpful suggestion that in sin we deny ourselves to God, we simply refuse to acknowledge and return God's love for us; we become unwilling to surrender to God in faith; we reject God as the center and foundation of our lives. When we speak of "sins," however, we refer to the conscious and deliberate substitutions that we make for God in our lives. In prideful assertion of ourselves as the ground of our own existence, we begin to act in misdirected ways by "misusing people and things."[8] In order to establish and protect our self-proclaimed independence from God, we relate to others and the world in a way that is manipulative; thus are born the acts of lying, stealing, greed, lust, gluttony, murder, etc. Sins, indeed, are the fruits of sinfulness, and whether we shall live in

---

[8]Franz Böckle, *Fundamental Concepts of Moral Theology*, trans. William Jerman (New York: Paulist Press, 1967), pp. 84-94.

sin or not depends upon a fundamental option that we make, namely, whether we wish to live for God and others or simply for ourselves.

II. Grace and Sin as Relational Realities

In an effort to provide a broader theological context for what we have said so far, we will have to consider further the basic issue of the very meaning of sin. Pope Pius XII once remarked that the greatest sin of our times is that we have lost the very sense of sin. We must honestly face the possibility that this is indeed the case, but we must also investigate other possibilities concerning the modern predicament. One such possibility is that today we have a new sense of sin which receives its meaning from the basic appreciation of Christian existence as a way of life lived in *continual conversion.* In other words, our lives as Christians should be expressed in a daily, growing love-relationship in which we show concern for God and for our fellow human beings.[9]

Because the ideal Christian life is basically a love-relationship spelled out in the service of God and neighbor, it makes sense to speak of grace and sin only as *relational realities.* At the deepest level, our lives are lived either in grace, inspired and informed by a love of God and our neighbor, or they are lived in selfishness and sin. Precisely because of this nature of our lives as a relationship, it seems more accurate to speak of the severing of the basic love-relationship in terms, not of mortal sins in the plural, but of serious sinfulness in the singular.[10]

Life is a pattern, a continuity, a process which moves over a period of time in a definitely discernible direction; basically, it is either an outgoing, giving, loving life-process, or it is turned

[9]In the development of this chapter my thinking has been greatly influenced by Charles E. Curran, *Contemporary Problems in Moral Theology* (Notre Dame: Fides, 1970), pp. 14-23; John W. Glaser, S.J., "Transition between Grace and Sin: Fresh Perspectives," *Theological Studies* 29 (1968), 260-74; John G. Milhaven, *Toward a New Catholic Morality* (Garden City, N.Y.: Doubleday, 1970), pp. 82-94.

[10]Curran, *op. cit.*, p. 21.

inwardly as a selfish, and thus sinful, life-process. Given this structure of life, we prefer today to speak of sinful orientations, dispositions or tendencies in one's life rather than of sinful actions, which in themselves are easily identifiable and subject to moral evaluation as individual and isolated events. This distinction between acts of sin and sinful tendencies is not new in the history of Christianity. The distinction, it seems, was first appreciated by Christ who had the unpopular habit of associating with tax collectors and others generally known as sinners and offenders against the law. The explanation for Christ's association with those whose actions violated specific precepts of the law lies, according to Eugene Maly, in the fact that despite their unlawful actions, these people continued to manifest an openness to God's healing love and thus they escaped the self-righteous sinfulness of those Scribes who considered themselves already saved through their observance of the law, and thus closed their hearts to the person of Christ.[11]

The distinction between sins and sinfulness suggests that in making moral evaluations the basic questions come down to these: "To what extent is my life a loving one?" and "To what extent is there a failure to love in my life?" Now obviously, both a loving life and a selfish life do reveal themselves in a series of concrete actions, but the point is that these acts cannot always be easily, quickly, and correctly identified as either morally good or evil. The truth of the matter seems to be that we choose to help or to hurt, to love or to be selfish, through numerous small decisions over a period of time.[12] What we have to do is to try to situate individual actions within the context of our whole lives, and in this way to determine how any act is related to the general orientation or direction of our lives as either generous or selfish. The question that is put to any action is: does this action indicate that my life is still moving in the general direction of self-giving love, or does it rather indicate that I have made a turn away from the love of God and neighbor and thus become too self-oriented and self-concerned?

[11]Eugene H. Maly, *Sin: Biblical Perspectives* (Dayton: Pflaum/Standards, 1973), p. 38.

[12]Milhaven, *op. cit.*, pp. 90-91.

These considerations suggest that the transition from leading a self-giving, loving and grace-filled life to leading a self-centered, selfish and sinful life does not take place suddenly and with frequent reversals. Put simply, we do not do flip-flops from grace to serious sin and back again. We do not find genuine, mature, loving relationships or commitments which allow for weekly or daily reversals from affirmation to complete rejection. This is not to say that love cannot die; but it is to say that love does not die suddenly; it is also to say that love does not climb into and out of its grave with the same frequency with which one climbs into and out of a bathtub, or up and down a flight of stairs.[13]

III. Life in Grace, Life in Sin

The human condition is such that we exist on many levels, but at the deepest level we establish ourselves either as caring, giving, and loving persons or as people who are selfish and self-centered. We live, in other words, basically either for God and for others, or for ourselves; thus our individual actions are to be evaluated precisely as expressions or indications of where our priorities lie. It is important to know whether any given action arises from our very heart or core, that is, whether it comes from the depths of our freedom and thus truly reveals the direction in which we are desirous of moving our lives. If an action is the expression of our deepest self, if our whole heart is in the act, then it does reveal where we stand in relationship to God and our fellow human beings. But is every action expressive in this way? Is it true that we *always* are what we do? Can we say that our actions always express the deepest orientation of our lives? Or is it rather the case that many of our actions come, not from the core or depths of our being, but from its periphery, from its edges, and thus hide as much of our basic life-orientation as they reveal?

[13]Glaser, *op. cit.*, p. 260.

This latter case seems closer to the truth. Our external acts do not always flow directly from our deepest freedom and thus do not always express that freedom; they do not always show where we really are, heart and soul. Thus, on the deepest level of our existence, at the center of our being, we may be dedicated to a life of love, committed to God and others, while on a more superficial and more visible level we at times hold back from our commitment — out of fear or laziness, or out of self-pity, pride or human respect. Deep-down, however, we want to keep our lives moving in the direction of God and neighbor. What we are saying, then, is that we do not fall into and out of serious sin any more often or more easily than we fall in and out of true love. For example, the relationship between husband and wife, or between parents and children, can often become strained without there being any serious threat to the quality and reality of their love for one another. However, should the tension-filled atmosphere produced by stubbornness or pettiness become the pattern of family life, we can only expect that in time the quality of life, and of love itself, will change; finally, love itself may die. On the part of every person, the same kind of stress can occur in the basic relationship between God and self, with the person remaining at heart a truly moral person. At the same time, however, the individual must remember that love does not flourish in a vacuum; it must be sustained in loving deeds. Finally, a person must be sensitive to what can weaken and destroy the love-relationship.

Speaking more positively, we can say that perseverance and growth in grace is like perseverance and growth in love. Now, while true love is, and must be, manifested in action, not every act which appears harsh and unloving is necessarily so; as we all know, we often say and do hurtful things to the people we love most, things that we really do not mean and often cannot explain. Through it all, our love for these dear ones goes on and even grows. What we are saying, then, is that life in grace and life in sin are determined by reference to the presence or absence of a deep relationship between a person and God, a relationship which consists primarily, not in isolated acts, but in a basic orientation toward God and neighbor, or away from them and toward self.

The basic distinction between a life in grace and a life in sin appears in the letter of Paul to the Galatians (5:16-26), where he distinguishes between life in the spirit (*pneuma*) and life in the flesh (*sarx*). Commenting on this distinction, Joseph Fitzmyer notes that the basic contrast is between a person "under the influence of the Spirit" and an individual "subject to his earthly tendencies." Whereas "*pneuma* suggests the knowing and willing self of man and as such reveals him to be particularly apt to receive the Spirit of God," by contrast, *sarx* refers to a person "subject to all that withdraws him from God."[14] Paul's insight was later appropriated by Augustine in his view of the Two Cities populated either by people who are moved by the love of God to contempt of self (City of God), or by those who are moved by the love of self to the contempt of God (City of Man). The heavenly city lives according to the Spirit (love), while the earthly city lives according to the flesh (self-centeredness). This, then, is the basic option confronting man.

It is not our intention to dismiss totally the importance of our actions, and this for several reasons. First, the whole New Testament is insistent on the fact that our relationship to God is manifested, known and embodied in our relationships with our fellow human beings. Secondly, it would be foolish to deny how difficult it is to attain to real self-knowledge and the knowledge of our personal motivations apart from a consideration of our human activities. Thirdly, we recognize that actions do in fact have consequences and repercussions, some of which are quite drastic in their effects upon society, upon other individuals, and upon ourselves, and thus cannot simply be ignored.[15] In an effort, then, to take account both of our theological traditions and of the data revealing our psychological make-up and the sociological reality in which we live, it seems necessary to distinguish between two different questions arising from a consideration of human actions.

[14]Joseph A. Fitzmyer, S.J., "Pauline Theology," *The Jerome Biblical Commentary*, pp. 820-21.

[15]Curran, *op. cit.*, pp. 18-19.

IV. Moral Good and Evil versus Right and Wrong

On one level, our actions raise the question of moral good or evil. As was already suggested, this question has to do with the basic orientation or direction of our lives, arising from decisions involving our core, our heart, our deepest freedom. Serious sinfulness in a person's life indicates and expresses a radical or deep-seated orientation of his existence selfishly toward himself and away from God and the service of others. The person finds himself deeply involved in this decision for self and against God and neighbors; he must, therefore, assume responsibility for being where he is. Here is formal or real sin; it may best be identified with what has traditionally been known as mortal sin. When we sin mortally, we choose a basic selfish identity for ourselves, we make a fundamental option, we take a basic stance which subsequently may be either confirmed or altered.

We turn now to the second question arising in relation to human actions. If we want to reserve the words "sin" or "moral evil" to the free breaking of the fundamental love-relationship which ought to bind us to God and others, then we must use other words, like "right" and "wrong," to speak of external actions when these actions are viewed apart from, or without regard to, the question of the degree of personal involvement, or intentionality, or responsibility of the person who is acting. Actions, in other words, are "right" or "wrong" insofar as, in and of themselves, they are either promotive or destructive of persons. Thus, an action must be regarded as objectively "wrong" or as an "objective moral wrong" when its nature or character is such as to render that action actually or potentially harmful to, or destructive of, the well-being of others and/or of self.[16]

Traditionally, theology has been fond of speaking of objective versus subjective morality. In this context, a distinction is made between objective or material sin and subjective or formal sin, the difference being that formal or subjective sin is the only sin for which a person bears moral responsibility for the action

[16] *Ibid.*, pp. 19-20.

precisely as a sin, because only in this instance has the individual acted with a sufficient degree of the required knowledge, freedom and consent. Today, many theologians consider the concept of material or objective sin unhelpful and a source of pedagogical confusion. Thus, in place of this notion, they prefer to talk simply of "objective moral wrongs" when referring to those actions which, in and of themselves, are humanly frustrative or destructive of self or others. Of course, if such acts are intentionally and freely done, they are sinful because they signal a deliberate rejection of the God-given challenge to love; when the same acts, however, are done unintentionally, without awareness of their significance, or with some notable curtailment of freedom, they retain their status as objective moral wrongs, but the agents of the actions cannot be said to have sinned, even though the actions clearly remain attributable to them, often with sad consequences to themselves and/or others. The point being made by theologians who reject the idea of objective or material sin is precisely this — that acts are not sinful in themselves; sins require sinners; sins spring from people who know that some intended course of action is wrong and nonetheless consciously and freely undertake it. In expressing this theological view, George Regan writes:

> The moral person is one who *intends* to do the morally good; his erroneous judgment about *what* is good does not make him immoral. In ordinary usage, however, we frequently objectify morality and speak of the act as being immoral "in itself," that is, as it stands in relation to the objective moral order prescinding from the person's intentions and emotions. This language factor causes untold difficulty in speaking clearly about morality. It seems preferable to reserve terms such as immoral, sin, and guilty to the area of personal involvement where free and conscious decison-making comes into play.[17]

[17]George M. Regan, C.M., *New Trends in Moral Theology* (New York: Newman Press, 1971), p. 162.

In line with Regan's suggestions, then, it might be said that certain acts, for example, like masturbation, the excessive use of alcohol, and various forms of racial, economic and sexual discrimination may indeed be objectively wrong without necessarily involving a person in what traditional theology would call moral evil or sin. These acts cannot be immediately and outrightly condemned as sins or moral evils simply because they cannot automatically be identified as actions which express a person's decision not to live for God and others, but rather for self. To the extent, however, that these actions, by their very nature, threaten the welfare of self or others, or isolate an individual, or establish in him or her a disposition toward the formation of unrealistic and immature relationships with people and the world, they are objectively wrong.

These actions retain their status as objective moral wrongs —as opposed to being moral evils or sins — when it happens, as it not infrequently does, that the people performing them are not nearly as personally involved in them as they might be. Thus, it might be said, for example, that certain of my actions do not reflect my deepest being, the true "me." Rather, these actions spring more from the edges of my being than from its center. Certain so-called impediments or obstacles have come to intervene in my life with the result that the actions in question, while admittedly harmful to others and/or myself, are not the expression of my truly informed, reflective and free self. These impediments may constitute, in effect, either temporary or some rather perduring *internal* or *subjective* extenuating circumstances in my life; the point is, that when and where these impeding or extenuating circumstances exist, they prevent objective moral wrongs from being also moral evils or sins, but they do so in varying degrees which cannot be easily and precisely determined.

At the very least, however, the following general observation is well rooted in traditional moral theory: while certain of my actions may clearly be regarded as objective moral wrongs whose effects weigh heavily upon myself and others, these actions, nonetheless, must not be immediately and unequivocally charged to me as moral evils or sins in light of the fact that, on occasion, my freedom may have been seriously diminished, or I may have been honestly mistaken in evaluating the moral status of a particular action, or given insufficient attention to its meaning and implications. To speak more specifically, it might be suggested that the curtailment of my knowledge and/or freedom, which explains why my performance of a particular objective moral wrong is not also a sin, has many possible explanations: more remotely, it may be the result of certain temperamental characteristics, ingrained habits, prejudices or neurotic anxieties and obsessions; more immediately, the impediments to my knowledge and freedom may arise from the passion of anger, lust or fear.[18]

In addition to the idea of impediments or *internal* and *subjective* extenuating circumstances, theological speculation, it should be noted, also employs another notion which is helpful in trying to evaluate human actions; it is the concept of physical, ontic or *premoral* evil. The theory behind this concept is that some actions we perform contain elements of non-good, involving, as they do, some threat or harm to the well-being of self or others; but these actions remain on the level of physical or *premoral* evil provided there are sufficient or proportionate reasons for their being performed or tolerated. Thus, it can be said that what might, in ordinary circumstances, be considered an objective *moral* wrong, remains or becomes only a *premoral*, physical or ontic wrong in the presence of definite *external* or *objective* extenuating circumstances which are seen as providing a proportionate or sufficient reason for the action to be initiated.[19]

In later chapters, we will further explore the notions of *premoral* evil, objective *moral* wrong, and sin or moral evil; for now, however, several more points should be made about the

[18]See Timothy E. O'Connell, *Principles for a Catholic Morality* (New York: The Seabury Press, 1978), pp. 45-6 for a fine treatment of what he calls "actual" and "habitual" impediments.

[19]The notion of premoral evil is well explained by Philip S. Keane, S.S., *Sexual Morality. A Catholic Perspective* (New York: Paulist Press, 1977) pp. 46-51; also see p. 200, notes 32-36.

question of right and wrong versus that of moral good and evil. Both dimensions of human activity are important and they are closely related, but they do not perfectly coincide. Thus, while moral evil or living in the "state of sin," that is, in chosen self-sufficiency and self-isolation from God and others, is always harmful to the individual and destructive of his authentic growth as a human being, we cannot say that every objectively wrong action or involvement is always and neces-sarily morally evil or sinful, always indicative, that is, of a lapse or break in the basic love-relationship with God and neighbors.

At the same time, we cannot falsely separate moral good and evil from all other aspects of human existence. For too long we have presumed to isolate theology and moral determinations from all other realms of human wisdom and experience. If we are going to insist that the crucial moral consideration concerns the status of our love-relationship with God and other persons, then we must also insist that real love is born, grows, and dies, not in a vacuum, but in the real world where people are actually helped and harmed by what we as individuals and as members of society do for and against one another. People can be profoundly hurt also by what we allow to be done, or by what we fail to do, while we feign ignorance and helplessness.

What we are saying, then, is that there is scarcely any issue —psychological, sociological, political, economic—which does not have moral overtones and implications insofar as it has an effect upon the quality of individual and corporate human life. We show our love, our hatred, our indifference, both by what we do and by what we leave undone. Partici-pation in warfare, open-housing legislation, proportionate geographical dispersion of low-income housing, equal job opportunities, quality education for all children, pollution-control legislation, determination of national priorities and government expenditures, provision for just political repre-sentation for minority groups — all these are not solely political or social issues. On the contrary, to the extent that they involve our decision to love or to refrain from loving, these are critical moral issues. Indeed, it is in issues like these that our love-relationship with God and our neighbor is tested and proved by the challenge, "I tell you solemnly, insofar as you did this to one of the least of these brothers of mine, you did it to me .... I tell you solemnly, insofar as you neglected to do this to one of the least of these, you neglected to do it to me" (Mt. 25:40, 45).

To summarize our discussion of moral good and evil, and the question of right and wrong, we can say that moral good and evil have to do with the conscious, deliberate, and free living of our lives, either lovingly or selfishly. Right and wrong have to do with the real but unintentional harm we cause ourselves and others, the damage, present or future, we do to our own or someone else's potential as loving human beings. If, because of our ignorance and insensitivity to human dignity, we are not guilty of sin or moral evil, we still have no cause for self-satisfaction and complacency for the less sensitive we are, the less human we are. Whatever stands in our lives as an obstacle to our free commitment in love is to be seen as a challenge to be overcome in our movement toward maturity as human beings and as Christians; in no way should this obstacle be valued or relished as an excusing cause from sin and its guilt. As Regan wisely observes, "unjustified warfare, racial prejudice, marital infidelity, or stealing from big businesses may have little moral culpability about them in some cases, but the carnage of warfare, indignities suffered, wrecked marriages, and lost investments bear eloquent testimony to the importance of promoting correct insights into moral values."[20] The proper perception of moral values is, of course, the function of a well-informed conscience, and thus it is imperative, as indicated in the previous chapter, that serious effort and careful attention be given to the formation of a correct conscience.

V. Reality of Sin

Let us ask one more question: Is it hard to break our basic love-relationship with God and thus to be seriously sinful? It is as hard to sin seriously as it is to love seriously, but it is also as

easy to sin seriously as it is to love seriously. There is no doubt
that the pain and hurt of sinfulness are very real. To love
someone is to live and to work so as to create an atmosphere in
which that person is encouraged and helped to reach his or her
full potential. If sin is seen as a deliberate failure to love and as a
contribution to the stifling of true human growth, then sin is
very real today, for men and women are still being crushed by
hatred and indifference, by educational, economic, and political injustices, by selfishness, and greed, and war. To the extent
that we play at love or allow it to be mocked, we enhance the
power of sin. At the same time, however, Thomas Aquinas
himself did not think it likely that a person who is seriously
trying to live as a good Christian would easily or frequently
rupture his or her love-relationship with God by recourse to sin:
"Although grace is lost by a single act of mortal sin, it is not,
however, easily lost. For the person in grace does not find it easy
to perform such an act (mortally sinful) because of a contrary
inclination" (*De Ver.*, q. 97, a. 1, ad 9). If we are truly in love, in
other words, we find it hard to deliberately hurt our loved ones,
and we do not want to do anything that would place our
relationship with those we love in jeopardy.

The Christian dispensation is a call to love; what is more,
Christianity frees people to love in confidence. In a love-
relationship we can never say that we have proved our love
sufficiently once and for all. There is always room for growth in
love. It is true, moreover, that in a love-relationship we do not
live in fear and trembling, and without confidence in the one we
love. We live in love with peace and joy, knowing we are
accepted, warts and all, with all our limitations and failings.
This is the way it is between God and us. From this perspective,
we do not determine the gravity of sin by listing various
categories. Rather, the pertinent questions are: Who is knowingly and willingly hurting others and thwarting their potential?
Who is freely destroying or failing to develop his or her capacity
to love? Who is freely doing more harm to himself or herself
and allowing others to be harmed? Is it the nosey backyard
gossip, the rebellious adolescent, the nagging and frigid wife
who refuses psychiatric aid, the ambition-driven executive who

lives only for his work, the promiscuous homosexual, the lazy or drunken priest, the puritanical nun?[21]

We remain sinners; but we are sinners within a dispensation of love. We sin against love and against life, against peace, and against justice. A person in grace, whose life is love-filled, lives with his heart and soul for God and others. Often, though, out of fear or laziness, or for some other reason, such a person does not love as fully as he should and as he really wants to; he acts inconsistently with his deepest love and weakens the love-relationship but does not break it. He is distracted from love, but does not alter his radical commitment.

In traditional terms such a person might be said to have sinned venially, but within the context we have described this would be sin only in some analogous sense, because the individual still belongs to God and the things of God. What he has done comes from the edges of his life and not from the center of his being. What we have traditionally known as venial sin illustrates, according to Curran, "the condition of man who constantly falls short of the total love union with God, neighbor and the world to which he is called."[22] Such a person is living proof of the tear in human existence, the inner contradiction of a person's human nature. To the extent that a person consciously and freely puts a strain on the love-relationship, more than objective wrong occurs, but insofar as this relationship of love remains unruptured, the person has not entered into the state of sin.

When, however, a person takes back his heart, turns away from God and others, and lives only for himself, then the direction of his life is radically changed; he takes back his decision and his desire to live as a giving and loving person; he stands against God and neighbor and in this he sins seriously. But his sin is known and experienced from within himself; it does not come from outside himself, and it is not announced or

[21] Milhaven, *op. cit.*, p. 94.

[22] Curran, *op. cit.*, p. 22.

judged by any other human individual.[23] Lest there be any doubt concerning this issue, let it be said that theologians generally agree that it is quite possible for a person to sin mortally in one particular act, but they deny that it is a simple or easy matter to identify that particular act. Moreover, it is not likely that a person sins mortally in an act that is totally out of character for him or her. In other words, mortal sin is not likely to be any act that is unprepared for. Rather, the *quality* of our relationship of love with God and others will probably change before any outright rejection or rupturing of the union. The truth of what is being suggested here might be illustrated this way: the physical act of adultery which serves to betray one's spouse is preceded usually by a lack of caring and concern; complacency, neglect and lack of communication between spouses are warning signs to be heeded that the relationship needs attention if it is to survive and thrive.

VI. Conclusions

If the reality of human sinfulness is to be properly understood, it must be viewed within the context of the very meaning of Christian living. The purpose of the teachings of Christian morality is to inspire the Christian to live even now with the life of Christ: "We can be sure that we are in God only when the one who claims to be living in him is living the same kind of life as Christ lived" (1 Jn. 2:5-6). As Bernard Häring sees it, the life lived by Christ, and hence the life to which Christians are called, is basically a eucharistic life, a life, in other words, of gratitude to the Father and of service to human beings and their world.[24]

The Christian life of love in gratitude and service is, of course, difficult; it must be tested and proven. One of Christ's last exhortations to his friends was: "If you love me, you will keep my commandments" (Jn. 14:15). What is remarkable here is

---

[23]Charles Davis, "Theological Asides: Announcing Mortal Sins," *America,* 112, 6 (February 6, 1965), 193.

[24]Häring, *op. cit.*, p. 15.

that Christ did not say, "If you want to be loved by me you will keep my commandments." His love for us is unqualified, unconditional. Our failure to keep his commandments does not destroy his love for us; rather, in our chosen sinfulness we betray his love for us; we spurn it, and put the lie to any protestation that we truly love.

The tragedy of sin is not that God decides to reject or deny the sinner, but that the sinner takes it upon himself or herself to reject God. God's love does not cease; ours does. The covenantal relationship of love is broken by us, not by God whose jealousy in love is exceeded only by his fidelity. It is the Christian's duty and privilege, then, to acknowledge that only through his love of others does he fulfill the law of God. "All the commandments: 'You shall not commit adultery, you shall not kill, you shall not steal, you shall not covet,' and so on, are summed up in this single command: 'You must love your neighbor as yourself.' Love is the one thing that cannot hurt your neighbor; that is why it is the answer to every one of the commandments" (Rom. 13:9-10). Thus, in a very real sense all sins of commission are expressions in fact of "the one great sin of omission, failure to love."[25]

Inasmuch as human sinfulness is a refusal of God's love, sin offends God, but it is we who suffer most from our own sinfulness because it opens up a tear in our nature as God's people who are free to desire and to do good; by reason of our sinfulness, our freedom to rejoice in what is good flows away from us.[26] Life in Christ is the liberty to love God and all the things of his creating love. When this freedom is wrongly used in the refusal to love, sin occurs and we threaten to enslave ourselves within the narrow and myopic confines of self-centeredness. This is a confinement that brings with it the death-penalty, for when we fail to love we become members of the living dead (1 Jn. 3:15). This human destructiveness of sin is acknowledged by Thomas who maintains that sin is indeed an offense against God, but that God is offended only by that

---

[25] Maly, *op. cit.*, p. 32.

[26] Häring, *op. cit.*, pp. 42-44; 74-75.

which is opposed to our true welfare.[27] What God commands is only for our good, which is why the gospel is invariably good news, even if it is not always immediately safe and comforting news.

Because God does indeed love us so much that he wants and commands only what is best for us, we ought to wonder why we would ever go against his will, since to go against it, is in fact to work against our own welfare, which is something God finds offensive. If we could only learn to take seriously God's best wishes for us, our whole perspective on God and sin would change, for no longer would we be inclined to view God as a heavenly kill-joy or spoil-sport who delights in making laws against everything we find pleasing and attractive. Instead, we would understand that certain actions do not become evil because they are forbidden by God and his law; the truth is, rather, that God establishes a law forbidding certain activities only and precisely because he sees that these actions are already evil in that they are simply harmful to, or destructive of, our well-being. And who, we may ask, knows better either what is really for our good or what can seriously harm us, than God who is our creator? Objectively speaking, of course, no one does, but when we sin, we stand in opposition to God and presume to suggest, as it were, that he should take lessons from us regarding what it is that can truly make us happy and fulfilled. Sin, in short, signals our rebellion against God's call to love, a call which he issues not for his own sake, but for ours, since it is only by loving that we move toward a lasting and ultimate joy.

When our effort at moral living is seen as a response to God's invitation to love, there is no propriety in the attitude which anxiously tries to weigh out the difference between "mortal" and "venial" sins, and then feels relieved when some failing proves not to be of mortal weight. What is expected of Christians, and what we must desire, is total conversion. We quickly recognize the travesty of love which is expressed in any

---

[27]"*Non enim Deus a nobis offenditur nisi ex eo quod contra nostrum proprium bonum agimus.*" *Summa Contra Gentiles*, III, c. 122.

human relationship where lovers ask each other only, "What must I do to avoid hurting you?" We expect lovers to share but one ambition: what more can I do to show my love for you? Thus sincere Christians are those who direct their attention not primarily to avoiding the step that would move them from "venial" to "mortal" sin, but rather to fostering that continual dedication of mind and heart whereby they always do more to embody their love of gratitude and service.

What, then, is the structure of Christian life within which we can properly consider sin? Insofar as innocence is an overly individualistic and non-historical concept that implies freedom not only from guilt but also from experience, we may argue that the task of the moral life for the Christian is the movement from innocence to righteousness which takes place under the constantly shaping hand of love. But this righteousness, it must be emphasized, has nothing to do with that individual smugness that revels in isolated splendor, or prides itself on its personal achievements in the face of the law. On the contrary, Christian righteousness is a relational reality which takes form only as a person, in response to the gospel of Christ, and strengthened and encouraged by His invitation to love, orients his or her life properly vis-à-vis God, neighbors and the world. To speak of the proper orientation of life implies, moreover, that what characterizes the Christian is not abstention from life, but rather dedicated involvement.

These reflections provide no easy morality; they demand and presuppose a mature and honest Christian. When sin is understood not as an isolated act but as a relational reality, that is, as a broken love-relationship, it becomes clear that we must be careful not only of what we actually do to harm or to destroy this relationship, but also of what we leave undone to improve the relationship. Over a period of time the relationship can suffer and die from thoughtless neglect in which we acquiesce and with which we eventually become satisfied. We can sin both by what we are and by what we fail to be, by our commitments and by our omissions. In the effort to live the Christian life we must make decisions *for ourselves* but we must not fall into the trap of making them *on our own.*[28] Now, more, perhaps, than ever before, we must seek counsel. We may approach the Sacrament of Reconciliation less frequently; it is to be hoped, however, that we will enter into it more seriously, more wisely, and with more incentive toward living a full Christian life.

The practice of sacramental confession is undeniably under fire these days; many sincere Catholics question both the usefulness of, and the need for, the rite of reconciliation. Such questioning must be addressed. I personally am convinced that behind Catholicism's centuries-old practice of sacramental confession there is a wisdom whose depth can only be more appreciated in light of the theological and psychological insights which have surfaced in recent times.

Today, for example, we have a deeper sense of the social nature and implications of our sinfulness; no sin is totally or solely private because, however much we yield to sin, we produce a change within ourselves that invariably shapes and influences our dealings with others. No sin really remains "secret"; its effects will somehow out. It is important, therefore, that in expressing our sorrow and in seeking forgiveness, there must be some appropriate expression of the fact that in our sinfulness we have alienated ourselves from both God and our neighbors. On one level, the sacrament of reconciliation serves this purpose, for as penitents, through our encounter with the priest, who is both the servant-representative of God and the minister to God's people, we testify to our desire to be re-integrated into the community of God's love and the company of his people.

Moreover, precisely as human beings who live as body-spirits, it is tremendously useful and helpful for us to incarnate or "act out" our sorrow and our need for forgiveness through recourse to sacramental confession. Fortunately, too, I think, many priests today are deeply sensitive to the essentially social and incarnational dimensions of Christian living; as a result, in their designation of a sacramental penance, they ask penitents

---

[28]John A. T. Robinson, *Christian Morals Today* (Phila.: The Westminster Press, 1964), p. 44.

to move beyond recitation of formal prayers and to pursue reconciliation with God and neighbor through specific acts of caring and concern.

Finally, the practice of sacramental confession seems to me to make eminent sense in terms of its positive psychological impact upon our human and spiritual development. I am speaking here not simply of the sense of joy and relief that replaces the burden of guilt; rather, I want also to suggest that confession can be a source of great inner strength because our sinfulness likes the darkness of concealment; it does not want to be owned up to, which is exactly what we do in confession. In the articulation and revelation of our sins we come to own our sinfulness more deeply, but at the same time we also possess more richly the redemptive power of Christ's love; in this way, sin's hidden power over us is loosened.

In light of the theology of sin presented in this chapter, I would argue for the advisability of having a regular confessor who comes to know us and can thereby help us to unravel and make sense of the stop-and-go movement that so often characterizes the effort to grow in love as a Christian. If there is any truth in the image of a priest-confessor as a doctor of the spirit, then we should be as judicious and discerning in the selection of a confessor as we are in the choice of a medical doctor. At the same time, however, we ought not to make a practice of shifting from one confessor to another; this is no more wise than to be regularly choosing different physicians. As with a physician, so also with a confessor, it is helpful and important to establish some kind of history so that a more accurate interpretation may be given to what is happening in one's life. We have to be reminded, finally, that confessors, like doctors, are not infallible; neither are they all equally competent or compassionate. If we have had a bad experience with a confessor, if we have been somehow mistreated or demeaned, the proper response is not to write off the whole notion of confession; this would be as irresponsible as the decision never again to seek medical advice and attention simply because we have in the past been the object of a physician's misdiagnosis or mistreatment.

It might not be inappropriate at this point to reflect briefly on the new Rite of Reconciliation. The substitution of a "reconciliation room" for the traditional "black box" confessional as the setting for the sacrament is more likely to allow for a true celebration of the event. Having been provided with an atmosphere in which they can be more comfortable, people may be naturally encouraged to engage in a dialogue that enables both penitent and priest to understand better their status before God. In this setting, neither penitent nor priest is likely to settle for, or be satisfied with, the simple narration of the proverbial "laundry list" of sins. Moreover, neither priest nor penitent is as easily able simply to play his respective role or to hide behind his "mask." In the "open confession" both penitent and priest are vulnerable; their shared humanity lies revealed and provides the context for the intervention and mediation of Christ whose presence is acknowledged in faith, whose love is cherished, and whose affirming forgiveness is sought.

Lest people, either out of embarrassment or because of fear that they will be less well thought of by a priest, mourn the loss of anonymity afforded by the customary confessional box, they should prayerfully reflect on the fact that their participation in the sacrament of reconciliation is a faith-event, an expression of their faith, and as such it bears witness to the mystery of God's graciousness toward them. Any priest will testify, moreover, that in celebrating the sacrament of reconciliation, he is both humbled and edified by the overwhelming goodness of God's people, and that his own life of faith is gloriously strengthened and enhanced. Every priest who serves as a confessor knows also that he himself stands as a sinner before God; as such, the priest is no stranger to the life of the penitent. Thus there is no reason or justification for a confessor to be self-righteous or condemnatory in his dealings with penitents. In the person of the penitent, the confessor comes face to face not so much with a liar, an embezzler or an adulterer; the priest, rather, meets and responds to someone who is loved by God and who is struggling, like the confessor himself, to grow in the ability to answer love with love in an ever more generous way. Rather than being fearful, then, let us as penitents be grateful for the miracle of sacramental reconciliation where we can confess our sins to a fellow human being and receive in response the forgiveness of Christ himself.[29]

As human beings and as Christians we are faced with the fact that in love-relationships an invitation or request to further growth together is often more binding than a command, and our coolness or indifference in responding is often more hurtful than outright betrayal. Thus, no one of us prays with false humility when we plead: "O Lord, be merciful to us, sinners." In order to realize more fully how significant our sinfulness, as a refusal to love, must be to God, it may help to consider the reality of human love-relationships. We know the joys and excitement of love, but we also know the pains of disillusionment and human rejection. When our human relationships do not work out, we can, over a period of time, re-channel the vitality of our love; we can slowly forget the love that goes unrequited; we can dull the pain of unanswered love by learning to love others. As human beings we can be distracted from those we love and go elsewhere to new loves.

God, it seems, can do none of this, for while human love is limited, God's love is not, and the greater the capacity to love, the greater the capacity to be loved and to be affected by unanswered love. Thus our refusal and hesitation to love God, our demands to be left alone and untouched, deeply and constantly affront him. Whereas human beings who love us can find their fulfillment elsewhere if we refuse their love, some part of God's infinite capacity to be loved finds no satisfaction in someone else if you or I reject him. Thus, just as there is no place for us to escape God's love for us, so also there is no place where God can escape our refusal to love him. Given our unique identity as a son or daughter of God, each of us is in a position to love God as he has never been loved before. Somehow God wants our love and somehow he can receive it. We can refuse to give it, however. In doing so, we frustrate ourselves and give offense to God. Somehow he is affected and vulnerable. Love brings him to this predicament. It is indeed strange, but so too is a God on a cross.

[29]See John O'Donnell, S.J., "The Need to Confess," *America*, 144, 12 (March 28, 1981), 252-53.

IV

Human Sexuality:
A Context for Its Meaning
and Morality

I. Introductory Observations: Religion and Sexuality

For a number of years I have had the opportunity to participate, along with a biologist and a psychologist, in a team-taught course in human sexuality. In the earliest days of this new undertaking the general scuttlebutt among the students was that the biologist would tell them what to do and how to do it, the psychologist would tell them who is doing what and why it is being done, and I, the moral theologian, would tell them not to do it. While the comment was made good-naturedly, I trust, it nonetheless indicated the not unusual expectation that people harbored when they concerned themselves with organized religion's involvement with human sexuality. The scene is changing, however.

The consensus today seems to be that religion is having less and less effect upon the everyday lives of people. More specifically, fewer individuals now regard the teaching of the churches as relevant to sexual activity. If various forms of sexual expression are avoided today, it is not because of religious condemnation, but because of various personal, social and aesthetic considerations.[1]

Notwithstanding the alleged relegation of religion's views on sexuality to the sidelines of human concern, the fact remains that over the long haul of history the impression instilled by Christianity in most people has been that, at best, physical sexuality is permissible under certain very specific conditions and for very specific reasons; and at worst, sexuality is demonic or animalistic. Sex was presented somehow as a regrettable necessity and sexual sins were regarded as the worst kind. How effectively this teaching took hold is evident even today in the fact that when we hear or speak of someone "living in sin," we almost always have in mind or imagine something to do with sex. We practically never mean or imagine that someone is full of pride or economic greed, or is responsible for some gross social injustice.

Religion's preoccupation with sexuality and sexual morality was captured in the remark of Josef Goldbrunner when he observed that "Christianity seems to have changed from a religion of love into a religion of chastity."[2] This is an expression of the criticism that Christianity has tended to exalt chastity above all other virtues. Lest I add fuel to the fire of this criticism, I ought explicitly to disassociate myself from any position which would maintain that an individual necessarily errs or sins most seriously, most often, or most easily in areas of sexual morality. While sexuality is an inherent and pervasive aspect of human existence, it is not the exclusive nor even the primary area for moral reflection. Admitting this, however, still leaves unchanged the fact that many people, especially adolescents and young adults, and regardless of the intensity of their religious affiliation, are very concerned about the proper role of sexual expression in their lives. I suggest that at least one

---

[1]Richard F. Hettlinger, *Living With Sex: The Student's Dilemma* (New York: The Seabury Press, 1966), pp. 23-25.

[2]Goldbrunner's remark appears in *Holiness Is Wholeness* (Notre Dame, 1965), and is quoted in *The New Morality. Continuity and Discontinuity*, ed. William Dunphy (New York: Herder & Herder, 1967), p. 69.

reason for this concern is that existentially it is most frequently in the area of sexuality that an individual first uncovers and confronts the terror and the task of establishing his or her self-identity and integrity. During adolescence we become very aware of, and self-conscious about, our own desires, needs, expectations and demands upon others. We are also exposed to the desires, needs, expectations and demands of others with respect to ourselves. We consciously stand as persons in front of other persons and must grapple with the questions: What kind of person am I? What kind of person do I wish to become? What kind of person should I become? What direction am I moving in? Do I need a change of direction? The perceptions that emerge and the answers that we give to these questions will greatly influence the expression we give to our sexuality and this, I think, is as it should be.

If it so happens that we profess Christianity, then it necessarily follows that our lives should be spent in the effort to grow and relate to others in a loving way. Sexual expression, whatever else it may involve, must be for the Christian an externalization of love; it must be love-in-action. Explicit physical sexual relationships should be a way of expressing love, but they are not the only way, nor the way for all times, places, and people. We must be loving always, and we cannot avoid being sexual in our relationships, but we simply are not always engaged in, nor desirous of, explicit genital or physical sexual unions. There is something special about the physical love-expression of human sexuality, and later we shall try to discover the nature of this distinctiveness. Before doing that, however, it might be helpful to look at some of the general movements in the history of ideas regarding the human body and sexuality.

II. Philosophy and Sexuality

It is no secret that until recently a lot of Christians viewed the human body and sexuality with suspicion. But why? In general, as Christianity began to spread beyond the borders of Israel

orgasm. What needs emphasizing today is the fact that the genitals are simply important symbols of our sexuality, but they are not its only focus. As Frederic Wood puts it, ". . . to make such symbols exhaustive of the reality to which they point is to practice the same kind of idolatry as those who confuse symbols of God with that reality itself." We may conclude from this that what is necessary for sexual and human fulfillment is "not simply the occasional use of someone's genitals" but the establishment of relationships with others precisely as persons.[12] What this means is that there is a whole other dimension to human sexuality; it is what may be called the social or affective dimension which shows itself in the human capacity to relate to others with emotional warmth, compassion and tenderness. All of these human qualities are rooted in sexuality and are true expressions of it, but they are not specifically genital in nature or focus.[13]

Surely, when we act as loving individuals, we are acting as sexual beings, but we are not necessarily involved genitally. In fact, in some loving relationships (between parents and children, or between friends) there is never any question of genital involvement, while in other relationships the genital expression of love may be more or less important and imperative depending on how well developed the human affectivity of the partners is. In other words, it is not unusual to find that to the extent that these affective qualities are undeveloped and unappreciated, we tend to become preoccupied with the genital or physical aspects of our sexuality.[14] This often leads to behavior which is destructive and/or futile because although physical sexual needs surely are real, they are not our highest needs. In fact, if our highest human needs go unrecognized and remain unmet, no satisfaction of our physical sexual needs is likely to result in a sense of human fulfillment.

[12]Frederic C. Wood, Jr., *Sex and the New Morality* (New York: Association Press and Newman Press, 1968), p. 23.

[13]Donald Goergen, *The Sexual Celibate* (New York: The Seabury Press, 1974), pp. 52-3.

[14]Marc Oraison, *Being Together* (New York: Doubleday, 1970), pp. 112-16.

It is crucial, therefore, to realize that sexual desire is not simply the need for genital relations, even though often enough this need for genital expression is what we are most consciously aware of. Also, as Donald Goergen reminds us, "it is easy to confuse the need for genital sex with the need for sexual identity, the need for self-acceptance, or the need for closeness."[15] Speaking in the same vein, Rollo May makes the point that "for human beings the more powerful need is not for sex, *per se*, but for relationships, intimacy, acceptance, and affirmation."[16] When these higher, greater, or more powerful human needs are met, our lower needs are more manageable. Abraham Maslow puts it this way: "Loving at a higher need level makes the lower needs and their frustrations and satisfactions less important, less central, more easily neglected. But it also makes them more wholeheartedly enjoyed when gratified."[17] Experience has often enough proven that genital relationships are no guarantee for a sense of intimacy. Experience, likewise, bears witness to the fact that intimacy is possible without genital expression.[18] The key to keeping the physical or genital dimension of a relationship in proper perspective is to develop the affective dimension of sexuality. It is possible to live fully, healthfully and happily without genital sexuality. It is not possible to do so without developed affective relationships.

Sexual passion, that is, the passion of genital relations, is human, not animal, precisely insofar as it embodies and expresses the pervasive and perduring quality of sexual affectivity. Unfortunately, however, genital expression is often a cop-out, an escape, because both inside and outside of marriage, it is far easier to "sleep with" someone than to live together with and for someone in a completely human way, that is, emotionally and psychologically, as well as physically. Too many people, it seems, neither appreciate nor capitalize upon

[15]Goergen, *op. cit.*, p. 61.

[16]Rollo May, *Love and Will* (New York: W. W. Norton and Co., 1969), p. 311.

[17]Abraham Maslow, *Motivation and Personality: Religion, Values, and Peak Experiences* (New York: Harper & Row, 1970), pp. 177-78.

[18]Goergen, *op. cit.*, p. 120.

the unique richness of human sexuality. In animals, the act of copulation is a brief, business-like, and rather routine interlude. Human beings, however, have the capacity, perhaps greatly under-utilized, to introduce variety into their sexual relationships. In this regard, Andrew Greeley makes the interesting suggestion that in point of fact genital fidelity in marriage means "the commitment to increasing both one's own pleasure and the pleasure of the spouse." He goes on to assure us, of course, that in its broadest sense there is much more to human fidelity in the marriage relationship. Greeley suggests that marital fidelity consists in the "permanent, public, solemn, and irrevocable commitment to dedicate one's life to bringing out the best in both one's partner and one's self." It is noteworthy, says Greeley, that while married people may experience a great degree of guilt for sleeping with someone other than their spouse, not much guilt at all is experienced when they allow their spousal sexual relationships to become dull and routine. And yet, concludes Greeley, static and stagnant genital relationships between spouses constitute a real ongoing infidelity.[19]

What I would like to suggest in this regard is that the tendency to allow one's spousal genital relationships to become dull and routine is often an expression of the failure to develop one's affective sexuality. In other words, too often, I think, genital relationships are turned to simply as a release from felt sexual tension rather than as a celebration of the tender, caring, compassionate, and loving relationship which, it is hoped, is being shared by spouses day by day. We tend to forget that people change gradually, and that it is incumbent upon those who are in love, and especially upon spouses, to discover the new person that the beloved becomes, day by day, week by week, month by month, and year by year. When two people relate creatively to each other on the level of affectivity, it is not unusual for that creativity to be carried over into their sexual genital relationships. This is the truth contained in the observation made by Kevin Axe: "It is no trick at all to have

[19]Andrew Greeley, *Sexual Intimacy* (Chicago: The Thomas More Association, 1973), pp. 177-78.

intercourse with five thousand women in the course of a lifetime. The real trick is to have intercourse with the same woman five thousand times."[20] When, of course, this ongoing genital relationship brings happiness and fulfillment to the two parties, it is most probably because they are experiencing the true miracle of mutual love.

V. Sexuality, Chastity and Love

What people want and need today, and what many theologians are arguing for, is a sexual morality that makes sense in terms of personal relationships. More and more, it is acknowledged that sex does not create a relationship; rather it expresses a relationship that already exists. The question to be asked is whether or not the physical sexual relationship corresponds to the depth of intellectual, emotional and interpersonal involvement that is shared by two people.[21] Living as a chaste person requires that the physical and external expressions of our sexuality be "under the control of love, with tenderness and full awareness of the other."[22] John A. T. Robinson has made the suggestion that chastity is honesty in sex, that is, chastity implies that we have "physical relationships that *truthfully express* the degree of personal commitment" that is shared with another.[23] What this means is that two people, in their physical sexual relationship, should not transcend, or go beyond, the degree of activity that would be appropriate for the commitment that actually exists between them.

It should be noted here that the criterion of honesty is not verified by what two people tell each other about the level of

---

[20]Kevin H. Axe, "Sex and the Married Catholic," *U.S. Catholic,* 41, 11 (Nov., 1976), 6-11 at 8.

[21]Gregory Kenny with Edward Wakin, "Sex and the Young Catholic," *U.S. Catholic/Jubilee,* 36, 10 (Oct., 1971), 9.

[22]W. Norman Pittenger, *Making Sexuality Human* (Philadelphia: Pilgrim Press, 1970), p. 50.

[23]John A. T. Robinson, *Christian Morals Today* (Philadelphia: The Westminster Press, 1964), p. 45.

their mutual commitment, but rather by whether or not their physical sexual expression exceeds or goes beyond their overall level of mutual commitment, regardless of what, or how much, they tell each other. Thus, just because two people openly admit to each other that they are in the relationship simply because of the fun or the pleasure involved, does not mean that they can, therefore, legitimately engage in genital expressions of their sexuality. The reason for this is that there is still a great discrepancy between their level of commitment and what the act of sexual intercourse itself says.

We will investigate the meaning of sexual intercourse a bit later in our reflections. For the time being, let us simply admit that once chastity is described as honesty in sex, it becomes necessary to distinguish between chastity and virginity. There are obviously people who give up their virginity but who in no way abandon their lives of chastity. Among such people are spouses whose physical relationships give honest testimony to the deep commitment and love which they share. Chastity is for all people and not just for those who are single. Spouses are, ideally, chaste non-virgins. At the same time, however, it is possible to be an unchaste virgin, which means that a person may retain his or her physical virginity but still be involved in a relationship that is not honest in terms of physical sexual expression. Thus the question of chastity should arise in a relationship before the question of virginity because often chastity is forgotten long before virginity is lost.

Goergen locates the virtue of chastity within the context of humanity and Christianity. He suggests that chastity is a virtue which "helps us to utilize the totality of our sexuality and put it at the service of our becoming Christian."[24] Far from being in any way opposed to sexuality, chastity rather accepts a person's striving for pleasure and "attempts to put that striving in the service of other human and Christian values." More specifically, a chaste person is the one who "places the intense pleasure associated with the genital interaction at the service of love."[25] Quite simply, concludes Goergen, "chastity moderates

---

[24]Goergen, *op. cit.*, p. 96.
[25]*Ibid.*, pp. 100-01.

or orders one's sexuality. It does not make sexuality the end of man nor the enemy of man."[26] In the context of Christianity it makes eminent sense, therefore, to suggest that the highest goal of any sex education is "to introduce human beings to a knowledge and exercise of truly responsible and partner-oriented behavior. Put another way, the goal is to develop in people the ability to give and receive love."[27]

Of course, not everyone agrees with the idea that there is a necessary or even a proper connection between sex and personal commitment or love. As a prime, although extreme, example of some thinking which explicitly rejects such a relationship between sex and love, we need only mention "The Playboy Philosophy" as developed by Hugh Hefner, who draws profit from the idea that it is quite possible and desirable for sexual activity to occur in a relationship that is kept recreational, that is, on the level of entertainment, and thus carries no evidence or implication of personal commitment or love. Hefner testifies: "I certainly think that personal sex is preferable to impersonal sex because it includes the greatest emotional rewards; but I can see no logical justification for opposing the latter unless it is irresponsible, exploitative, coercive, or in some way hurts one of the individuals involved."[28] The question must be asked of Hefner: How is it possible for sex to be impersonal without it at the same time being irresponsible, exploitative and hurtful? For it would seem that as soon as we treat a person impersonally, that is, as a non-person, we are treating him or her in a way that is inappropriate precisely because it does not acknowledge who he or she really is. This kind of behavior opens up a tear in reality. It smacks of dishonesty and introduces injustice into the relationship.

[26] *Ibid.*, p. 99.

[27] Klaus Breuning, "Responsible Sexuality as an Educational Goal: Problems and Prospects," in *Sexuality in Contemporary Catholicism*, part of *Concilium*, Religion in the Seventies, eds. Franz Böckle and Jacques-Marie Pohier (New York: The Seabury Press, 1976), 89.

[28] Hugh M. Hefner, "The Playboy Philosophy" Part 19, appearing in *Playboy* (December, 1964), 164.

There are two pertinent critiques of "The Playboy Philosophy" which deserve to be heard at some length. One of these critiques is developed from the viewpoint of the human and psychological meaning of human sexuality, while the other engages in a theological analysis of this philosophy. Let us look first at Hettlinger's objection that "The Playboy Philosophy" does not take account of the full psychological and human amplitude of human sexuality; men are told lies about women; thus, women are mistreated and men are misled:

> By depicting sex as a simple, uncomplicated, easily controllable exercise in the enjoyment of the good life, *Playboy* misleads its readers into assuming that real women are as pliable, convenient, and usable as the playmate of the month—quite prepared to be folded up in three sections when the next attraction comes along. And the male reader is equally wrongly encouraged to suppose that he can approach sex in this manner without danger to his own integrity and maturity.
>
> In fact, *The Playboy Philosophy* falls into precisely the same error as the traditional religious mores, which it castigates most vigorously: it denies the contemporary psychological understanding of the depths of sexuality in the human person. . . Yet if we have learned anything from Freud and his successors, it is surely that we are not people with or without sex, as we choose, but sexual beings—and that to deny or degrade our sexuality is to degrade our very selves.[29]

Responding as a theologian, Harvey Cox regards *Playboy* as a futile attempt to address the male's fascination with, and deep-set fear of, sexuality. *Playboy* wants to turn sexuality into a packageable consumption item by reducing the proportions of human sexuality, its power and its passion. Within the confines of the magazine, "the nude woman symbolizes total sexual accessibility but demands nothing from the observer." Thus, the male is supposed to feel unthreatened and reassured, for he is in charge and there is nothing to fear in human

---

[29] Hettlinger, *op. cit.*, pp. 41-42.

sexuality. But Cox contends that tearing the heart out of human sexuality is no way to solve the problem of being a man, because "sexuality is the basic form of all human relationships and therein lies its terror and its power." The way to becoming fully human, therefore, does not lie in "having the other fully exposed to me and my purposes—while I remain uncommitted—but exposing myself to the risk of encounter with the other by reciprocal self-exposure." Cox concludes that "any theological critique of *Playboy* that focuses on its 'lewdness' will misfire completely. *Playboy* and its less successful imitators are not 'sex magazines' at all. They are basically anti-sexual. They dilute and dissipate authentic sexuality by reducing it to an accessory, by keeping it at a safe distance."[30]

Among the college students with whom I am in contact, very few subscribe to "The Playboy Philosophy." The great majority, by far, talk about the ideal of responsible sexual relationships. By this, they mean to restrict physical expressions of sexuality to relationships of love. There are, however, wide-ranging discussions as to just what the meaning of love is, and it is to this question that we must now turn our attention.

VI. Love, Sexuality and Responsibility

To relate physical sexual expression to love is not without its problems. To love someone has certain prerequisites, not the least of which is the capacity to love oneself. Unless I have a basic sense of who I am and who I would like to be, and am able to find value in myself, accept myself, and love myself, it is likely that I will try to derive my value from someone else; in doing so, there is a terrible danger that in my relationships with others I will be manipulative and exploitative. This, of course, undermines any possibility of true love of another person. In addition, truly loving someone is an enterprise undertaken from a position of strength, at least in the sense that I am

---

[30]Harvey Cox, *The Secular City* (New York: The Macmillan Company, 1965), pp. 203-04.

sufficiently at one with myself to have a basic perception of my strengths and weaknesses, such that I know what I can and cannot offer the one whom I love. Moreover, love, as I understand it, is not an accident that befalls me. It is not something I fall into. Rather, love is my free response, my free decision to respond to the beauty and potential that I see in my loved one. This decision involves also a willingness to make the effort to create an atmosphere in which my loved one can reach the fullness of his or her potential. Erich Fromm puts it this way:

> Love should be essentially an act of will, of decision to commit my life completely to that of one other person... To love someone is not just a strong feeling—it is a decision, it is a judgment, it is a promise. If love were only a feeling, there would be no basis for the promise to love each other forever. A feeling comes and it may go.[31]

All of this suggests that true love involves work, an investment of self. Therefore, two people who love each other do not so much "fall for" one another; rather, they "stand in" with respect to each other. To capture the significance of this distinction, it is necessary to reflect on the fact—too little understood and appreciated today—that there is a lifetime of difference between true love and being "in love." While the experience of being "in love" tends to be quite romantic, true love must struggle with reality. One writer marvelously contrasts the two experiences:

> Being in love is the high-voltage, circuit-blowing infatuation we've all experienced when we connect with someone new. It's the intoxication of being accepted and desired. It's the thrill of taking a leap, shedding clothes and inhibitions, being dazzled by the private magnificence of another. Being in love is awesome and enthralling, but in the end, sadly, it's an emotional sprint.

[31]Erich Fromm, *The Art of Loving* (New York: Bantam Books, 1963), p. 47; also see p. 18.

Like a blossoming flower, it's simply too phenomenal to last longer than a season.

Love, by contrast, is a marathon of the heart. It requires training, discipline, endurance and work. It is not a spectator sport or an event whose outcome can be decided in seconds. It is pushing up hills and suffering pain and resisting the temptation to drop out.... When love is viewed as an act of will,... it can survive as long as your heart beats. Put another way, while being in love may sometimes lead to marriage, it's love that makes a marriage last. More specifically, it's the deliberate, active commitment implied by love that lies at the core of conjugal bliss.[32]

Being "in love" is unquestionably a valid or authentic human experience. That really is not the point at issue. Rather, what is important is to understand the nature of this experience and be able to distinguish it from the experience of true love. At root, it seems that being "in love" is something that can happen to us from time to time; it is not something we do on our own. In describing the experience a person might say, "I was swept off my feet," "I was beside myself with love," or "I was carried off my feet." These expressions indicate that the person "in love" is not the primary actor or agent in the experience; somehow or other, the person "in love" is on the receiving end of the experience as though being "in love" were an experience to be endured because it is beyond our control. By contrast, the experience of real love is quite otherwise; the person who truly loves another is not at a loss to manage the situation, but rather decides actively, positively and freely to live and work for the well-being of the beloved.

When I truly love another, I desire not only to be *with* my loved one, but also to be and live *for* him or her. Real love entails the desire to share a common destiny with a loved one, and a willingness to do what is necessary to enable my beloved to have the room to achieve fulfillment. What this means is that

[32]Art Carey, "In Defense of Marriage," *The Philadelphia Inquirer Magazine* (February 20, 1983), 29.

in love the focus of my attention and of my action is my loved one, not myself; and yet I, of course, do not go unaffected by this love-relationship. In giving, I receive. But my own growth is not the reason, the motive or purpose of my loving someone. In love, moreover, I seek no domination of my loved one. I desire only his or her freedom and growth. My loved one, I trust, desires the same for me. There is nothing forced about love. Love has no ulterior motives.

Healthy and moral love-relationships do not consist simply in the satisfaction of needs. Needs are involved, certainly, and they obviously should be acknowledged, but the satisfaction of these needs is not the reason of my love for someone. It is, in fact, when my own needs occupy too central a position in my relationship with another that my lust is likely to be discovered. For lust is the desire for another person who is seen as capable of satisfying my need for pleasure by providing me with an outlet for the release of tension. In lust, I am concerned with the fulfillment of my own needs and desires, with little or no thought being given to the needs, interests, and desires of the other. Fromm has commented on the interplay of love and needs when he observed that there is a mature and an immature form of love. "Immature love says: 'I love you because I need you.' Mature love says: 'I need you because I love you'."[33] In the first instance, needs have priority; in the second, the commitment of love is primary.

How we express ourselves sexually and genitally depends to a large extent, I think, upon how we see ourselves as persons and how, more specifically, we see the relationship between our body and our spirit. When I engage myself sexually with a person, I am giving more than my body. I give myself. So also, do I receive more than a body. I receive another person. As a person, I live in my body, which I both have and am. So also, does the other person live in his or her body. But I must be careful. I do not live in my body as a ghost lives in a machine. The relationship between my spirit and my body is not the same as that which exists between a driver and his or her car. The

[33]Fromm, *op. cit.*, p. 34.

distinction between a driver and a car is a clear and distinct one; more importantly, the driver may be separated from his or her vehicle. Such is not the case, however, in the relationship between the individual human spirit and the human body. Although our body and our spirit are distinct realities, they cannot be separated one from the other without destroying the very reality we know as a human being or person. If I were to physically mistreat someone, I would be establishing some kind of a relationship, not only with that person's body, but also with his or her very personhood. Quite simply, the human spirit permeates, penetrates into, and humanizes the entire human body.

This view of the relationship between the human spirit and the body has profound implications for sexual activity. Sexual intercourse is not fully or adequately understood as simply body-to-body contact and penetration. Rather, as John Dedek puts it, "sexual intercourse is a sign of total, unreserved giving of self. At the moment of orgasm, the individual's personality is lost in an interpenetration of the other self. Sexual intercourse is expressive of one's person. To be authentic and not a lie it must correspond to the existing relationship between the persons."[34] In addressing the question of the meaning of sexual intercourse, James Gaffney speaks in a similar vein. For him, both the mutual self-giving and the acceptance of another which occur in the act of sexual intercourse constitute the physical symbols of a spiritual achievement, the essence of which "consists in the uniting of two human personalities by mutually assuming an unconditional responsibility for one another." The practical meaning, in fact, of a couple's mutual self-giving lies precisely in their assumption of this unconditional responsibility for each other.[35] If sexual intercourse proclaims a gift of self, then, in effect, two people, through this action, are embodying a mutual profession which says something like this: "Not only do I care for you, but I also want to

---

[34]John F. Dedek, *Contemporary Medical Ethics* (New York: Sheed and Ward, Inc., 1975), pp. 82-83.

[35]James Gaffney, *Moral Questions* (New York: Paulist Press, 1974), p. 26.

take care of you. Not only do I respond sensitively and physically to you, but I also want to be responsible for you unconditionally."[36]

It happens, unfortunately, that quite often the gift of self to another, which is symbolized by the act of intercourse, turns out to have been merely a loan. When this occurs, a radical discrepancy is created between the relationship as it is symbolized by the act of intercourse and the relationship as it exists in reality. The very meaning of sexual intercourse as an act of human communication is compromised. This is not a healthy situation, either for individuals or for society as a whole. For if we accustom ourselves to say, whether in word or in action, more than we really mean, we will find over a period of time that we have greatly compromised our ability to mean as much as we say.[37] What I am suggesting is that the only time sexual intercourse tells the truth is when it signifies that two people have united themselves as one to start a new life together. Sexual union should occur within the context of a life-commitment because the body-giving of physical intercourse symbolizes the self-giving which is the essence of love.

It so happens, however, that the rumor is spreading that before any commitment is entered into, the relationship must be tested for mutual compatibility. By this line of argumentation, sexual intercourse and/or "live-in" arrangements come to be regarded as necessary and justifiable. This rationale contains a fallacy which reflects a serious inadequacy in the understanding of the nature of physical sexual pleasure. The bodily pleasures of sexual involvement are so powerful and enthralling that they tend to become attention-consuming and preoccupying; one sexual interlude sets the stage and predisposes a person for the next. Heat is generated in the relationship but not necessarily any light. When two people are trying to find out if they can please each other physically, they may well find out nothing else; mutual discovery of each other as persons

---

[36] I am paraphrasing here some ideas of William H. Masters and Virginia Johnson in association with Robert J. Levin, *The Pleasure Bond* (New York: Bantam Books, 1976), p. 268.

[37] Gaffney, *op. cit.*, p. 27.

is replaced by body-exploration; it is all so pleasurable, but so blinding and so distracting, that the quest for knowledge of self and of the other is stymied. The situation is described well by James Burtchaell:

> ...it is so powerful and influential an experience that a continued sexual relationship summons forth from a couple the feelings of being one, while they are still very much two. The feelings are artificially elicited but, like all things counterfeit, they feel like the real thing, especially to one who has not felt the real thing. I can hardly think of a way for two people better to conceal from themselves their true relationship and prospects for marriage than becoming sexually involved. And there is no time in their lives when reliable self-evaluation is more crucial.[38]

With Burtchaell, I would take strong exception to the idea of "testing for sexual compatibility" as an argument for premarital sex. A man and woman are more likely to be blessed with sexual compatibility within the context of a mutual commitment and a willingness to work at the strengthening of their relationship. As one student recently put it: "If two people genuinely love one another, their physical relationship should take care of itself with time and with tenderness."

VII. Summary

To conclude this chapter, let us briefly highlight what we have seen. It is clear, first of all, that for many centuries the meaning and morality of human sexual expression were defined primarily in terms of the natural law with its emphasis on procreation. Only in more recent years have we come to a fuller, richer, and more personal understanding of human sexuality, an understanding which makes clear who we are, not only biologically, but also psychologically, socially, affectively

---

[38]James T. Burtchaell, (ed.), *Marriage Among Christians: A Curious Tradition* (Notre Dame: Ave Maria Press, 1977), p. 33.

and theologically. Sexuality is an integral or essential element in the task we face of becoming fully human. It is also a crucial factor in the mission we enjoy as Christians, namely, to continue or extend the reality of God's love for all people. For it is our nature as sexual beings that enables us to be lovers, and it is love which must be the context for our expression of sexuality.

It is for this reason that we have tried to show what the meaning of love is, and have discovered in this effort that any human relationship which deserves to be known as loving, involves concern and caring for the other and demands a willingness to assume responsibility for the other. The desire, the willingness, the promise, the decision, to live not only with my loved one, but also *for* my loved one, is a critical part of the truth that is proclaimed in the act of sexual intercourse. It is for this reason that such an act must not be entered into lightly. The richness of the meaning of sexual intercourse has been well expressed by a former male student of mine: "Sexual intercourse is an act of self-revelation, self-expression, and self-giving which is so complete that it bears the potential of creating another human life. As such, this act is too awesome to be risked with a person who is not understanding of both one's beauty and one's faults."

This insight into the meaning and implications of sexual intercourse goes a long way toward explaining why the context of a mutually shared life-commitment provides the proper moral atmosphere for this form of full sexual expression. The mutual self-giving of sexual intercourse is supposed to be an in-the-flesh reflection of the self-giving contained in a couple's commitment to one another. For Masters and Johnson, commitment means that two people entrust their physical and emotional well-being to one another; such commitment "is an act of faith and an acceptance of vulnerability."[39] For this reason, neither commitment nor sexual intercourse should be entered into lightly; if either is, it is not likely to be done with impunity. Let another male student's comments on love and

[39]Masters and Johnson, *op. cit.*, p. 274.

marriage as the appropriate context for the physical expression
of sexuality serve as a transition to the next chapter:

> In marriage, two people make emotional, psychological, and
> physical contributions to a union that is greater than the sum of
> its parts. Only in this total organism of living and loving does
> sexual intercourse, the ultimate physical act of pleasure, find a
> supportive base. It is the emotional and spiritual unity of
> marriage which properly nourishes the physical union of sexual
> intercourse. When sex is simply recreational, it is not likely to
> afford an opportunity for personal and spiritual growth. As
> Woody Allen might have it: "Sex without love is an empty
> experience, but as empty experiences go, it is one of the best."
>
> When, however, sex arises out of love, we are brought out of
> ourselves, out of our self-preoccupation, into the light of a
> dynamic relationship that integrates all parts of our humanity.
> Sex is no longer a dead-end experience, that is, one of mutual,
> but isolated and separable, self-gratification. In love, rather, sex
> is allowed to become the gift-to-the-other that it really is. Surely,
> sex without love is quite pleasant, but it leaves us ungrown. Sex
> without love is somewhat like masturbation, except that instead
> of being physically alone, the two people are only affectively or
> emotionally alone. The human spirit is still somewhat self-
> contained and cold. Sex without love, it seems, comes off as
> selfish and, as such, it bears its own frustration as all selfishness
> does. The selfish person, the person who seeks to possess, is
> ultimately left possessing only himself.

V

The Issue of Premarital Sexuality

I. Introduction

The purpose of the preceding chapter was to provide a background for the discussion of specific issues of sexual morality. It has been suggested that a loving commitment establishes the proper context for genital sexual expression. While it is one thing to say that genital sexual expression should be limited to those relationships which embody a living commitment of love, it would be quite another thing to say that relationships of love are limited to those in which physical or genital sexual expression would be appropriate. Such a stance, in fact, could never be maintained, because the reality of love is far more inclusive or more comprehensive than the reality of genital sex. In other words, even though we might argue that genital sexual expressions should be limited or confined to relationships in which the commitment of love has come to life, love, as should be obvious, is certainly not confined or limited to expressions of physical or genital sexuality. In fact, I may come to the decision, or I may be obliged to reach the conclusion, that while I truly do love someone, there are reasons why I should not, or do not want to, express that love genitally because of my or my loved one's other commitments or responsibilities. Quite simply, genital expression in some love-relationships may be temporarily or permanently out of the question. This point has been well made by James Burtchaell:

> There may be many people whom one loves profoundly, yet without sexual expression. Sex is not the only expression of love, nor the necessary one. It is not even the greatest: you love your parents as deeply as anyone but you do not have sex with them; that does not mean that you love them less than your spouse. It does mean that your love for them is of a specifically different sort. Sex is appropriate, not simply to exquisite love, but to a very special kind: pledged love.[1]

Burtchaell is here refining the idea expressed in the previous chapter that love provides the context that is required for moral expressions of our physical or genital sexuality. Thus, while it is true that love is always a necessary condition for expressions of genital sexuality, Burtchaell is making the point that love is not always a sufficient condition for these expressions, but rather that a special form of love must provide the setting for genital sexuality. According to him, "What is truthful, proper, distinctive, and defining about sexual union is that it means: 'I take you, for better, for worse, until death'." The uniqueness of the genital union consists in this: that it embodies "the love between two persons who can say to each other, and to no other living person: 'I am yours, and all that I have is yours. All that each of us has is not "mine" or "yours" but "ours".' This is a love-pledge one does not make even to one's children."[2] I would like to suggest that Burtchaell's position on the pledged love that should constitute the proper setting for intimate physical expressions of sexuality complements Gaffney's articulation of the practical meaning of sexual intercourse as an act which testifies to a couple's mutual and full self-giving that does not hesitate to assume even an unconditional responsibility for each other.

[1] James T. Burtchaell, (ed), *Marriage Among Christians. A Curious Tradition* (Notre Dame: Ave Maria Press, 1977), p. 34.

[2] *Ibid.*, pp.34-35.

Up to this point we have simply adverted to the fact that there are many love-relationships, many forms of love, which do not provide the appropriate context for moral genital expressions of sexuality. Another point must be made now, namely, that even between spouses who are involved in a pledged or committed relationship, genital relationship must sometimes be judged morally inappropriate. We generally think of love as tending toward union, whether that union be simply spatial or physical or, more intimately, genital. But there are instances when love requires, instead, that union of one kind or another be sacrificed precisely for love's sake. Thus, for example, a man may sometimes leave his wife and family for the sake of doing them and others a service (participation in military service for their protection); an alcoholic wife may leave her husband and family because she realizes that she is unable to be of help to them until she regains her self-composure and sense of identity and purpose; or a husband may refrain from sexual intercourse with his wife out of consideration for her physical and/or emotional well-being.

For our purposes, the point to be made here is simply this, that although genital expression should indeed reflect the level of personal commitment present between two people, love itself may very well decide sometimes that such expression would be inappropriate, precisely because it would be unloving and must, therefore, be curtailed or sacrificed. This idea is not new. It rests upon one of the central insights of the Christian tradition, namely, that true love is distinct from physical sex. Sex is not the primary language or ultimate proof of love; rather, for Christians, the greatest proof of love is caring for others even to the point of self-sacrifice: "A man can have no greater love than to lay down his life for his friends" (Jn. 15:13). In one way or another, then, the lover must die to self so as to live for the beloved. This is, of course, a struggle to the death.[3]

---

[3]John F. Harvey, O.S.F.S., "The Controversy Concerning the Psychology and Morality of Homosexuality," *The American Ecclesiastical Review,* 167 (1973), 617.

II. A Norm for Human Sexual Expression

We have seen that there are many truly loving relationships which involve no desire for or interest in genital expression. There are other truly loving relationships which are motivated precisely by that love to sacrifice genital involvement, either temporarily or permanently. The point to be made, however, is that while true love does not necessarily or always include genital involvement, genital relationships must always occur within the context of true love. Moreover, this true love is of a special character. It takes the form of a pledge or commitment. There are two reasons for this. One has to do, as we have seen, with the very meaning of sexual intercourse as a mutual self-giving and receiving of the other; such an interaction as this symbolizes the couple's willingness to assume unconditional responsibility for one another. The other reason for the pledge-character of the love which should serve as the context for genital expression is theological in nature.

Just as we have received from Christ the radical charge that we are to love one another even as he has first loved us, so also, within the specific area of physical sexual expression, we have received a charge that the quality of our love is to be a manifestation of the quality of God's love for us. In this way, God's creative and faithful love for humanity becomes the model for human expressions of sexuality. It provides the norm against which such expressions are to be measured. This is to say, that in its full richness, when it fully reflects its ideal, human sexual love is supposed to be both *procreative*, just as God's love for us is creative, and also *unitive*, which means that it should be expressive of a commitment to exclusive and permanent fidelity in imitation of God's promise of fidelity to his people. These characteristics of procreativity and unitive fidelity are suggested in the creation accounts of the first two chapters of the Book of Genesis.

In the first chapter of Genesis, man and woman are recorded as having been created male and female in the image of God. After having been blessed by God, they are given the mission of being fruitful, of multiplying, of filling the earth and conquering it (Gen. 1:27-28). The second chapter of Genesis, which contains the older account of creation, portrays God as being concerned over the loneliness of the one whom he has made in his own image; thus God creates woman to be with man, and the two shall be for each other: "This is why a man leaves his father and mother and joins himself to his wife, and they become one body" (Gen. 2:24).

Once we understand that the qualities of God's love for humanity as being both creative and eternally faithful are meant to be reflected in the full richness of human sexual love through the characteristics of procreativity and permanent fidelity, we can perhaps come to better appreciate why a committed love-relationship has traditionally been regarded as the required setting for genital sexual expression. For in this matter, Christians are responding not so much to the stipulations of an impersonal natural law, but more, rather, to the promptings and exhortations of a personal God whose manner of loving we are called to incarnate. It is true, of course, as we shall see in the next chapter which deals with the issue of contraception, that according to the official Roman Catholic teaching, these procreative and unitive dimensions of human sexuality are to be kept united in every act of sexual intercourse. This means that genital expressions of sexuality are to occur only within the context of a committed love-relationship and that when such genital expressions are used to express and enhance the love between two people, there is to be no direct or positive interference that would serve to prevent or curtail sexuality's procreative potential from being realized.

Many theologians, however, both Catholic and Protestant, take issue with the idea that the procreative and unitive dimensions of human sexuality must be kept joined in every act of sexual intercourse; they maintain, rather, that it is necessary only that these two dimensions be kept together *in principle*. This means that the sexual expression of committed love might occur in intercourse with the procreative possibility being intentionally blocked on certain occasions without the unity of the spheres of personal, unitive love and procreation being necessarily ruptured thereby. Thus, according to Paul Ramsey, a married couple engaging in contraceptive sexual intercourse "do *not* separate the sphere or realm of their personal love from the sphere or realm of their procreation, nor do they distinguish between *the person* with whom the bond of love is nourished and *the person* with whom procreation may be brought into exercise."[4] A husband and wife are in effect still testifying to each other: "If and when I procreate it will be with you whom I love. I will not procreate with anyone else. And I will not enter into the one-flesh unity of love with anyone but you whom I want to have as the mother or father of my child." Such testimony explains what is meant by the idea of keeping the procreative and unitive dimensions of human sexuality together *in principle*, if not in every act of intercourse.

Even if the demand regarding the unity of the procreative and unitive dimensions of sexual love is interpreted to mean that this unity is preserved provided that the two dimensions are kept together in principle, although not in every act of intercourse, such a stipulation nonetheless succeeds in posing two hard and real questions to people who are contemplating premarital sexual intercourse. It calls them to a great test of personal integrity. Before engaging in premarital expressions of genital intercourse, every person should raise these questions about his or her prospective sexual partner: "Can I honestly say that if I ever have a child it will be from my flesh-unity with you so that I will not procreate apart from our union? Can I honestly say, moreover, that I will not exercise love's one-flesh unity with anyone but you whom I desire to have as the mother or father of any child of mine?" Or the questions to be addressed might be put more simply: "Are you the one I want to be the mother or father of any child of mine? Are you the one I want to be with, to care for, and to be cared for

---

[4]Paul Ramsey, *Fabricated Man. The Ethics of Genetic Control* (New Haven: Yale University Press, 1970), p. 34.

by, for the rest of my life?" It would be difficult, I think, to overestimate the decline in the incidence of premarital intercourse were it to occur only after such questions were answered affirmatively by both people involved after honest and prayerful reflection. And yet, unless such questions are in fact answered affirmatively, with sincerity and after prudent consideration, I do not see even the possibility for premarital sexual intercourse being morally acceptable.

In view of what has been said so far, I would maintain that genital sexual expression is properly reserved to the stable relationship of marriage. There is another reason why I am taking this stance. I am convinced that in order for an act to be moral, it must be truly human; and in order for an act to be truly human, it must be socially sensitive. Thus for sexual intercourse to be morally justified, it must express a truly human relationship, that is, the relationship must be, among other things, an embodiment of social sensitivity. This implies that intercourse should occur within the context of marriage which is a social structure by means of which "we try to provide the possibility for true humanity by protecting each other" from the abuses of a person's immaturity and self-centeredness. When two people enter into marriage, they put all their talk of mutual love for each other on the line. They are willing to profess publicly that they have certain ambitions, desires and expectations with respect to each other, and by their public action they implicitly anticipate that society will both encourage them in their new state in life and hold them responsible for the pledge they share. As a social reality, marriage testifies to the personal commitment of love between two people; as such, marriage tells us something of the depth of the relationship and of its durability, for if the commitment of love means anything, it involves more than the present. Two people must share more than the momentary now if they are committed to each other; they must have a common past and they must seek a common future. Marriage, in fact, is the announcement that in the lives of two people a past has been shared, a present is being enjoyed, and a future is hoped for and will be worked for together.[5]

The issue is anything but trivial. According to Ramsey, marriage as a social institution may be said to testify to the very facts of the human condition: "Man's capacity for responsible fidelity to the being and well-being of another of opposite sex makes marriage possible...; yet man's inclination toward unfaithfulness and irresponsibility makes marriage necessary...." Thus, while marriage celebrates the beauty of the human spirit and the heights to which it can soar, it is intended also to assist in protecting men and women from "undue harm and from harmfulness" that can occur through the misuse of God's gift of sexuality. When two people enter seriously into the marital commitment, they proclaim that they know and trust themselves well enough so as to be able to promise today what they will be and do tomorrow.[6] On just one level, love has indeed been described as "the promise that the pleasure of today will also be tomorrow's."[7]

The self-trust of each spouse that takes shape in the promise for the future inspires the confidence and trust of the other; their life together becomes, of course, no less one of mutual faith and of risk, but it now also bears the mark of prudence. Some people today, of course, proclaim their impatience with the legalities of marriage; they see no need for their love in all its richness, strength and uniqueness, to be "licensed". They do not wish to insult their love by employing the social and legal supports of marriage. I make no judgment on the good faith or sincerity of conviction with which such people speak, but I entertain some doubt

[5]Joseph C. Hough, Jr., "Rules and the Ethics of Sex," *Moral Issues and Christian Response,* ed. Paul T. Jersild and Dale A. Johnson (New York: Holt, Rinehart and Winston, Inc., 1971), pp. 129-30.

[6]Paul Ramsey, "A Christian Approach to the Question of Sexual Relations Outside of Marriage," *The Journal of Religion,* 45 (1965), 114-15.

[7]James B. Nelson, *Embodiment. An Approach to Sexuality and Christian Theology* (Minneapolis: Augsburg Publishing House, 1978), p. 88.

about their wisdom, their degree of self-knowledge, and their sensitivity to the foibles of our wounded human nature.

III. Theological Tradition and Development

Any number of Catholic theologians today are trying to reflect on matters of sexual morality in a way that pays more than lip-service to the fact that in human beings sexuality cannot be reduced to or equated with a biological or physical phenomenon. Rather, sexuality is a fundamental and integral dimension of the human personality such that, as Donald Goergen puts it, "a *sexual* person is primarily a sexual *person.*"[8] This means that we must try to make moral evaluations about sexual activity as a personal and human reality; we cannot and should not make moral determinations about sexual activities, or any other activities, in isolation from the person or persons placing such acts. Quite simply, what these theologians are trying to do is to move away from what is tagged as "physicalism" or the tendency to identify the human moral act completely with the physical structure of the act, and to rest one's moral evaluations or determinations solely on an analysis of the physical act itself, without paying any attention to the intention behind the act or to the circumstances in which the act is performed.

Catholic moral theologians are simply suggesting that the break from physicalism must occur in our reflections on matters of sexual morality just as this break has in fact occurred in our moral reflection in other areas of human conduct where it is recognized first, that the intention of the person acting and the circumstances in which the action takes place influence and determine the *human* meaning of the act, and secondly, that the *human* meaning of the act must be appreciated before a moral evaluation of that act can be made. Thus, for example,

[8]Donald Goergen, *The Sexual Celibate* (New York: The Seabury Press, 1974), p. 51.

traditional theology acknowledges that not every act of killing is murder; killing another in self-defense, or in defense of an innocent third party, or during participation in a just war is allowed; also acknowledged is the fact that not every falsehood is a lie, which means that the truth may be kept from someone who has no right to it; finally, our tradition recognizes that in certain circumstances (e.g., in danger of death from starvation) taking another's property is not stealing. In short, not all killing carries the *moral* malice of murder, not all falsehood bears the *moral* malice of lying, and not all taking of another's belongings constitutes the *moral* malice of stealing.

Each of these acts retains, of course, the element of ontic, physical or premoral evil, but it has traditionally been thought that under certain specified conditions, in particular circumstances as indicated in the examples, there are sufficient or proportionate reasons for perpetrating such premoral or ontic wrongs. The question being asked today is why can this mode of thinking not be applied in dealing with issues of sexual morality. Why, for example, must every act of premarital intercourse be judged in isolation from circumstances and intention and immediately tagged or weighted with the moral malice associated with the term "fornication"? Can there not be any premarital sexual intercourse that bears only the weight of ontic or premoral evil? Before proposing an answer to this specific question, it might be helpful to look briefly at the history that has contributed to Catholic moral teaching on this issue.

As was mentioned in the previous chapter, the natural law tradition has probably been the single most influential factor in shaping Roman Catholicism's moral evaluations of human sexual expression. It was on this basis that Thomas Aquinas developed what eventually became the standard argument in Catholic manuals of theology against premarital sex: "it is opposed to the natural purpose of sexual intercourse, which is the generation and education of a child."[9] Commonly referred

---

[9]In the following treatment of Thomas' view of premarital sex I am greatly indebted to John F. Dedek's informative article, "Premarital Sex: The Theological Argument from Peter Lombard to Durand," *Theological Studies*, 41, 4 (Dec., 1980), 643-67, especially 652-60, 667.

to as the "*bonum prolis*" argument (the good of procreating and educating a child), this mode of thinking is directed against both contraceptive premarital sex which would be intended to prevent the generation of a child, and non-contraceptive premarital intercourse which would constitute a threat to the education of a child who might be born outside of the stable and nurturing atmosphere of marriage. The difficulty with this line of reasoning is that it does not appear cogent enough to result in a universal prohibition of premarital intercourse, insofar as it is possible to imagine situations where such sexual expression will not in fact injure the welfare of a child, either because no child can or will be conceived or because the child can and will be properly educated without the marriage of his parents.

To meet this objection against the universal prohibition of fornication, Aquinas proposed what might be called "the principle of *per-seity*" which can be paraphrased in different ways: here, as in other matters, the law "is determined by what usually occurs *per se*, not by what sometimes happens *per accidens* [accidentally];" "the law does not consider what can occur in any one instance but what can occur usually and conveniently;" "natural or moral rectitude in human actions is not determined according to what happens *per accidens* in one individual but according to what results for the whole species." These texts would seem to indicate that Thomas' approach is not to say, as has commonly been thought, that certain acts like premarital intercourse or fornication are intrinsically evil, that is, "so deformed in themselves that they never can be good or licit in any circumstances." Rather, there is a different emphasis.

As Dedek maintains, Aquinas' position is best summarized this way: human reason indicates that premarital intercourse is generally harmful to people; therefore, the natural law, insofar as it is itself ordered to the common good and exists to prevent a common danger, prohibits every act of premarital intercourse. This prohibition by the natural law allows for no exceptions to be made on one's own private authority or individual discretion, even if it is certain that the harm which the law seeks to prevent will not occur in a specific case at hand. The common good is not to be jeopardized by private discretion, individual exception-making or self-exemption from the law. In effect, then, says Dedek, Thomas' view is that the natural-law prohibition of premarital intercourse is analogous to a prohibition based on a positive law that is promulgated on the broad presumption of a common danger.[10] An example of such a positive law might be one which forbids all outdoor fires during times of drought because the presumption is "that the threat to the common welfare cannot be sufficiently averted if private citizens are allowed to decide for themselves what precautions are adequate."[11]

If this analysis of Thomas' line of reasoning is correct, namely, that he did not condemn acts of premarital intercourse as intrinsically evil, that is, as evil in and of themselves, but claimed rather that a universal prohibition of such acts was justified and demanded by reason of their general nature as a serious threat to the well-being of possible offspring, then the issue must be further explored. Does Thomas go too far in absolutely excluding the question of premarital intercourse from an individual's discretionary powers? Using his own line of reasoning alone, I personally think that Thomas' conclusion is overdrawn; to say nothing of the fact that his argument must especially ring hollow to couples or individuals who know themselves to be infertile, there would, in addition, seem to be at least one group of people, namely, engaged couples, who could possibly express their mutual love in sexual intercourse without posing any threat to a child who might be conceived, provided that, having first discussed the matter, they honestly concluded that together they had both the willingness and the ability to provide for the possible child's welfare. It goes without saying, of course, that in their consideration of premarital intercourse, the engaged couple under discussion would have eliminated abortion from their list of possible responses should pregnancy occur; the couple would, moreover, have to be anticipating, within months, a life of marital sex in which their one-flesh unity will be both life-giving and love-giving.

[10]Here I am conflating Dedek's conclusions as they appear *Ibid.*, 659-60 and 667.

[11]This example is used by Richard A. McCormick, S.J. to show why the norm against direct killing of terminal patients is virtually exceptionless; see "The New Medicine and Morality," *Theology Digest*, 21, 4 (1973), 319-20.

I am not claiming that sexual intercourse in the lives of engaged couples is always or easily justifiable; I am simply suggesting that in the circumstances just described, sexual intercourse would be such a circumscribed reality that it would constitute little realistic threat to the welfare of a possible child; for this reason, it might be said that using only his own line of argumentation, Thomas' universal censure of premarital intercourse is over-extended, unwarranted, and overly cautious. I personally am not persuaded by his prudential evaluation that the act of premarital intercourse is so essentially dangerous to the common good that the natural law demands that there be no exceptions to its prohibition. The exclusion of premarital intercourse in this mode of thinking appears to be not so much a matter of intrinsic immorality as of external discipline.

Earlier in this chapter I commented to the effect that unless two people could honestly and prayerfully say that they would enter into love's one-flesh unity and would procreate only with each other and not with anyone else, I could not see even the possibility for the moral acceptability of their premarital intercourse. I think now that if any unmarried people are capable of making such a profession, it would most probably be engaged couples who are on the threshold of publicly proclaiming their mutual love and who privately make such a promise to each other before the public ceremony and thus, in effect, maintain in principle the integrity of the spheres of procreative love and unitive fidelity. If, therefore, premarital intercourse were ever judged morally acceptable, I perhaps could imagine it to be so only within the supportive structure of a couple's engagement and only after the couple has agreed to provide love and care for any child who might be conceived. Nonetheless, were I approached by an engaged couple who were contemplating premarital intercourse, I would challenge and encourage them to patience. Circumstances change, engagements are broken, promises are not vows and a couple's whispered words of love need the strengthening that comes from the willing support of the community of faith and the sacramental grace of marriage.

Reference to the sacramental grace of marriage leads to another point. I think that the Roman Catholic teaching regarding premarital sex makes eminent sense and is most persuasive when considered from a faith-inspired view of marriage as a sacrament. To say that marriage is a sacrament is to say that it is a special point of contact between God and his people. But marriage as a sacrament says more than this. It says that in loving each other, two people intend to enter into and share the quality of love that exists between Yahweh and Israel and between Christ and his people. A couple who enter into a sacramental union of love want their love for each other to reflect God's love; they want the reality of Christ and his love to be mediated by husband to wife and by wife to husband; then, Christ's love can be extended through them, as spouses, to their neighbors and community, and especially to their own children.

The significance of Christian marriage is well stated in Vatican II's *Pastoral Constitution on the Church in the Modern World*:

> For as God of old made himself present to his people through a covenant of love and fidelity, so now the Savior of men and the Spouse of the Church comes into the lives of married Christians through the sacrament of matrimony. He abides with them thereafter so that, just as he loved the Church and handed himself over on her behalf, the spouses may love each other with perpetual fidelity through mutual self-bestowal.
>
> Authentic married love is caught up into divine love and is governed and enriched by Christ's redeeming power and the saving activity of the Church. (no. 48)

It is no exaggeration, then, to say that when a Christian couple enter into marriage they are professing that it is their desire, hope and intention to be "the touch of God" in each other's life. In this way, "as each partner strives to 'make flesh' for the other the self-giving love of Christ, each is capable of sanctifying and enriching the other for a lifetime."[12] Seen in this light, the dignity of life as a Christian spouse is obvious.

Christians regard married life as a true vocation, a personal calling from God, who promises that those who honestly respond to that call will have the help of his grace as they generously strive to meet their responsibilities as married people. Indeed, without such help, the intent to live and love as God does would be presumptuous, just as the attempt to do so would be futile.

In a deeply theological sense, moreover, it is more accurate, and closer to the reality of things, to say that on their wedding day, a man and a woman *become sacraments* or living and effective signs of God's love rather than to say simply that they receive the sacrament of matrimony. For, in truth, by means of Christ's graciousness, they do become sacraments or signs, first to each other and then to all the believing community, of God's abiding love. What they promise, pledge and affirm concerning their life together is now immeasurably supported and facilitated by the very covenant of Christ before whom and in whose name they are joined. The richness of Christ is theirs to draw upon ever after in their daily struggle to put flesh upon the words they use to speak of love. Quite simply, if we believe that through his own graciousness the reality of God's love and life is shared in by couples who are joined in sacramental unions, then we believe also that such couples have unlimited help available to them in their efforts to live out their commitments of love.

The accessibility of God's loving assistance to spouses in the sacrament of matrimony has been marvelously explained by Ladislas Orsy, who reminds us that as a sacrament, marriage is a saving event and that, like all such events, it arises out of "a unilateral covenant: God gives, human beings receive." This means, quite simply, that: "In Christian marriage God covenants with the couple before they can covenant with each other....God promises to stand by the couple, to be their

---

[12]Gerald S. Twomey, *When Catholics Marry Again. A Guide for the Divorced, Their Families and Those Who Minister to Them* (Minneapolis: Winston Press, 1982), p. 27.

strength in their weakness, so that they can initiate a union, grow into it through successes and failures, and consummate it in grace, and bring it to maturity in love."[13]

This is not to say, of course, that there is anything magical about the sacrament of marriage; two Christians must still work at their marriage and at loving each other. But the truth remains that by virtue of their sacramental union, the reality of God's grace is available to them in a new way; what is required of the couple, however, is that they make use of the grace that is offered them; in an attitude of faith they must remain open and receptive to the daily gift of God's love which can vitalize their marital life. Something, indeed, does happen when a man and a woman enter into the sacrament of marriage; they are changed; they are sparked with a new energy to love.

When a couple is encouraged to refrain from premarital sex, they sometimes respond with the question: "Why? Will we love each other more after our wedding day than we do now?" The answer to that question surely is, "No, not necessarily," and yet, of course, it is to be hoped that a couple will in fact grow in love for each other day by day. The couple, however, responded with the wrong question. The more pertinent thing for them to ask, I think, is this: "Will we be further helped after our wedding in our love for each other?" The answer to this question is most certainly yes: by the grace of God. All the good will and desire in the world do not make up for the empowerment to love which a couple receives through God's grace in the sacrament of marriage, just as a man's years of prayer, study, training and yearning must await the day of ordination before he is empowered to celebrate the eucharist and to offer God's forgiveness to sinners.

Besides wanting to highlight the fact that in the sacramental view of marriage a couple is seen as coming to share in the strength and richness of Christ's love for his people, another reason for commenting here upon the nature of marriage as a sacrament has been to illustrate that precisely because marriage is a sacrament, and because a husband

---

[13]Ladislas Orsy, S.J., "Faith, Sacrament, Contract, and Christian Marriage: Disputed Questions," *Theological Studies,* 43 (1982), 379-98 at 382-83.

and wife themselves become sacraments, marriage is inherently a sign-event or sign-reality. It testifies to the presence of God's love but it must also reflect that love outwardly, for a sign not only gives witness; it must itself be witnessed. There is, therefore, and there must be, a social dimension to marriage as a sacrament. This is why the marriage ceremony is so significant. To be sure, the essence of marriage lies in the exchange of vows and the mutual consent of the couple; but in order for the full richness of marriage as a sacrament or sign of God's creative and faithful love to be exposed and appreciated, it is necessary for a man and a woman to proclaim their love in a social context so that the sign may be seen and heard, and so that through this new promise of love, people may be reminded of the greatness of God and of his love and therein rejoice. It is true that in her early centuries the Church recognized the validity of secret or clandestine marriages, but it is also true that during those centuries the Church had no developed theology of marriage as a sacrament in the strict sense. It is also true that even today in extreme circumstances, for example, in danger of death or given a priest's unavailability for an extended period of time, two Catholics may be validly married without a priest or other official witness being present, but there must always be at least two other witnesses. The Church thus has come to be insistent on giving recognition to the essentially social character of marriage.

It is because of the sacramental and, hence, social character of marriage that I take issue with those theologians who claim that in the case of an engaged Christian couple, it is possible and perhaps even necessary to distinguish between premarital and preceremonial sexual expressions of love. In other words, according to some theologians, an engaged couple's physical expressions of love might not be premarital expressions at all, but simply preceremonial. Thus, says Paul Ramsey, if an engaged couple, by means of genital relations, intend "to express the fact that their lives are united and that they now are willing to accept all that is entailed in sexual intercourse as their unity in one-flesh and possibly *into* the one flesh of a child, then it is simply impossible for them to engage in premarital sexual relations...."[14] In Ramsey's eyes, this couple is in some sense already married and therefore their genital involvement is only preceremonial, not premarital. I would object to this view in light of what I see as the implications and requirements of the sacramental character of marriage. If marriage is really a sacrament or sign, then it is necessarily social; it requires witnesses. Thus an engaged couple who privately profess their love in a genital way cannot, I think, be considered married, whatever else might be said about the good faith of their mutual commitment.

In taking this position I am making no final judgment regarding the moral status of sexual intercourse that might be shared by such an engaged couple. I would maintain, in fact, that in light of the personalist approach which is required in making moral evaluations, the degree of personal commitment between two people is a critical factor to be weighed when discussing the moral status of premarital intercourse. I agree with Curran's observation that, in general, the moral gravity or impropriety of such activity "is inversely proportionate to the degree of personal commitment involved."[15] But we must insist that other considerations do enter into the discussion: our actions have unavoidable repercussions upon ourselves and others, and we must not avoid asking whether or not we and others are prepared to face these repercussions; we must also contend with the difficulty of knowing our true motives and intentions in our protestations of love. Is the commitment as strong and real as we think, or are we really not thinking, but merely feeling? Will our "commitment" survive the passing of such feeling? With these cautions in mind, I nonetheless think that the distinction being suggested today between non-marital and premarital sexual intercourse is helpful and significant for our moral reflections.

---

[14]Ramsey, "A Christian Approach," 113.

[15]Charles E. Curran, *Contemporary Problems in Moral Theology* (Notre Dame: Fides Publishers, Inc., 1970), pp. 177-80.

IV. Theological Speculation

Non-marital sex implies no commitment to marriage; it is sex with a prostitute, or the sex that is sought and occurs in a series of casual affairs; it might even be the sexual relations that are shared with someone whom you enjoy and whom you have been dating for several months. Premarital sex is that which occurs in a relationship which is definitely directed toward marriage, but which is "not yet realized or capable of being realized in a public marriage ceremony."[16] The reality of premarital sex, therefore, is most likely to be found only in the lives of engaged couples. This distinction between non-marital and premarital sex suggests that there is a significant difference between casual intercourse and the sexual relations shared by an engaged couple. The same physical act performed in different circumstances is simply not the same moral act; the same act, viewed externally or physically, cannot be evaluated identically in terms of morality in every situation.

In the chapter on sinfulness, you will recall, we differentiated between an objective moral wrong and sin or moral evil. Applying this distinction to the issue of sexual intercourse, it can be said that traditionally the Catholic Church regards intercourse outside of marriage as an objective moral wrong; but we cannot immediately say that every person who engages in sexual intercourse outside of marriage has committed a moral evil or is a sinner. As a general rule, however, it is safe to say that non-marital sex is much more likely than premarital sex to involve subjective guilt and sinfulness in addition to objective wrong. Nonetheless, given the fact that sin requires elements of knowledge, reflection and consent, it is still possible that expressions of non-marital sex are not subjectively sinful because of the very definite limited perspectives, undeveloped moral sensitivities or infringements on personal freedom that may be part of a person's life.

---

[16]Gregory Kenny (with Edward Wakin), "Sex and the Young Catholic," *U.S. Catholic/Jubilee,* XXXVI, 11 (Nov., 1971), 10.

It is not difficult to give recognition to the *subjective* extenuating circumstances which come to bear in an individual's life and have the effect of reducing or minimizing a person's understanding and freedom. Acknowledging such circumstances has given rise to a definite, time-honored approach in dealing with moral issues, namely, the "objectively wrong but subjectively not sinful or culpable" method of categorizing various actions. As we saw earlier, however, in our discussion of sinfulness, some Catholic theologians are not content with the recognition only of *subjective* or internal extenuating circumstances; these theologians go further to suggest that there are some circumstances which may be so significant that they can change the substantive or objective moral character of an action, and not just a person's subjective moral relationship to that act.[17] In other words, due to certain *objective* or external extenuating circumstances, an act like sexual intercourse before marriage might not be an objective *moral* wrong, as it usually is, but rather a significant *premoral, ontic,* or *physical wrong.* Such an act (intercourse before marriage) would be a *premoral* rather than a moral wrong only because the objective circumstances are such that they constitute or provide a proportionate or sufficient reason for the act's occurrence. Moreover, these objective circumstances can, on occasion, be of such a nature as to create a situation in which a couple committed to each other do not "experience themselves as genuinely free to take the more ideal route of abstaining from that intercourse that cannot be publicly proclaimed as part of a marriage."[18]

As should be obvious from the preceding analysis, it is not a simple matter to determine the moral status of an action. Some remarks may be helpful, however, in summarizing the various categories into which a questionable act may fall. Depending upon the circumstances in which the action is performed, three possibilities exist: the action may be an

---

[17]Philip S. Keane, S.S., *Sexual Morality: A Catholic Perspective* (New York: Paulist Press, 1977), pp. 86, 190.

[18]*Ibid.*, p. 107; also see p. 225, n. 22.

objective *moral* wrong, it may also be a moral evil or sin, or it may constitute a *premoral*, ontic or physical evil. Any action which, in and of itself, is harmful to, or destructive of, self or others, is an objective *moral* wrong. When such an action is done without significant involvement of a person's reflection and freedom, it remains on the level of an objective *moral* wrong; as such, it is still attributable to the person as its agent, but the action does not constitute a sin; it is because of some prevailing impediments or *internal, subjective* extenuating circumstances (curtailment of knowledge, reflection or freedom) that the agent of the action is not guilty of having sinned. Should, however, the same harmful, destructive, and, hence, objectively wrong action be intentionally and freely done, the action would indeed involve the agent in sin and the action would be regarded as a moral evil. Finally, it can sometimes happen that the presence of significant *external* or *objective* extenuating circumstances will so alter a situation that two things occur: the action in question, which is ordinarily an objective *moral* wrong, is transformed into an action that is, instead, a *premoral* or physical evil, and a sufficient or proportionate reason now exists for the action to be performed.[19]

In order to understand properly the notion of premoral evil, two points should be made. First, premoral evil is something generally to be avoided; premoral evil is not to be seen as morally "neutral." In fact, the moral "non-neutrality" of premoral evil illustrates why the choice of a premoral evil without sufficient reason constitutes *moral* evil or sin. Thus, for example, we can say that killing a human being is never a neutral act; even when the killing is justifiable, as Christian tradition says it sometimes is, it constitutes a premoral evil; when, however, the killing is wanton, lacks sufficient cause and, hence, is unjustified, it becomes an objective moral wrong which would also be sinful if done with knowledge and consent.

---

[19]For Keane's development of this notion of premoral or ontic evil, see *Ibid.*, pp. 47-51.

The second thing to be noted with respect to premoral evil is this: the argument is never that good consequences or a sufficient reason justify an action that is morally evil. Rather, the idea being proposed is this: an act cannot be morally evaluated simply by looking at its structure or object in a narrow or restricted sense; instead, we must view the act in the context of all its morally relevant circumstances because such circumstances can in fact transform an action which is usually an objective moral wrong into one that is now premorally evil and thus justifiable. For example, there is a moral world of difference, as is obvious, between arbitrary mutilation of the human body through the performance of unnecessary surgery, and the amputation of a cancerous limb to save a patient's life or the removal of a person's kidney so that it can be donated to another in need. The moral difference lies in the circumstances, intentions, motivations and consequences which transform what would be moral wrong (bodily mutilation) into premoral evil (loss of bodily integrity, experience of anxiety or inconvenience). In contrast to premoral evil, moral wrong is found in harm that is unjustifiably caused; the presence of a proportionate reason, however, would preclude the existence of a moral wrong, and presents us, instead, with premoral evil.[20]

Keeping in mind these descriptive definitions of sin, objective moral wrong and premoral or ontic evil, the following scheme emerges: (1) when a person freely performs an action that is known to be objectively morally wrong, that person is responsible or subjectively culpable for the act and is involved in sin or moral evil; (2) no sin occurs, however, when an objectively morally wrong action is performed by an individual under some *subjective* extenuating circumstances, that is, when there are significant infringements upon, or impediments to, the person's free and / or reflective involvement in the action; (3) a premoral,

---

[20]See Lisa Sowle Cahill, "Teleology, Utilitarianism, and Christian Ethics," *Theological Studies,* 42, 4 (Dec., 1981), 601-29 at 614. Also see Richard A. McCormick, S.J., "Notes on Moral Theology," *Theological Studies,* 43, 1 (March, 1982), 81-6.

ontic or physical evil occurs when an action that is usually considered to be an objective moral wrong is performed under *objective* extenuating circumstances which together serve as sufficient reason for the action's occurrence.

It might be helpful at this point to indicate briefly and concretely how the three distinct realities of sin, objective moral wrong, and premoral or ontic evil might be verified or identified in trying to make a moral evaluation of sexual intercourse prior to marriage. To begin with, such activity would seem to be both an objective moral wrong and subjectively sinful or morally evil in a situation where two people meet and within several weeks become genitally involved; they realize they are not ready for a permanent relationship and they do not ask for any promises; they acknowledge that their sexual relations are premature; nonetheless, because they find each other so stimulating and pleasing, they intend to continue to relate genitally so long as the relationship remains mutually interesting and fulfilling.

Secondly, intercourse outside of marriage might be seen as an objective moral wrong but subjectively not sinful in each of the following two scenarios: a) after dating steadily for three years, two young adults become engaged with plans to be married within the year; at this time, after prayerful reflection and careful discussion, they honestly believe that given their mutual love, intercourse would not be wrong for them; this is their sincere judgment. Objectively, they may be mistaken in their evaluation and an objective moral wrong may be involved, but there would probably be no serious sin on their part; b) two teenagers who have been bombarded by the sexual fireworks of our society and who find themselves pushed to false sophistication may wind up in a relationship that stirs their feelings far more than they understand or can cope with; their passions prevail and become their master, leading the couple into periodic episodes of genital involvement; here again, objective moral wrong exists but if there is truly a curtailment of the couple's freedom, the reality of serious subjective guilt or sin seems unlikely. Pastorally, of course, these teenagers need to be informed of the human and spiritual harm associated with their activity. It is to be hoped, too, that they can be brought to a change of behavior.

Thirdly, regarding the possibility of sexual intercourse outside marriage being only an ontic or premoral evil, and not a moral wrong, Keane says this situation could be realized when society or social conditions "unreasonably impede people's right to marry." Keane offers two examples of such a situation. The first occurs when two elderly, retired people fall in love and wish to marry but are honestly too fearful to do so, lest they suffer a serious loss of economic security as a result of having pension-benefits cut or social-security payments reduced. The second instance might occur in the lives of a couple in their early-to-mid-twenties, who are "mature, deeply committed to each other, and fully intending to marry;" but, says Keane, before they are free to do so, a steady series of structured delays must be worked through: "college, military service, graduate school, the achievement of financial independence, etc."[21]

In discussing this issue of premarital intercourse, Keane makes three significant points. First, he freely admits that the instance is very rare where premarital intercourse could be morally justified, that is, where such intercourse is an ontic or premoral evil, but not an objective moral wrong and, therefore, of course, not a subjective moral evil or sin. Secondly, Keane maintains, however, that it more frequently happens that premarital intercourse is objectively a moral wrong, while the persons involved are not guilty of sin or subjectively culpable of committing a moral evil. Thirdly, and most importantly, Keane argues the position that genital sexual activity is most likely to be honest, is most properly expressed, and is best protected, within the committed love-relationship of marriage.[22]

On one matter I take issue with Keane. His suggestion that sexual intercourse outside of marriage might sometimes be only a premoral or ontic wrong seems to have its greatest plausibility when it is restricted to instances like that described in the example of the elderly, retired couple who are committed to

[21]Keane, *op.cit.*, pp. 106-09
[22]*Ibid.*, pp. 105-108.

each other, but for whom marriage would mean economic and human insecurity. The anxieties of old age are clearly not insignificant for many people, and it would seem unnecessarily harsh to impose additional hardships upon them as a consequence of marriage. Of course, the moral situation would change if their economic stability could be protected by lifting the financial penalty incurred by marriage. This would involve altering legislation concerning social security and pension payments. Another observation might be pertinent here, especially if the couple happen to be religiously sensitive: Keane most cautiously suggests that they might have their love-relationship secretly or privately blessed by a priest or minister. This would, of course, not be a valid or legally recognized marriage and no record would be kept of the event, but pastorally it might be tremendously helpful to the couple whose love is genuine, but who are convinced that their freedom to marry has been snatched away by the economic realities of old age.[23]

The situation is different, I suggest, in Keane's example of the two young adults who are in love and who fully intend to marry when certain social and economic obstacles are overcome. Whereas Keane is of the opinion that their genital activity might sometimes be regarded in these circumstances as an ontic or *premoral* wrong, I am inclined to say that genital activity in their situation is more likely a *moral* wrong, but depending on the sincerity of their decision, may not be subjectively sinful. Even granting Keane's premises, it is hard to see how the young couple have a sufficient or proportionate reason for their genital activity.

Unlike the young couple, the elderly cannot see any time in the future when they will reach economic security. They can anticipate no change in their status except one for the worse. In addition, the young couple would seem to have a

[23] *Ibid.,* pp. 108-09.

broader range of options open to them; they have the time and space to make some choices which, while admittedly difficult, are nonetheless realistic: they can interrupt their formal education, graduate school can be postponed, career goals can be altered, loans can be negotiated, and so on. Finally, in the case of the young adults, the vibrancy of sexuality's physical passion may be such as to override clear human judgment, and thus, due to the power of personal infatuation, the illusion of abiding love can often be mistaken for the real thing. For all these reasons, I am skeptical of the prospect that objective extenuating circumstances will ever be such as to verify premarital intercouse as simply a *premoral* or physical evil—as opposed to an objective *moral* wrong—in the lives of people like the young and caring couple described by Keane.

Before bringing this chapter to a conclusion, something should be said about the question of premarital petting. In general, the issue should be viewed within the context of the observation made in the last chapter to the effect that chastity is a matter of honesty in sex; therefore, no physical expressions of love should go beyond the degree of interpersonal commitment that is found in a relationship. Two people who are striving to be honest with each other must be concerned that their physical manifestations of affection and love always remain appropriate, and this is a matter of much broader concern than simply confronting the issue of sexual intercourse. Even though, as Keane points out, many people engage in petting precisely in order to avoid sexual intercourse, and despite the fact that such recourse to petting often reflects a couple's effort "to deal with their sexual tensions in a way that respects the fact that intercourse ought to be reserved for marriage,"[24] the truth remains that it is possible to be an unchaste virgin; retaining physical virginity by refraining from sexual intercourse is not a guarantee of premarital chastity or sexual honesty.

[24]*Ibid.,* p. 110; for a helpful treatment of premarital petting, confer Keane, pp. 110-13.

Not all petting, of course, is the same. Some forms of petting are quite mild; kissing, hugging and embracing are often meant to be no more than signs of true affection; they are not intended to be a means to sexual arousal, although some arousal might unintentionally occur on occasion. In general, such mild forms of petting certainly seem to be appropriate ways in which to give expression to true feelings of affection and love, and to manifest the human need for intimacy. Other forms of petting are much more intense and seem clearly designed for the purpose of moving the participants toward ever greater sexual arousal. Included among these forms of petting would be such things as deep (soul or "French") kissing, undressing to the point of partial or total nudity, and the fondling of breasts or genitals.

Such activity is not uncommonly referred to as "foreplay"—and with good reason, because it is an enjoyably appropriate and provocative way of preparing two people for the shared pleasure of sexual intercourse. But if it is true, as I would maintain, that sexual intercourse is best and morally expressed only in a marital relationship where two people have pledged themselves to mutual unconditional responsibility for each other, then I see something unwise and frustrative in heavy premarital petting; it is even dishonest, perhaps, in that two people are dangerously toying with each other by making overtures that they know they should not, or may not even want to, follow through on.

The question, "How far may we go in physically expressing our feelings and love for one another?", can hardly be put aside facilely. This issue seems to be of special concern to young people; in a recent discussion I had with some college students, the comments of one of them struck me as being reflective of some practical wisdom which recognized the need for both honesty and caution in trying to assess the role of sex in a loving personal relationship:

> Sex is just a very small part of love. It's a part which can't be allowed to dominate a relationship. Once a relationship

becomes dominated by sex, you know you've gone too far. So in my eyes, going too far will be easy to measure. If I ever want to see my girlfriend solely or primarily because of some previous episode of "making out," then I have gone too far.

V. Conclusions

The whole idea of premoral or ontic wrong in the area of sexual morality needs more analysis, reflection and articulation than can be provided here, but some comments and questions are in order. To say that an act contains ontic, physical or premoral evil means that it has elements of non-good which can be incurred or tolerated under certain conditions. We may do a physical or premoral wrong in order to achieve a moral good or prevent a moral evil. Thus it is sometimes necessary to kill (a physical evil) in order to protect one's own or another's life from the attack of an unjust aggressor. Or we may be obliged to tell a falsehood (a physical or ontic wrong) regarding the where-abouts of a friend who is being terribly harassed by an insistent and brash suitor. Or, finally, in order to provide for his family, it may be necessary for an unemployed man whose compensation has run out, to take food-goods that do not belong to him. In all of these instances, it seems assumed (1) that the course of action pursued is the only one possible in the immediate circum-stances, and (2) that the circumstances cannot reasonably be altered. In each case, moreover, some moral evil is being curtailed and some moral value fostered in what is judged to be the only way possible given the situation. Thus this particular killing is not murder, this falsehood is not lying, this taking of another's property is not stealing.

In turning to sexual morality we now ask the question: when, if ever, is sexual intercourse between two unmarried people not fornication; when, in other words, would such activity not carry the weight of moral wrong usually associated with it? We would have to know what moral value is being pursued by the act of premarital intercourse or what moral evil is being resisted by it; and we must ask, finally, in the circumstances is sexual intercourse the only way by means of which the intended moral good may be achieved and the moral evil avoided? At this point I can only say that there is not much evidence that these questions have been of sufficient concern to those who are hypothesizing about the possibility of premarital intercourse sometimes being a premoral rather than a moral wrong; there is even less evidence that these questions have been satisfactorily answered.

I see what the elements of non-good are in premarital intercourse, namely, that such intercourse must be contraceptive in acknowledgment of the demand for responsible parenting; also, such intercourse is not occurring in a sacramental love union, that is, in a love-relationship that has publicly proclaimed its existence and its desire to reflect God's love among his people. I know that premarital sex can be intended to foster love between two people, but the warning bears repeating that sex cannot create a relationship; it should express only what has already honestly come to life between two people. Finally, I doubt seriously that the moral good (mutual growth in deepening love) which is said to be pursued through premarital intercourse can be achieved only in this way—or even that this is the best way.

Despite these hesitations, would it not be difficult to argue that all acts of premarital intercourse necessarily express and embody only, or mainly, selfishness, self-seeking, pleasure-fascination, lust, and need-satisfaction? Yet these are the realities which seem so often to be implied in the term "fornication," and these are the realities that help to convey the meaning of fornication's moral malice or immorality. As our previous discussion of the theological meaning of sin has indicated, the reality of human sinfulness is verified when a person freely and deliberately acts in an unloving way that is hurtful to others and/or self. With this understanding, it is not possible to maintain that every act of premarital intercourse is, in and of itself, morally evil or sinful. Nonetheless, there is no question but that there are significant elements of non-good in such activity so that it must be considered an objective moral wrong. I would acknowledge, however, that the theoretical possibility, in isolated instances, of premarital intercourse being only a premoral, ontic or physical wrong needs to be discussed further. But for this theoretical possibility to be verified, it must be clearly indicated just what moral good is being achieved and what moral evil is being avoided or curtailed by recourse to sexual intercourse outside of a marital union. Such indications are scarcely available.

In the course of this and the preceding chapter, several lines of reasoning have been pursued which indicate that sexual intercourse is properly reserved to marital relationships in which the shared love of two people takes the form of a pledged commitment. Four strands of thought may be isolated as contributing to this conclusion: (1) any truly honest sexual intercourse is an act of mutual self-giving by means of which two people express their willingness to assume unconditional responsibility for each other; (2) human sexual love in its full richness is to reflect the qualities of God's love for us; therefore, just as his love is creative and faithful, so also must human sexual love, when fully realized, be open to procreation and permanent fidelity; marriage is the context in which this full richness can be best achieved; (3) premarital sex is not sufficiently appreciative of the fact that for human activity to be moral, it must be socially sensitive; marriage is an institution which is intended to enhance personal relationships by offering some defense against human immaturity, self-seeking and false protestations of love; (4) finally, the perception of chastity as honesty in sex—such that physical relationships must truthfully express the degree of personal commitment between two people—would seem to be of special pertinence to those Christians who regard marriage as a sacramental reality and thus appreciate the fact that in marriage God's grace is available to assist them in their efforts both to be faithful to their promise of love and to make their physical expressions of love ever more honest and creative. The combined strength of these four lines of thinking suggests that the burden of proof for its moral legitimacy lies upon those who would engage in premarital intercourse. Of course, once such people are honestly convinced of the moral propriety of their contemplated action, it remains for them only to make their case before God.

VI

Marital Sexuality: Contraception and Beyond

I. Introduction

"Would Augustine or Thomas be surprised if he were to return and see what Catholic theologians are teaching today?" After posing this question in the conclusion of his masterful work on the history of the Church's views regarding contraception, John T. Noonan, Jr. goes on to suggest that were lack of surprise established as the test of orthodoxy, then the whole development of the Church's teachings "on the purposes of marital intercourse would have been unorthodox."[1] Whatever the bearing which the presence or absence of surprise has upon the verification of truth, Noonan's reminder may serve us well: "...it is a perennial mistake to confuse repetition of old formulas with the living law of the Church. The Church, on its pilgrim's path, has grown in grace and wisdom."[2]

That there has been an evolution in the Church's understanding of the purpose of conjugal intercourse is undeniable.

[1] John T. Noonan, Jr., *Contraception: A History of Its Treatment by the Catholic Theologians and Canonists* (New York: Mentor-Omega Books, 1967), p. 630.

[2] *Loc.cit.*

189

From the thirteenth to the fifteenth centuries, largely due to the continuing influence of Augustine's views, it was the popular opinion of theologians that loving married couples committed a venial sin if they engaged in sexual intercourse without the intention of procreation, but simply for the pleasure derived from the act, or as a way to resist the temptation to marital infidelity. It was also commonly taught that intercourse during the time of menstruation or during pregnancy was morally prohibited because the possibility of procreation was then precluded.[3]

Such teachings have long been abandoned, of course. In fact, by the middle of the nineteenth century we can identify three stages in the development of the Church's official stance regarding married couples' proper motivation for engaging in sexual intercourse. It was initially taught that couples must positively entertain a procreative intent in intercourse; later, it was proposed that other motives for intercourse are morally acceptable so long as couples do not positively exclude the intention of procreation, especially by any attempt to frustrate, interrupt, or prevent the procreative power of the sex act.

Finally, it was acknowledged that in certain situations married couples might morally engage in intercourse with a definite intention and desire to avoid procreation, but they must not directly or deliberately attempt to thwart or interfere with the procreative potential of sexual intercourse. In other words, in this third stage of evolution in the Church's teaching, the moral acceptability of periodic abstinence is clearly recognized, but as we shall see, this teaching was not officially publicized until the middle of the twentieth century.[4] Nonethe-

---

[3]*Ibid.*, pp. 300-01, 630.

[4]For a brief discussion of this evolution in teaching see Richard A. McCormick, S.J., *Health and Medicine in the Catholic Tradition* (New York: Crossroad, 1984), pp. 90-1. As early as 1853 the Sacred Penitentiary in Rome, in response to private inquiries made by various bishops, approved of spouses restricting intercourse to the times of infertility, but as Noonan observes, this practice was seen only "as an alternative to be cautiously proffered to onanists [couples engaging in *coitus interruptus* or withdrawal];" confer Noonan, *op. cit.*, p. 530. There was no public approval or affirmation of rhythm as a method of birth-control until 1951 in Pius XII's Address to Italian Midwives.

less, approval of periodic abstinence means that, for good reasons, married couples may purposely confine sexual intercourse to those periods of time when the wife is thought or known to be infertile. Abstention from intercourse during the time of a woman's fertility is considered to be a natural method of contraception, whereas, apart from recourse to sterilization, all other attempts to prevent procreation, while still engaging in intercourse, are regarded as forms of artificial contraception.

In this chapter our attention is focused on the Catholic Church's teaching regarding contraception and some other issues related to marital sexuality. The Church traditionally has maintained the position that every act of sexual intercourse must be left open to the possibility of procreation; this stance has led the Church to ban the use of all so-called artificial contraceptives, while giving qualified approval to the practice of rhythm or what are regarded as natural methods of family planning. The Catholic Church's teaching differs, then, from that of other Christian Churches which require only that the procreative and unitive dimensions of sexuality be kept together *in principle,* but not in every act of intercourse. As we saw in the previous chapter, this latter view means that a husband and wife will procreate only from within their relationship of mutual love, and that they will enter into the one-flesh unity of love with no one but each other, because each desires the other to be the parent of his or her child.

In its unfolding, this chapter will take the following course: (1) the official views of the Church on contraception will be presented as these have been articulated in some key documents of the twentieth century; (2) some of the theological responses to the Church's position, especially as it was presented in *Humanae Vitae,* will be analyzed; (3) an attempt will be made to morally evaluate artificial contraception in light of some of the theological criticism provoked by *Humanae Vitae;* (4) a critique of specific contraceptive devices or techniques and of methods of natural family planning will be offered; (5) we will investigate the possibility of dissent from the official teaching on contraception; (6) finally, before concluding, we will look at some special questions pertaining to sexual intercourse and love-making in the context of a marital union.

II. Contraception in the Twentieth Century

In an attempt to understand the present official Roman Catholic position on contraception, we will begin by looking at four Roman Catholic documents of this century which pertain to this issue. Before doing so, however, we must first make note of the fact that contraception itself is a narrower reality than birth-control, for this latter concept has unfortunately come to be understood as including any means employed to limit the number of live births; even abortion is frequently regarded as a last-ditch method of contraception, which, of course, it is not. Contraception, even when it takes the permanent or quasi-permanent form of sterilization, comprises any and every action undertaken to prevent conception or fertilization (contraception=contra-conception), whereas abortion is an action initiated after conception has in fact taken place. As distinct realities, contraception and abortion involve different moral issues and questions, as we shall see. With this understanding of contraception in place, we can now present the Catholic Church's teaching on this issue.

POPE PIUS XI AND *CASTI CONNUBII*

It is the Roman Catholic Church which today bears the weight of heavy criticism for its stand against contraception. In our present mode of thinking we tend to overlook the fact that up until well into the twentieth century, the Christian Churches were generally agreed that contraception was a threat to the institution of marriage. In 1930, however, after failed attempts to do so in 1908 and 1920, the Lambeth Conference of Anglican Bishops gave qualified and cautious approval to contraception in the lives of Christian spouses. In a resolution adopted in August, the bishops, while abandoning the absolute prohibition of contraception, nonetheless called for restraint and Christian sensitivity:

> Where there is a clearly felt moral obligation to limit or avoid parenthood, the method must be decided on Christian prin-

ciples. The primary and obvious method is complete abstinence from intercourse (as far as may be necessary) in a life of discipline and self-control lived in the power of the Holy Spirit. Nevertheless, in those cases where there is such a clearly felt moral obligation to limit or avoid parenthood, and where there is a morally sound reason for avoiding complete abstinence, the Conference agrees that other methods may be used, provided this is done in the light of the same Christian principles. The Conference records its strong condemnation of the use of any methods of conception-control from motives of selfishness, luxury, or mere convenience.[5]

In reaction, at least in part, to this revised teaching of the Anglican Church as reflected in the resolution above, Pope Pius XI, in December of 1930, issued the encyclical, *Casti Connubii* (On Chaste Marriage), in which Catholicism's traditional teaching on contraception was forcefully maintained.[6] In his letter, the Pope made several important points: he defended the institution of marriage against the abuses of the popular doctrine of "free love," and he argued against the notion that women needed to be freed from the "slavery" of children, for implicit in this idea is the perception of children as constituting a burden in life rather than a blessing.

In considering the specific question of marital sexuality, *Casti Connubii* clearly sees intercourse as having two purposes, one of which is primary, while the other is secondary: "...the conjugal act is destined primarily by nature for the begetting of children.... [but] in the use of the matrimonial rights there are also secondary ends, such as mutual aid, the cultivating of mutual love, and the quieting of concupiscence which husband and wife are not fobidden to consider so long as they are subordinated to the primary end and so long as the intrinsic nature of the act is preserved."[7] In this context, the point is made

---

[5]This is resolution #15; confer Noonan, *op.cit.,* pp. 486-87.

[6]The full text of *Casti Connubii* may be found in Odile M. Liebard (ed.), *Official Catholic Teachings.* Vol.4 *Love and Sexuality* (Wilmington, North Carolina: McGrath Publishing Company, 1978), pp. 23-70.

[7]*Ibid.,* #80,85, pp. 41-2.

that any time a couple engages in sexual intercourse "in such a way that the act is deliberately frustrated in its natural power to generate life," we are then faced with an offense against the law of God and of nature, "and those who indulge in such are branded with the guilt of a grave sin."[8]

In prohibiting the deliberate frustration of sexuality's procreative power, the encyclical does not specify by name what particular forms of contraception are banned. In general, however, at this time, as noted by Noonan, the term most often used by theologians when talking about contraception was "onanism," or the sin of Onan. The evil done by Onan was his refusal to follow the Old Testament law of levirate marriage (Deut.25:5-6), whereby a man was supposed to try to provide an heir for his brother who had died childless. In Onan's case, he slept with his sister-in-law, Tamar, but each time he "spilt his seed on the ground," whereupon Yahweh brought about his death (Gn.38:6-10).

Thus onanism refers specifically to *coitus interruptus* or the act of "withdrawal" whereby the penis is withdrawn from the vagina prior to ejaculation, but in the realm of theological discourse preceding the appearance of *Casti Connubii,* the term, onanism, came to have an expanded meaning. Included under the sin of onanism was not just withdrawal followed by ejaculation, but also every exercise of the conjugal act that involved any attempt to prevent or impede procreation by some positive means like the use of mechanical devices or chemicals ("onanism by instrument"). In Noonan's judgment, then, a strict reading of *Casti Connubii* would see as forbidden both *coitus interruptus* and the use of a condom, while a broader interpretation would call also for the prohibition of post-coital douches, as well as diaphragms and other products later to be designated as the "barrier methods" of contraception.[9]

[8]*Ibid.*, #82, p. 41.
[9]Noonan, *op.cit.*, pp. 509-10.

POPE PIUS XII'S ADDRESS TO THE ITALIAN CATHOLIC SOCIETY OF MIDWIVES

In 1951, Pope Pius XII, for the first time, gave public, explicit and official approval for the practice of periodic abstinence or continence whereby married couples refrain from sexual intercourse during the woman's fertile period and thus limit intercourse to the times of non-fertility in the wife's cycle. In his address to Italian midwives, the Pope made it clear that married couples must have a good reason for limiting intercourse to those periods of time when it is judged that procreation cannot occur.[10] He cited medical, eugenic, social and economic considerations as possible grounds that might morally justify spouses' recourse to this practice. He also recognized that such medical, eugenic and socio-economic indicators might be of such a nature as to warrant the practice of periodic abstinence for a considerable length of time and "even for the duration of the marriage." In insisting that there must be a good reason for restricting marital intercourse to the times of infertility, Pius XII made it clear that in so limiting their sexual activity, it is also possible that spouses may be acting irresponsibly and hence immorally:

> If, however, in the light of a reasonable and fair judgment, there are no such serious personal reasons, or reasons deriving from external circumstances, then the habitual intention to avoid the fruitfulness of the [sexual] union, while at the same time continuing fully to satisfy sensual intent, can only arise from a false appreciation of life and from motives that run counter to true standards of moral conduct.[11]

One final thing should be noted about Pius XII's Address. Once the possibility is acknowledged that periodic abstinence or the use of rhythm or natural family planning can be morally legitimate, we must affirm also that it can be morally permissible for spouses to engage in intercourse with the explicit

[10]The complete text of the Address may be found in Liebard, *op.cit.*, pp. 101-22.

[11]*Ibid.*, #301, p. 113.

intention and desire of not conceiving a child. Assuming that spouses have legitimate reasons for not wanting to procreate, the question then presses for attention: is periodic abstinence the only moral way for spouses to implement their desire not to conceive? As we shall see, the debate surrounding this question peaked in some sense during the decade of the Sixties.

VATICAN II ON MARRIAGE AND THE FAMILY

In 1965, at the close of its fourth and final session, the Second Vatican Council promulgated the *Pastoral Constitution on the Church in the Modern World (Gaudium et Spes),* in which a number of important points were made about Christian marriage and the meaning of family life:[12]

1) As a "community of love" (#47) and as an "intimate partnership of life and love" (#48), marriage both reflects and shares in the loving covenant which unites Christ with the Church. The beauty and significance of the Christian family lie in the expectation that "by the mutual love of the spouses, by their generous fruitfulness, their solidarity and faithfulness, and by the loving way in which all members of the family work together," the living presence of Christ in the world will be made manifest to all (#48).

2) Coital expressions of conjugal love are regarded as having a substantial value independent of procreation. Marital acts of love are titled "noble" and "worthy," and in their truly human expression, they "signify and promote that mutual self-giving by which spouses enrich each other with a joyful and a thankful will" (#49).

3) At the same time, however, conjugal love is not unrelated to the procreation and education of children. Both matrimony itself and conjugal love "are ordained for the procreation and education of children, and find in them their ultimate crown" (#48). Moreover, precisely as "the supreme gift of marriage,"

---

[12]The full text of *Gaudium et Spes* may be found in Walter M. Abbott, S.J., (ed.), *The Documents of Vatican II* (New York: The America Press, 1966). The discussion of marriage appears in sections 47-52 of the document, pp. 249-58 of Abbott's text.

children "contribute very substantially to the welfare of their parents" (#50).

4) When married couples fruitfully exercise their procreative power, they come to enjoy a certain special participation in God's own creative work. In elaborating upon the place of children in married life, *Gaudium et Spes* urges that, "while not making the other purposes of matrimony of less account, . . . parents should regard as their proper mission the task of transmitting human life and educating those to whom it has been transmitted" (#50). On this point, we must take note of the fact that the document steadfastly refuses to employ the traditional terminology of a "hierarchy of goals or ends" whereby the procreation and education of children is referred to as the primary purpose of marriage and conjugal sexuality, while the expression and fostering of love between spouses is designated as the secondary purpose of marital sex.

According to the official legislative history of the Council, various amendments to this text were proposed, calling for a re-assertion of the idea of a "hierarchy of ends," that is, the distinction between primary and secondary purposes or goals. Nonetheless, all of these amendments, one of which stated explicitly that "conjugal love is ordained to the primary end of marriage, which is offspring," were rejected.[13] Thus, marriage and conjugal sexuality are seen as having dual purposes, but the Council Fathers refused to render a judgment on the relative importance of these purposes by ranking them first and second.

5) Married couples are to carry on the task of procreating and educating children "with human and Christian responsibility." In planning their families, Christian spouses should "thoughtfully take into account both their own welfare and that of their children, those already born and those which may be foreseen." Responsible parenting means that married couples "will reckon with both the material and the spiritual conditions of the times as well as of their state of life;" spouses will, in addition, "consult the interests of the family group, of temporal

[13]See John T. Noonan, Jr., "Contraception and the Council," *Commonweal*, 83 (March 11, 1966). 657, 659. See also note 168 in Abbott's text, p. 254.

society, and of the Church herself." Parents who raise a relatively large family are accorded special mention, but they are reminded of their duty to raise their children "suitably," and it is expected that the decision to have a large family entails "wise and common deliberation" (#50).

As the preceding paragraph makes clear, the Catholic Church is not opposed to responsible or planned parenthood. *Gaudium et Spes* does not glorify uncontrolled procreation, nor does it offer any praise for the procreation of children without reminding us of their need to be educated. For Christian spouses, then, responsible parenting would seem to entail three things: they must be open to procreation, and they must properly care for children already born; finally, when and as necessary, spouses must establish appropriate limitations to their power to conceive.[14] How they do so, of course, is still the object of ongoing debate.

6) Regarding the decision to transmit human life, "the parents themselves should ultimately make this judgment, in the sight of God," but they are to realize "that they cannot proceed arbitrarily." Rather, Christian spouses must come to their decision in a responsible or conscientious way, which is to say, that "they must always be governed according to a conscience dutifully conformed to the divine law itself, and [they] should be submissive toward the Church's teaching office, which authentically interprets that law in the light of the gospel" (#50). We will reserve comment on this matter of responsible decision-making until later in the chapter.

7) Finally, it is recognized that married couples often "find themselves in circumstances where at least temporarily the size of their families should not be increased." Thus parental responsibility to avoid procreation comes into conflict with the desire to express conjugal love in a physical way. In such circumstances, spouses feel pulled in two different directions: responsibility requires both that they avoid conception and that they maintain "the faithful exercise of love and the full intimacy of their lives." Failure to preserve "the intimacy of married life"

---

[14]McCormick, *op.cit.,* p. 96.

is clearly a threat to the spouses' mutual fidelity, but it may also endanger the welfare of their children already born and undermine parental courage and generosity to accept new ones (#51).

In offering guidance to spouses as they attempt to "harmonize conjugal love with the responsible transmission of life," *Gaudium et Spes* warns against "dishonorable solutions" and advises married couples that the moral propriety of their conjugal expressions of love is determined by objective standards which are based on the nature of human persons and their actions and which "preserve the full sense of mutual self-giving and human procreation in the context of true love" (#51). What is most significant in this statement is the fact that acts of conjugal love are not to be judged simply with reference to their biological dimension, but rather by their relationship to the whole human person. Quite simply, the document chooses to move away from the oft-repeated argument against contraception which looks only to the biological structure of the coital act considered in isolation from the persons performing the act. The norm for morality is seen rather as rooted in the nature of human persons, not in the isolated purposes of specific actions.

The Council Fathers end their discussion of marriage and family life by encouraging spouses to the practice of conjugal chastity, which means, in part, that in attempting to regulate births, married couples are to avoid those methods "found blameworthy by the teaching authority of the Church in its unfolding of the divine law" (#51). No further guidance is given by way of distinguishing between acceptable and nonacceptable forms of contraception, but in a footnote to the text the Fathers explain the reason for their silence: "Certain questions which need further and more careful investigation have been handed over, at the command of the Supreme Pontiff, to a commission for the study of population, family, and births, in order that, after it fulfills its function, the Supreme Pontiff may pass judgment. With the doctrine of the magisterium in this state, this holy Synod does not intend to propose immediately concrete solutions."[15]

[15]Abbott's text, p. 256, n. 173.

"HUMANAE VITAE" AND ITS BACKGROUND

This special papal commission established to study the issue of contraception was initiated in 1963 by Pope John XXIII; in 1964, Pope Paul VI appointed a large number of additional members to the commission. Both laity and clerics comprised the 60 to 70 members of the group, and their number included physicians, social scientists, married couples, priests, bishops and cardinals. At the conclusion of the commission's deliberations in June, 1966, two separate reports were submitted to Pope Paul VI; in the minority opinion, signed by four theologians, the traditional prohibition of all forms of artificial contraception was maintained; the majority opinion, which was shared by all the remaining members of the commission, recommended a change in the Church's official teaching on methods of contraception.

In February, 1966, prior to having received the papal commission's reports, Paul VI addressed the National Congress of the Italian Women's Center. In his speech, the Pope referred to the complexity and delicacy of the issues being considered by the commission which had been set up specifically "with the task of going into these problems more deeply from all points of view — scientific, historical, sociological and doctrinal—while making abundant use of the advice of bishops and experts." In urging his audience "to await the results of these studies and to accompany them with ... prayers," the Pope noted the Church's need for caution and careful study in its attempt to teach the people of God:

> The magisterium of the Church cannot propose moral norms unless it is sure that it is interpreting God's will. In reaching this certitude, the Church is not excused from carrying out research nor from examining all the many questions proposed for its consideration from every corner of the world. Sometimes these operations take a long time and are anything but easy.[16]

---

[16]The full text of the Address is found in Liebard, *op.cit.,* pp. 288-95; this quote is from #290, p. 290.

With these expressed sentiments of Pope Paul VI as a background, once the recommendations of the papal commission's majority report became known, there was more than a fair amount of expectation within the Catholic Church that the prohibition against so-called artificial methods of contraception would be modified. People awaited Paul VI's response to the commission's suggestions. It came two years later when he issued his encyclical letter, *Humanae Vitae* (Of Human Life), in July, 1968.

In the opening section of his letter, the Pope thanks the commission for its work but says that its conclusions cannot be considered as definitive, nor do those conclusions dispense him from a personal examination of the questions at hand. The Pope then remarks that the papal commission had reached "no full concordance of judgments concerning the moral norms to be proposed;" furthermore, he says that in the commission's report, certain criteria for solutions to the question of contraception had indeed emerged "which departed from the moral teaching on marriage proposed with constant firmness by the teaching authority of the Church." Finally, with the assurance that he has "attentively sifted the documentation" presented to him, the Pope, "after mature reflection and assiduous prayers," maintains that there can be no change in the Church's opposition to the use of artificial contraceptives (*HV,* #6).

The encyclical offers the following rationale: "Each and every marriage act must remain open to the transmission of life" (*HV,* #11), because God has willed "the inseparable connection ...between the two meanings of the conjugal act: the unitive meaning and the procreative meaning." By virtue of its intimate structure, "the conjugal act, while most closely uniting husband and wife, capacitates them for the generation of new lives, according to laws inscribed in the very being of man and of woman" (*HV,* #12). Thus, it is "intrinsically dishonest" (*HV,* #14). and "always illicit" (*HV,* #16) for spouses to engage in sexual intercourse while at the same time attempting deliberately and positively to frustrate the act's procreative potential.

In commenting on these basic assertions of the encyclical, Richard McCormick observes that the letter's primary contention is this: sexual intercourse "is a single act with two aspects or inner meanings, the unitive and procreative;" moreover, these two meanings "are by divine design inseparable," so that anyone who deliberately tries to render the act of intercourse sterile also "attacks its meaning as an expression of mutual self-giving."[17] McCormick notes that such an analysis is not new. Several moralists had already written along these lines, and McCormick admits to having earlier made the point himself that "by excluding the child as the permanent sign of the love to be expressed in coitus, one introduced a reservation into coitus and therefore robbed it of that which makes it objectively unitive."[18] But McCormick no longer argues for this position.

According to the mode of thinking represented in *Humanae Vitae,* the unitive and procreative meanings of sexual intercourse are so intimately joined as to be inseparable. This means that any deliberate physical interference with one of these meanings must necessarily have a disruptive or destructive influence upon the other, so that the moral significance of the sexual act as a whole is undermined. Thus the inseparability of the unitive and procreative dimensions of conjugal love lies at the root of the Church's prohibition against any use of sexual intercourse which involves the positive attempt to prevent the act from resulting in procreation; at the same time, it should be noted that the same argument, namely the inseparability of the two dimensions of conjugal love, plays a large part in the Church's objections to any attempts by spouses to procreate apart from the intimate expression of their mutual love in sexual intercourse. Thus the Church maintains an official stance against not only AID (artificial insemination using a donor's sperm) but also AIH (artificial insimination using the husband's sperm) and *in vitro* fertilization where both the ovum and sperm belong to the spouses.

---

[17]Richard A. McCormick, S.J., "Notes on Moral Theology," *Theological Studies,* 29, 4 (Dec., 1968), 726. Also see McCormick's remarks in *Theological Studies,* 44, 1 (March, 1983), 82-3, n. 36.

[18]*Ibid.,* 727-28; McCormick is here paraphrasing a position he adopted in two of his earlier articles written in 1964; cf. n. 136.

III. Theological Responses to Humanae Vitae

Many theologians and others have thought it necessary to criticize the analysis offered by *Humanae Vitae* as an explanation for prohibiting the conjugal practice of contraceptive intercourse.[19] Some of this criticism focuses on what is seen as a problem of basic inconsistency in the text of the encyclical itself; other critics have challenged the legitimacy and moral relevance of the distinction between periodic abstinence (or the practice of rhythm), which the Church accepts as a "natural" method of limiting or spacing children, and all other methods of contraception which the Church rejects as "artificial." A sampling of both types of criticism follows. We begin with a challenge to one of the encyclical's basic assertions.

ARE THE PROCREATIVE AND UNITIVE MEANINGS OF CONJUGAL SEX INSEPARABLE?

As noted earlier, *Humanae Vitae* claims that God has willed an inseparable connection between the two meanings of the conjugal act (#12). On this very point, however, McCormick finds that the encyclical seems to be in contradiction to something it had previously affirmed: acts of conjugal love "do not cease to be lawful if, for causes independent of the will of husband and wife, they are foreseen to be infecund [infertile], since they always remain ordained towards expressing and consolidating their [the couple's conjugal] union" (*HV,* #11). McCormick rightly points out that here the encyclical is approving of acts of sexual intercourse even when it is known that these acts cannot be procreative, and the justification for these acts is simply this: the acts remain directed toward the expression and furthering of conjugal love. But the text seems clearly to imply here that the "ordering toward procreation" ceases and is absent precisely whenever spouses engage in intercourse during the periods of infertility. If the act of

---

[19]For a fine overview of the reactions to *Humanae Vitae* see William H. Shannon, *The Lively Debate: Response to Humanae Vitae* (New York: Sheed & Ward, 1970).

intercourse loses its directedness or ordering toward procreation during times of natural infertility, then clearly this ordering or directedness is separable from the conjugal expression of love in sexual intercourse. McCormick concludes by saying:

> In these infertile acts the unitive and procreative aspects are separable. This means that at one point [#11] the encyclical seems unwittingly to imply a factual separation of the unitive and procreative aspects of individual coital acts during the infertile period. At another (#12) the doctrine that each act must remain open to new life is said to rest on the inseparable connection between the procreative and unitive meanings...[which exist together in the conjugal act].[20]

It should be noted that in the very section of the encyclical under discussion (#11), the text goes on to say that "God has wisely disposed natural laws and rhythms of fecundity which, of themselves, cause a separation in the succession of births." It can be legitimately argued, I think, that in keeping with the line of reasoning established a bit earlier in this paragraph of the letter, the sentence quoted might just as well read as follows: "God has wisely disposed natural laws and rhythms of fecundity which, of themselves, cause a separation *in the two meanings of the conjugal act as procreative and unitive."* God, it seems, through the laws of physical nature as revealed in the ordinary rhythms of a woman's body, has seen to it that the two meanings of conjugal sex not only can be separated but in fact are separated during a woman's recurring periods of infertility. Clearly, then, not each and every act of intercourse is open to the transmission of life. This being the case, the Church's argument against artificial contraception, which is based on the premise that "God has willed the inseparable connection between the two meanings of the conjugal act" (#12), seems to be open to question.

The grounds for resisting artificial contraception must be found elsewhere. Artificial contraception cannot be ruled out

---

[20]McCormick, *Theological Studies,* 29, 4 (1968), 728.

simply on a predicated "inseparability" between the procreative and unitive dimensions of sexuality, when in fact God at times makes such separation a reality. There is now, rather, a new question at hand; the issue at stake is a different one: granted that God, through the laws of nature, provides for the separation of the procreative and unitive meanings of conjugal sex, may human beings attempt to bring about or ensure such a separation on their own initiative? The Church may insist on answering this question negatively, but it cannot legitimately do so by simply affirming, by way of explanation for its position, that God has willed the inseparable connection of the procreative and unitive dimensions of love in every act of intercourse.

In reaction both to the idea of the inseparability of the procreative and unitive meanings of conjugal sex and to the Church's admonition that "each and every marriage act must remain open to the transmission of life" (*HV*, #11), an interesting line of reasoning appeared recently in *The Tablet*. Professor Adrian Hastings points out that sexual intercourse, in fact, is not of its nature always "open to life;" it is not just an accident that conception does not always follow upon intercourse; it is rather the case that nature has been so devised by God that conception cannot always follow upon intercourse.[21] Nature, then, has made two types of intercourse: one that is biologically "open to life," and one that is not. Hastings goes on to say that both types of intercourse have positive functions in nature's purposes; both, in fact, "have a basic biological purpose: the one type, conceptive and rather rare, brings a baby into existence; the other, non-conceptive and frequent, provides it with a stable home and upbringing."

The sense of Hastings' observation would perhaps be better conveyed had he said, as he does later, that both types of intercourse are related to the good and welfare of children in that conceptive intercourse provides for their entrance into existence, while non-conceptive intercourse allows for their education and rearing. Clearly, both types of intercourse have a

---

[21] Adrian Hastings in a letter to *The Tablet* (2 March, 1985), 238-39. Here and in the following several paragraphs all references are to Hastings' letter.

necessary and integral role in married life since, as we saw earlier in our discussion of *Gaudium et Spes,* the call to responsible parenting sounds in two echoings: there is praise neither for unlimited procreation nor for procreation without provision for the subsequent care of children.

Given the fact that both types of intercourse bear some positive relationship to children, one to their procreation, the other to their overall education and welfare, Hastings suggests that it is permissible to guarantee, preserve, and even enhance, the distinction between the two types of intercourse in order to ensure "that one kind of intercourse does not take place when what is needed is the other kind." Therefore, just as spouses are justified in using hormone pills in an attempt to enhance fertility and render an otherwise "non-conceptive act conceptive," so are they justified in using contraceptives in order to guarantee "that a particular act of intercourse should be ensured to belong to the natural category of the non-conceptive when that is appropriate." Hastings concludes by saying that his argument is irrefutable. It is not clear to me, however, precisely what it is that Hastings has demonstrated. Married couples are to be free, he says, to ensure that a particular act of intercourse does in fact belong to the natural category of the non-conceptive *when that is appropriate,* but it must be asked when exactly is it appropriate to ensure, without begging the question, that an act of intercourse belongs to the category of the non-conceptive.

Put simply, I am not sure what extent of justification Hastings thinks he has established for artificial contraception. I wonder if his argument is suasive in the lives of childless spouses, and also if it warrants, for sound reasons, recourse by parents to an unrestricted use of artificial contraception. It seems more likely to me that the logic of his thinking establishes just this: at times—when ovulation is occurring—God and nature intend intercourse to be procreative; in keeping with the call to responsible parenting, married couples may assist in achieving this goal by the use of hormones which enhance fertility; at all other times, God and nature determine that intercourse is not directed toward procreation, and married couples may see to it, through the use of contraceptive devices, that their intercourse during these times retains its non-conceptive meaning. I think, in other words, that Hastings has made a good case for the moral use of artificial contraceptives, but only in those situations where, in recognition of the implications of responsible parenthood, married couples make use of contraceptive devices in an attempt to guarantee the non-conceptive nature of those acts of intercourse legitimately shared during the expected or foreseen times of natural infertility.

Hastings' argumentation allows spouses to be involved in assisting nature to maintain both conceptive and non-conceptive types of intercourse, but I doubt that, in itself, the force of his reasoning justifies their using contraceptives during the time when it is intended by nature that the wife be fertile. Hastings' comments suggest at most the following scenario: when spouses are morally justified in restricting acts of intercourse to the wife's "safe" or infertile periods, they may morally make use of contraceptive devices to ensure that these non-conceptive acts of intercourse do indeed remain such. Spouses may find some comfort and reassurance in this practice, but it leaves untouched the requirement that they must periodically and regularly refrain from conjugal expressions of love when the wife is fertile. So the question remains: may married couples use contraceptives during those times when it is thought that the wife is fertile?

IS PERIODIC ABSTINENCE NATURAL?

In addition to the arguments against its own internal logic, *Humanae Vitae* provoked another line of criticism, one which questioned the validity and moral relevance of the distinction between natural and artificial forms of contraception. The encyclical echoes the teaching of Pope Pius XII to the effect that when there are serious motives deriving "from the physical or psychological conditions of husband and wife, or from external conditions," it is then licit for spouses "to take into account the natural rhythms immanent in the generative functions" and to limit acts of conjugal love to the infertile periods only. This practice is distinguished from that of having intercourse during periods of fertility while using devices designed to prevent conception. "In reality," says the letter, "there are essential differences between the two cases: in the former, the married couple make legitimate use of a natural disposition; in the latter, they impede the development of natural processes" (#16).

The difference, in other words, between rhythm or periodic abstinence and all other forms of contraception is this: rhythm capitalizes upon, or takes advantage of, the natural infertile periods in a woman's cycle and restricts intercourse to these times; other forms of contraception allow intercourse to occur at any time but try to interfere with the effects of the act in some way so as to prevent any possible conception. Moreover, spouses who legitimately engage in periodic abstinence and renounce intercourse during periods of fertility are seen as giving proof "of a truly and integrally honest love" (#16). Thus it seems clear that at least part of the explanation for the Church's singular approval of periodic abstinence arises from the fact that this practice ensures and requires that spouses maintain a routine of self-discipline and asceticism in their conjugal relationship.

Regarding this last point, it certainly would be foolish to minimize the role discipline must play in spouses' personal growth and in their lives as a couple, but there is doubt that more can or should be demanded of them beyond that daily dying-to-self which allows them to fulfill, in a gracious and generous way, their responsibilities as husband or wife, mother or father. To the extent that periodic abstinence places additional emotional or psychological strain upon spouses, especially wives, and constitutes a threat to marital fidelity and thus, ultimately, to the welfare of children, some would suggest that the Church reconsider her insistence that rhythm is the only legitimate way whereby Christian spouses may engage in family planning.

Certainly, the distinction between natural and artificial contraception has been challenged frequently. James T. Burtchaell well expresses the difficulties generally raised against periodic abstinence as a "natural" form of contraception. It is only "a base theology," he says, "that would want intercourse to harmonize with the involuntary endocrine rhythm of ovulation and menstruation, while forsaking the greater spiritual and emotional ebbs and flows which should also govern sexual union."[22] Burtchaell's point is not to deny the biological rhythms that are part of female sexuality; rather, his intention is to affirm the fact that human sexuality is so much more than merely a biological reality.

In human beings, sexuality reflects the affective, emotional and psychological dimensions of people, not simply their physical or biological ones. It has been shown, moreover, that the great majority of women experience a peak in sexual desire and are more sexually sensitive and responsive at the time of ovulation and immediately before and after the onset of their menstrual period.[23] Yet it is precisely at the times of ovulation and menstruation that spouses must refrain from sexual intercourse if they wish to abide by the church-approved form of contraception or natural family planning. Burtchaell sees nothing natural in this. On the contrary, he says that compared to the other methods of contraception, he is tempted "to think of rhythm as the most unnatural of all, since it inhibits not only conception, but the expression of affection." [24]

[22]James T. Burtchaell, "'Human Life' and Human Love," in Paul T. Jersild and Dale A. Johnson (eds.), *Moral Issues and Christian Response* (New York: Holt, Rinehart and Winston, Inc., 1971), pp. 139-47 at 140. The article appeared originally in *Commonweal*, 89, 7 (15 November, 1968), 245-52.

[23]In 1965, Dr. John R. Cavanagh, a Catholic psychiatrist, prepared and distributed a questionnaire to be answered by married couples using rhythm; he wanted couples to share the story of their success; confer "Is Rhythm Better Than We Think?," *Marriage*, 47 (November, 1965), 1-4; the results were not as he expected. Many respondents spoke against rhythm as a satisfactory method of family planning. Cavanagh later reported that women often were frustrated because they could not engage in intercourse at the time of ovulation when their sexual desire was greatest. Confer "Special Marriage Report on Rhythm," *Marriage*, 48 (August, 1966); "Rhythm of Sexual Desire in Women," *Aspects of Human Sexuality*, 3 (February, 1969); "The Rhythm of Sexual Desire in the Human Female," *The Bulletin of the Guild of Catholic Psychiatrists*, 14 (1967), 87-100; Cavanagh gives six reasons, in this 1967 article, why rhythm is more psychologically harmful than other methods of contraception. For an overview of Cavanagh's ideas on responsible parenting, see Charles E. Curran, *Critical Concerns in Moral Theology* (Notre Dame: Univ. of Notre Dame Press, 1984), pp. 216-24. It should be noted that Cavanagh was originally a strong advocate of rhythm, but the responses to his questionnaire and his membership in the special papal commission on contraception led him to call for a change in the Church's prohibition of other forms of birth-control.

[24]Burtchaell, *op.cit.*, pp.139-40.

Burtchaell goes on to suggest that there is no "imposing intrinsic ethical difference" between periodic abstinence and any other means of contraception. He faults *Humanae Vitae* for "quibbling" over methods to prevent conception instead of challenging "the illusory motives which lead so many families to adopt contraception." For Burtchaell, the real evil to be avoided in marriage is not artificial contraception, but rather the surrender to selfishness which, at least in this rich country, "is perhaps the most frequent excuse for contraception." Married couples are in constant danger of yielding to a "contraceptive mentality" which blinds them to the value of children who consequently are placed quite low on the spouses' list of priorities;[25] thus many things come to outrank children in the order of importance: two careers, two houses, two cars, new furniture, new-model appliances, trips and uninterrupted social lives. From this perspective, children are viewed as burdens, not as blessings and God's gifts.

With Burtchaell, I believe that Christian spouses need reminding that in sharing their lives they will encounter surprises that will demand of them a love and generosity which they can "in no way calculate or control." Certainly, married couples should be encouraged to recognize and appreciate how the presence of children may challenge them, "in ways that surprise even themselves, to be greater men and women than they had planned."[26] When this attitude prevails, when children are cherished, generously anticipated and graciously welcomed, and when contraception of any sort is practiced only as the requirements of responsible parenting so dictate, then spouses ought not to strain unduly in their effort to decide between periodic abstinence and other methods of avoiding conception. This position is, and can be, advanced only to the extent that it can be reasonably maintained that the use of so-called artificial methods of contraception is not necessarily morally evil and hence is not always illicit. It is to this question of the moral evaluation of artificial contraception that we must now turn.

[25] *Ibid.*, pp. 139, 143-44.
[26] *Ibid.*, pp. 146-47.

IV. Toward a Moral Evaluation
of Artificial Contraception

Any attempt to develop a coherent and comprehensive position on the matter of conjugal sexuality must first recognize that Christian spouses are called to lives of genital intimacy as an expression of their generous and self-giving love which is most richly blessed when it not only strengthens the personal bond of marital unity but also gives birth to new life in the creation of children. For this reason, *Humanae Vitae* is rightly seen as challenging married couples to preserve the most ideal human possibilities for intercourse when it calls them to keep their love open in intention, desire and action to the procreation of children. Nonetheless, the circumstances in which married couples find themselves are rarely ideal; spouses must realistically assess their personal, physical and emotional resources, and cope, as well, with the social and economic conditions in which they find themselves. Accordingly, the encyclical assures spouses that they may well be morally justified in deciding to limit sexual intercourse to those times of the month when it is fully expected that procreation cannot occur; by doing so, the spouses are giving proper expression to their legitimate desire and moral intention to avoid conceiving a child. After recognizing that it is morally permitted to engage in sexual intercourse while maintaining the desire and intention to avoid conception, the question arises as to whether or not any means other than periodic abstinence may be used morally to achieve the intended goal of not procreating.

The answer offered both by *Humanae Vitae* and by the longstanding Catholic tradition is no. The argument offered is that contraceptive intercourse is against the natural order of things as established and intended by God, who wills that the procreative and unitive dimensions of the conjugal act be kept inseparable. As we saw earlier, however, this line of reasoning would seem flawed in that God through nature has in fact seen to it that in no small measure the procreative and unitive dimensions of human sexuality are separable and separated— in cases of sterility, or during a wife's periods of infertility.

Certainly, in these latter instances, where the conjugal act may rightly be said to have lost its natural directedness to procreation, there should be no objection to spouses employing some contraceptive device or technique to ensure that the time-periods of non-procreative sex as designed and intended by nature actually remain such. The real question is whether or not spouses are ever morally justified in separating and eliminating the procreative meaning of sexuality from its unitive meaning outside those times established in God's ordering of nature. As we shall see, any number of Catholic theologians now maintain that, assuming spouses are responsibly motivated and are not acting out of a selfish or materialistic contraceptive mentality, the use of artificial contraception does not constitute a moral evil or sin and is not an objective moral wrong.

It must be immediately noted, however, that in saying artificial contraception is not necessarily immoral, there is no intention to claim that the practice of contraceptive intercourse is a completely neutral act. On the contrary, many theologians who concede that spouses may responsibly have recourse to contraceptive devices are explicit in pointing to the disvalues which the use of these devices embodies. These disvalues, however, are seen as belonging not to the realm of moral evil, but rather to the sphere of premoral or ontic evil which we discussed in earlier chapters. In referring to contraceptive devices, McCormick describes them as "non-moral evils" which can be fairly seen as "nondesirable interferences" in the lives of spouses who "would welcome the chance to limit their families without them."[27]

As an explanation of the nonmoral, ontic or premoral evil which contraceptive intercourse entails, Philip Keane points to the fact that the act is deliberately closed to the possibility of procreation; he also notes the physical and emotional problems and side-effects which are associated with various contraceptive devices and techniques. Keane, however, comes to this conclusion: "If a couple face serious medical, psychological, or

---

[27]Richard A. McCormick, S.J., "Notes on Moral Theology, *"Theological Studies,* 40, 1 (March, 1979), 86-7.

economic problems [which warrant avoidance of procreation], their need for the human values involved in sexual communion would seem to give moral justification to their use of birth control devices." Introducing such a disvalue or premoral evil into their lives is not something which these spouses should do lightly or complacently; nonetheless, even though regretful of their need to do so, they may proceed "with a good conscience and with the conviction that, all things being considered, their action is objectively moral."[28] In stating, as he does, that the couple's action is moral, "all things being considered," Keane is reminding us that there must be a serious reason for permitting the premoral evil of artificial contraception; in fact, if couples cause or allow a premoral evil to occur unnecessarily or in the absence of any such sufficient or proportionate reason, they indeed then move into the realm of moral evil. In other words, it is the objective extenuating circumstances in which the spouses find themselves that render the act of contraceptive intercourse a premoral evil and not an objective moral wrong.

Picking up on this idea, McCormick indicates that the distinction between moral evil and evil that is nonmoral, ontic or premoral has long been acknowledged in our tradition and should be pertinent in our decisions about artificial contraceptives:

> Catholic tradition has always said that not every killing is murder, not every falsehood is a lie, not every taking of another's property is theft,.... It has insisted that before an action can be branded as a *moral* evil, a closer look is demanded. This close look will reveal that, at root, our tradition has been saying that the evils associated with human action are *moral* evils precisely in so far as they lack proportionate justification. Why is the same not true of the fecundity of sexual intercourse? If there can be a proportionate reason for taking human life itself, at times, why can there not be a reason for "taking" the fecundity of the sexual act, or even the faculty, at times? This is all that is being argued. To say anything else is to

---

[28]Philip S. Keane, S.S., *Sexual Morality. A Catholic Perspective* (New York: Paulist Press, 1977), pp. 124-25.

say that integral intercourse is in all conceivable situations of conflict the highest value, a thing we will not say of human life itself.[29]

Compatible with these observations is another extremely helpful and illuminating approach to the moral evaluation of contraceptive intercourse which has been taken by John H. Wright, S.J. He suggests that in its contention that spouses must not directly interfere with the procreative potential of sexual intercourse, *Humanae Vitae* is presenting them with what might be called an "obligatory ideal" which "makes a positive and enduring claim" upon their consciences.[30] In explaining his position, Wright first acknowledges that four types of obligatory ideals exist. The first kind of obligatory ideal is impossible of realization in any perfect way in this life. Thus, as human beings, we never give a totally adequate response to the biblical injunction to love God with all our mind, heart, soul and strength—indeed, with our whole being; neither are we ever as perfect as our Father in heaven (Mt. 5:48).

Belonging to the second type of obligatory ideals are those which in themselves are capable of realization; we find, however, that "extrinsic circumstances make their actual achievement impossible." Thus, although the world has sufficient resources to feed the hungry, to clothe the naked, to shelter the homeless, and so forth, it nonetheless happens that "accumulated problems of communication and transportation, compounded by human greed and insensitivity, along with other claims on our time and energy make the actual achievement of these ideals impossible." The third type of obligatory ideals consists of those which "are genuinely and fully realizable, at least at times." The ideal of fidelity is realized, for example, by people who persevere until death in their commitment to their "religious or marriage vows." Finally, comprising

---

[29]Richard A. McCormick, S.J., in a response to critics, *America*, 129,12 (Oct. 10, 1973), 290.

[30]John H. Wright, S.J., "An End to the Birth Control Controversy?," *America*, 144,9 (March 7, 1981), 175-78 at 175. Also see his follow-up article, "The Birth Control Controversy, Continued." *America*, 145, 4 (August 22, 1981), 66-8.

the fourth type of obligatory ideals are those which "are capable of realization both intrinsically and extrinsically" when "viewed in abstraction from the total situation;" however, when "considered with all attendant circumstances," it can happen that these ideals "ought not or need not be realized."[31]

In Wright's opinion, the ideal of "intercourse open to the possibility of conception" belongs to this fourth category of obligatory ideals. He compares it with, among others, the ideal of telling the truth at all times and thus never intentionally deceiving anyone. But sometimes, in order to preserve a higher or more urgent value such as protecting a third party from an unjust assailant, it becomes necessary to set aside this ideal of truth-telling and so I deliberately mislead the would-be attacker. In this situation, to be sure, the ideal of truth-telling retains its claim upon me, but only in this sense: I do not regret *actually deceiving* the potential assailant; I do, however, regret *having to* deceive him.[32] I regret, in other words, the circumstances which make it incumbent upon me to depart from the truth-telling ideal.

Wright provides a comparable analysis of the situation in which married couples may find themselves. The ideal of intercourse open to the possibility of conception makes a claim upon them, but for sufficient or proportionate reasons over which they have no control, this claim "may and sometimes should be set aside." When it is, and thus when spouses either render "fertile periods unproductive" by engaging in contraceptive intercourse or purposely try to avoid procreation by limiting sexual intercourse to determined infertile periods, it may be said that "they regret having to do this, but not actually doing it. They regret having to separate the unitive and procreative aspects in their expression of conjugal love, but not the separation itself."[33]

It should be noted that Wright sees both periodic abstinence and contraceptive intercourse as departures

---

[31] *Ibid.*, 175-76.

[32] *Ibid.*, 176; see also Richard A. McCormick, S.J., "Notes on Moral Thelogy," *Theological Studies*, 43, 1 (March, 1982), 72-74.

[33] *Ibid.*, 177.

from the ideal of intercourse open to conception. In other words, in fact and in intention, sexual intercourse restricted to periods of infertility is not "intercourse open to the possibility of conception;" neither is intercourse which involves the use of so-called artificial devices. Yet both types of intercourse can be morally justified; nor does Wright suggest that intercourse involving the use of contraceptives requires greater justification than intercourse intentionally restricted to periods of infertility. In either case, however, spouses will "regret the reasons which make the departure [from the ideal of intercourse open to the possibility of conception] necessary or advisable, even if not the departure itself."[34] Finally, we might offer the suggestion that when spouses do responsibly depart from the ideal of intercourse that is open to the procreative possibility, they are then involved in what we have referred to as premoral or ontic evil, but these terms are not employed by Wright.

We conclude this discussion of the moral status of contraceptive intercourse with the following comments. The Christian tradition clearly maintains that the fullest and richest expressions of human sexuality are those which remain open to both its unitive and procreative dimensions. There is also no question but that contraceptive intercourse often frustrates the immediate biological purpose of the marital act. But we must remember that in its fullest sense the procreative dimension of human sexuality is directed toward the overall good and welfare of children, and thus it involves much more than just the conception of new life. Spouses are responsible for new human life beyond its conception and birth; children must be educated and lovingly reared. If spouses cannot preserve this full meaning and purpose of the procreative dimension of sexual intercourse from serious harm without sometimes limiting or frustrating the act's immediate biological goal of conception, then their decision to do so might be judged morally legitimate, for it seems wise to judge individual acts of intercourse by the manner in which they contribute to the

[34] *Loc.cit.*

overall stability of marital and family life.[35] But this line of thinking finds no favor in *Humanae Vitae:* "...it is an error to think that a conjugal act which is deliberately made infecund and so is intrinsically dishonest could be made honest and right by the ensemble of a fecund conjugal life" (#14).

In the opinion of some theologians, it is possible for a married couple to decide morally to engage in some form of contraceptive intercourse, but surely these moralists would have to accept two major stipulations: (1) the spouses must agree that contraception is a moral option given their circumstances, and the method decided upon must be mutually acceptable; (2) the couple must remain open and honest in periodically re-evaluating their situation so as to avoid entrapment in the contraceptive mentality, which remains a constant and basic threat to marital and family life. Of course, contraceptives have already become acceptable to many Catholic spouses. In 1980, Archbishop John Quinn of San Francisco referred to a study which shows that 76.5 percent of the American Catholic women who are married and of child-bearing age use some form of contraception; of these women, 94 percent are using methods officially prohibited by the Church.[36] But these statistics should not be allowed to settle the question of whether any or all of the contraceptive devices being employed are morally valid or acceptable.

In the following section of this chapter, some comments will be made about the moral issues associated with specific contraceptive devices, but first some recognition must be given to the question of contraception in the lives of those who are unmarried. As the high incidence both of unwed motherhood and of abortions among young unmarried women makes clear, the occurrence of premarital and

[35]See John Farrelly, O.S.B., "The Principle of the Family Good," *Theological Studies*, 31 (1970), 262-74; also see his paper, "An Introduction to A Discussion of Human Sexuality," *CTSA Proceedings*, 32 (1977), p. 226.

[36]Archbishop John R. Quinn, "New Context for Contraception Teaching," *Origins: N.C. Documentary Service*, 10 (October 9, 1980), 263-67.

nonmarital intercourse is a sad and unfortunate reality; it is not something to be morally condoned or in any way encouraged.

Certainly, there is a need for more and better sex education of youth, but sex education alone, without appreciation of the meaning, dignity and beauty of human sexuality and without some attempt to establish norms for proper sexual expression, is powerless to curtail premarital intercourse. So long as this remains the case, adolescents, young adults and anyone else who cannot be dissuaded from engaging in premarital or extra-marital intercourse, should be encouraged to a careful and effective use of some kind of contraceptive device.[37] Moral responsibility would seem to demand this course of action, for contraceptive intercourse here appears less morally harmful than the subsequent decisions either to avoid unwed parenting by recourse to abortion, or to enter into a precipitous, premature and unloving marriage or, finally, to bring a child to birth under circumstances which seriously jeopardize his or her well-being.

V. Artificial and Natural Contraception: Various Techniques and Devices

My intention here is to indicate that not all the methods employed in an attempt to avoid procreation have the same status from a moral standpoint. Some devices, moreover, which are generally referred to as contraceptive, are not such in fact. Rather, they are abortifacients or abortion-causing agents and have to be judged accordingly.

STERILIZATION PROCEDURES

According to a recent study conducted by the Population Crisis Committee, the most common recourse of Americans

[37]Keane, *op.cit.*, p. 109.

who wish either to limit the size of their families or to avoid procreation altogether is sterilization. Of the Americans wishing to avoid parenthood or an increase in family-size, 34.6 percent get sterilized either by tubal ligation (23.2%) or by vasectomy (11.4%); 30 percent use oral contraceptives, 12.9 percent employ condoms, 7.9 percent make use of intrauterine devices, while 14.6 percent turn to one of the other available devices such as diaphragms, cervical caps, vaginal sponges and spermicidal foams and jellies. Preferred recourse to sterilization is not limited to America; in China (50.4%), India (80%) and Latin America (39.4%), surgical procedures to induce sterility stand as the most frequently used technique to avoid procreation.[38]

This high incidence of sterilization is terribly disconcerting, for the sterilization procedures, whether they be tubal ligations, hysterectomies or vasectomies, do not result simply or solely in the temporary avoidance or prevention of fertilization; rather, those who are sterilized are rendered permanently incapable of parenting. Even when sterilization techniques are used that allow for some possibility of reversal, no guarantee can be given that such reversal is indeed achievable; people seeking sterilization are therefore told that they must consider the procedure as permanent and irreversible.

What should be said of the morality of sterilization procedures? In its traditional response to this question, the Catholic Church distinguishes between "direct" and "indirect" sterilization. Direct sterilization, which the Church finds morally unacceptable, is understood as any sterilization that is specifically directed toward contraception, either as an end in itself or as a means to some other end. Thus, for example, the Church opposes sterilization when it is sought simply because children are not desired (here contraception is desired as an end in itself), or when it is proposed as a way to avoid any future pregnancy which might be judged as dangerous to the life or health of a woman who is afflicted with some heart or kidney disorder (contraception is intended here as a means to another end,

---

[38]The results of this study appear in *Newsweek,* March 11, 1985, p. 70.

namely, preserving the woman's health). In short, direct sterilization is identified as having a clear contraceptive intent.

By contrast, indirect sterilizations, which the Church permits, are those which are required specifically for the preservation of a person's health or life. Thus, for example, cancerous ovaries, uteri or testes may be removed; the intent here is clearly therapeutic, not contraceptive, as is obvious from the fact that were it possible to undergo these procedures without surrendering fertility, such would be the desire of the people requiring such surgery. Perhaps the best way to distinguish between indirect or therapeutic and, hence, permitted sterilization and that which is direct or contraceptive and, hence, prohibited, is to pose this question: would the proposed or sought sterilization still be considered as medically required or advisable even if infertility or avoidance of conception were not an issue in the person's life, either because he or she were committed to celibacy or were past child-bearing or child-producing age? If the answer to this question is affirmative, then clearly there is no contraceptive intent in the sterilization and it is morally permitted.

Some Catholic moralists regard the Church's distinction between direct and indirect sterilization as insufficiently responsive to the ethical complexities of human living.[39] There is a consensus, however, that given the assumed permanent and irreversible nature of sterilization, much more serious reasons must prevail if spouses are to be morally justified in resorting to such procedures, rather than to less extreme measures, in an attempt to avoid pregnancy. Later, in the chapter on abortion, I will present some circumstances which may be thought to warrant recourse to contraceptive sterilization, but for now one final observation should be made: the Church maintains that should a spouse seek and achieve sterilization for purposes of avoiding procreation, that person, upon repentance, is morally permitted to resume sexual intercourse, and is not morally

---

[39]See Keane, *op.cit.,* pp. 128-34; for a fuller discussion of sterilization see John P. Boyle, *The Sterilization Controversy. A New Crisis for the Catholic Hospital?* (New York: Paulist Press, 1976).

bound to attempt a reversal of the sterilization;[40] likewise, an unmarried person who has been sterilized may legitimately enter into marriage, but before doing so, he or she has an obligation in conscience to inform the future spouse that the sterilization has taken place.

COITUS INTERRUPTUS

Withdrawal or *coitus interruptus* is one of the most ancient forms of contraception. As seen earlier, it is referred to in the book of Genesis as the sin of Onan. Obviously, the effective use of this method presupposes and demands a great deal of discipline and self-control on the part of the male. Even granting such discipline, however, the fact remains that sperm may be contained in the pre-ejaculate fluid which is emitted before male orgasm, in which case the possibility exists that fertilization may occur even though ejaculation itself takes place outside the vagina. Moreover, beyond the question of its effectiveness, *coitus interruptus* raises a specific moral concern.

In attempting to exercise self-discipline, the husband may experience significant psychological strain and tension because of his concern to withdraw before the onset of sexual climax. At the very least, the husband's attention seems necessarily to be focused more on himself and on what is happening to him than on loving and pleasing his wife, who is thus frequently left feeling unsatisfied. For this reason, Bernard Häring has suggested that *coitus interruptus,* at least when adopted as a regular method of trying to avoid procreation, may be "more unnatural than other methods which, while using artificial means, nevertheless leave inviolate the physiological and psychological integrity of the marriage act."[41]

---

[40]See Noonan, *Contraception,* pp. 511, 537-46.

[41]Bernard Häring, C.S.S.R., *Love is the Answer* (Denville, New Jersey: Dimension Books, 1970), pp. 91-2.

ORAL CONTRACEPTIVES

To begin with, it should be noted that the very expression, "oral contraceptives," is itself problematic, for it fails to recognize the fact that there are various types of pills which function in quite different ways. Recent editions of the *Physician's Desk Reference* speak of four basic kinds of pills. In the first category are some high-dosage pills which contain synthetic forms of both estrogen and progestogen; these pills work primarily to suppress the normal ovulation process, and insofar as they succeed in doing so, they are properly regarded as anovulents and, as such, constitute a form of temporary sterilization; these high-dosage pills, however, may also have the effect both of thickening cervical mucus to prevent passage of sperm into the uterus, and of affecting the uterine lining (the endometrium) in such a way as to reduce the likelihood of implantation of any ovum which might happen to be fertilized. It should be noted that these high-dosage-type pills are less used today because of their high-risk side effects.

The second and third types of pills are the low-dose, combined pills and the low-dose, mini-combined pills; as their designations indicate, both of these types of pills contain compounds of estrogen and progestogen, but in smaller amounts, especially of estrogen. These pills work in ways comparable to the higher-dosage pills, except for the significant fact that they are much more likely to allow ovulation to occur regularly, and hence pregnancy is avoided by greater reliance upon the buildup of cervical mucus to block the entrance of the uterus and upon the prevention of uterine implantation should fertilization of an ovum occur. The fourth type of pill, finally, is the mini-pill which contains only progestogen and almost always functions simply by rendering the endometrium hostile to implantation by a fertilized egg; only occasionally and incidentally do such pills thwart ovulation.

The point of this discussion is to indicate that the so-called "oral contraceptives" are to no small extent rather misnamed; thus, for example, any pills which truly thwart ovulation (the anovulents) should be seen as agents of temporary sterilization, since they constitute an intervention against a woman's general reproductive capacity, as opposed to interfering immediately in some way with the act of intercourse itself. To the extent that truly anovulent pills cause only temporary sterilization, not permanent, their use would not seem to require any further moral justification beyond that needed for any of the strictly contraceptive devices. Many pills, however, especially the mini-pills, defy being referred to as contraceptives insofar as they do not in fact prevent fertilization from occurring but, rather, directly thwart the development of fertilized eggs by preventing their uterine implantation; these pills, then, must properly be regarded as abortifacients or abortion-causing agents. Strictly speaking, the only pills which should be called contraceptive in nature and functioning are those which would allow ovulation to occur, while interfering with fertilization by thickening the cervical mucus and thus depriving sperm of access to the newly released ovum.

Given the variety of types of pills and the continuing uncertainties with regard to their precise modes of operation, no simple or universal moral evaluation is possible. By way of a general observation, however, it might be said that in order for the use of a particular type of pill to be considered a moral option in the effort at family planning, that pill's functioning must be clearly anti-ovulatory and/or contraceptive. Recourse to those types of pills which function most probably as abortifacients is, in my judgment, morally unacceptable. Moreover, since, as we have seen, the abortifacient potential seems to be inherent, to a greater or lesser degree, in all forms of the pill, I would urge that couples look to other methods of family planning when they judge that they must curtail the procreative capacity of their sexual activity.

In general, I maintain that all abortifacient devices or techniques must be avoided as methods of regular family planning, even though there are, as we shall see later in the chapter on abortion, solid reasons for thinking that in the early days and weeks following upon fertilization, the developing zygote is not yet a human person. Assuming for now that this is indeed the case, we must be guided, nonetheless, by the realization that from the time of fertilization itself, we are immediately presented with the zygote's potential for human personhood and, morally, this potential may not be casually disregarded or thwarted, as would seem to be the occurrence when it is known that a fertilized ovum might regularly be prevented from implanting as the result of a decision to use a particular method of family planning.

It should be noted that in addition to the moral complexities and ambiguities associated with the use of the pill, spouses may find other good reasons for deciding in favor of a different method of regulating births. The debate over the safety of the pill is not ended, although today there seems to be a consensus that women who are young and generally healthy can use the pill with little physical risk. Recent studies indicate that the pill does not increase the risk of breast cancer and seems, in fact, to offer some protection against forms of cancer affecting the ovaries and the endometrium. Still, the pill does involve other health-concerns; its use is sometimes linked to blood clots, strokes and heart attacks, and there are strong indications that women who smoke or who are over 35 should use other methods of family planning. It is assumed, of course, that physicians will not prescribe any form of "the pill" until after a woman's medical history has been taken and a physical examination completed. It should be mentioned, finally, that sometimes the pill is prescribed on a temporary basis for specifically non-contraceptive purposes: to help, for instance, in regulating a woman's cycle, or as a means to producing a "lighter" period, or as an aid in reducing cramping. Such uses of the pill create no cause for moral concern when taken by women who are sexually inactive; sexually active women, however, should seek assurance that the prescribed pill is not an abortifacient.

As might be expected, research into new methods of limiting the number of children born is continuing. In France, a new type of pill is under development and is already being used experimentally in several countries, including the United States. Referred to at present simply as RU-486, this pill in no way claims to prevent ovulation but, rather, is classified as an "anti-progesterone," which means that it works against the hormone, progesterone, that prepares the lining of the uterus to receive a fertilized egg and retain it during the early stages of pregnancy. By preventing the production and action of progesterone, the pill induces menstruation, thus preventing a fertilized ovum from implanting, or causing "the expulsion of any fertilized egg that may have implanted in the wall of the uterus." RU-486 is being praised as a scientific breakthrough since a woman would be required to take it only four days a month to ensure the onset of menstruation, regardless of whether or not fertilization has occurred, whereas the conventionally-marketed pills must be taken for 21 or 28 days every month. Or the woman might choose to take RU-486 only when and if she misses her period and comes to believe that she is pregnant.[42]

As should be obvious from the description of the way in which RU-486 works, this pill is neither a true contraceptive nor a form of temporary sterilization; it does not prevent conception or fertilization of an ovum; it guarantees, rather, that the implantation of any ovum which happens to be fertilized will be prevented or interrupted. In its mode of operation, then, RU-486 is comparable to the so-called "morning after" pills and, along with them, must undoubtedly be regarded as abortifacient in nature. Any moral evaluation of such pills must proceed accordingly. Indeed, some further discussion of the use of such pills, and of comparable hormonal injections, in the treatment of rape victims appears later in the chapter on abortion.

Finally, notice should be given to the fact that many countries, America among them, are experimenting with a contraceptive implant called Norplant, which was developed in Finland. Norplant consists of six match-size rubber tubes filled with synthetic progestin; the tubes are implanted

---

[42]Reported in *Newsweek*, May 3, 1982, p. 85 and March 11, 1985, p. 70. When first tested, RU-486 was administered to eleven women who were six to eight weeks pregnant; nine of these women aborted after four days of treatment; possibly because they had received inadequate dosages of the pill, the other two women underwent abortion by conventional means.

in a woman's upper arm and the progestin is slowly and gradually released over a period of five years. The effect of the implant is said to be two-fold: to inhibit ovulation and, as added protection, to thicken the cervical mucus, thus rendering passage of sperm into the uterus more difficult. It is estimated that Norplant will be approved for more general use in the United States in about a year at the cost of approximately $60, which means that women would have five-year contraceptive protection for roughly the same price as a six-month supply of the pills presently marketed as oral contraceptives. Of course, no final moral evaluation of Norplant is possible until fuller and more definitive information on its method of operation is available.

INTRAUTERINE DEVICES

The use of variously shaped intrauterine devices, commonly referred to as I.U.D.'s, is the object of much debate today, and the concern over their medical safety seems only to grow. It is known that I.U.D.'s do sometimes produce discomforting side-effects like uterine cramps or a heavy menstrual flow; they also are associated with an increased risk of pelvic inflammatory disease (PID) which can result in such damage to the Fallopian tubes that sterility ensues. It is especially recommended, therefore, that I.U.D.'s not be used by women who either are still childless or have multiple sex partners.

The intrauterine device's precise mode of operation is not known; the most common explanations of its working, however, are the following: the presence of an I.U.D. causes a newly released egg to move through the Fallopian tube so quickly that the egg, even if fertilized, enters the uterus before it is possible for implantation to occur; or it may be that the I.U.D. irritates the lining of the uterus (the endometrium) to such a degree that it is rendered unsuitable for the egg's implantation or nidation. As both these explanations make clear, I.U.D.'s do not prohibit fertilization or conception; only implantation is prevented, so that any ovum which becomes fertilized is simply sloughed off during the next menstrual period.

That the use of an I.U.D. does not prevent fertilization is verified by studies which have revealed the presence of human chorionic gonadotropin (HCG) in women fitted with I.U.D.'s. This hormone, HCG, is one which is detected in the urine of pregnant women. Thus, the conclusion seems unavoidable: women wearing I.U.D.'s do conceive, but the implantation of the fertilized egg is prevented. The I.U.D. should, therefore, be viewed as an abortifacient, not as a contraceptive device. Many physicians, however, object to this designation of the intrauterine device; they insist— wrongly, in my judgment—that nothing should be termed an abortifacient unless it brings about the expulsion of an egg which has already been implanted. Despite this medical contention, the majority of moralists regard the I.U.D. as an abortifacient and thus would judge its use to be a morally unacceptable method of family planning.

This certainly is my judgment, even though, as will be seen later in our treatment of abortion, there are serious reasons to question whether the newly fertilized egg in its first days and weeks is a human person. This question notwithstanding, I maintain, as indicated earlier, that we cannnot ignore the fact that from the moment of conception, there exists a new being with the full potential for personhood, and this potential deserves to be respected, protected and nurtured. Only rarely, if ever, may this potential be deliberately thwarted or destroyed; yet when I.U.D.'s are used, the attitude toward the loss of this potential for personhood is far too cavalier: it is freely accepted that however often an egg is fertilized, it will simply be made to slough off during the next menstrual period. Such casualness cannot be morally condoned.

BARRIER METHODS

The remaining contraceptive devices are designed to establish some kind of barrier or blockage to the cervix of the uterus so that sperm will be unable to effect fertilization.

Included among the so-called barrier methods of contraception are condoms, diaphragms, cervical caps, and spermicidal sponges, suppositories, creams, foams and jellies. These various devices have some distinct advantages: when used carefully and consistently, they are rather effective (90-95% on the average), and their effectiveness is increased when various devices are used simultaneously (e.g., condom or diaphragm together with a spermicide); except for diaphragms and cervical caps which require proper fitting, these devices are available without prescription; they are, moreover, considered safe and free of harmful side-effects, although bladder irritation sometimes is associated with use of a diaphragm; finally, spermicides and condoms offer partial protection from sexually transmitted diseases.

Commonly heard complaints about the barrier methods of contraception are that they are "messy," or that they diminish physical sensation and pleasure, or that they interfere with the spontaneity of the sexual relationship since a woman must be sure that she has prepared herself for intercourse or must do so in the midst of foreplay, and a man must achieve an erection before putting on a condom. Despite these objections, I nevertheless suggest that of all the so-called artificial forms of contraception, the barrier methods present the least moral and medical difficulty to those who judge that they are morally justified in trying to inhibit the procreative potential of their sexual activity. This is so for two reasons: first, because, when used properly, these barrier methods are not only generally devoid of any serious side-effects, but also quite effective; secondly, these barrier methods are clearly contraceptive in their functioning; they are directed to the prevention of fertilization, and thus they are morally far less problematic than the devices (I.U.D.'s and pills) which clearly or possibly function as abortifacients. To emphasize a point made earlier, I believe that in selecting a method of family planning, couples have an obligation in conscience to make every effort to avoid recourse to any abortion-causing devices or pills.

NATURAL FAMILY PLANNING

As indicated in this chapter, many Catholic theologians believe that married couples may responsibly decide that contraceptive intercourse is a legitimate moral option. Moreover, there are those who see periodic abstinence as a psychologically and emotionally frustrating experience for spouses, and one that could threaten their marital union and thus the well-being of their children. This concern notwithstanding, I believe the practice of periodic abstinence deserves further attention and should not be dismissed out of hand.

Unquestionably, the methods for determining the onset of a woman's fertile period have become much more sophisticated and accurate. If spouses wish to postpone or delay pregnancy, no longer must the time of fertility, the wife's "unsafe" period, be projected or estimated simply by reliance upon her past "calendar rhythms" or the continued regularity of her menstrual cycle. According to this theory, it was assumed that the same fluctuations which had occurred in the wife's cycle over, say, the past year would continue to do so; and thus her fertile periods could always be expected to fall within a certain range of days of her cycle, during which intercourse would have to be avoided.[43]

Today, however, the regularity or irregularity of a woman's cycle is no longer of such relevance for the practice of periodic abstinence, because it is now possible for a woman to detect in an ongoing way, and on a day-to-day basis, the various changes in her body, especially as these changes pertain to the process of ovulation. Various techniques allow a woman to familiarize herself with the physiological signs that accompany her alternating periods of fertility and infertility. One such technique that is receiving great attention, is known as the ovulation method or the Billings method. Drs. John and Evelyn Billings came

---

[43]For a fuller explanation of the rhythm method and determination of the time of fertility, see Committee on Human Reproduction, "The Control of Fertility." *JAMA*, 194,4 (October 25, 1965), 468.

to the realization that a woman's vaginal mucus serves as a reliable indicator of the hormonal changes which occur at the time of ovulation. Women are easily taught how to use this method, and an international group, World Organization of the Ovulation Method-Billings (WOOMB), is engaged in the dissemination of this information.[44]

A basic description of the ovulation method for discovering the time of fertility follows:

1) The menstrual period at the start of each cycle is considered to be fertile. The reason for viewing the time of menstruation as fertile is that if a woman should have an unusually or unexpectedly short cycle such that the ovulation process were to begin toward the end of menstruation, she would have no warning of this fact since the presence of the menstrual flow would make it difficult for her to examine her vaginal mucus. Thus, as a precaution, women are advised to regard the menstrual period as fertile.

2) After menstruation, there is a noticeable absence of any vaginal discharge of mucus, and a woman experiences a definite sensation of dryness. During these days of dryness, the woman is infertile.

3) At the conclusion of this period of dryness, cervical mucus begins to be discharged from the vagina. At first, this mucus is a kind of cloudy, sticky discharge, but it gradually becomes a clear, egg-white, stretchy and lubricative substance. The "peak" or main sign of ovulation is the last day on which this clear and stretchy mucus is present. The woman's period of fertility, however, is defined as starting with the first day of the cloudy mucus discharge and continuing up until three days past the peak symptom of ovulation.

4) Finally, from the fourth day after the peak symptom until the start of the next menstrual cycle, a period of infertility occurs.[45]

[44]See Elise B. Martinez, "The Ovulation Method of Family Planning," *America*, 144, 13 (April 4, 1981), 277-79.

[45]I am using a description based on that provided by Thomas W. Hilgers, M.D., "The Ovulation Method: Ten Years of Research," *The Linacre Quarterly*, 45, 4 (November, 1978), 383-87 at 384.

In addition to learning the meaning of the changes in vaginal secretions, a woman also comes to discover the pre-ovulatory, the ovulatory and the post-ovulatory differences in the positioning and firmness of the uterine cervix. A woman's familiarity with the signs of oncoming fertility provides her with sufficient information to know in advance when she is about to ovulate. It must be noted, of course, that no woman should attempt to use this method of natural family planning unless she has received instructions in it from fully trained personnel. The method is easy to learn, however, and most dioceses have ongoing programs of instruction which usually consist of two sessions scheduled about six weeks apart. Knowledge of this method is helpful, of course, not only to couples wanting to delay pregnancy, but also to those who may be having difficulty conceiving. For this latter group, knowing when ovulation is occurring enables them to focus or time their efforts at procreation.

Because the success or effectiveness of natural family planning depends so much on the strong motivation and cooperation of both husband and wife, it is generally expected that both spouses will attend the learning sessions. I personally would like to see instruction in natural family planning seriously encouraged as part of the pre-marriage preparation expected of engaged couples. If those who are engaged knew more about the method, and if the fiancées had several months during which to gain experience with the method, newly-wed couples might be more inclined and confident to use it. It might also be the case, of course, that given the earnest exuberance of young love, the earliest months or years of a marriage are the least appropriate or likely times for spouses to be strongly motivated or drawn toward the practice of natural family planning and periodic abstinence. Be that as it may, however, I am uncomfortable with the easy readiness sometimes demonstrated by couples to dismiss natural family planning as simply being outside the realms of possibility or consideration.

Proponents of the modern methods of natural family planning offer a number of positive considerations in their favor: (1) because couples must be well motivated and mutually cooperative in the use of such methods, the responsibility for family planning clearly comes to rest on both spouses, which is where it belongs; (2) as a result of their increased awareness of, and sensitivity to, their bodies and their natural biological rhythms, many women experience an enhanced sense of personal dignity; (on the other hand, it should be noted that some women claim that the need to examine their vaginal mucus or to probe for the location of their cervix is aesthetically repugnant to them; so long as that attitude persists, these women are not likely to practice the ovulation method very effectively); (3) the need for periodic abstinence in their lives may encourage spouses to explore and deepen the affective dimension of their sexual lives so that they come to find a true sexual and human fulfillment even when their expressions of love are intentionally directed away from any genital involvement that would encourage or provoke orgasm; (4) finally, the presence of periodic abstinence in their lives may help to ensure that spouses do not fall victims to a dull sexual routine; the joyful anticipation of renewing their genital relations after a period of abstinence may inspire married couples to more vibrant, exciting and creative acts of love.[46]

Reservations about natural family planning often center today not on the issue of its effectiveness, but rather on the fact that there are so many unpredictable occurrences in ordinary living that "limited abstinence" can tend to become "limitless." In other words, during the anticipated periods of infertility, circumstances may be such that spouses find sexual intercourse impossible, inconvenient or unthinkable. For example, one of the spouses may be ill, or the spouses' attention may be focused on sick children or on a crisis at work or home; or it might happen that one of the spouses is away on a business trip, or that out-of-town relatives are visiting and ordinary sleeping arrangements are disturbed.[47]

[46]Benedict M. Ashley, O.P. and Kevin D. O'Rourke, O.P. *Health Care Ethics: A Theological Analysis* (St. Louis: The Catholic Hospital Association, 1978), p. 278.

[47]See Mary Beth Benecke, "Rhythm: Ideal and Reality," *America*, 137,11 (October 15, 1977), 240-41.

The possibilities are many, but the effect is the same: a time of infertility passes, the fertile period begins and spouses must await the next "safe" period.

Some moralists insist that such practical considerations are not irrelevant to the moral decision-making process which spouses should undertake before choosing any method of family planning. Realizing, moreover, that the modern forms of natural family planning can be very effective for strongly motivated couples, these moralists are nonetheless not surprised that for many spouses such effectiveness is seen as exacting too high a price insofar as it creates an excessive strain upon their marital union and the harmony of family life. It would be terribly rash for anyone to conclude that any married couples who prefer some method of family planning other than that officially approved by the Church must therefore be undisciplined in love or unwilling to live under the shadow of the cross.

VI. Responsible Dissent from Authentic Fallible Teaching

Earlier in this book we considered the role which the magisterium plays in the area of moral teachings. We indicated that the Church clearly has a right and a duty to address any issue of personal or public morality; we noted, moreover, that the clear theological consensus today maintains that in the area of morality the magisterium has never exercised its official teaching authority in an infallible way by means of any solemn definition issued either by a pope or by the college of bishops gathered together in an ecumenical council. There is still some discussion, however, about whether or not the magisterium *could ever* teach infallibly in the area of morality. In his book, *Magisterium: Teaching Authority in the Catholic Church*, Francis A. Sullivan, S.J., claims that most Catholic theologians and moralists now judge that the particular norms of a morality based on the natural law are simply not proper matter for irreformable or infallible teaching; as Sullivan rightly observes, if this is the case, then we must rule out "not only the possibility of the infallible definition of such a norm, but also the claim that such a norm has ever been, or could be, infallibly taught by the ordinary universal magisterium."[48]

Sullivan's observation makes reference to the two ways in which the Church's ability to teach infallibly has in fact been exercised in the past concerning matters, not of morality, but of faith: the Church, in other words, can and does teach infallibly either in an extraordinary manner through papal definitions (*ex cathedra*) or through the solemn decrees of an ecumenical council; likewise the Church can teach infallibly in an ordinary manner through its universal magisterium. Sullivan describes the notion of the "ordinary universal magisterium" this way: it is "the concordant teaching of the whole Catholic episcopate together with the Pope, apart from the rather rare occasions when the bishops are gathered in an ecumenical council."[49] This ordinary universal magisterium can sometimes teach infallibly as is made clear in Vatican II's *Dogmatic Constitution on the Church, Lumen Gentium* (#25):

> Although the individual bishops do not enjoy the prerogative of infallibility, they can nevertheless proclaim Christ's doctrine infallibly. This is so, even when they are dispersed around the world, provided that while maintaining the bond of unity among themselves and with Peter's successor, and while teaching authentically on a matter of faith or morals, they concur in a single viewpoint as the one which must be held conclusively.

[48]Francis A. Sullivan, S.J., *Magisterium: Teaching Authority in the Catholic Church* (New York: Paulist Press, 1983), p. 152; see also pp. 227-28, n. 46 where Sullivan lists many of the theologians who deny that there can be an irreformable teaching regarding the particular norms of natural law morality. It should be noted that the Church clearly has authority to teach on issues pertaining to natural moral law such as contraception (*Gaudium et Spes*, #50, *Dignitatis Humanae*, #14). The question to which a negative response is given here, is whether the Church can teach infallibly on such issues. Sullivan (pp.140-41) points out that in its first draft, *Lumen Gentium* claimed infallibility in interpreting the natural law, but this claim does not appear in the final draft or in any other document of Vatican II.

[49]*Ibid.,* p. 122. Sullivan points out that this expression was first used by Pius IX in 1863 in his letter "Tuas Libenter"; it also appears in Vatican I (D-S 3011).

The fact that the Church can teach infallibly through its ordinary universal magisterium has come to play a part in the theological debate that arose after *Humanae Vitae's* reiteration of the ban on artificial contraceptives. In 1978, ten years after the encyclical, two theologians, John C. Ford, S.J., and Germain Grisez, wrote an extended article which argued that even though there had never been an infallible proclamation on the matter of contraception, nevertheless the Church's position on the issue should be regarded as having been proposed infallibly because all the requirements have been met that were outlined in *Lumen Gentium* as being necessary for teaching infallibly through the exercise of the Church's ordinary universal magisterium. As Ford and Grisez put it:

> . . . the conditions articulated by Vatican II for infallibility in the exercise of the ordinary magisterium of the bishops dispersed throughout the world have been met in the case of the Catholic Church's teaching on contraception. At least until 1962, the Catholic bishops in communion with one another and with the Pope agreed in and authoritatively proposed one judgment to be held definitively on the morality of contraception: acts of this kind are objectively, intrinsically and gravely evil. Since this teaching has been proposed infallibly, the controversy since 1963 takes nothing away from its objectively certain truth. It is not the received Catholic teaching on contraception which needs to be rethought. It is the assumption that this teaching could be abandoned as false which needs to be rethought.[50]

Despite the fact that the thesis proposed by Ford and Grisez received wide attention and serious consideration, most Catholic theologians have rejected it; thus they deny, as does Sullivan, that "according to the official Catholic doctrine on the infallibility of the ordinary universal magisterium, the sinful-

[50]John C. Ford, S.J., and Germain Grisez, "Contraception and the Infallibility of the Ordinary Magisterium," *Theological Studies,* 39,2 (June, 1978), 258-312 at 286. For a brief summary of the article's line of argumentation, see Russell Shaw, "Contraception, Infallibility and the Ordinary Magisterium," *Homiletic and Pastoral Review,* 78,10 (July, 1978), 9-19.

ness of artificial contraception has been infallibly taught."[51] Ford and Grisez openly admit that at the press conference at which *Humanae Vitae* was released, the Pope's spokesman, Monsignor Ferdinando Lambruschini, made it clear that the encyclical was not an *ex cathedra* pronouncement; Lambruschini went further, however, and seemed also to rule out the possibility that the letter "was a reaffirmation of a teaching already infallibly proposed."[52] In the context of this denial that the prohibition of artificial contraception had ever been infallibly defined (an extraordinary exercise of the magisterium's teaching authority by solemn decree of a pope or ecumenical council), it seems to me remarkable that no one thought to suggest that the traditional teaching was nonetheless infallible by virtue of the constant and repeated teaching of the ordinary universal magisterium.

[51]Sullivan, *op.cit.*, pp. 120, 226 n.3; chapter six (pp.119-52) of Sullivan's book deals in detail with the concept of the ordinary universal magisterium and with the Ford and Grisez thesis; see also Joseph A. Komonchak, "'Humanae Vitae' and Its Reception: Ecclesiological Reflections," *Theological Studies*, 39.2 (June, 1978), 221-257, especially 238-50. It should be noted that in support of their claim that the official Church doctrine has been taught infallibly by the ordinary universal magisterium, Ford and Grisez cite the view presented in the minority report of the special papal commission on contraception. Ford was a member of this commission and helped to draft the minority report which claimed that the traditional teaching was unchangeable: "The Church cannot substantially err in teaching a very serious doctrine of faith or morals through all the centuries—even through one century—a doctrine constantly and insistently proposed as one necessarily to be followed in order to attain salvation. The Church could not substantially err through so many centuries—even through one century—in imposing very heavy burdens under grave obligation in the name of Jesus Christ as it would have erred if Jesus Christ does not in fact impose these burdens. The Catholic Church could not in the name of Jesus Christ offer to the vast multitude of the faithful. . . for so many centuries an occasion of formal sin and spiritual ruin on account of a false doctrine promulgated in the name of Jesus Christ. If the Church could err as atrociously as this, the authority of the ordinary magisterium in moral matters would be stultified; and the faithful henceforth could have no confidence in moral teaching handed down by the magisterium, especially in sexual matters" (quoted in Ford and Grisez, *art. cit.*, 302-03). In response to this line of reasoning, Sullivan notes (pp. 141-42) that God could permit such an evil situation to occur just as he has permitted the spiritual harm to the faithful that is caused by the scandalous conduct of church leaders; so, also, has God permitted the harm brought on by the Great Schism between the Western and Eastern Churches, and the later "rending of Christendom at the time of the Reformation"—a point made by Garth L. Hallett, S.J., "Contraception and Prescriptive Infallibility," *Theological Studies*, 43,4 (December, 1982), 629-50 at 649.

[52]Ford and Grisez *art.cit.*, 260-61 and n.8.

Even in the many pastoral letters which were prepared by the various national conferences of Catholic bishops to guide Catholics throughout the world in their response to *Humanae Vitae*, nowhere was it suggested that the traditional teaching on contraception had been proposed infallibly by the ordinary universal magisterium of the Church. Ford and Grisez argue that no national hierarchy took any position on this question; rather, it was an issue to which the bishops "simply did not address themselves."[53] But the matter cannot be dismissed so cavalierly. In the atmosphere of theological debate and pastoral turmoil that followed *Humanae Vitae*, the bishops had every opportunity to provide guidance. That they never proposed the view that the ban on artificial contraception had been infallibly taught without being solemnly defined requires explanation. Were they simply too cautious or afraid to take this stance? Were they ignorant of the fact that the teaching could be interpreted in this manner? Such moral hesitance or ignorance would seem to reflect a level of irresponsibility that is simply unworthy of the hierarchy. I suggest, therefore, that the reason why the bishops never presented the teaching on contraception as infallible by virtue of the Church's ordinary universal magisterium, is simply because they were well aware that such is not the case. The ban on contraceptives belongs rather to the category of authentic (or authoritative) fallible Church teachings; this means, as we saw earlier in this book, that the possibility of responsible dissent exists here, as it does whenever we are confronted with noninfallible teachings.

Something further should be said about the many statements by national hierarchies which were issued in response to *Humanae Vitae*. Joseph Komonchak makes reference to the fact that there were three types of hierarchical responses: "clear acceptance" of the document was seen in twenty-five statements originating from eighteen countries; sixteen episcopal statements from thirteen coun-

[53]*Ibid.,* 311; also see Komonchak, *art.cit.,*249-50, n.87.

tries revealed an attitude of "clear mitigation" of the encyclical's teaching, and an "uncertain" stance was adopted in eleven statements coming from ten countries.[54]

With reference to these three types of responses, I find it difficult to classify the American bishops' pastoral letter, *Human Life in Our Day*, which appeared in November, 1968. In a section of their letter entitled "The Encyclical and Conscience," the bishops' thinking reflects, I think, some unresolved tensions and wants to move in opposite directions. The bishops first affirm: "*Humanae Vitae* does not discuss the question of the good faith of those who make practical decisions in conscience against what the Church considers a divine law and will of God. The encyclical does not undertake to judge the consciences of individuals but to set forth the authentic teaching of the Church which Catholics believe interprets the divine law to which conscience should be conformed." Then the bishops acknowledge that spouses may face "agonizing crises of conscience" because of "conflicting duties" which make it difficult for them "to harmonize the sexual expression of conjugal love with respect for the life-giving power of sexual union and the demands of responsible parenthood." These conflicting duties notwithstanding, married couples are told "that however [much] circumstances may reduce moral guilt, no one following the teaching of the Church can deny the objective evil of artificial contraception itself." Finally, spouses who have used artificial contraceptives are told "never to lose heart but to continue to take full advantage of the strength which comes from the Sacrament of Penance and the grace, healing, and peace in the Eucharist."[55]

---

[54]Komonchak, *art.cit.*, 249-50 in n.87; the author there refers to a study by Joseph A. Selling, *The Reaction to "Humanae Vitae", A Study in Special and Fundamental Theology* (Unpublished doctoral dissertation, Katholieke Universitei te Leuven, Faculty of Theology, 1977), pp. 132-37.

[55]*Human Life in Our Day,* U.S.C.C., November 15, 1968, pp.15-16.

Briefly, let me indicate the difficulties I see with the position articulated by the American bishops. To begin with, the bishops support *Humanae Vitae's* view that the use of contraceptives is an objective *moral* wrong, and can never be a *premoral* evil, as many theologians now maintain. Next, the bishops are inclined to recognize the traditional distinction that acknowledges the difference between sinning, and sinlessly doing something that the Church regards as an objective moral wrong. But then they seem to suggest that any use of artificial contraceptives (an objective moral wrong in their eyes) must also always involve some degree of subjective moral culpability or guilt (sin) on the part of spouses. The bishops, in other words, do not affirm the possibility of spouses deciding in good conscience, even if erroneous, that it is sometimes moral for them to use contraceptives. If the bishops do so recognize the possibility of contraceptives being used without sin, why do they imply that spouses are always bound to confess the matter? The clear inference, both of the American bishops and of *Humanae Vitae* itself (#25), is that no matter what the circumstances, spouses sin to some degree in using contraceptives. Given this inference, it would seem that both the encyclical and the American bishops are indeed "judging the consciences of individuals." Catholics simply are not told in any clear or explicit way that they could ever in good conscience decide to use contraceptives in such a responsible or honest way that no sin is involved and thus there is no need for them to confess this matter, or to seek sacramental absolution for any moral wrong-doing on their part.

As I read the pastoral letter of the American bishops, I see no clear presentation of the fact that spouses may responsibly, and without guilt, disagree with *Humanae Vitae* and make use of artificial contraceptives. Later in their statement, in a context different from the one we have been looking at, the bishops do, however, speak in general terms of the possibility of theological dissent: "The expression of theological dissent from the magisterium is in order only if the reasons are serious and well-founded, if the manner of dissent does not question or impugn the teaching authority of the Church and is such as not to give scandal."[56]

In contrast to the American bishops, a number of other national conferences of Catholic bishops (the bishops, for example, of Holland, France, Canada, Scandinavia, Austria, Belgium and South Africa) wrote letters which clearly advised Catholic spouses of their rights in conscience and of the possibility for legitimate moral disagreement with the teaching of *Humanae Vitae*. We will close this discussion with a sampling of some of the bishops' remarks:

> *1. The Canadian Bishops:*
> It is a fact that a certain number of Catholics...find it either extremely difficult or even impossible to make their own all elements of this doctrine....
> . . . .
> Since they are not denying any point of divine and Catholic faith nor rejecting the teaching authority of the Church, these Catholics should not be considered, or consider themselves, shut off from the body of the faithful. But they should remember that their good faith will be dependent on a sincere self-examination to determine the true motives and grounds for such suspension of assent and on continued effort to understand and deepen their knowledge of the teaching of the Church.
> *2. The Scandinavian Bishops:*
> ...it is self-evident that no one should doubt the content of the encyclical without entering into its way of thinking and intention thoroughly, honestly and with consciousness of his responsibility before God.
> However, if someone, from weighty and well-considered reasons, cannot become convinced by the argumentation of the encyclical, it has always been conceded that he is allowed to have a different view from that presented in a noninfallible statement of the Church. No one should be considered a bad Catholic because he is of such a dissenting opinion.

[56] *Ibid.*, p.18.

Everyone who, after conscientious consideration, believes himself entitled not to accept this teaching and considers himself not bound to obey it in practice, must be responsible before God for his attitude and way of acting.[57]

3. The South African Bishops:

Situations will, no doubt, arise in which another pregnancy is unacceptable for reasons such as health or difficult domestic conditions, and where a regime of continence would threaten family peace, marital fidelity or the future of the marriage itself. Here, in common with many other hierarchies, we would say that it is best for the parents to decide what in their given circumstances is the best or only practical way of serving the welfare of the whole family. In this conflict of duties, their responsible decision, though falling short of the ideal, will be subjectively defensible since the aim is not the selfish exclusion of pregnancy but the promotion of the common good of the family.[58]

VII. Conjugal Sexuality: Some Special Questions

Before concluding this chapter, I want to address briefly two other issues pertaining to conjugal sexuality. It happens at times that married couples raise questions about the moral permissibility of such alternate forms of genital contact as oral sexual intercourse and anal intercourse. According to the Church's traditional teaching, it is neither unnatural, perverted nor immoral for couples to seek sexual stimulation and arousal by means of oral or anal intercourse, but such activity should not be continued to the point of orgasm. Thus, assuming both partners desire, and agree to, these expressions of love, oral and anal sex are morally legitimate forms of foreplay serving as

---

[57]These two excerpts, as well as others from the Dutch, French, Austrian and Belgian Bishops' Letters, appear in John Giles Milhaven, *Toward a New Catholic Morality* (Garden City, N.Y.: Doubleday Image, 1970), pp.176-92, especially pp.178-81.

[58]This excerpt is quoted in Kevin T. Kelly, *Divorce and Second Marriage* (New York: The Seabury Press, 1983), p.111. The full text of the South African Bishops' Letter appears in *The Tablet* (March 3, 1974).

preludes to vaginal intercourse; sexual climax, however, is to occur only after vaginal penetration.[59]

For spouses who are comfortable with the types of foreplay mentioned above, other possible scenarios present themselves. In the event that a woman is multi-orgasmic and thus would not be inclined to lose interest in the love-making episode should she achieve sexual climax prior to coitus, there would not seem to be cause for great moral alarm were this to occur, say, for example, during an episode of oral sex. Moreover, in situations where these same spouses have responsibly, honestly and prayerfully decided that they must employ some form of contraception, they find themselves awaiting a good explanation for why they might not, on occasion, justifiably achieve sexual fulfillment by means of oral or anal sex that is turned to in place of contraceptive vaginal intercourse.

On another matter of marital sexuality, some wives may need reassurance. Should it happen that she fails to achieve sexual fulfillment in the act of sexual intercourse, a woman is morally permitted, according to the Church's teaching, to seek and achieve orgasm by other means. The traditional moral view is articulated as follows: "Although a woman is not obliged to do so, she may immediately after her husband's ejaculation in the vagina or immediately after his withdrawal upon ejaculation obtain her own complete satisfaction through her own or her spouse's efforts performed by means of touches or in some other manner."[60]

By way of commentary on this situation, I would suggest that a wife's regular or habitual failure to achieve a desired orgasm through sexual intercourse would seem to highlight the need for better, more open and honest communication between spouses concerning their sexual expressions of love. Given a woman's generally slower response to sexual stimulation, it may be necessary for a husband to prolong the period of foreplay out of

[59]Keane, *op.cit.,* pp.117-18.

[60]Nicholas Halligan, O.P., *The Ministry of the Celebration of the Sacraments.* Vol 3. *Sacraments of Community Renewal: Holy Orders and Matrimony* (New York: Alba House, 1974), p. 199; see also Joseph and Lois Bird, *The Freedom of Sexual Love* (Garden City, N.Y.: Doubleday Image, 1967), pp. 177-78.

concern for his wife and her sexual fulfillment. At the same time, a wife should freely tell her husband what actions please her, and she should better inform him as to whether or not she is ready for the initiation of vaginal intercourse.

VIII. Conclusion

This chapter has been concerned with a number of specific moral issues related to conjugal sexuality. In the midst of such technical discussion it would be unfortunate and unwise for us to forget that it is marital love which both brings spouses together in the intimacies of genital expression and draws them beyond themselves into a generous openness to children. Like all true love, marital love is sensitive to its responsibilities, and so at times it is moved to express its most private and personal feelings while its valued power to create a new life is held in abeyance. At such times as these, the intimacies of conjugal love remain an expression of the spouses' ongoing desire to pledge their permanent and mutual fidelity. And then there are other times when marital love's sense of responsibility impels and inspires a husband and wife to refrain from the embrace of genital sex. But whether spouses at times withdraw from procreation or whether they remain apart from the union of genital sex, what continues to bind them together is the mutual commitment of love, and it is only through this commitment that a man and woman can come to fulfill all the obligations of marriage.

VII

Morality and Homosexual Expressions of Love

I. Introduction

It is not unusual for discussions of homosexuality to be initiated in an atmosphere that is uncomfortably tense. This is largely due to the fact that many of us have misconceptions about, and stereotypical images of, homosexually oriented men and women and their sexual behavior which make us suspicious of them or fill us, at least, with a sense of disdain; also, we tend to reject out-of-hand what we do not understand, and we often wish to distance ourselves from that which causes us fear or anxiety. It is probably true, moreover, that the ravages of AIDS (acquired immune deficiency syndrome), which are being experienced in most instances, at least in America, by homosexual men, are likely to confirm and strengthen any predisposition we may have either to judge homosexuals harshly or to discriminate against them.

If the situation is at all as I have described it above, I suggest that before offering a moral evaluation of the genital behavior of homosexual men and women, we should first try to "clear the air" by identifying any overt or hidden prejudices which may be operating in our thinking about this issue. With this goal in mind, our discussion will focus on the following points: (1) an explanation for why there are so many myths and stereotypes regarding homosexuals; (2) a presentation of some definitions and distinctions needed for entering into a moral analysis of homosexual behavior; (3) a review of some significant psychological data; (4) an investigation into, and assessment of, the arguments against the moral acceptability of homosexual behavior; (5) a sampling of present-day moral evaluations of same-sex genital activity; and (6) some observations and conclusions regarding pastoral advice to homosexually oriented men and women.

II. Why the Myths and Stereotypes?

"The 'problem' of homosexuality is primarily one of *straight* liberation—liberation from myths, stereotypical thinking and the consequent forms of discrimination that, in turn, engender defensive postures among gays."[1] This statement may perhaps strike us as exaggerated, and yet it suggests a kernel of truth which is hard, unrelenting and unavoidable: if the amount of homophobia or fear of homosexuality which presently characterizes so much of heterosexual society is ever going to be reduced, the myths, the stereotypes, and the misunderstandings which heterosexuals harbor and nurture regarding homosexuals must first be exposed, challenged and discarded. But before trying to unmask the myths that surround homosexuality, we might rather ask how the myths and misunderstandings have come to gain such prominence in the first place. Perhaps a more probing version of this question has been posed by James Harrison, a minister and clinical psychologist practicing in New York: "Considering that one in twenty persons around us is homosexual, why is it that people know so little about homosexuality and about homosexual people—and that so much of what they think they know is false?"[2]

The reason, says Harrison, for both our ignorance and our misconceptions regarding homosexuality is society's intolerance; he explains that, due in large part to the discrimination and ridicule to which they know they would be subjected, many homosexuals try to deny or hide their sexual orientation. If they wish to live peacefully and without risk to their civil rights, homosexuals often feel required to maintain a kind of "invis-

[1]Richard Woods, *Another Kind of Love* (Garden City, N.Y.: Doubleday Image, 1978), p. 60.

[2]James Harrison, "The Dynamics of Sexual Anxiety," *Christianity and Crisis,* 37 (1977), 136-40 at 137.

ible" existence, but it is largely because of this invisibility that stereotypical characterizations of homosexuals develop and persist. Thus, for example, when society thinks of homosexuals at all, it is usually in terms of those individuals who, either in defiance of society or in self-defense or both, have "come out of the closet" and are making much of their sexual orientation by participating in parades and public demonstrations.

What we do not realize, however, and what Harrison wishes to call to our attention, is simply this fact: "gay people are our co-workers whom we respect, our relatives whom we love. They are our friends, parents, children, siblings, uncles and aunts. To the extent that we are unaware of this, we are ourselves victims of the... [discrimination] which causes gay people to be silent."[3] And precisely to the extent that our homosexual friends, relatives and acquaintances find it necessary and prudent to remain unidentified and thus "invisible," many heterosexuals who would choke on such derogatory expressions as "nigger," "wop" and "hebe," feel quite justified in unhesitatingly referring to homosexuals as "fags," "perverts," or "queers," all of whom, moreover, are thought of as promiscuous bed-hoppers and are perceived as "drag queens," "limp-wristed flits," or "dykes."

Distorted, misguided and unfair as these designations and categorizations are, they nonetheless often go unchallenged even by more discerning and sensitive people simply because they themselves fear that any defense of homosexuals will arouse suspicions about their own sexual orientation. In this kind of atmosphere, the myths about homosexuals are self-perpetuating and the stereotypical descriptions go unchecked; as a result, great numbers of heterosexuals simply remain oblivious to the real situation as described by Morton Kelsey: "While a small proportion of homosexuals do have bodily characteristics of the opposite sex, and some occasionally affect the mannerisms or clothes of the opposite sex, the great majority have no outer physical characteristics that identify them in their sexual predilections. Indeed, many feminine-appearing men are exclusively and enthusiastically heterosexual. The great majority of homosexuals, the best adjusted,

[3]*Ibid.,* 138.

pass through society with none of the heterosexuals knowing that they are different."[4]

We have suggested so far that a great many homosexuals feel pressured into remaining invisible and that this very invisibility allows the myths and stereotypes about homosexuals to flourish since, in the usual course of everyday living, people now have difficulty finding much evidence to counter those very same stereotypical portrayals of gays as irresponsible, sick or dangerous, which to a great extent explain society's homophobia. Of course, this problem of stereotyping affects the attitudes, not only of heterosexuals, but of homosexuals as well, since they themselves often absorb, internalize, and accept as true, the negative stereotyping before they fully realize their own homosexuality. Thus, quite simply, much of the personal struggle experienced by homosexuals arises from the fact that "they have to deal with the stereotype-induced negative feelings about themselves before they can take even the first steps toward self-acceptance."[5] By the time people with a homosexual orientation do indeed come to realize this fact, they have also most usually been made aware of their "difference" from the majority of people and, as pointed out by the Catholic bishops of England and Wales, this self-perception takes its toll upon them:

> [The] consciousness of being "different," of belonging to a minority, leaves the homosexual person suffering from the same problems as all minority groups with the added factor that their "difference" is secret. This leads to a deeper alienation. In a society that can see them as objects of cruel jokes and contempt, homosexuals commonly suffer from lack of self-esteem and a loneliness that heterosexuals find difficult, if not impossible, to comprehend. In ordinary mixed society, homosexuals feel like strangers.... Many homosexuals are reserved and even withdrawn, not anxious to draw attention to their difficulties.[6]

[4]Morton T. Kelsey, *Prophetic Ministry. The Psychology and Spirituality of Spiritual Care* (New York: Crossroad Publ. Co., 1982), p. 127.

[5]Darrell Sifford, "Society's Fears of Homosexuals," *The Philadelphia Inquirer* (March 8, 1984), p. K1.

[6]In 1981, the Catholic Social Welfare Commission, a working committee of the Catholic bishops of England and Wales, prepared a document entitled *An Introduction*

It seems, then, that society is trapped in a vicious circle: its largely intolerant reaction to homosexuality induces many homosexuals to remain "invisible," and this invisibility, in turn, permits the stereotypical characterizations of homosexuals both to dominate our awareness and to cloud our judgments to such an extent that society's fear of homosexuality is reinforced and its discriminatory attitude and behavior are maintained. I do not suppose that there is any one way to escape this circle of myths, fears and suspicions, but certainly any breakthrough would seem to require at least two things: on the one hand, the courage of more homosexuals who will let it be known that they are in no way represented by the stereotypes of "the gay life," and on the other, the sincere effort of more heterosexuals to restrain their emotional reactions to the stereotypical portrayals of homosexual lifestyles long enough to try honestly to understand that homosexuals manifest no less diversity and no more predictability in the conduct of their sexual lives than do heterosexuals. In an attempt to unravel some of the complexities that stand in the way of an adequate understanding of homosexuality, the next section of this chapter will provide some needed definitions and distinctions.

III. Some Definitions and Distinctions

It is best to begin by reviewing some of the definitions used in describing what it means to be a homosexual:

> 1) homosexuals are "those individuals who more or less chronically feel an urgent sexual desire towards, and a sexual responsiveness to, members of their own sex, and who seek gratification of this desire predominantly with members of their own sex."[7]
>
> 2) a homosexual is someone "who is motivated,

---

to the Pastoral Care of Homosexual People. As an extremely fine example of episcopal teaching, it has been made available by New Ways Ministry, 4012 29th Street, Mt. Rainier, Md. 20712. The quote here is from pp. 10-11.

[7]Isidor Rubin, "Homosexuality," *SIECUS,* Discussion Guide, No. 2 (New York: 1965), p. 1.

in adult life, by a definite preferential erotic attraction to members of the same sex and who usually (but not necessarily) engages in overt sexual relations with them."[8]

3) a homosexual is an adult whose "primary affectional and genital orientation is toward the same sex."[9]

4) homosexuals are persons "who feel comfortable and affirmed when intimate with other members of the same sex, while, with the other sex, they feel weak, resentful, scared, or simply indifferent or less comfortable when genital intimacy is possible or occurs."[10]

With these definitions in mind, it seems fair to say that a homosexual is an adult person who basically remains erotically indifferent to the physical attractiveness of the opposite sex and thus is consistently and primarily inclined to seek and find his or her sexual satisfaction and/or emotional fulfillment and human happiness in relationships with members of the same sex.

Several observations immediately suggest themselves in light of this description of a homosexual. To begin with, having isolated or periodic homosexual experiences does not mean someone is a homosexual; adolescents, especially, may experience sexual attraction to members of the same sex and may occasionally engage in overt sexual activity with partners of the same sex, but these experiences in themselves are most often simply reflections of sexual curiosity and manifestations of one of the phases of psycho-sexual development; as such, they do not indicate that these adolescents are or will become homosexuals for life. At the same time, of course, there are people who never have explicit sexual or genital contact with members of their own sex and yet who are truly homosexual in that their predominant erotic attraction is toward members of the same

[8]Judd Marmon (ed.) *Sexual Inversion* (New York: Basic Books, 1965), p. 4.

[9]James B. Nelson, *Embodiment: An Approach to Sexuality and Christian Theology* (Minneapolis: Augsburg, 1979), p. 201.

[10]William F. Kraft, "Homosexuality and Religious Life," *Review for Religious,* 40 (1981), p. 371.

sex with whom alone they are able to find affectional fulfillment.[11]

In light of these observations, two additional remarks are pertinent: (1) we must acknowledge the distinction which exists between a person's homosexual orientation and any explicit sexual activity which may or may not result from the physical attraction which that person experiences for members of the same sex; (2) since not all explicit homosexual activity reflects a true homosexual orientation, we must also recognize the existence of what may be referred to as the phenomenon of pseudo-homosexuality. I would like now to expand on each of these remarks.

Regarding the distinction between a person's sexual orientation and his or her sexual activity, it should first of all be noted that while specific sexual actions arise, for the most part, from conscious choices or decisions, this is not true of one's sexual orientation. People, in short, do not choose their sexual orientation; nobody makes up his or her mind to become or to be a homosexual or a heterosexual; homosexuals, therefore, no more make a conscious choice to be physically or sexually attracted to members of the same sex than heterosexuals consciously choose to be erotically attracted to members of the opposite sex. Rather, at some point in their development, homosexuals "discover" that they are sexually drawn to members of the same sex in just the same way that heterosexuals "discover" that members of the opposite sex are physically attractive to them.

One additional point should be mentioned about a person's discovery of his or her homosexual orientation: in the face both

[11]It is not easy to estimate what percentage of the population is homosexually oriented, but Kinsey's 1948 and 1953 statistics have, in general, borne the test of time. According to him, 4% of males and 2-3% of females are exclusively homosexual throughout their lives; 18% of males are more homosexually oriented rather than heterosexually oriented after adolescence, while 37% of males and 13% of females have "at least one overt homosexual experience to the point of orgasm after puberty." See A. Kinsey *et al., Sexual Behavior in the Human Male* (Phila: Saunders, 1948), pp. 636-41 and *Sexual Behavior in the Human Female* (Phila: Saunders, 1953), pp. 468-72, where the authors suggest that people are located at various positions along a sliding seven-point scale ranging from exclusively heterosexual (zero) to exclusively homosexual (six). Individuals can be found with a basic heterosexual orientation but with some same-sex attraction, with a bi-sexual attraction, or with a fundamental homosexual orientation accompanied by some inclination toward the opposite sex.

of society's generally phobic reaction to homosexuality and of the strong cultural pressures which push toward heterosexuality, it seems fair to say "that only those whose orientation is firmly homosexual are likely to accept the embarrassment, shame and humiliation involved in deviance from the societal norm."[12] Thus, a person's own discovery of his or her homosexual orientation is not about to be accepted easily or lightly and without some sense of confusion as to how one reached the point of his or her present disposition.

Of course, in light of the fact that a person's sexual orientation is not the result of any conscious decision-making process on his or her part, there is absolutely no justification for the discrimination to which homosexuals are often subjected solely because of their sexual orientation. The American Catholic bishops have, in fact, insisted on this point: "Some persons find themselves through no fault of their own to have a homosexual orientation. Homosexuals, like everyone else, should not suffer from prejudice against their basic human rights. They have a right to respect, friendship and justice. They should have an active role in the Christian community."[13] It should be stressed, furthermore, that a person's sexual orientation, whether it be heterosexual or homosexual, is in itself not a matter for moral analysis or evaluation; thus a person who is heterosexually oriented is not, by virtue of this fact alone, any more moral than a homosexually oriented person. It simply makes no more sense to ask whether it is immoral to be homosexually oriented than it does to ask whether it is moral to be heterosexually oriented.[14] Moral questions do arise, however, and are appropriate, when people, be they heterosexual or

[12]Richard Hettlinger, *Sex Isn't That Simple. The New Sexuality on Campus* (New York: Seabury Press, 1974), p. 142.

[13]See *To Live in Christ Jesus,* A Pastoral Reflection on the Moral Life by the National Conference of Catholic Bishops (Wash. D.C.: USCC, 1976), p. 19.

[14]The distinction between homosexual acts and the homosexual orientation has been made repeatedly in statements by members of the Catholic hierarchy. See *Homosexuality and the Magisterium. Documents from the Vatican and the U.S. Bishops, 1975-1985,* edited by John Gallagher (Mt. Rainier, Md.: New Ways Ministry, 1986). It must be noted, however, that in October, 1986, the Sacred Congregation for the Doctrine of the Faith, with the approval of Pope John Paul II, issued a statement on homosexuality maintaining that although the homosexual orientation itself is not sinful, nevertheless, it is "ordered toward an intrinsic moral evil, and thus the inclination itself must be seen as an objective disorder" and as "essentially self-indulgent."

homosexual, face real choices in deciding whether or not, and under what circumstances, they should express their sexual orientation in specific genital activity.

Since people do indeed make choices about engaging in sexual activity, and since some people who are basically heterosexually oriented do at times decide to become sexually active with members of their own sex, something further must be said about the phenomenon of pseudo-homosexuality. This term is used to indicate the fact that when some people, whose basic sexual orientation is heterosexual, are deprived of sexual contact with members of the opposite sex, they at times are drawn to seek sexual release through contact with members of the same sex. This happens, for example, among prisoners and military personnel who are isolated from members of the opposite sex for long periods of time. As mentioned earlier, sexual activity with members of one's own sex can also occur among young adolescents who spend most of their time with same-sex peers; because they still feel most comfortable and safe with one another, they sometimes are led to satisfy their sexual curiosity by means of sexual activity that involves only members of the same sex.

But in all or nearly all of these instances, the truth remains that whatever physical attraction there is toward members of the same sex, and however this attraction translates into explicit sexual activity with same-sex partners, these people have or will develop a more fundamental desire for relating sexually to members of the opposite sex. Their sexual interest in members of the same sex is only temporary or transitory and thus reflects a form of pseudo-homosexuality. There are other people, however, whose homosexual orientation is experienced in a quite different manner; for reasons that are, as we shall see, unclear, many and varied, these are the people who come to discover that their physical attraction to members of the same sex is so deeply rooted in them, and is so much a permanent and consistent element of their existence, that it forms an essential part of their very nature. These are the people who are truly homosexually oriented.[15]

[15]The American bishops acknowledged the distinction between "temporary" and "permanent" homosexuals in their 1973 statement, *Principles to Guide Confessors in Questions of Homosexuality,* (Wash. D.C.: USCC, 1973), pp. 9-11. So also did the

Having acknowledged the difference existing not only between sexual orientation and sexual activity, but also between pseudo-homosexuality and homosexuality which is a constitutive or integral dimension of one's being, we are now in a position to review some of the latest psychological reflections on the true homosexual orientation.

IV. Sorting Psychology's Data

Before going any further in this discussion, however, we should at least advert to a suggestion made recently that it is probably best not to talk simply of "homosexuality," for this is only an abstraction which exists in the mind, while in the real world, there are only individual homosexuals who are "concrete human beings with whom we interact, knowingly or not, every day."[16] In line with this suggestion, it makes sense to say that much good might result were we also to use the word "homosexual" less often as a noun and to employ it instead more often as an adjective; this point has, in fact, been made by Gabriel Moran who maintains that using the word "homosexual" as a noun only serves to equate people with, or reduce them to, their sexual orientation, whereas, of course, people are so much more than this.[17]

We rarely, if ever, think of identifying someone as a "heterosexual," probably because we realize how precious little this term reveals about anybody. And yet, upon hearing that someone is a "homosexual" or a "lesbian," we too often think that we have heard the most significant thing that can be said

1975 *Declaration on Certain Questions Concerning Sexual Ethics* put out by the Sacred Congregation for the Doctrine of the Faith, #8.

[16]Michael D. Guinan, "Homosexuals: A Christian Pastoral Response Now," in Robert Nugent (ed.), *A Challenge to Love. Gay and Lesbian Catholics in the Church* (New York: Crossroad Publ. Co., 1983), pp. 67-77 at 68.

[17]Gabriel Moran, "Education: Sexual and Religious," in Nugent (ed.), *op. cit.,* pp. 159-173 at 170. It might be noted that in an extremely sensitive paper, "Ministry and Homosexuality in the Archdiocese of San Francisco," the San Francisco Senate of priests always uses the word "homosexual" as an adjective. The pastoral plan adopted by this priests' senate in 1983 reflects, to a large extent, the thinking of the Catholic bishops of England and Wales and has the approval of the Archbishop of San Francisco, John R.Quinn. The paper may be found in *Homosexuality and the Magisterium,* pp. 55-78.

about that individual, with the result that we neither want nor need to know anything more about the person before writing him or her off, or allowing that individual to be made the object of ridicule, scorn, injustice and even violence. This, of course, is a most deplorable situation, reflecting a distorted perception of reality, for people cannot and should not be equated with, or reduced to, either their sexual orientation or any specific form of sexual activity. It might even be argued, in fact, that to identify a person simply in terms of sexual orientation is as superficial as identifying a person merely as a sex object. Any honest attempt, then, to appreciate another human being must begin by realizing the complex totality which every individual is. Both this last point and others mentioned in this paragraph have been stressed by the Washington State Catholic Conference in its 1983 letter on ministry to homosexual men and women:

> ...the Church, which considers a person as a whole, can find much good to be praised and affirmed in any homosexual person. Although one's sexuality affects to some extent all that one is and does, just as does any basic quality, homosexual orientation and homosexual acting out [i.e., homogenital activity or genital activity with a person of the same sex] constitute but one aspect, and not the most important aspect, of concrete gay and lesbian persons. Accordingly, no matter what one thinks about their homosexuality, one is never justified in labeling such persons as homosexual and then condemning them under that category. No person is merely a category. He or she is composed of many good attributes that outstrip any single category.[18]

Whether we refer to someone as a "homosexual" or as "an individual with a homosexual orientation," the truth to be kept in mind is simply that every person who is attracted to members of the same sex is unique, no less than is every person who is attracted to members of the opposite sex. It is important, as well, to remember that the great majority of homosexual men and women are children of heterosexual parents, and that most

---

[18]See "The Prejudice Against Homosexuals and the Ministry of the Church," in *Homosexuality and the Magisterium*, pp. 46-54 at 47.

of them have brothers and sisters who are heterosexual. Together, these two facts would seem to put the lie to any theory which claims that homosexuality itself is a kind of sickness that is dangerous to others by reason of "contagion"; in other words, heterosexuals do not become homosexuals merely by associating with people who are homosexually oriented; and neither do homosexuals become heterosexuals—however great the pressure to do so—simply by relating to people who are heterosexually oriented.

All that we have seen up to this point serves to suggest that a person's sexual orientation—whether heterosexual or homosexual—is a complex human and psychological reality which admits of no easy explanation. Indeed, it should be noted that when any attempt is made to explain the homosexual orientation, the question is often raised as to why we are so intent upon discovering the causes of homosexuality when no comparable effort is made to uncover the causes of heterosexuality. Most probably, this question is being used to articulate the lingering suspicion and fear that any investigation into homosexuality is undertaken not simply in acknowledgment of homosexuality as a departure from what is the statistically normal form of sexual orientation, but rather out of the conviction that homosexuality represents an emotional or psychological abnormality.

Obviously, as we struggle to grow in our understanding of the homosexual orientation, we need to be aware not only of the acute sensitivities of many members of the homosexual community, but also of the fact that, for a long time, much of the available psychological data regarding homosexuality presented a rather slanted or distorted view of homosexuals, in that the great mass of information had been gathered from homosexual individuals who were seeking one or another form of therapy because they either regarded themselves as sick, or were dissatisfied and unhappy with their situation, and/or felt that they needed help in order to function as responsible members of society. None of these people, however, could or did speak for the great percentage of homosexual individuals who are well-adjusted and experience neither the need nor the desire for therapeutic assistance.

IS HOMOSEXUALITY A MENTAL DISORDER?

Remaining mindful of the preceding cautionary observations, what may be said of homosexuality as a psychological reality? To begin with, Freud did not view the homosexual orientation as a neurotic illness. In 1935, he wrote: "Homosexuality is assuredly no advantage, but it is nothing to be ashamed of, no vice, no degradation, it cannot be classified as an illness; we consider it to be a variation of the sexual function produced by a certain arrest of sexual development."[19] Precisely to the extent that homosexuality reflects some interference with, or interruption and frustration of, the normal process of psycho-sexual development toward heterosexuality, it came to be regarded as a form of sexual inadequacy. We should quickly point out, however, that to say that a person has been prevented from attaining the fullest degree of sexual development is a far different thing from saying that he or she is emotionally sick or psychologically disturbed. As human beings, all of us are confronted with our various inadequacies, but these "do not necessarily or usually prevent us from living reasonably happy, socially constructive lives, and many homosexuals are as integrated and mature as any heterosexuals."[20]

This last point has been substantiated by the outstanding work of Dr. Evelyn Hooker who has conducted a number of comparative studies of homosexuals and heterosexuals. Hooker administered a series of personality tests—designed to recognize various psychotic and neurotic traits—to sample groups of male heterosexuals and homosexuals who were not in therapy and who were leading "relatively stable" and "occupationally successful" lives; clinical psychologists were then asked to analyze and evaluate the test results "blindly," that is, without knowing in advance which of the research-subjects were homosexually oriented and which were heterosexually oriented. On the basis of their analysis, the psychologists were unable to determine the sexual orientation of the individual subjects, nor could they find "evidence of any demonstrable pathology"

---

[19]"Letter to an American Mother," in Hendrick Ruiteenbeek (ed.), *The Problem of Homosexuality in Modern Society* (New York: Dutton, 1963), pp. 1-2.

[20]Hettlinger, *op. cit.,* p. 148.

among those later identified as being homosexually oriented.[21]

In light of such data, one writer has concluded that, whatever the "neurotic" traits typically ascribed to homosexual individuals, these traits "are essentially the same for members of any oppressed minority groups, and in cultures where homosexual behavior has been fully accepted such traits do not discernibly appear."[22] Indeed, recognition of the oppression and prejudice to which homosexuals are subjected has led Richard Hettlinger to observe: "The social, religious and personal opprobrium under which homosexuals have suffered for so long may be a major factor in causing their emotional problems, not the homosexuality itself." Furthermore, "it is interesting," continues Hettlinger, "that lesbians, who have always been less persecuted for their sexual behavior than male homosexuals, present themselves much less frequently for psychiatric treatment."[23]

It should be noted, finally, that in 1974, the American Psychiatric Association (APA) voted to remove "homosexuality" from its list of "mental disorders" or "sexual deviations." In its statement, the Association commented that "homosexuality *per se* implies no impairment in judgment, stability, reliability, or general social or vocational capabilities." The APA went on to distinguish homosexuality, "which by itself does not necessarily constitute a psychiatric disorder," from the phenomenon of "sexual orientation disturbance," a diagnostic category used in referring to "individuals whose sexual interests

[21]Hooker's report appears in *Foundations for Christian Family Policy* (New York: New York Council of Churches, 1961). See also her article "Homosexuality," in *International Encyclopedia of the Social Sciences* (New York: Macmillan, 1968). For a good overview of the spectrum of psychological and psychiatric opinion regarding homosexuality, see John J. McNeill, S.J., *The Church and the Homosexual* (Kansas City: Sheed Andrews and McMeel, 1976), pp. 109-25.

[22]Nelson, *op. cit.*, p. 194.

[23]Hettlinger, *op. cit.*, p. 147. It has been suggested, however, that factors other than diminished societal prejudice may also explain why lesbians are less likely than male homosexuals to seek professional treatment. For example, many lesbians have heterosexual experiences first, and often differ from male homosexuals: (1) by not identifying themselves as being homosexually oriented until after attempting heterosexual genital relationships; (2) by placing lesser emphasis on genital activity and being more amenable to a life of continence; and (3) by more frequently achieving stable homosexual relationships. See John F. Harvey, O.S.F.S., "An In-Depth Review of *Homosexuality and the Christian Way of Life*," *The Linacre Quarterly*, 50, 2 (May, 1983), pp. 122-43 at 125. Similar observations regarding lesbians appear in *Principles to Guide Confessors*, p. 14.

are directed primarily toward people of the same sex and who are either disturbed by, in conflict with, or wish to change their sexual orientation."[24] At least one implication of the APA's decision is that therapy would in no way be indicated for all homosexuals, but rather only for those who are somehow perturbed by their sexual orientation.

ATTEMPTS TO EXPLAIN THE HOMOSEXUAL ORIENTATION

Just as psychologists and psychiatrists have long differed in their professional judgments as to whether or not homosexuality represents an emotional abnormality, so too is there a continuing attempt to explain why certain individuals find themselves attracted primarily to members of the same sex. It seems well established by now that there is indeed no one "cause" of homosexuality. It is probably better, in fact, not to speak at all of "causes" in the strict sense, but rather of "factors which contribute to the genesis and growth of homosexuality," for the origins of our sexual orientation—whether heterosexual or homosexual—are deeply rooted in our early experiences, and they undoubtedly reflect a convergence of many biological, psychological and sociological circumstances.[25]

Over the years, the suggested explanations for homosexuality have generally fallen along one of two lines: its appearance was regarded as due either to biological or to psycho-social factors in a person's life. The issue, in other words, was whether homosexuals were such by nature as a result of some genetic anomaly or some pre- or post-natal hormonal imbalance or deficiency, or whether they were so nurtured by their environment that they learned to be attracted to members of the same sex. It is not for us, of course, to settle this debate, but reference should be made to a study concluded by the Kinsey Institute for Sex Research in 1981.[26]

---

[24]See McNeill, *op. cit.*, pp. 117-18. Approximately 10,000 of the APA's 17,000 members participated in the vote referred to; the decision to drop homosexuality from the list of mental disorders reflected a 60%-40% split among the voting members, with several hundred abstentions.

[25]See the American bishops' 1973 statement, *Principles to Guide Confessors,* pp. 5-8.

[26]Alan P. Bell, Martin S. Weinberg, and Sue Kiefer Hammersmith, *Sexual Preference: Its Development in Men and Women* (Indiana Univ. Press, 1981).

In their research, the study's authors (a psychologist and two sociologists) and their staff conducted several hours-long interviews with 979 homosexuals and 477 heterosexuals who were questioned about such things as their early relationships with their parents, their childhood friendships, their emotional and sexual feelings as youths, and traumatic sexual incidents. As a result of their investigations, the researchers concluded that the importance of the role of parents in determining a child's sexual preference has, in general, been "grossly exaggerated." Boys, for example, who had dominant mothers and weak fathers were found to be almost as likely to turn out heterosexually oriented as homosexually oriented. The study did report, however, significant differences between homosexuals who had ever been under therapeutic treatment and those who had never been in treatment. Those in the first group did tend to have parental relationships traditionally regarded as typical for homosexuals (i.e., detached/hostile fathers for males and rejecting/detached mothers for females), but for the homosexuals who had never been in therapy, such parental relationships were not at all typical. This information simply serves to highlight the fact that in the past "clinical descriptions of homosexual persons have been based on the study of only those persons in treatment, rather than on a more representative sample"[27]—a point made earlier in this chapter.

In further attempting to isolate and identify other potential factors in the development of homosexuality, the Kinsey-Institute researchers also measured and eventually downplayed such things as: childhood isolation from peers or an inability to form effective relationships with them, early traumatic heterosexual experiences or homosexual seduction, and a lack of heterosexual dating experience. Insofar as they were unable, in fact, to discover any strong connection between specific childhood experiences and adult homosexuality, the researchers suggested finally that the homosexual orientation "may arise from a biological precursor that parents cannot control." Given the present state of our knowledge, then, it is safe only to say that no one should imagine that the last word has been spoken

[27]Marguerite Kropinak, "Homosexuality and Religious Life," in Nugent (ed.), *op. cit.*, pp. 245-56 at 247.

or heard concerning the factors contributing to homosexuality's appearance.

Assuming that it were indeed possible to explain the existence of homosexuality, we need to ask, of course, what exactly is it that we would have explained since, in fact, its manifestations are so diverse, as has been pointed out by Alan Bell of the Kinsey Institute for Sex Research: "Our data appear to indicate that homosexuality involves a large number of widely divergent experiences—developmental, sexual, social, and psychological—and that even after a person has been labeled 'homosexual' on the basis of his or her preferred sexual object choice, there is little that can be predicted about the person on the basis of that label."[28] This means, therefore, that just as we are not blind to the differences found among heterosexuals and the various ways in which they express their sexuality, so also must we acknowledge the diversity existing among homosexuals and their patterns of sexual behavior.[29] If some physical expressions of heterosexual attraction embody the deepest form of life-long love and commitment, there are surely others which are nothing or little more than insensitive manifestations of instinctual bio-chemical urges in which the sex-partners are simply reduced to the status of mutually available pleasure-machines; can any less be said, then, of the physical expressions of homosexual attraction?

An impartial review of the empirical data would seem to justify the conclusion that there are many homosexually oriented men and women who are no less healthy, well-adjusted, responsible, and desirous and capable of sensitive, loving sexual relationships than the majority of the heterosexual population. At the same time, however, there are some homosexuals whose overt sexual activity occurs under such

[28]"Homosexuality: An Overview," in Ruth T. Barnhouse and Urban Holmes III (eds.), *Male and Female: Christian Approaches to Sexuality* (New York: Seabury, 1976), p. 142. For further confirmation of the divergent experiences of homosexuals see Alan P. Bell and Martin S. Weinberg, *Homosexualities. A Study of Diversity Among Men and Women* (New York: Simon and Schuster, 1978). It is interesting to note that, according to this report, about 20% of homosexual men and one-third of lesbian women have been in heterosexual marriages, and that about half of these have had children. The authors concluded that only 12% of gay men and 5% of lesbian women can be regarded as dysfunctional.

[29]See Kelsey, *op. cit.*, p. 128.

circumstances and with such a multiplicity of partners that their actions seem somehow pathological in that they are "unreasonable," "excessive," or "extreme," and do not appear as the freely chosen expressions of a wholesome and humanly integrated sexuality. Habitual sexual activity that is performed, rather compulsively, simply in reaction to an urge that is viewed as intolerable and irresistible scarcely indicates that a person's emotional and psychological life is healthy and sound.

Homosexuals, like heterosexuals, surely manifest different degrees of freedom in controlling their sexual desires, yet the American bishops have drawn attention to a compulsion which they see as operative in much homosexual activity; according to the bishops, "the compulsive nature of many homosexual acts may be surmised from the squalid circumstances, coupled with risk, in which many meetings take place. Reciprocal masturbation in a public washroom is hardly the sort of thing which would appeal to a normally free agent."[30] Without taking exception to the bishops' observation, I, nonetheless, must ask how they would explain the even more blatantly public demonstrations of heavy heterosexual petting—and even intercourse—that are sometimes witnessed on beaches and city streets, or on public transportation vehicles. Is this also compulsive behavior, or is it just simply that some heterosexuals consciously and freely choose to demonstrate their lack of regard for the human, aesthetic and moral sensitivities of others?

I raise these questions only to suggest that the sexual behavior of some heterosexuals is surely neither more "normal" nor less "bizarre" than the behavior of some homosexuals. At the same time, even while granting that the behavior patterns of some homosexuals, like those of some heterosexuals, must clearly be associated with some kind of neurosis, I nonetheless have to agree with Lisa Cahill's observation that "same-sex preference as such is not in principle incompatible with psychological health, or with the capacity to enter into loving and faithful relationships."[31] It needs to be said further,

---

[30] *Principles to Guide Confessors*, p.8.

[31] Lisa Sowle Cahill, "Moral Methodology: A Case Study," in Nugent (ed.), *op. cit.*, pp. 78-92 at 85.

however, that while the empirical sciences have indeed contributed much to our understanding both of the complexity of the homosexual orientation itself, and of the various human meanings which homosexual genital behavior can have, the truth remains that in trying to evaluate such behavior from the perspective of Christian morality, we must be aware not only of what has been learned empirically from the experiences of God's people who happen to be homosexually oriented, but also of the scriptural data and of the views traditionally and commonly held by the Christian community of faith regarding homosexual genital activity.

V. Arguments Against the Morality of Homogenital Activity

Over the centuries, two arguments have been presented against the moral acceptability of homogenital or homo-erotic behavior (i.e., the various forms of genital contact and stimulation between two members of the same sex: mutual masturbation, fellatio, cunnilingus, sodomy). To begin with, the sacred writings of the Judeo-Christian tradition are seen as condemning such activity and, secondly, these actions are prohibited by the natural law because they frustrate and essentially contradict the primary purpose of the sexual faculty which is procreation; homogenital activity must therefore be regarded as intrinsically disordered.[32] In recent years, a third argument has been offered against homogenital activity, namely, that such behavior should be avoided not because it violates the procreative design of the sexual faculty, but rather because it somehow contributes to the human frustration of the very persons engaging in such activity. Let us examine and comment on each of these arguments.

SCRIPTURAL PROHIBITIONS

Before looking at the specific texts usually cited in support of the view that Scripture prohibits all homogenital activity, I offer two prenotes. First, we should be aware of the observation

---

[32]cf. *Declaration on Certain Questions*, #8.

made by New Testament scholar Victor Furnish, that people "have not always agreed on *how* the Bible's authority should be understood, particularly in its concrete teachings about morality." What Furnish goes on to say about Paul's teaching regarding specific moral issues, may, I suggest, probably be said just as well about all the examples of concrete moral teaching found in the Scriptures, namely, that such teaching should neither be venerated as a "sacred cow" nor dismissed as a "white elephant."[33]

In rejecting the idea that Paul's stance on concrete moral issues should be automatically revered and accepted as a "sacred cow," Furnish explains that Paul was writing to specific Christian communities, and that, "since we are *not* the readers Paul had in mind, we must *interpret* his letters, including his moral instructions. They cannot possibly be automatically, and without remainder, applicable to us in our situations." Thus, because the sociopolitical-cultural conditions facing Paul's various congregations are not the ones we confront, we must be wary of blindly accepting, in any fundamentalistic way, the "literal" moral conclusions reached by Paul on specific issues.[34] But, of course, a similar caution is needed in our dealing with all the works of Scripture insofar as each of the various authors was historically and culturally conditioned and had a definite purpose and audience in mind when writing.

While Furnish is clearly intent upon pointing out the dangers of a "sacred cow" view of Paul's specific moral conclusions, he is just as convinced that we must not adopt the "white elephant" mentality which is inclined to write off Paul's moral teachings as simply "outmoded, irrelevant, maybe even a little ridiculous."[35] In an attempt to strike a balance between these two extreme positions, Furnish maintains that the proper and most helpful attitude for us to adopt is to value Paul's concrete moral instructions not so much for "the particular patterns of conduct" which they prohibit or promote, but rather for "the underlying concerns and commitments" which they reveal.

[33] Victor Paul Furnish, *The Moral Teaching of Paul* (Nashville: Abingdon, 1979), p. 13.
[34] *Ibid.,* pp. 16-17.
[35] *Ibid.,* pp. 18-19.

Furnish concludes, finally, by observing that treating Paul's moral teaching "*as if it were a sacred cow*" is exactly what most exposes us to "*the risk of turning it into a white elephant.*" In other words, "if we regard the particulars of Paul's moral instructions as automatically applicable and binding in *our* times and circumstances, we are sure to end up with a good many requirements that are either irrelevant or, what is worse, clearly inappropriate."[36] I want to suggest that Furnish's conclusion regarding Paul's moral teaching is pertinent as well to the specific ethical instructions found elsewhere in Scripture.

The second prenote to our investigation into the scriptural texts usually cited in reference to homogenital activity pertains directly to the fact that the concepts "homosexual" and "homosexuality," as such, were unknown during the time of the Bible's composition. In fact, "these terms," says Furnish, "like the terms 'heterosexual,' 'heterosexuality,' 'bisexual,' and 'bisexuality,' presume an understanding of human sexuality that was possible only with the advent of modern psychological and sociological analysis."[37] What Furnish is suggesting here, I think, is that Scripture simply does not recognize or speak at all about homosexuality (or heterosexuality, for that matter) as a sexual orientation as distinct from specific genital activity. This would mean that the biblical writers simply took it for granted that all people were created with a natural attraction to members of the opposite sex and that their genital activity would and should reflect this fact; given this mentality, any homosexual behavior was likely to be judged as the capricious and malicious rejection of God's designs for human beings.

In line with the point made by Furnish, James Nelson maintains that Scripture's references to homosexuality "are— without exception—statements about certain kinds of homosexual *acts.* Our understanding of homosexuality as a psychosexual orientation is a relatively recent development. It is crucial to remember this, for in all probability the biblical writers in each instance were speaking of homosexual acts undertaken by persons whom the authors presumed to be

[36]*Ibid.,* pp. 28, 27.
[37]*Ibid.,* pp. 65-6.

heterosexually constituted."[38] Insofar as this last observation is correct, we might conclude, at the very least, that Scripture condemns all homogenital actions performed by those individuals whom we have referred to earlier in this chapter as pseudo-homosexuals (i.e., people who are basically or primarily heterosexual, yet who sometimes engage in homogenital activity), but we might still wonder then whether the biblical writers would also have adopted the same attitude toward those people who are truly, constitutively and permanently homosexually oriented. We are, however, getting somewhat ahead of ourselves, so let us look now at the scriptural texts in an attempt to uncover their contemporary relevance.[39]

Old Testament Texts

Discussions about the morality of homogenital activity usually refer to three texts found in the Hebrew scriptures. The first of these appears in Genesis 19, where it is reported that one evening two angels disguised as men were offered lodging in Lot's house in the city of Sodom. After a while, before Lot's guests had retired for the night, all the men of Sodom surrounded the house and began shouting to Lot, "Where are the men who came to you tonight? Send them out to us that we may abuse them" (v.5). Lot refuses this demand and, intent upon safeguarding his guests, he pleads with the crowd to do nothing to the two men "for they have come under the shadow of my roof" (v.8). Lot even offers to send out his two virgin daughters whom the men of Sodom may treat as they please, but the crowd rejects Lot's offer and angrily tries to enter his house. At this point, however, the men of Sodom are struck blind (v.11), and Lot's guests warn him to take his family and leave Sodom because the city is going to be destroyed by Yahweh (v.14). But what exactly is the offense for which Sodom was to be punished?

[38]Nelson, *op. cit.*, p. 182; see also McNeill, *op. cit.*, p. 42 and D. Sherwin Bailey, *Homosexuality and The Western Christian Tradition* (New York: Longmans, 1955), p. 10.

[39]For an analysis of the biblical data on homogenital behavior, consult: McNeill, *op. cit.*, pp. 37-66; Nelson, *op. cit.*, pp. 181-88; Cahill, *art. cit.*, pp. 80-5; Furnish, *op. cit.*, pp. 53-8, 63-4, 67-78, and Anthony Kosnik *et al.*, *Human Sexuality: New Directions in American Catholic Thought* (New York: Paulist Press, 1977), pp. 188-96.

For many centuries, Christian tradition has accepted the view that this passage serves notice of the fact that the sin for which the city of Sodom was destroyed was, plainly and simply, homosexual behavior, and especially sodomy. That this view should ever have become commonly accepted seems a rather remarkable phenomenon, for when we look at Scripture's references to the evil that is associated with Sodom, we find a number of different offenses mentioned. Thus, for example, Jeremiah says that Sodom's sins were adultery, persistent lying and an unwillingness to repent (23:14); Ezekiel claims that the crimes of Sodom's people were "pride, gluttony, arrogance, [and] complacency"; moreover, the inhabitants of Sodom "never helped the poor and needy; they were proud and engaged in filthy practices..." (16:49-50); the Wisdom literature identifies the evils of Sodom as folly, insolence and inhospitality (19:13-14). Finally, Ecclesiasticus says simply that God "did not spare the people with whom Lot lived, whom he abhorred for their pride" (16:8).

In turning to the gospels of Luke and Matthew, we see that when Jesus refers to the city of Sodom, he does so within the context of his instructions to his disciples and apostles as he sends them out to preach the good news. Should it happen that some town or village not receive them hospitably, Jesus tells his disciples how they are to react: "...whenever you enter a town and they do not make you welcome, go out into its streets and say, 'We wipe off the very dust of your town that clings to our feet, and leave it with you. Yet be sure of this: the kingdom of God is very near.' I tell you, on that day it will not go as hard with Sodom as with that town" (Lk. 10:10-12; also Mt. 10:14-15). Thus Jesus himself seems to associate Sodom with the evil of inhospitality. There are, however, two late New Testament texts (2 Pet. 2:4-10 and Jude vv.6-7) which do give a predominantly sexual interpretation to the Sodom story. Nonetheless, we cannot avoid asking the questions: if the people of Sodom were notorious for their homosexual behavior, why is this never clearly stated in all the other texts where Sodom's evil is detailed, and why is Sodom never mentioned in those scriptural texts which, as we shall soon see, do in fact make specific reference to homogenital activity?

To suggest that the citizens of Sodom were involved in numerous offenses does not in itself deny that homogenital activity is indeed a partial, even primary, explanation for their destruction, but, as the Genesis text itself makes clear, the action which the men of Sodom were contemplating would have been an instance of outright sexual lust and homosexual gang rape. As such, the behavior deserves to be condemned, but this text alone can scarcely be used as a justification for prohibiting all homogenital activity. Furthermore, Lot's offer to expose his virgin daughters to the pleasure of Sodom's men suggests either that he was desperate and confused, or that he valued the laws of hospitality more than the safety and virtue of his daughters, or that he considered heterosexual rape less evil than homosexual rape, or that he knew well enough that the men of Sodom were not what we would call today "truly homosexually oriented" and that, therefore, their lustful desires might just as likely be satisfied by means of heterosexual intercourse as by homosexual relations. (See Judges 19:11-30 for the story of the crime committed by the men of Gibeah; it has many parallels to the incident at Sodom).

Whatever one finally concludes about the role which homogenital activity played in bringing about God's harsh judgment against Sodom, there is no question but that such behavior is clearly the object of condemnation in two other Old Testament passages. Leviticus 18:22 says "You must not lie with a man as with a woman. This a hateful thing," and Leviticus 20:13 goes on to say that when two men lie together as with a woman "they have done a hateful thing. . .; they must die, [and] their blood shall be on their own heads." Before saying anything further about these specific texts, we should note that they are part of the same so-called Holiness Code which imposes death as the penalty for cursing one's mother or father (20:9), for adultery (20:10), and for various forms of incest and bestiality (20:11-17); the Code also prohibits uncovering "the nakedness of a woman who is unclean by reason of her monthly periods" (18:19), and couples who engage in intercourse during the time of the woman's menstruation "must be outlawed from their people" (20:18). I mention these various stipulations of the Code only in order to suggest that we are confronted here "almost exclusively with cultic and ritual matters."[40]

In other words, since Yahweh had commanded the Israelites not to "behave as they do in Egypt where once you lived" nor "as they do in Canaan where I am taking you" (Lev. 18:3), the Holiness Code was designed to specify numerous requirements for maintaining cultic purity or cleanliness lest Yahweh's people be tainted by their contact with neighboring tribes. With respect specifically to homosexual behavior, what the concern for cultic purity suggests, is that among the Israelites all such activity was prohibited in an attempt to avoid and outlaw any practice that might be identified with the occurrences of male and female prostitution which was commonly part of the temple services honoring the gods of fertility who were worshipped by various nearby mid-East religious cults. The Israelites were clearly severe in their judgment against the practice of sacral male prostitution (Dt. 23:18; 1 Kgs. 14:24, 15:12, 22:47), but they considered it an "abomination" precisely because of its connection with the fertility rites of the Canaanites; in this context, then, the suggestion seems quite justified that Leviticus' condemnation of homosexual activity is not primarily or precisely an ethical judgment regarding sexual behavior; rather, such activity is prohibited because of its association with idolatry.[41]

In concluding our discussion of the Old Testament's attitude toward homosexual behavior, we should note that all the textual references are to actions involving only males. In a patriarchal society and culture, great emphasis was placed upon the preservation and fostering of male dignity; this would help to explain why there was such great opposition to those actions in which one man used another man as a woman, while the second man allowed himself to be so used. The point might be made, finally, that as a people who were quite conscious of the dangers they faced from their numerous enemies, the Israelites were strongly committed to the values of marriage, procreation and family life, for only in this way could they increase their numbers and thereby ensure their ability to resist future attacks

[40]Martin Noth, *Leviticus, A Commentary* (London: SCM, 1965), p. 16.

[41]cf. Kosnik *et al., op. cit.,* p. 190 and Norman H. Snaith, *Leviticus and Numbers, The Century Bible* (London: Nelson, 1967), p. 126.

and possible annihilation. Such values, of course, were seen as being obviously contradicted by homosexual behavior; this would have been a particularly unacceptable situation to the Israelites if they thought, as they probably did, that such behavior was being resorted to by individuals who were simply freely choosing to act in a way that violated and rejected the "natural" and universal (heterosexual) inclinations or attractions of human beings.

New Testament Texts

Although Jesus himself never mentioned homogenital activity, there are three New Testament texts which refer to such behavior. In 1 Corinthians 6:9-10, Paul lists some types of people who will not inherit the kingdom of God; cited here are "people of immoral lives, idolaters, adulterers, catamites, sodomites, thieves, usurers, drunkards, slanderers and swindlers ...." Then in 1 Timothy 1:9-10, Paul, or one of his followers, reminds us that the Law is not intended for those who are good but rather for such people as "... criminals and revolutionaries, for the irreligious and the wicked, for the sacrilegious and the irreverent; ... for people who kill their fathers or mothers and for murderers, for those who are immoral with women or with boys or with men, for liars and for perjurers...."

In reflecting upon these two texts, we are interested only in trying to capture the idea or meaning originally intended by the terms which have been translated above as "catamites," "sodomites," and those who are immoral "with boys or with men." The words "catamites" (generally understood as the passive partners in male homosexual intercourse) and "sodomites" (the active partners in male homosexual intercourse) are translations of the Greek words *malakoi* and *arsenokoitai*; the latter word, along with *pornoi* and *andrapodistai,* appears also in 1 Timothy. Suffice it to say that none of the translations given above is universally accepted; among alternate renderings for the Greek words we find the following expressions: "the sexually immoral," "sexual perverts," "homosexual perverts," "male prostitutes," and "the weak, soft, or effeminate." It is not at all easy, then, to know exactly what is being criticized here as far as homogenital behavior is concerned.

In recent years, however, it has been suggested that in light of Paul's knowledge of the widespread practice of pederasty in Greco-Roman culture, it is quite possible that it is really this practice which he intends to condemn. Although Platonic love relationships between an adult man and a young boy had often been praised by philosophers in the centuries before Christ, by the time at which Paul was writing, such relationships had lost their Platonic or a-sexual character and were strongly criticized by ancient secular writers such as Seneca, Plutarch, Philo and Dio Chrysostom as being among "the grosser forms of self-indulgence."[42] In the typical pederastic relationship, the male youth, who was prized mainly for his female characteristics, was the passive partner in the sexual relationship, while the adult man was the active sexual partner; once the youth reached puberty and began to develop the male secondary sex-characteristics (beard, etc.), he was replaced by a new younger lover and would himself go on later to become the active partner in another relationship.

As New Testament scholar Robin Scroggs points out, even the secular philosophers found much to criticize about the Greco-Roman practice of pederasty. To begin with, the relationship was marked by inequality and a lack of mutuality, and whatever sexual activity occurred was intended simply for the pleasure of the adult; in addition, the physical and emotional exploitation of the young male was inevitable in view of the fact that he was desired only for his fleeting physical attractiveness, and the relationship held no possibility or hope for personal commitment and permanency. It is possible, moreover, that most of the adult pederasts were not what we would call today "true homosexuals." Since they were either already married men or would go on to be such, and since the youths they turned to as "lovers" were found attractive mainly because of their feminine qualities, it is conceivable that these pederasts were really heterosexually, or perhaps bisexually, and not basically homosexually, oriented. But whatever the pertinence and validity of this last bit of speculation, the fact remains that we cannot simply discount the possibility that, in the passages cited above, what Paul condemns, along with many

[42]cf. Furnish, *op. cit.,* pp. 58-63, 65-7.

other actions, is not all homogenital behavior as such, but the specific practice of pederasty as it appeared in Greco-Roman society, along with male prostitution and other forms of dissolute sexual activity.[43]

The third and most extended New Testament reference to homogenital activity appears in the first chapter of Paul's letter to the Romans, and this is the only place in the Bible where mention is made of female homosexual behavior, as well as of male. Once again, however, in attempting to understand Paul's position on this matter, we must first expose the theological context in which it appears.

In Romans 1:18-32, Paul's basic thesis is that because the pagans have freely refused to acknowledge and honor the true God who is clearly revealed through the marvelous wonders of creation, God's anger is now being manifested against them. Their worshiping of idols has resulted in God's abandonment of the pagans "to degrading passions"; thus, says Paul, "their women have turned from natural intercourse to unnatural practices and ... their menfolk have given up natural intercourse to be consumed with passion for each other, men doing shameless things with men and getting an appropriate reward for their perversion" (vv.26-7). This is not all, however; Paul portrays the pagans' deliberate rejection of God as having many other dire consequences. Thus, for example, people who turn away from the true God become "steeped in all sorts of depravity, rottenness, greed and malice, and addicted to envy, murder, wrangling, treachery and spite. [They are] libellers, slanderers, enemies of God, rude, arrogant and boastful, enterprising in sin, rebellious to parents, without brains, honor, love or pity" (vv.29-31).

What, then, are we to make of Paul's teaching regarding homogenital acts? In reflecting upon Paul's overall perspective

[43]The ideas in this paragraph are derived from Robin Scroggs, *The New Testament and Homosexuality* (Phila.: Fortress Press, 1983), pp. 24-43, 145-49. Scroggs maintains that Paul is not speaking out against all homogenital activity, but he goes on to suggest also that Paul is in fact castigating an especially sordid and degrading form of pederasty in which the young male is a "call boy" or boy prostitute who is trained to imitate the mannerisms of girls and who is hired to satisfy an older man's desires. Thus Scroggs translates the pertinent words in 1 Timothy as follows: "male prostitutes [*pornoi*], males who lie with them [*arsenokoitai*], and slave dealers who procure them [*andrapodistai*]"; cf. Scroggs, pp. 101-09, 118-22, 126.

on homosexual behavior, Furnish maintains that for Paul such activity "represented a rebellion against the Creator and his creation, a surrender to one's own lusts, the debasement of one's own true identity and the exploitation of another's." Furnish then goes on to conclude that, while "it is no longer possible to share Paul's belief that homosexual conduct always and necessarily involves all these things," it can nonetheless "be said with certainty that whenever a homosexual *or* heterosexual relationship does involve one or more of these, it stands under the judgment of scripture."[44] Thus Paul's teaching would clearly oppose any kind of forced genital relations (rape), any involvement with male (and female) prostitution and, in general, any sexual relationship, including pederasty, which is essentially lacking in mutuality and equality.

What seems overdrawn, however, is any conclusion that Paul's teaching must remain as a condemnation of all homo-genital activity, even that which occurs between two committed people whom we would describe today as being constitutively or permanently homosexually oriented. Indeed, this point is mentioned only because when Paul speaks in Romans 1 of people "giving up" or "turning away from" heterosexual relations, he does not seem to be describing and condemning the actions of true homosexuals, but rather those of people whom we referred to earlier as pseudo-homosexuals, people, that is, who are really heterosexually oriented but who engage in homosexual acts and thus behave in a perverted way by choosing to defy their "nature."[45] The thought thus suggests itself that, at least under certain conditions, the homogenital behavior of true homosexuals might not stand under Paul's negative judgment, or that of Scripture in general.

The reader should note, however, that the proposition that, in Romans 1, Paul is denouncing only homosexual acts

[44]Furnish, *op. cit.,* pp. 73-82 at 81.

[45]True homosexuals are sometimes referred to as "inverts" and homosexuality has been described as "inversion"; likewise, those whom we have called "pseudo-homosexuals" are at times referred to as "perverts," that is, heterosexuals who engage in homosexual practices, but the latter term might just as well be used to designate homosexuals who engage in heterosexual activity; McNeill, *op. cit.,* p. 42, says the "distinction between the condition of inversion and the behavior of perversion is indispensable for a correct interpretation of biblical and traditional sources."

performed by pseudo-homosexuals or by individuals who are apparently or predominantly heterosexual, emerges, not as an explanation of Paul's text, but rather as an interpretation of it. We are clearly involved, in other words, not in exegesis, but in hermeneutics, when we make such a statement regarding the scriptural text. This is a point that is stressed by New Testament scholar Richard B. Hays, who correctly observes that the notion of "sexual orientation" is an anachronism when applied to Paul's text, and thus "to suggest that Paul intends to condemn homosexual acts only when they are committed by persons who are constitutionally heterosexual is to introduce a distinction entirely foreign to Paul's thought-world..."[46]

Unable to distinguish between sexual orientation and sexual activity, Paul unambiguously indicts all homosexual behavior as immoral. This leaves contemporary Christians who now see and appreciate a distinction between sexual orientation and genital acts with the task of determining the normative relevance of Paul's text for judgments regarding homogenital activity. What, in other words, is the "authority" of the biblical text, or how are we to appropriate Paul's teaching, given our expanded understanding of the complex reality of human sexuality? Hays has no definitive answer to these questions, but he does offer two cautions. First, he reminds those who follow the Christian tradition "by upholding the authority of Paul's teaching against the morality of homosexual acts" that they must do so with proper humility and without any self-righteous condemnation of homosexual behavior (cf. Rom. 2:1; Gal. 6:1-5). Turning next to those "who decide that the authority of Paul's judgment against homosexuality is finally outweighed by other considerations," Hays advises them to have "a due sense of the gravity of their choice."[47]

THE NATURAL LAW ARGUMENT

Throughout the centuries the argument most frequently used by philosophers and theologians against the moral accepta-

---

[46]Richard B. Hays, "Relations Natural and Unnatural: A Response to John Boswell's Exegesis of Romans 1," *The Journal of Religious Ethics,* 14, 1 (Spring, 1986), 184-215 at 200-01.
[47]*Ibid.,* 210-11.

bility of homogenital activity has been that such behavior frustrates the primary purpose of sexuality which, according to the natural law, is procreation. The magisterium of the Roman Catholic Church continues to use this natural law argument in explaining its prohibition of all homogenital acts, even though, as we saw in the previous chapter, Vatican II's *Gaudium et Spes* abandoned the idea that when speaking of the twofold purpose of human sexuality, we must continue to rank the procreation and education of children as of greater value or importance than the mutual fostering of love between spouses.

Given the constancy with which the natural law argument against homosexual acts appears, it is necessary and important for us to consider its validity or cogency in this context. Unquestionably, there is, and there is meant to be, some relationship between human sexuality and procreation, but as Charles Curran observes, "that relationship is very difficult to define and very difficult to use as a criterion for absolute moral condemnations."[48] May we continue to say, then, that all homogenital behavior is morally unacceptable simply because it lacks any and all possibility or potential for procreation?

We know, of course, that not all heterosexual expressions of vaginal intercourse are, or can be, procreative since, realistically, such acts are biologically open to the possibility of procreation only during the period of time surrounding a woman's ovulation. Beyond this, we know, too, that the Catholic Church does not require of heterosexuals that they be blessed with fertility or the ability to procreate as a condition for entering into marriage and the subsequent joys of physical sexual union. Thus sterility on the part of a man or woman or both is simply no impediment or obstacle to their marriage or to their morally legitimate sexual intercourse as spouses. Even if a person's or a couple's infertility is not due to causes beyond their control, but rather is the direct result of their having undergone some sterilization procedure with the deliberate intent to render themselves incapable of procreating, they are not prohibited by the Church from marrying or—in the event that they are already married—from continuing to engage in sexual inter-

---

[48]Charles E. Curran, *Critical Concerns in Moral Theology* (Notre Dame: Univ. of Notre Dame Press, 1984), p. 84.

course, provided that they are now sorry for their previous decision to be sterilized; it is not clear, however, that this person or couple would be expected or morally obliged even to attempt to have the effects of the sterilization procedure reversed before initiating or resuming sexual relations.[49]

We may recall, as well, that the Catholic Church officially approves of the practice of periodic abstinence, thus recognizing that, for serious reasons, spouses may legitimately and morally decide that it is necessary for them temporarily or permanently to intend positively to have no children; in keeping with their intention and desire to avoid procreation, these spouses then deliberately restrict sexual intercourse to the wife's infertile periods which are determined as carefully as possible. Some Catholic theologians go even further, of course, and maintain that, for serious reasons, the use of artificial contraceptives by spouses is morally permissible; finally, various national conferences of bishops have acknowledged that spouses may, without sin, act on their dissent from the Church's ban of artificial contraception.

The examples and teachings reviewed in the preceding two paragraphs are presented only to indicate that in fact neither the potential nor the desire and intent to procreate need be present in every act of sexual intercourse between spouses, or, indeed, even in any such act as an absolute or indispensable condition for the moral acceptability of the spouses' genital expressions of love. When such expressions of love do indeed lack any possibility for procreation, they do not embody and reflect the full richness and power which God intended for human sexuality, but they are not, for that reason alone, said to be even objectively wrong from the perspective of morality.

In light of the fact, then, that the procreative possibility is not an absolute moral requirement for all heterosexual intercourse,

---

[49]See John T. Noonan, Jr., *Contraception* (New York: Mentor-Omega Books, 1967), pp. 318, 511, 546; also see John L. Clifford, S.J., "Marital Rights of the Sinfully Sterilized," *Theological Studies*, 5 (1944), 141, 158. We might note here that, according to the canon law of the Catholic Church, in order to enter into a valid marriage, a man and woman must be potent; this means simply that a woman's vagina must be able to receive semen, and that a man must be able to maintain an erection sufficient to penetrate a vagina and then to ejaculate some kind of seminal fluid (but not necessarily sperm) into the vaginal cavity. People who are, without a doubt, permanently unable to engage in such genital activity are considered impotent and cannot enter into a valid marriage.

the objection might be raised that it seems inconsistent to establish the absence of any procreative potential as the basis for saying that all homogenital acts are unnatural and hence objectively wrong and immoral. It should be noted, however, that Catholic moral teaching has tried to meet this objection by employing Aquinas' distinction between those genital acts which are only *accidentally* deprived of procreative potential and those which are *essentially* or *generically* lacking such potential; those genital acts which are only accidentally or incidentally nonprocreative, Thomas regards as natural, whereas the essentially nonprocreative acts are seen as unnatural. But what exactly is the criterion or norm for distinguishing between accidentally nonprocreative acts, which are natural, and essentially nonprocreative acts, which are unnatural? For Thomas, the norm is simply this: if the genital act allows for and results in insemination, that is, in the depositing of semen in the vagina—which is seen as the only suitable vessel or receptacle for receiving semen—, then the act, no matter what other circumstances or conditions may prevail, is seen as essentially open to procreation and as only accidentally nonprocreative; as such, the act is natural; but any genital activity which allows for no possibility of insemination is regarded as essentially nonprocreative and hence as unnatural.[50]

On the basis of this distinction, Thomas and Catholic tradition can regard as only accidentally nonprocreative many instances of heterosexual vaginal intercourse in which procreation itself is known or is considered to be impossible: e.g., intercourse after menopause or among the elderly, intercourse involving people who are naturally infertile or who have purposely undergone sterilization in order to avoid procreation, intercourse that is carefully restricted to the well-defined periods of a woman's infertility. Because all these actions allow for insemination, they are seen as natural, and spouses can morally engage in them.[51] Spouses must avoid as unnatural,

---

[50]*Summa Contra Gentiles,* 3, 122. Using the inability to inseminate as the mark of an essentially nonprocreative, and hence unnatural, sex act, Thomists can regard contraceptive practices like coitus interruptus and the use of condoms as unnatural. However, in calling the modern forms of artificial contraception which allow for insemination (into the vagina) unnatural, Catholic teaching seems to have gone beyond Thomas' understanding of the term, if not beyond his intention.

[51]Noonan, *op. cit.,* pp. 294-95.

however, any genital activity which does not allow for insemination; thus masturbation, fellatio, cunnilingus and sodomy may not be engaged in to achieve sexual orgasm, but may serve, rather, only as the preludes to vaginal intercourse during which insemination will occur.

Within the context of this traditional teaching regarding the difference between acts that are accidentally nonprocreative and those which are essentially so, the reason for prohibiting all homogenital actions as unnatural is clear: all such actions exclude the possibility of insemination, and hence they are essentially nonprocreative and unnatural. By way of comment, however, it might be argued that the validity of the distinction between accidentally and essentially nonprocreative actions is not beyond question, for there seems to be something fanciful and contrived in saying that just because insemination can occur through them, acts of vaginal intercourse in the lives, for example, of elderly, infertile or sterilized spouses are really only accidentally deprived of procreative possibilities and thus may be permitted, whereas all other forms of complete genital activity (e.g., oral and anal intercourse) must be avoided in all spousal relationships, even where sterility is a proven fact, simply because these actions allow for no insemination and are thus essentially nonprocreative. Anyone not convinced of the legitimacy of the distinction between accidental and essential deprivation of procreative potential might consistently suggest that, when serious reasons prevail, spouses may legitimately engage in alternate forms of sexual intercourse even to the point of achieving orgasm. Likewise, someone not convinced that the possibility for insemination is or should be a requirement for the moral acceptability of all acts of spousal intercourse might not be persuaded that all homogenital actions can or should be morally prohibited simply because it is impossible for insemination to occur by means of them.

It is possible, of course, that there are other reasons for prohibiting homogenital acts as immoral; Thomas himself speaks of some violations of chastity as sins "according to nature," but these, by definition, are not condemned as "unnatural." The proposal seems warranted, therefore, that any attempt to explain or justify the universal prohibition of homogenital acts should look elsewhere than to the natural law.

HOMOGENITAL ACTIVITY AND HUMAN FRUSTRATION

The basic thrust of the argument that homogenital activity is wrong, not because it frustrates the purpose of the sexual faculty, but rather because it brings about harm to the whole person, and thus violates the criterion of love which must govern all human relationships, seems to be this: that if a person loves himself or herself as well as others, then homogenital actions will be avoided because they somehow contribute to the human frustration of the individuals who engage in them. There are two different lines of reasoning used in connection with this argument, however.

In some instances, the case has been argued that in choosing to engage in homogenital acts, homosexuals are opting to behave in ways which simply express, confirm and deepen feelings which are themselves profoundly immature and disordered, and which reflect an arrested or stunted psycho-sexual development resulting in a mental or emotional disturbance. In this scenario, it is being suggested that homogenital behavior should be avoided because it is only likely to nurture a person's homosexual make-up which itself is viewed here as inherently disordered. Precisely because the homosexual orientation is a sickness, love requires that homosexuals make every effort to contain or control it out of consideration for self and others. The focus, then, is not so much on homogenital acts themselves, but rather on the underlying "neurotic" homosexual condition which may have to be tolerated, but should not be fostered or supported by overt homogenital behavior.

In summary, then, the argument just outlined claims that homogenital acts are unloving and wrong insofar as they nurture a condition which itself must be resisted because it reflects an inherent frustration of human development. In reaction to this line of reasoning, I can only submit that the empirical data presented earlier in this chapter challenge the conclusions either that homosexuality itself is an illness, or that the conflicts, fears, anxieties and neurotic tendencies which some homosexuals may exhibit are due precisely and or exclusively to their homosexual orientation, and not to the external pressures often exerted upon them by the discrimination and ridicule of a hostile society. Of course, if a person's homosexual orientation, in and of itself, is not a sickness, then there is no reason to prohibit all homogenital actions *simply* because such actions are seen as confirming or nurturing that individual's homosexual inclination.

Quite a different approach to the question of homogenital behavior is taken by psychologist William Kraft, who admits both that authentic love is quite possible between two people of the same sex, and that such love does indeed foster the healthy growth of the people involved. Kraft maintains, however, that authentic love is necessarily incompatible with homogenital activity which "cannot be healthy because it lacks and excludes permanent commitment...." In contrast to heterogenital relations, homogenital acts never "go beyond themselves" and thus "what many homosexuals are really seeking—to feel permanently at home and to grow perpetually in love—is not possible in homogenital relations."[52]

Kraft grants that people can have homosexual feelings, desires and fantasies and still be healthy, provided that they never or only rarely engage in homogenital actions, which he sees as simply providing self-gratification and need-reduction without any enhancement of personal human development. Homogenital intimacy does not "promote progressive and transcendent growth" as heterogenital relationships are able to do; more than this, however, such homogenital intimacy "impedes and violates healthy growth" and thus "is incongruent with authentic love...."[53] It is Kraft's contention, then, that if two homosexuals are truly in love, they will try to foster not only each other's growth but also their own by avoiding all homogenital actions because these actions are simply frustrative of human development and thus are unhealthy.

We might note that Kraft is not claiming that homosexuality or the homosexual orientation itself is unhealthy, but only that homogenital behavior is. Thus the cost of being a healthy homosexual is the pursuit of a life of celibacy which precludes, ideally, all homogenital actions. While I agree with Kraft's judgments that homosexuality itself is not unhealthy and that

[52]Kraft, *art. cit.,* 372.
[53]*Ibid.,* 373.

homosexuals are indeed capable of authentic love relationships, I do not think that he has offered sufficient grounds for
saying that homogenital behavior is inherently frustrative of
human growth. His affirmations about such behavior seem to
me, in fact, to be largely gratuitous.

Other writers have a more nuanced view of homosexuality in
that their reservations about the homosexual condition do not
result in an absolute and unequivocal prohibition of homogenital activity. Psychiatrist Ruth T. Barnhouse, for example,
maintains that homosexuality is not a sickness but rather a
retarded stage of psychological development, and hence a form
of immaturity. The context within which she reaches this
conclusion is intriguing, however. Barnhouse regards human
sexuality as normatively symbolic and reflective of the ideal
relationship between God and humanity, and it is this insight
into the meaning of sexuality which is preserved "not only in the
image of the Church as the bride of Christ, but in the institution
of marriage as a sacrament." Because sexuality is, and is meant
to be, indicative and expressive of profound unity and
wholeness, its goal, from the human perspective, is not mere
personal satisfaction, but completeness without which, satisfaction too easily deteriorates into lust. This completeness
requires, however, an integration of opposites which is simply
impossible in homosexual relationships. Thus it may be said
that any genital activity between two people of the same sex
introduces symbolic confusion into the meaning and reality of
human sexuality.[54]

Writing in a similar vein, moralist Edward A. Malloy
maintains that "a homosexual person should be considered
mentally ill only if he or she is unable to function as a
responsible member of society."[55] He goes on to lend strong
support to the general analysis of homosexuality as proposed
by Barnhouse. According to Malloy, because of the participants'
physical and psychic similarity, homosexual relationships are
"an exercise in narcissism." Indeed, it is only the mystery of the

---

[54]Ruth T. Barnhouse, "Homosexuality," *Anglican Theological Review,* 58 (1976),
107-34 at 129-30; also see her *Homosexuality: A Symbolic Confusion* (New York:
Seabury, 1977), pp. 172-74.
[55]Edward A. Malloy, *Homosexuality and the Christian Way of Life* (Lanham, Md.:
University Press of America, 1981), p. 88.

other as found specifically in the opposite sex which can sustain two people in "the ongoing task of self-giving and mutual domestic responsibility."[56] For Malloy, no matter how different two persons of the same sex may be, they can simply never offer each other "the same opportunity for complementary fulfillment" that is possible between two people of the opposite sex. Hence, homosexual relationships are likely only "to breed boredom and dissatisfaction."[57] This would explain, at least in part, why homosexually oriented people, especially men, find it difficult, even when desirable, to maintain exclusive sexual relationships for long periods of time.

Neither Barnhouse nor Malloy regards homosexuality as "a normal alternate lifestyle." Thus, says Barnhouse, in order to minimize the effects of their condition, homosexuals have a responsibility either to involve themselves in an attempt at heterosexual adaptation or to choose a celibate lifestyle. She admits, however, both the serious difficulties and the limited success associated with therapeutic efforts at heterosexual reorientation. She acknowledges, likewise, that complete sexual abstinence is not possible for all homosexuals "without crippling them in other ways, and it is unreasonable and cruel to demand it." She suggests, therefore, that homosexuals "who cannot change or abstain must make the attempt to express their sexual nature in the most stable and responsible and loving forms of which they are capable." Barnhouse concludes, finally, with this observation: "If one speaks of homosexual acts taking place between two consenting adults in private in the context of an ongoing relationship between the partners, even though the homosexual disposition itself constitutes an immaturity, it surely ranks well below many other immaturities in the amount of social or moral harm which is done."[58]

A similar conclusion seems to be reached by Malloy who reasons that for those constitutive homosexuals who are incapable of living a celibate life, which is always the moral norm, some preservation of Christian values is most likely to be found only in a homosexual relationship that is consciously

[56]*Ibid.*, p. 234.
[57]*Ibid.*, pp. 339, 234.
[58]Barnhouse, "Homosexuality," 131, 128.

intent upon, and committed to, the establishment of a permanent and exclusive union. Although objectively disordered, the genital activity involved in such a union remains preferable, says Malloy, to the other alternatives with which a homosexual is confronted when sexual abstinence is impossible.[59] At this point we might note that if one takes seriously and literally Barnhouse's and Malloy's reference to some homosexuals' incapability of living a life of celibacy or complete sexual abstinence, then it is inevitable that serious doubts arise regarding the moral culpability associated with the failure of these individuals to achieve the ideal of complete abstinence. As the remainder of this chapter will indicate, however, granting the possibility, or even the likelihood, of significant curtailment of moral culpability in the lives of some sexually active homosexuals in no way diminishes the discussion concerning the moral status of homogenital activity itself. Is such behavior always an objective moral wrong, or is it morally neutral, or does it, finally, sometimes exist as a premoral or ontic wrong?

VI. Current Moral Evaluations of Homogenital Acts

With all that has been said so far as a background, we can now review several of the various ways in which homogenital activity is being morally evaluated today. After looking briefly at the positions maintained by the Roman Catholic Church and by the Quakers, we will focus on the views proposed by a number of Catholic theologians.

OFFICIAL ROMAN CATHOLIC TEACHING

The long-held and current official or magisterial teaching of the Roman Catholic Church is that all homogenital actions are intrinsically evil because they cannot fulfill the procreative purpose of the sex faculty, and thus they constitute a disordered or unnatural use of the power given us by God to continue the species. This is the position developed both in the 1973 statement of the American bishops, *Principles to Guide Confessors in Questions of Homosexuality,* and in Rome's 1975

[59]Malloy, *op. cit.,* pp. 359-60.

Declaration on Certain Questions Concerning Sexual Ethics.[60]
It is also the position consistently proposed by Fr. John Harvey,
a well-known writer on this issue of homosexuality.

For the proponents of this view, while the homosexual
orientation itself is not regarded as morally evil, homogenital
acts must always be judged as objective moral wrongs which are
always unacceptable even though those who engage in such acts
are not always guilty of sin, due to the presence of extenuating
subjective circumstances within their lives. Furthermore, within
the context of the official teaching of the Church, homosexuals
must be counseled to pursue a celibate life, which is possible
with God's help. In insisting on this point, Harvey remarks that
"...the Catholic doctrine on the sufficiency of grace to do the
explicit will of God in the observance of appropriate chastity
demands that we do not accept the presumption that free
homosexuals cannot live the life of complete abstinence from
genital intercourse."[61] By way of comment on this traditional
absolute rejection of homosexual behavior, I would only note
that, insofar as it is linked to a particular interpretation of the
natural law, the questions raised earlier about this law's
prohibition of all homogenital activity suggest that this view is
not beyond legitimate criticism.

THE QUAKER VIEW

The basic thesis put forth a number of years ago by the
English Quakers is that homogenital acts are in themselves
morally neutral. Thus, genital acts are to be judged not by their
outward appearance, or in isolation from the personal relationship within which they occur, for "surely it is the nature and
quality of a relationship which matters." The one thing that
cannot be tolerated, however, is any kind of sexual activity

---

[60]See also the 1983 statement of the Sacred Congregation for Catholic Education, *Educational Guidance in Human Love*, #101-03.

[61]Harvey, *art. cit.*, 143; for a synthetic treatment of the official Catholic teaching on homosexuality see Harvey's article, "Homosexuality," *New Catholic Encyclopedia* (New York: McGraw-Hill, 1967), vol. 7, pp. 116-19. Harvey is the moderator of *Courage,* an organization that tries to provide spiritual and psychological support for homosexuals attempting to live a life of complete abstinence from genital relations. This group was established as an alternative to *Dignity,* a national organization for gay Catholics, which Harvey views as less than committed to the Roman Catholic teaching regarding homogenital behavior.

which depersonalizes or exploits another. Therefore, whether among homosexuals or heterosexuals, the Quakers condemn "seduction and even persuasion and every instance of coitus which, by reason of disparity of age or intelligence or emotional condition, cannot be a matter of mutual responsibility."[62]

In response to the Quaker position, I offer these observations. I agree with the insistence upon the need for mutual responsibility in all sexual activity; I would also maintain, of course, that ultimately any moral evaluation of genital activity must consider the nature and quality of the personal relationship within which this activity occurs, but I must say that in claiming that homogenital behavior is, in itself, morally neutral, the Quaker view goes too far.

Such a proposal seems, indeed, to be entirely forgetful of the fact that Christian thinking about physical expressions of love is guided by this basic insight, namely, that the true richness of human sexuality is revealed only insofar as its expressions reflect the qualities of God's love for humanity; this means, as we saw earlier, that, ideally, full expressions of human sexual love are to be open to procreation (even as God's love for us is creative), and are to occur within a personal relationship that involves a commitment to permanent fidelity in imitation of God's covenantal love for his people. Such references to procreative potential and to a pledge of faithful love remind us that the Judeo-Christian understanding of human sexuality has been fundamentally shaped and governed by the norm of marital love that is shared by a man and woman. This norm is, moreover, accepted and universally emphasized by the Roman Catholic theologians whose views we will now consider.

ROMAN CATHOLIC THEOLOGICAL OPINIONS

Although the Catholic theologians whose thoughts will be presented here propose views that in one way or another are at variance with the official teaching of the Church that homogenital acts are always objective moral wrongs and thus may never be permitted, they, nonetheless, are generally convinced that we cannot dismiss out-of-hand what Lisa Cahill has

---

[62]Alastair Huron (ed.), *Toward a Quaker View of Sex* (London: The Society of Friends, 1963), pp. 26 ff. A similar viewpoint is adopted by Gregory Baum, "Catholic Homosexuals," *Commonweal*, XCIX, 19 (Feb. 15, 1974), 479-82.

described as our tradition's "positive heterosexual, marital, and procreative norm for sexual love." As the Genesis accounts of creation make clear, says Cahill, "humanity is constituted male and female, so that sexual differentiation is definitive of humanity from the beginning." As equal but distinct creations made in the "likeness" and "image" of God, men and women are capable of a physical union with one another that guarantees the continuation of the human race. Furthermore, insofar as it is true that Christianity claims that the aim of human sexuality is not simply personal satisfaction, but rather human completion, the heterosexual relationship takes on added significance for "neither man nor woman alone is complete humanity; only their duality, complementarity, and union give human nature its fullness."[63]

We might note, however, that despite the basic validity of this notion that each sex is complemented, on many levels, by its involvement with the other, the fact remains that some individuals can simply find no adequate sense of fulfillment or completion through physical and/or human intercourse with members of the opposite sex. It seems to me that the Catholic Church herself gives explicit acknowledgment to this fact by her recognition of homosexuality as grounds for the annulment of a marriage. Sadly and unfortunately, a number of homosexually oriented men and women, for various reasons (e.g., in order to gain respectability, or to avoid suspicion, or because they have no sense of being called to a life of celibacy and yet are fearful of the condemnation and ridicule inspired by homogenital behavior), attempt heterosexual relationships and marriage. Even with the best of intentions, however, and despite great effort, what these people often find, is that they are simply incapable of establishing the true marital community or intimacy of life and love that is expected of spouses; in these situations, there is no mutual completion or fulfillment of two human beings, and the judgment must simply be rendered that no valid marital union exists between them.

The question, then, is unavoidable. If a truly homosexually oriented person finds it impossible to give or receive the human completion usually provided by a singular and deep relationship with a member of the opposite sex, may he or she, in an

[63]Cahill, *art. cit.,* p. 82.

attempt to establish a mutually fulfilling union, enter into a same-sex relationship that would involve the possibility of moral homogenital behavior? Cahill suggests an affirmative response to this question. She maintains that while "the consistent positive contribution of the Christian tradition on sexuality is that 'normative' human sexuality is heterosexual, marital, and has an intrinsic relation to procreation, love, and commitment," it still remains the "sticky task" of Christian ethics to determine "when, why, and how to make exceptions to norms."[64]

For Cahill, acknowledgment of the heterosexual, marital and procreative norm for sexual love does not require that we render "a negative moral judgment on homosexual persons, on their potential for praiseworthy relationships," or "necessarily on homosexual acts." Thus, she suggests "that while heterosexual marriage is the normative context for sexual acts for the Christian, it is possible to judge sexual acts in other contexts as *nonnormative but objectively justifiable in the exceptional situation,* including that of the confirmed homosexual." It is Cahill's considered judgment, finally, that while homogenital acts are generally to be avoided as "evil," conditions may prevail in the lives of true homosexuals such that, for them, homogenital behavior may legitimately be seen as a "premoral" rather than a "moral" evil.[65] Presumably, however, this possibility is limited to the genital acts which occur within stable and committed relationships of mutual love.

Other Catholic theologians propose ideas similar to Cahill's. Thus Edward Vacek, for example, observes that while homogenital acts are obviously "biologically deficient" since they are not open to the possibility of procreation, it nonetheless seems inhuman ". . . automatically to deprive homosexuals of the values that Christians have found in sexuality. Such values include pleasure, romantic feelings, companionship, mutual support, sexual outlet, ecstacy, intimacy, and interpersonal communication." If we must insist that all homogenital behavior is to be avoided, even by true homosexuals living in a stable and faithful relationship of mutual love, then we are reduced to saying that to be a homosexual is necessarily to be biologically

[64] *Ibid.,* pp. 87-8.
[65] *Ibid.,* pp. 90-1.

fated to a life of involuntary celibacy. Unconvinced that all homosexuals are so fated, Vacek concludes that, in itself, the biological deficiency of homogenital behavior does not seem "serious enough in our time to justify" the view that true homosexuals, of necessity, are and must be deprived of any moral opportunity to experience the positive values of a committed, loving, sexual relationship.[66]

The procreative and heterosexual norm for genital activity also grounds the conclusions drawn by Philip Keane in his analysis of the morality of homogenital behavior. Keane makes several important observations: (1) homosexuals whose sexual orientation is not firmly established or irreversible should attempt growth toward heterosexuality; moreover, if a person "who is free to develop as a heterosexual is not seeking to do so, but is deliberately seeking homosexual acts, these acts are objectively immoral"; (2) any "manifestly irresponsible" actions like the seduction of youth or involvement with homosexual prostitution are objectively immoral, even for true or irreversible homosexuals; (3) any true homosexual "who feels genuinely free to live a life of perfect chastity. . . ought morally to take this option"; and (4) in the case of a true homosexual who has no experience of being free to choose perfect chastity, homogenital behavior within the context of a stable and committed love relationship that desires permanency may be viewed not as an objective moral evil, but rather as a premoral or ontic evil.[67]

In explaining his position on homogenital acts within stable loving relationships involving true homosexuals, Keane admits that permanency in such unions is difficult to achieve, given the fact that there is no civil or religious recognition or support of

[66]Edward Vacek, S.J., "A Christian Homosexuality," *Commonweal,* CVII, 22 (Dec. 5, 1981), 681-84 at 684.

[67]Philip S. Keane, S.S., *Sexual Morality. A Catholic Perspective* (New York: Paulist Press, 1977), pp. 84-5. Keane also maintains that bisexuals should attempt to move toward heterosexuality; if this is not possible, movement toward homosexuality is preferable to remaining in the state of bisexuality; cf. pp. 90-1, 207, n.33. I call attention to the fact that even McNeill, who, unlike the other Catholic theologians being considered here, contends that the notion of male/female complementarity need not be viewed as normative for sexual relationships (cf. *Church and the Homosexual,* pp. 62-3), advises true homosexuals to attempt to live without an active sex life. He offers this counsel, however, only because of the violence and discrimination to which active homosexuals are exposed; he says also that because of the feelings of guilt and self-hatred which are often associated with homogenital acts as a result of religious

such relationships. Despite this difficulty, Keane nonetheless suggests that within the context of these stable unions the premoral evil, which homogenital acts necessarily involve "because of their lack of openness to procreation and to the man/woman relationship as it functions in marriage," is prevented from becoming an objective moral evil. The reason for this, is that within such stable and loving relationships, the sexual acts involve the proportionate good of contributing "to the growth and development of both parties." Moreover, such relationships are seen as strengthening "the homosexual couple's sense of self-worth" and as enabling "them to contribute more effectively to the good of society."[68]

Keane goes on to say that the premoral evil involved in homogenital actions warrants society's and religion's refusal to permit or recognize homosexual marriages; at the same time, however, he believes that society and the Catholic Church "should be open to finding other ways of supporting stable homosexual unions." Finally, Keane remarks that in light of society's and Christianity's long-standing instinct that "the heterosexual family is the best atmosphere for the rearing of children," he considers it justified that we continue "to bar the adoption of children by homosexual couples." I am not exactly sure what Keane's rationale here is, especially since he is not opposed to single adults adopting children, presumably even if they are homosexual adults.[69] Possibly, Keane is concerned that children raised by two members of the same sex will be confused and embarrassed by this arrangement when it is contrasted with the family-constellation common to most other households. Perhaps, too, he is fearful that adoption by a homosexual couple would provide role-modeling that would entice a child into a homosexual lifestyle, but I am not aware of any evidence that would support or validate this fear, especially since the influence of role-models upon others seems mostly, if not exclusively, limited to those matters involving the exercise of free choice; but the creation or establishment of a person's

teaching and societal ridicule, it is likely that any active homosexual relationship may prove harmful to the individuals involved. Notice, however, that these cautions do not imply that homosexual behavior is seen as being evil in itself (cf. pp. 164-72).

[68] *Ibid.*, pp. 87, 85.

[69] *Ibid.*, pp. 89, 207 n.31.

basic sex orientation is not the result of any free-choice decision.[70]

We turn finally to the thoughts of Charles Curran, whose basic position regarding homogenital behavior has been clear for a number of years.[71] Like Keane, Curran maintains that homosexuals whose sexual orientation is not firmly established and irreversible "have a moral obligation to strive for a loving heterosexual union."[72] In the case of true homosexuals, however, whose sexual orientation is irreversibly defined, homogenital acts within "the context of a loving relationship striving for permanency are objectively morally good." Curran believes that such stable and faithful relationships of sexual love must be accepted insofar as they are the only way in which some irreversible homosexuals "can find a satisfying degree of humanity in their lives."[73] But in no way is the acceptance of these homosexual unions meant to deny the fact that the ideal and normative meaning "of human sexual relationships is in terms of male and female."[74]

In further delineating his position, Curran notes that he does not think all homosexuals are called to celibacy. He suggests, moreover, that the reason why, under the conditions outlined above, homogenital acts can be objectively good in the life of a true homosexual is that they are grounded in that person's homosexual psychic structure and humanity, which differ from the psychic structure and humanity of a heterosexual. And, quite simply, if "morality follows from our being," then "we should act in accord with who and what we are"; this means that a true homosexual's activity "can and should correspond" to his or her homosexual nature and orientation. Not all

[70]See Letha Scanzoni and Virginia Ramey Mollenkott, *Is the Homosexual My Neighbor? Another Christian View* (New York: Harper & Row, 1978), p. 100. The authors are here speaking against the argument that teachers known to be homosexuals might cause harm to children who admired them as role-models; later, the authors suggest, in fact, that homosexual teachers can have a very positive influence upon the lives of some students (pp. 101-03).

[71]Curran's views on homosexuality may be found in three of his books: *Catholic Moral Theology in Dialogue* (Notre Dame, Ind.: Fides Publishers, 1972), pp. 184-219; *Transition and Tradition in Moral Theology* (Notre Dame: Notre Dame Univ. Press, 1979), pp. 59-80; and *Critical Concerns in Moral Theology* (Notre Dame: Notre Dame Univ. Press, 1984), pp. 73-98.

[72]Curran, *Transition and Tradition*, p. 77.

[73]Curran, *Theology in Dialogue*, p. 217.

[74]Curran, *Critical Concerns*, pp. 92-3.

homogenital acts of true homosexuals are justified, however, but only those which occur "within the context of a loving, faithful relationship striving for permanency."[75]

Curran must now confront the task of reconciling the idea that heterosexual genital relationships remain the Christian ideal and norm with his view that at least for some people (true homosexuals), some homogenital actions (those that occur between faithfully committed lovers) are objectively morally good. He believes that such a reconciliation is indeed possible if his position on homogenital acts is viewed within the broader framework of his theology or theory of compromise, according to which we must take serious account of the fact that all of us have been born into a world that in many diverse ways has been fragmented and ravaged by sin. This "sin of the world" affects people in different ways, and sometimes so profoundly that, through no fault of their own, they find themselves prevented from being as they would want to be; as a result, they must acquiesce to a way of acting which, under ordinary circumstances, they would not and should not want to choose.

This, for example, is the situation, says Curran, of irreversible homosexuals, whose psychic structure may be seen as but one of the effects of the sin of the world. Since these individuals bear no personal moral guilt for their sexual orientation, and since they have a desire and need for human fulfillment which they find cannot always be realized through celibacy, it seems unwarranted to deny them any moral possibility for genital activity. At the same time, however, there are limits to what can be justified by the theology of compromise. There is no place, therefore, for casual or exploitative sexual relationships in the lives of any persons, homosexual or heterosexual, nor for any activity which would violate the rights either of innocent people or of society. Finally, acknowledgment of the sin of the world does not change the fact that procreative and heterosexual expressions of love remain as the human and Christian ideal.[76]

Indeed, the only thesis being proposed is this: insofar as one admits that, for serious reasons, spouses may either temporarily or permanently be morally justified in deliberately

---

[75]Curran, *Transition and Tradition*, p. 73; *Critical Concerns*, p. 94.

[76]Curran, *Transition and Tradition*, pp. 73-8; *Critical Concerns*, pp. 93-6; *Theology in Dialogue*, pp. 216-19.

engaging in contraceptive or nonprocreative genital acts, and insofar as one further admits that two truly homosexually oriented people are just as capable of a mutully loving and committed relationship as are two heterosexually oriented individuals, the possibility for objectively moral expressions of homogenital sex under certain limited conditions seems to be established.

SUMMARY REMARKS

The Catholic theologians whose views we have been considering are sometimes referred to as "revisionists" insofar as they "revise" official Catholic teaching by proposing that homogenital acts within the confines "of a faithful, stable, mutual relationship can be morally justified and acceptable."[77] Regarding the general stance of the revisionist moralists, several things should be noted. To begin with, it is never their contention either that active sexual involvement in a homosexual lifestyle is a morally neutral alternative to marriage and family living, or that homogenital activity itself should ever be viewed as a morally neutral or indifferent act. Undeniably, there are elements of the homosexual sub-culture which are simply irreconcilable with the Christian way of life. Thus, for example, all sexual activity which is violent or coercive, anonymous or impersonal, promiscuous or seductive of the young and innocent is clearly unacceptable, both humanly and morally, and to whatever extent the homosexual sub-culture encourages or condones this type of behavior, it needs and deserves to be criticized.[78] Furthermore, to whatever degree a homosexual's contact or involvement with the gay sub-culture usually leads to participation in the kind of sexual activity just described, that sub-culture must be regarded as dehumanizing and harmful to the individual's spiritual growth, in which case the homosexual has a responsibility to try to find some personal and social support-system that is more conducive to development as a human being and as a Christian.

As explained earlier, the revisionist position entails and intends no denial of the ideal of permanent and exclusive relationships of procreative heterosexual love, nor does it believe that this ideal is

---

[77]Curran, *Critical Concerns,* pp. 90-1.

[78]Malloy, *op. cit.,* pp. 328, 358.

necessarily undermined by the proposal that homogenital activity be seen as a ˌpremoral evil when occurring within the context of a committed love-relationship that is striving for permanence and exclusivity. In fact, say the revisionists, apart from the obvious and significant obligations associated with procreation and biological parenting, homosexuals are subject to the same criteria, and must face the same responsibilities, with which heterosexuals struggle when trying to give appropriate sexual expression to human love. And even spouses may be deprived of, or take it upon themselves to curtail, their procreative powers, either temporarily or permanently, without moral fault being attributed to their sexual expressions of love. For some couples, in other words, contraceptive marital intercourse itself exists as a premoral evil and not as an objective moral wrong.

Of course, critics of the revisionists' stance not only deny the moral permissibility of homogenital activity for constitutive homosexuals involved in stable and loving relationships that are seeking permanence; rather, they go further and claim that the revisionists' position is of little practical use in that it smacks of "unreality" since very few homosexuals find the revisionists' conditions or stipulations concerning homogenital activity's existence as a premoral evil desirable or attractive, and that even if they do, they remain incapable of fulfilling them. This is Malloy's view and he notes in support of it that "many observers of the gay scene remain unconvinced that the intimacy, commitment, and perseverance of the idealized gay couple is possible for the majority of homosexuals." Malloy maintains that homosexuals involved in loving relationships of an exclusive and permanent nature will always be the exception to the usual homosexual lifestyle. This is due, he says, not only to the lack of support, sympathy, understanding and encouragement shown such unions by either "straight" society or the gay sub-culture, but also, as mentioned earlier, to the general tendency of such relationships to inspire "boredom and dissatisfaction."[79]

In support of his position, Malloy makes reference to the study done by Bell and Weinberg in which the authors found that most homosexuals fall into one of five categories: close-coupled, open-

---

[79]*Ibid.*, p. 136; see also pp. 323-28, 234.

coupled, functional, dysfunctional and asexual.[80] Among male homosexuals, about 10% are involved in close-coupled relationships, while 28% of lesbians are in such unions. These close-coupled homosexuals are described as living in quasi-marriages with few regrets about their homosexuality and with few sexual problems. Only these close-coupled homosexuals approach the kind of relationship that the revisionists see as the required context within which homogenital activity may exist as a premoral evil rather than as an objective moral wrong, but even in these close-coupled situations, data on long-term permanence are hard to come by, and the failure to maintain exclusivity is common, at least among males.[81]

Confronted with this information, revisionists must indeed admit that the existence of exclusive loving relationships seeking permanence is rare among homosexuals, but, they say, the rarity of such unions does not in itself undermine the thesis that within the context of such relationships homogenital activity exists as a premoral evil. In response, moreover, to the criticism that their position is unrealistic because homosexuals find it too unattractive and/or too difficult, revisionists might well urge the point that in the life of the Church the propriety and validity of a moral challenge is not tested by the enthusiasm or ease with which that challenge is met. Clearly, then, most homosexuals may well find the establishment of permanent and exclusive relationships difficult and restrictive, but not as burdensome and frustrating, perhaps, as observance of the norm of complete genital abstinence. The revisionists might observe, finally, that when a constitutive homosexual involved in a stable loving relationship fails on occasion to maintain exclusivity and engages in genital activity with someone else, it is not clear that such "affairs," which are judged, at the very least, as objective moral wrongs, would automatically change the moral status of the genital activity which is part of the ongoing loving relationship in such a way that this activity ceases to be a premoral evil and would now have to be regarded as an objective moral wrong.

---

[80]The work referred to is *Homosexualities;* see note 28 of this chapter.

[81]For more information on the typology of homosexuals, see Malloy, *op. cit.,* pp. 126-31; Bell and Weinberg, *op. cit.,* pp. 132-33, 219-20; William H. Masters, Virginia E. Johnson, Robert C. Kolodny, *Human Sexuality* (Boston: Little, Brown and Company, 1982), pp. 328-29.

A few comments now seem warranted in light of some points made earlier. It should be said, first of all, that if homogenital acts were sometimes to be morally permitted, but only in the lives of true homosexuals, then it would seem imperative that people who experience homosexual attraction should take the steps necessary to discover whether they are indeed constitutively or permanently homosexually oriented or are only going through a temporary phase of psycho-sexual development. In their search for companionship and love, homosexuals, of course, face the same difficult task and moral obligation as heterosexuals to be restrained and circumspect in sexual expression. Furthermore, pseudo-homosexuals or those going through a transitory stage of sexual development would seem always to be involved in objective moral wrong were they to engage in homogenital actions, since there would be little or no likelihood of these actions ever being a part of a mutually helpful, stable and loving relationship that is geared to permanency and exclusivity.

In light of what was just said, it seems necessary and prudent to suggest that especially adolescents and young adults, who may be either experiencing homosexual inclinations or involved in homosexual activity, should be advised and encouraged to seek some kind of professional counseling in order to gain some insight and assurance regarding their true sexual orientation. They may not be truly homosexually oriented at all, or if they are, there is reason to say that the possibility for sexual reorientation is greater in the lives of young people who have had relatively little experience with overt homogenital behavior. Even in the case of young people, however, the process of sexual reorientation may be expected to be personally draining, time-consuming and costly, and therapy, of course, holds no guarantee of success. Nonetheless, even when reorientation does not occur, these people may come to view both their sexual being and themselves with more understanding and peaceful acceptance.

VII. Some Pastoral Observations

It is important that pastors and counselors be sensitive to some of the inner upheaval that may be part of the experience of the homosexuals whom they are called upon to help. As the Catholic bishops of England and Wales point out, "Homosexuals may feel that nature in some way cheated them and produced tensions which are undeserved...[They] can be shattered on discovering that...[they have] permanent tendencies through no personal fault [of their own] which arouse antagonism, ridicule and rejection in society....They may well feel that the Church is demanding impossible standards."[82]

It is helpful, too, for pastors and counselors to be aware of, and to inform others of, the following points: (1) it is simply not true that most homosexuals are physically attracted to children and adolescents and wish to have sexual contact with them; (2) "it is inaccurate to claim that all male homosexuals are easily identifiable as effeminate or all female homosexuals as masculine"; (3) homosexuals do not automatically recognize each other; (4) being homosexually oriented does not mean automatically that a person is unstable or promiscuous; (5) it is erroneous to say that homosexuals simply need will-power in order to re-direct their sexual interest; in fact, there is no easy way to effect sexual reorientation, and homosexuals, therefore, should not be too readily criticized if they are hesitant about attempting sexual readjustment through therapy; (6) not all homosexuals are associated with radical or progressive pressure groups; (7) "it is incorrect to assert that homosexual persons sustain a higher incidence of mental disorder"; and (8) it is inaccurate to assume that homosexually oriented people "are limited to only certain social classes or professions."[83]

The American bishops advise confessors and pastors to avoid both harshness and permissiveness when counseling sexually-active homosexuals; while it is noted that homosexuals should not be told that they are not responsible for their actions, the bishops nonetheless observe that in most instances homosexuals do not

[82]Catholic bishops of England and Wales, *op. cit.*, p. 13.

[83]These points appear both in the statement of the Catholic bishops of England and Wales, p. 5, and in the statement of the San Francisco Senate of Priests, found in *Homosexuality and the Magisterium*, p. 61. It should be noted here that while homosexuality is no longer regarded as a mental disorder, pedophilia is. According to the American Psychiatric Association's *Diagnostic and Statistical Manual of Mental Disorders* (DSM-III), pedophilia is "the act or fantasy of engaging in sexual activity with prepubertal children as a repeatedly preferred or exclusive method of achieving sexual excitement." The manual goes on to say that not all pedophiliacs are homosexuals; in fact, "adults with this disorder are oriented toward children of the opposite sex twice as often as toward children of the same sex."

have full freedom of will. Moreover, homosexually oriented individuals, who have been engaged in an active sex-life, should be encouraged to deepen their spiritual life; at the same time, however, they should be made aware of the fact that, despite any resolution to begin a new way of living, "very probably there will be relapses because of long-standing habit, but this must not be allowed to be an occasion for sterile self-pity."[84]

In speaking very directly to the situation of homosexuals who are involved in exclusive, stable and loving relationships, the Catholic bishops of England and Wales claim that it "is a false and unacceptable analogy" to compare such unions to heterosexual marriages. Any genital activity that occurs within these stable homosexual relationships remains objectively immoral, according to the bishops, but pastors and confessors may nonetheless "distinguish between irresponsible, indiscriminate sexual activity and the permanent association between two homosexual persons, who feel incapable of enduring a solitary life devoid of sexual expression." The bishops then make the point that since pastoral care must consider "the individual in his actual situation, with all his strengths and weaknesses," when pastors try to evaluate homogenital acts, it is important to interpret these acts, "to understand the pattern of life in which they take place, [and] to appreciate the personal meaning which these acts have for different people." At the same time, however, pastors cannot ignore the fact that homogenital acts in themselves are objective moral wrongs.[85]

In the statements of both the American and British bishops, we find clear use of the traditional distinction between objective moral wrongs and a person's subjective responsibility which results in sin; the same distinction is emphasized by the San Francisco Senate of Priests in its pastoral plan for ministering to homosexuals. We read there: "It is one thing to consider homosexual acts from an objective perspective; it is quite another reality to judge individual homosexual people and their subjective culpability in the face of pressures and the possible loneliness which they experience."[86] The Washington State Catholic Conference likewise recognizes the legitimacy of the distinction between objective moral judgments and subjective responsibility, and does not hesitate to draw the

---

[84] *Principles to Guide Confessors*, pp. 8-9.
[85] *An Introduction to the Pastoral Care of Homosexual People*, p. 8.
[86] "Ministry and Homosexuality," in *Homosexuality and the Magisterium*, p. 65.

conclusion that no human being can judge the moral culpability or guilt of another. In its statement on ministry to homosexuals, the Conference remarks:

> A person is guilty of sin only when she or he does not do what she or he is capable of doing in progress toward . . . [the norm of total love of God and others]. Because we cannot know just where another person stands and because we cannot know just how hard that person is trying to live up to the total norm of the two great commandments . . ., we are unable to judge the degree of responsibility the individual bears . . . . We cannot judge that a homosexual who engages in homogenital activity is committing subjective sin. What we can say is that this activity falls short of the ultimate norm of Christian morality in the area of genital expression.[87]

Helpful and important as this "traditional distinction between the objective [im]morality of the act and the subjective responsibility or culpability of the person performing the act" may be, revisionist theologians do not believe that recourse to this distinction is sufficient to cope with the full range of complexities involved in trying to lead a morally good life in the midst of a sinful world. What this distinction does successfully do, is acknowledge the presence of what are called "excusing causes," which "diminish or take away subjective culpability and responsibility," so that a person may not be guilty of sin when performing an act that is an objective moral wrong. These "excusing causes" can be seen as the "internal or subjective extenuating circumstances" we referred to earlier (in chapter three). Given their presence, it is entirely within the stream of traditional thinking to say that "even if an act is objectively morally wrong, the formal act or choice of the individual who is existentially unable to realize [or fulfill] the moral obligation is morally good [i.e., not sinful]." A person who is simply existentially incapable of meeting a particular moral obligation is said to be caught in "invincible ignorance" regarding that matter.[88]

What the traditional "objectively wrong/subjectively not culpable" distinction does not address, however, is the possibility that, in addition to "excusing causes," there are also "justifying

[87]"The Prejudice Against Homosexuals," in *Homosexuality & the Magisterium*, p. 49.
[88]Curran, *Critical Concerns*, pp. 239-47.

causes" which at times can make some act morally acceptable, even though most often that act would have to be regarded as an objective moral wrong.[89] In other words, the notion of "justifying causes" may be linked to what we earlier called "external or objective extenuating circumstances" which together constitute a proportionate or sufficient reason for viewing an act that ordinarily is an objective moral wrong as now a *premoral* or ontic wrong; as a *premoral* wrong, such an action, by definition, is not an objective *moral* wrong and hence may be seen as a morally acceptable act.

The official Catholic teaching that homogenital acts must always be judged as objectively immoral, no matter what the circumstances, necessarily has an impact on the pastoral advice that is given to true homosexuals who find themselves in exclusive, stable and loving relationships which may occasionally involve genital activity. The Church clearly recognizes and encourages the human and spiritual good that can be part of such close, loving relationships, and thus she does not require that homosexuals abandon them, even though the love shared in these relationships sometimes finds expression in explicit sexual actions. But since the Church always regards any homogenital activity as an objective moral wrong, she insists that homosexuals in such loving relationships that are striving for permanency must aim at, and struggle for, the elimination of all genital behavior from their lives. At the same time, however, the Church acknowledges that homosexual couples will probably not be able to achieve this goal immediately, but only gradually.[90]

In contrast to this official Church teaching, revisionist theologians propose that in light of the mutual support, love and enhancement of human growth that accompany such stable homosexual relationships which desire permanency, whatever genital activity occurs within these unions may be viewed as a premoral wrong, not an objective moral wrong; as such, this activity may be morally permitted for true homosexuals within the kind of relationships just described, even though it is never the moral ideal. Many revisionists, moreover, express the fear that the Church's continued insistence that true homosexuals must profess genital abstinence as their goal within stable, loving relationships,

---

[89] *Ibid.,* p. 239.

[90] *Principles to Guide Confessors,* p. 11; see also the "principle of gradualism" referred to by the San Francisco Senate of Priests, *Homosexuality and the Magisterium,* pp. 62-4.

will only serve to create and foster in these individuals an ongoing state of tension and a sense of inauthenticity, duplicity and frustration, insofar as they themselves often do not believe in their hearts that God is requiring of them a lifetime devoid of any genital expressions of love.[91] This is not to deny, of course, that at times heterosexuals must live without genital activity, i.e., before marriage, or when separated or divorced, or when widowed. But these people live with the hope, and very often with the real possibility, that the future will allow them to initiate or renew genital activity. Irreversible homosexuals are allowed no such hope or possibility, however, according to traditional Church teaching.

I wish, finally, to end this chapter with the sensitive reminder that appeared as part of the statement issued by the Roman Catholic Church of Baltimore when it announced the beginning of its formal and public ministry to the homosexual community in 1981:

> The ministry of the Roman Catholic Church to gays and lesbians . . . is always a pastoral ministry. It is a ministry which is not content merely to repeat the challenge Christ sets before each generation; it seeks to work with each individual, taking into account that person's particular strengths and weaknesses, and helping that person make the fullest response possible at this moment in his or her life. This pastoral concern for the individual has sometimes given people the impression that the Church no longer takes a stand on the meaning and demands of sexuality and that it allows the individual to do whatever he or she wants. Such is not the case, [but] . . . the only way the Church could make certain that such an impression would not be taken would be for the Church to stop using a pastoral approach to ministry. Should that be done, however, Christ's call to perfection could appear as a harsh, impersonal law that is blind to the weaknesses and limitations of the human condition; and the face of a merciful God, as revealed to us so powerfully through Christ, would be covered and lost to sight.[92]

---

[91]A similar fear might be associated with the Church's demand that a man and woman involved in what is seen as an invalid "second" marriage must either separate or strive to live together as brother and sister if they wish to be in good standing with the Church and to receive the sacraments.

[92]"A Ministry to Lesbian and Gay Catholic Persons," in *Homosexuality and the Magisterium*, p. 39.

VIII

Masturbation: Some Human Meanings, Moral Evaluations and Pastoral Advice

I. Introduction

As Father John Kirvan of Wayne State University points out in his book, *The Restless Believers*, it is usually in a bout with masturbation that the young male Catholic first confronts the challenge of Christianity in a meaningful way.... The problem of masturbation is a real scourge of the Catholic confessional. During the most sensitive years of their lives, the possibility of the "state of grace" for most young people depends—in the estimation of textbook theology and the young people themselves—upon the possibility of their refraining from masturbation.

The above statements are taken from the opening paragraph of a chapter on masturbation that appeared in a 1968 publication.[1] The sentiments expressed, however astounding they may appear to be, are hardly off-target in reporting on the attitude surrounding masturbation which seems to have prevailed up until the late sixties. The scene, of course, is far different today. The Catholic population, at least insofar as it is

---

[1]Robert P. O'Neil and Michael A. Donovan, *Sexuality and Moral Responsibility* (Washington; Corpus Books, 1968), p. 99; the authors make reference to J. Kirvan, *The Restless Believers* (Glen Rock, N.J.: Paulist Press, 1966).

represented in the college students with whom I have had contact, does not think much about masturbation; not much concern, worry or guilt seems to be experienced over masturbation, nor does it serve as a prime or central topic in the sacrament of reconciliation.

For the most part, young people do recognize that there can be something emotionally unhealthy and unfulfilling about masturbation but this, they judge, is true only when such activity becomes habitual and too self-preoccupying. I do not mean to imply that young Catholics are all of one mind regarding masturbation. Such, of course, is not the case. As we might expect, there are some variations in the views held on this issue by Catholics, and these reflect in large measure both the diverse understandings which professional psychologists and theologians have of masturbation and the different evaluations they make of it. In an attempt to make some sense of the teachings regarding masturbation, I suggest that we must be cautious not to dismiss the issue as inconsequential; at the same time, however, it must be admitted that serious questions have been raised about the stance which maintains that every act of masturbation, in and of itself, is morally wrong.

In this chapter we will be presenting the views of several different authors, some of whom emphasize the psychological dimension and meaning of masturbation, while others focus more directly on the moral assessment of the act. It should be said immediately that a good many writers would maintain that a moral assessment of masturbation, or of any act for that matter, should never be attempted, and will probably be inadequate, without reference to the action's psychological or human significance. The traditional teaching of the Roman Catholic Church on masturbation will be discussed, and the chapter will conclude with some pastoral advice on dealing not only with masturbation, but also with the whole matter of temptation and sexual frustration.

II. Some Psychological Interpretations of Masturbation

The psychologist, Eugene Kennedy, has remarked that "masturbation has suffered from a horrendous mythology for centuries"; it has been characterized as "a wicked and perverse experience, one capable of corrupting a person physically and psychologically." The effect of such mythology has been to burden people "with a great and unnecessary sense of guilt." Admittedly, in recent years a "more sensible and compassionate understanding of masturbation has been achieved," but, says Kennedy, if the whole truth be told, a new myth has in fact been born about masturbation, namely, that it is "something not to worry about at all, just 'the second best kind of sex'." People are told that they should feel quite free about masturbating because it is one of those actions that simply "don't hurt anybody."[2]

Kennedy does not buy into either of these myths; he is not satisfied with regarding masturbation as always sinful, but neither does he consider it honest or prudent to glorify masturbation or to regard it as virtuous. According to Kennedy, masturbation does indeed have different meanings. Sometimes the act can be expressive of a person's, especially an adolescent's, efforts to understand and integrate the various elements of his self-identity as a sexual being so that he can move on to the level of mature interpersonal relationships. At other times, however, masturbation can be stultifying and isolating. This occurs, for example, when a person "finds the locus of all pleasure in himself," with the result that "he cannot pass through the further stage of being able to share himself, which is essential to his complete growth." At the very least, says Kennedy, masturbation is a complex phenomenon, and to suggest otherwise is a serious disservice to people.[3]

Kennedy refuses to evaluate masturbation simply and immediately by means of the category of moral right or wrong; as was indicated above, however, this is not to say that

---

[2] The quotes in this paragraph are from Eugene C. Kennedy, *The New Sexuality: Myths, Fables, and Hang-Ups* (New York: Doubleday, 1972), pp. 121-22.

[3] *Ibid.*, pp. 123-26.

masturbation is insignificant, and Kennedy does not advocate masturbation as a "healthy outlet" for sexual tension.[4] He nonetheless does prefer to talk of masturbation as a question more of growth than of sin. Thus, while he is not sympathetic to the teaching that masturbation is an intrinsically evil act, he clearly acknowledges that there are moral dimensions or implications to masturbation insofar as it frustrates or impairs an individual's capacity for the joy of interpersonal living and loving. Yet Kennedy maintains that the moral question is probably best and properly addressed only within the broader context of attending to the psychological needs and blocks which are making their presence felt through a person's recourse to masturbation.[5]

Freud himself observed that "...the problem of masturbation becomes insoluble if we attempt to treat it as a clinical unit, and forget that it can represent the discharge of every variety of sexual component and of every sort of fantasy to which such components give rise."[6] For Freud, in other words, masturbation is not to be regarded as a problem or entity in itself, but rather should be seen as an action that expresses or reflects some internal psychosexual state. In recent years masturbation has been viewed in contexts broader even than those suggested by Freud. In adolescence, for example, masturbation is often symptomatic of many non-sexual conflicts. This has led *Siecus* (Sex Information and Education Council of the U.S.) to maintain that:

> Boredom, frustration, loneliness, a poor self-image, inadequate boy-girl relationships, conflict with parents, too many pressures in school, etc., can all create tensions that the adolescent tries to relieve through masturbation. In some cases it is not the

[4]Eugene Kennedy, *What a Modern Catholic Believes about Sex and Marriage* (Chicago: The Thomas More Press, 1975), p. 56.

[5]*Ibid.*, p. 60.

[6]S. Freud, "A Case of Obsessional Neurosis," in *Standard Edition of the Works of Sigmund Freud*, Vol. X, (London, The Hogarth Press, 1955), quoted by Peter Blos, *On Adolescence* (New York: The Free Press, 1962), p. 160.

masturbation that must be examined, but the conflict of which it is a symptom; and counseling or psychotherapy may be indicated.

The suggestion that masturbation has many meanings has found wide support. It is not uncommon today even to describe some masturbation in positive terms as an experience that can be healthy and mature. In his book, *The Sexual Celibate*, Donald Goergen reports with apparent approval on the view of those psychologists who maintain that apart from instances where the act is clearly abusive, masturbation is normal and healthy; this is certainly the case regarding infantile masturbation, and in large measure it holds true for adolescent and adult masturbation. Goergen maintains that masturbation does not cause any psychological disturbance; rather the opposite is true: such disturbance may cause masturbation. If, moreover, there are any psychological problems associated with masturbation, they "do not arise from the masturbatory activity but from the individual's attitude towards it." The practical conclusion Goergen reaches is this: "Only if masturbation is the exclusive sexual release where heterosexual relations are possible is it pathological. When masturbation is preferred to intercourse, something is wrong."[7]

Pursuing the same line of thought, the psychiatrist, Dr. Frederick Perls, believes that masturbation is healthy when it expresses an outgoing drive and serves as a substitute for intercourse when intercourse simply is not available: "The healthy masturbation fantasy would be that of approaching and having intercourse with a beloved person."[8] Quite a different position, however, is taken by another psychiatrist, Dr. Thomas Hora, who maintains that "masturbation as a substitution for intercourse with a beloved person when the opportunity for intercourse is not available is unhealthy and

[7]Donald Goergen, *The Sexual Celibate* (New York: The Seabury Press, 1974), pp. 197-99.

[8]Frederick Perls, *Gestalt Therapy* (New York: Dell Publishing Co., 1951), p. 178, as quoted by Bernard J. Tyrrell, S.J., "*The Sexual Celibate* and Masturbation," *Review for Religious*, 35, 3 (1976), 402.

inauthentic." Hora sees such masturbation as trivializing the sacredness and mystery of intercourse and as diminishing its significance. Rather than being simply a substitute for loving intercourse, masturbation is more a counterfeit of it; "masturbation allures and attracts but in the end it is an illusion which confers the opposite of what it promises: a sense of emptiness and non-being rather than fulfillment."[9]

Behind many of the varying psychological interpretations given to masturbation is a general principle that has been articulated by Goergen: "Insofar as any sexual expression is destructive of our physical, emotional, or spiritual growth, it is abusive. Insofar, however, as it is constructive and contributes to our physical, emotional and spiritual life, it is mature."[10] This principle itself, I believe, needs to be carefully nuanced, for I doubt that any masturbation, in and of itself, is directly constructive or promotive of our human or moral growth; this is not to say, of course, that all masturbation can be immediately written off as a serious moral evil. The issues of maturity and morality are surely related but they are not identical. Goergen does, in fact, have much to say about masturbation that is of value. In the following paragraphs we will take a more studied look at some of his observations on this issue before turning to the specific question of the moral evaluation of masturbation.

Although Goergen does not consider masturbation to be intrinsically immoral, the activity does, he says, raise some moral questions, not the least of which is the psychological danger that human sexuality might become a solitary and, hence, selfish experience rather than a shared one. According to Goergen, masturbation is neither necessarily nor even usually, perhaps, a selfish act; still, a definite possibility remains that such activity will lead a person "in the direction of narcissistic rather than interpersonal sexuality." Clearly, "masturbation is not in complete accord with the goal of sexuality, which is other-oriented love;" at the same time, however, Goergen can imagine situations in which this goal of other-oriented love

---

[9]Tyrrell, *op.cit.*, 403-04; the quotations indicate Tyrrell's summary analysis of Hora's position as derived from conversations, tapes and articles.

[10]Goergen, *op. cit.*, pp. 201-02.

need not be violated or betrayed by the act of masturbation. One example of how love might sometimes even be protected by masturbation is in the case of a married person who masturbates instead of having intercourse with someone else when sexual relations with his or her spouse are rendered impossible for some long period of time due to physical separation or illness.[11] It might be suggested also that another instance where masturbation would seem not to violate other-oriented love would be when a man masturbates in order to obtain sperm for fertility-testing so as to see if there is a way of enhancing the possibility of procreating with his wife.

When all is said and done, Goergen suggests that "it is as false to say that masturbation is always wrong as it is to say that it is never wrong."[12] What can be most safely maintained, perhaps, is that masturbation points to the unfinishedness of the process of a person's sexual and spiritual integration as a human being. Goergen develops this point with wisdom and sensitivity:

> To be unfinished is not to be immoral nor irresponsible. It is, however, to be challenged toward further growth. We must accept unfinishedness but not choose to remain there. There will always be the tension between accepting ourselves where we are and striving after the ideals of Christian life. . . . We should not be ashamed of our present stage of growth nor should we stagnate there.[13]

It should be noted that in the quotation above, Goergen is speaking specifically of masturbation in the lives of professed or vowed celibates. In his judgment, masturbation in the life of a celibate reflects a need which the celibate should hope to outgrow simply because genital expressions of sexuality are of no particular service to the lifestyle which has been freely chosen.[14] What Goergen says about masturbation as an indication of a celibate's unfinishedness in terms of human and

[11]*Ibid.*, p. 201.
[12]*Ibid.*, p. 201.
[13]*Ibid.*, pp. 203-04.
[14]*Ibid.*, p. 204.

spiritual growth, should be applied as well, I believe, to the experience of masturbation more broadly, for no one, I think, ought to be complacent over a period of time about the habitual presence of masturbation in his or her life. Progress toward full sexual integration may well be slow, and I would hope that the journey might be undertaken more peacefully than seems often to be the case, but I think everyone, not just vowed celibates, should be encouraged to move step by step beyond the unfinishedness reflected in masturbation. Along the way, help may be derived from the recollection that, for everyone, the gift of sexuality is meant to be of service to us in our relationships with God and our fellow human beings.[15] This truth is pertinent also in trying to morally evaluate masturbation.

III. Varying Moral Perceptions Regarding Masturbation

One looks in vain to the Old and New Testaments for any specific or explicit condemnation of masturbation. The Old Testament does make reference to seminal discharges (Lev. 15:16) and nocturnal emissions (Dt. 23:9-11) to say that they make a man temporarily unclean and ritually impure; in the New Testament, we are told to use our bodies in a way "that is holy and honorable, not giving way to selfish lust..." (1 Thes. 4:3-4), and "people of immoral lives" are warned that they will not inherit the kingdom of God (1 Cor. 6:9-10). Scripture scholars seem to agree, however, that there is no convincing proof that any of the passages cited pertain to the morality of masturbation as such.[16]

The lack of scriptural condemnation notwithstanding, there exists a long line of magisterial pronouncements against masturbation going all the way back to the eleventh century. Among other things, we find in the teachings a prohibition

---

[15]*Ibid..*, p. 204.

[16]See Anthony Kosnik, *et al., Human Sexuality: New Directions in American Catholic Thought* (New York: Paulist Press, 1977), p. 219; John Dedek, *Contemporary Sexual Morality* (Kansas City: Sheed Andrews and McMeel, 1971), pp. 49-51.

against masturbation as a means of obtaining seminal speci-
mens, and a warning against admitting into religious life or
sacred orders any candidate who has had a habit of masturbating and has not given consistent proof for a period of about a
year that the habit has been broken.[17] The traditional, present
and official teaching of the Roman Catholic Church on
masturbation is clearly and concisely stated in the 1975
Declaration on Certain Questions Concerning Sexual Ethics
which was prepared by the Sacred Congregation for the
Doctrine of the Faith:

> ... both the Magisterium of the Church — in the course of a
> constant tradition — and the moral sense of the faithful have
> declared without hesitation that masturbation is an intrinsically
> and seriously disordered act. The main reason is that,whatever
> the motive for acting in this way, the deliberate use of the sexual
> faculty outside normal conjugal relations essentially contradicts
> the finality of the faculty. For it lacks the sexual relationship
> called for by the moral order, namely the relationship which
> realizes "the full sense of mutual self-giving and human
> procreation in the context of true love."[*Pastoral Constitution
> on the Church in the Modern world*, #51] All deliberate exercise
> of sexuality must be reserved to this regular relationship.[18]

Over the years the arguments against the morality of
masturbation have taken different forms. Sometimes the
prohibition focused on the waste of sperm that is involved in
masturbation, but critics of this argument have been quick to
point out that most sperm are wasted anyway either through
nocturnal emission or through intercourse with a sterile woman
or in intercourse with a fertile woman during her non-fertile
periods. Besides, this argument is useless against female
masturbation. Even under the best conditions, of course,
procreation is the result of an ovum's fertilization by one sperm
only so that in some sense millions of sperm are lost or wasted

[17]The teachings of these magisterial pronouncements can be found in Kosnik *et al.*,
op. cit., pp. 220-23 and in Dedek, *op. cit.*, pp. 51-55.

[18]#9 of the *Declaration*.

even in an act of sexual intercourse which results in the creation of a new life. In the past it was also argued that unless masturbation were strictly forbidden, the good of the species would be endangered since people would not marry. This approach obviously falsely or gratuitously assumed that most people would find masturbation, more or less permanently, a suitable and fulfilling substitute for both sexual intercourse and the psychological fulfillment of an intimate personal relationship. Today, these arguments are regarded as largely unpersuasive and have, for the most part, been abandoned.[19]

Among contemporary Roman Catholic theologians there are varied opinions regarding the moral status of masturbation. Norbert Brockman has masterfully articulated four positions which currently indicate the spectrum of thought within the Church today. I quote Brockman at length because it would be difficult to improve upon his formulation of the different stances.[20] He first identifies the traditional moral understanding of masturbation:

> Masturbation is objectively a serious sin. Except in rare cases, it is also subjectively sinful, and the average person who gives in to masturbation, either as a teenager or as an adult, commits sin. Through confession and the sacraments, a person of good will can obtain the grace to overcome this habit, if he is willing to mortify himself and to avoid occasions of sin.

The next formulation describes what may be called "the diminished freedom view":

> Masturbation is far from being a simple sexual sin, but is part of the complex process of maturation. While it is always objectively sinful, habitual masturbation usually involves a significant diminishing of freedom, so that in many cases it is

---

[19]Dedek, *op. cit.* pp. 55-6.

[20]Norbert C. Brockman, S.M., "Contemporary Attitudes on the Morality of Masturbation," *The American Ecclesiastical Review*, 166 (1972), 597-614. All four of the views on masturbation are presented on pp. 602-03, or see Goergen, *op. cit.*, pp. 199-200.

unwise to consider the person who has this problem as being morally responsible, at least in regard to serious sin.

The third view is the one involving a person's "fundamental option":

> While masturbation is a moral question, for the average person it is not necessarily to be regarded as seriously sinful. A particular individual action has meaning insofar as it makes incarnate and intensifies the fundamental moral choice that man must make between God and creatures, which ultimately means self. It is difficult to imagine that an act of masturbation could be regarded as such a fundamental choice.

Finally, Brockman presents "the neutral attitude" toward the morality of masturbation:

> Masturbation is such a normal part of growing up that the only serious evil that can be attached to it arises from the unfortunate guilt feelings that come from early training and negative attitudes toward sexuality. Masturbation represents a phase through which a person grows toward interpersonal relationships.

By way of commentary on these various evaluations of the morality of masturbation, several observations are in order. To begin with, the official teaching of the Roman Catholic Church is reflected, for the most part, in what Brockman presents as the traditional teaching on masturbation, and yet the Church does recognize the fact that on occasion a person may truly experience a curtailment of freedom in his or her behavior (the second view), so that while the act of masturbation remains objectively a serious wrong, the individual is not subjectively responsible for, or guilty of, a serious sin. The 1975 *Declaration Concerning Sexual Ethics* does, however, state the Church's teaching on masturbation in such a way as to be more cautious than "the diminished freedom position" is in assuming that the person who masturbates is not morally responsible for serious sin:

On the subject of masturbation modern psychology provides much valid and useful information for formulating a more equitable judgment on moral responsibility and for orienting pastoral action. Psychology helps one to see how the immaturity of adolescence (which can sometimes persist after that age), psychological imbalance or habit can influence behavior, diminishing the deliberate character of the act and bringing about a situation whereby subjectively there may not always be serious fault. But in general, the absence of serious responsibility must not be presumed; this would be to misunderstand people's moral capacity.[21]

There may, indeed, be something of value in the view which attempts to determine the moral status of masturbation in terms only of what the act expresses about a person's "fundamental option" to act either on behalf of God and others or on behalf of self. Within this frame of reference, theologians do not immediately or automatically conclude that masturbation is seriously sinful or even that objectively it is a grave moral wrong. Rather, here the tendency is to take seriously the fact that masturbation can be and is symptomatic or reflective of many different personal states of being and thus has varying human meanings which must be uncovered and analyzed before a judgment can be rendered concerning its moral significance. Thus theologians might evaluate masturbation differently depending on the meaning and context of the act. Some of these meanings and evaluations may be seen in the study that was commissioned by the Catholic Theological Society of America.

Of the six types of masturbation which are reported on in that highly controversial study, we need refer to only a few. Hedonistic masturbation, which is performed "simply for the sake of the pleasure involved, without any effort at control or integration, can be indicative of self-centeredness, isolation, and evasion of relational responsibility." The study argues that to exploit one's sexuality in this manner deliberately and

[21] *Declaration Concerning Sexual Ethics*, #9.

consistently "creates a serious obstacle to personal growth and integration and constitutes the substantial inversion of the sexual order — an inversion that is at the heart of the malice of masturbation."[22]

The report speaks also of a psychological maladjustment which results in a kind of pathological masturbation where the impulse to masturbate "seems to be a compulsion, bringing little or no satisfaction and yet frequently repeated even though there is no rational explanation for the behavior." Both here and in the instances where masturbation is regularly preferred despite the availability of moral opportunities for intercourse, the individuals involved "seem to be operating out of a sexuality that has not been fully integrated." In these situations, counseling, more than moral prohibition, seems to be in order so as to discover the underlying causes of such behavior.[23]

When speaking of adolescent masturbation the authors of the *CTSA* study refrain from making any moral judgment of the act. They prefer simply to point out that at this stage of life, people are in need of "support and direction that will bring reassurance and foster growth and development in terms of reaching out to others." The report suggests that no direct attention be given to individual acts of masturbation since this could hamper human development "by focusing attention on self and deepening the youngster's sense of inadequacy." According to the report, what will be most helpful to the adolescent struggling with masturbation is that he or she be directed "to activities that strengthen self-confidence and encourage growth and interrelationship with others..." As personal development occurs, it is expected that "the masturbation in most cases will gradually disappear."[24] With reference, finally, to masturbation as a clinical procedure "for obtaining semen for fertility testing or for diagnosing certain venereal infections," the report concludes simply that this "should not be

[22]Kosnik *et al., Human Sexuality*, pp. 227-28.

[23]*Ibid.*, p. 227.

[24]*Ibid.*, p. 226.

viewed in any way as sinful or immoral."[25]

In the last several paragraphs we have seen that masturbation has been variously interpreted in human terms and, consequently, in moral terms. Thus before one makes the judgment that masturbation is subjectively sinful, it must first be determined whether or not the action accurately expresses the fact that a person's fundamental relationship with God and others is being deliberately and intentionally curtailed. In recent years, some Catholic theologians have pushed the issue even further and expressed serious doubts about maintaining the traditional and official view of the Catholic Church that, regardless of any extenuating circumstances which may excuse a person from the responsibility of sin, masturbation is always an objective moral wrong.

Philip Keane, for example, whose discussion of sexual morality we have referred to in earlier chapters, does not regard masturbation as always objectively morally wrong; the act does, however, always embody some significant premoral or ontic wrong insofar as it closes off "both the personal union aspect and the procreative aspect of physical sexual expression;" the following are some instances where Keane suggests that masturbation might be a premoral wrong but not necessarily a moral evil: adolescent masturbation, masturbation by an adult who has chosen "to remain single for some important reason (care of a sick parent, a worthwhile professional career, etc.)," masturbation by a married person whose spouse is absent or ill for a long period of time, masturbation for purposes of sperm testing.[26] When masturbation is turned to without proportionate or sufficient reason, it then carries the weight of an objective moral wrong and would be sinful if the individual knowingly and freely entered into the act.

To Keane's way of thinking, this view is faithful to "the deepest instincts and traditions of the teaching Church on

[25]*Ibid.*, p. 227.

[26]Philip S. Keane, S.S., *Sexual Morality: A Catholic Perspective* (New York: Paulist Press, 1977), pp. 66-9.

masturbation." At the same time, while his approach cannot be completely reconciled with the "Church's traditional formula that all venereal pleasure outside marriage is an objectively grave moral evil," Keane is confident that the view he maintains "stays with the tradition's main insight that directly acted-for venereal pleasure in a non-marital context is an occasion for notable human reflection and a challenge to human growth and integration." We are, in other words, simply not dealing with a minor or indifferent matter.[27]

If any consensus has emerged among Catholic theologians regarding the morality of masturbation, it would seem to fall along these lines. The immorality of masturbation does not consist in whatever obvious pleasure the act may involve; rather the action must be morally evaluated in terms of its compatibility or incompatibility with the meaning and purpose of human sexuality. If, in the full richness of its physical dimension, human sexuality is meant to be understood and valued as being not only love-giving, unitive and interpersonal, but also life-giving, procreative and heterosexual, then masturbation must necessarily be lacking in the ability to express faithfully sexuality's full meaning and purpose. In this inability, this failure, to reflect the richness of human sexuality, lies the moral problem with masturbation; "to stunt one's growth intersubjectively and heterosexually," as Dedek says, "is a serious matter."[28]

The point is obvious and indisputable, but what is not at all certain is how much any individual act of masturbation constitutes a significant distortion of the meaning of human sexuality. Years ago, Charles Curran expressed this concern: "Perhaps in the past theologians have illegitimately transferred to the individual act the importance that belongs to the sexual faculty. I am not saying that individual actions are never important; but in the total consideration of masturbation, individual actions do not always constitute a substantial

[27] *Ibid.*, pp. 70, 182.

[28] Dedek, *op. cit.*, p. 60.

inversion of human sexuality."[29] Dedek makes the same point; for him, too, "it is not clear how a single act of masturbation or a short series of these acts is a substantial inversion of growth or a substantive withdrawal from the human meaning of sexuality as unitive and procreative." Dedek can thus conclude that to the extent that masturbation neither "impedes intersubjective and heterosexual growth" nor constitutes an inversion of the meaning of human sexuality, it is not objectively immoral.[30]

In attempting to bring these thoughts on the morality of masturbation to a close, some final observations may be helpful toward obtaining an overview of the matter. All of us must learn to resist the urge toward immediate gratification of our sexual desires. Controlling our instincts, of course, is the work of a lifetime and it constitutes an integral part of the larger task of finding our true selves. The task, moreover, is successfully accomplished only to the extent that we persistently overcome the temptation to turn in upon ourselves and thereby fail to manifest a true love for others. If, as we saw earlier, our sexuality is God's way of calling us into communion with others, if it is, in fact, "both the physiological and psychological grounding of our capacity to love," then we must be on guard against the self-centeredness and self-preoccupation which can enter into our lives and become a part of our daily routine. In this context, the moral danger of masturbation is obvious: it can entrap a person in such a way that he becomes so fixed "on himself, on his body, and his own sensual pleasure that his capacity to show love in a relationship with a partner ceases to be functional."[31]

But while it may be easy to identify the moral threat involved in masturbation, honesty requires that we ask how often it

[29]Charles Curran, "Masturbation and Objectively Grave Matter," in his book, *A New Look at Christian Morality* (Notre Dame: Fides, 1968), p. 212.

[30]Dedek, *op. cit.*, p. 60.

[31]See Klaus Breuning, "Responsible Sexuality as an Educational Goal: Problems and Prospects," in *Sexuality in Contemporary Catholicism*, part of *Concilium*, Religion in the Seventies, eds. Franz Böckle and Jacques-Marie Pohier (New York: The Seabury Press, 1976), pp. 88-9, 92 n. 15 quoting R. Bleistein, *Sexualerziehung zwischen Tabu und Ideologie* (Würzburg, 1971), pp. 89-90.

happens that this threat is actualized or carried out. It is not at all clear that in the ordinary course of events masturbation does in fact give birth to such selfishness and self-centeredness that a person's desire or capacity to love is curtailed, thwarted or destroyed. Granting that the full richness and meaning of human sexuality lie in its potential to confer love and life, masturbation, without question, will always remain, objectively, an incomplete and inadequate expression of sexuality's value. But it seems that most often, especially among adolescents and young adults, recourse to masturbation indicates not a selfish or inverted aversion with regard to love, but rather a concession to the fact that one is presently prepared for, and capable of, neither love and its obligations nor parenting and its responsibilities. People who masturbate do so not because they fear or reject love, but because they have not yet discovered it; and yet, far more often than not, these people do eventually seek love, embrace it and come to learn the lessons it has to teach.

In keeping with the above, some would maintain that in order to arrive at a moral evaluation of any specific act of masturbation, it is first necessary to know within the context of a person's life what that act means as a human act for, as we have seen, masturbation can have many different human meanings. It can happen that masturbation may have little or nothing to do with sexuality and may simply serve as a response to various kinds of psychological or emotional pressures arising from school, work or inter-personal relationships; sometimes masturbation may be an expression of sexual curiosity, or function as an attempt to deal with sexual feelings and desires that have not yet been perfectly integrated. To some people, masturbation even appears as the better thing to do in the sense that it is "the lesser evil;" thus, for example, a person might masturbate rather than press his or her sexual attention on an unready partner or engage "in the full sex act without the depths of personal relationship which it properly expresses."[32]

[32]Richard F. Hettlinger, *Living With Sex: The Student's Dilemma* (New York: The Seabury Press, 1966), p. 92.

Both psychologists and theologians have come to emphasize the fact that the fantasies which quite frequently accompany masturbation are important and useful indicators of what masturbation means, first humanly and then morally. The gamut of fantasies is long and varied; they may be sadistic, incestuous, masochistic or unrealistically and ambitiously self-glorifying; a different story unfolds, of course, when a person fantasizes about his or her spouse with whom a sexual relationship has been rendered impossible or inappropriate. That fantasies in general ought to be taken very seriously when attempting to determine the human and moral significance of masturbation seems to be confirmed by a fact which has been verified by both clinical psychologists and priests engaged in pastoral counseling, namely, that the guilt "which arises as a result of masturbatory activity does not so much arise from the act itself as from the fantasies which accompany it."[33]

Thus on the basis of the fantasy-life involved in masturbation, people view themselves as desiring what is not permitted them in real life; they see themselves as being exploitative or manipulative of others; sometimes the fantasies reveal that a person yearns for and imagines a closeness with another individual without investing the work and making the commitment which such intimacy presupposes and requires; at other times the fantasies associated with masturbation highlight a person's need for control in a relationship because he or she fears, or has little capacity for, trusting another human being, or is simply unwilling to be vulnerable.[34] Such fantasy-attitudes do indeed reflect moral evil and the consequent guilt that flows from entertaining them would seem to be authentic and proper.[35]

Masturbation is especially problematical from the perspective of human and moral growth when it is chosen in preference to the fuller and richer forms of shared sexual

---

[33]Tyrrell, *op. cit.*, p. 404.

[34]James B. Nelson, *Embodiment: An Approach to Sexuality and Christian Theology* (Minneapolis: Augsburg Publ. House, 1978), pp. 160-63.

[35]Tyrrell, *op. cit.*, p. 404.

activities when these are readily and morally available. Even granting, however, the objective moral evil of masturbation —a concession which, as we have seen, some Roman Catholic theologians are unwilling to make—some strong evidence exists against the subjective sinfulness of the act in many instances. This evidence unfolds in the fact that acts of masturbation in the lives of people who, for one reason or another, regard such acts as objectively wrong, most often occur in a cyclic pattern as these people struggle to live the gospel of Christ. In other words, a period of regular and perhaps frequent masturbation alternates with a period of abstinence. This cyclic pattern is morally significant because it renders doubtful the likelihood that a person "has accepted masturbation into his life as an integral part of his growth and life-expression." The alternation between periods of masturbation and abstinence would seem rather to indicate that a person accepts the action unwillingly and with embarrassment; it is an expression of weakness, a sign of tested, tried and failed virtue. But a person's very lack of complacency, the unwillingness to grant masturbation a permanent and undisputed place in one's life, argues strongly that in such circumstances masturbation may more inspire a person to humility than be an expression of basic and serious sinfulness.[36]

IV. Concluding Remarks on Pastoral Advice

It is important as we bring this chapter and our ethical reflections on human sexuality to a close that certain truths be reiterated: sexuality is good, it is part of our nature and it plays a central role in the development of our personality. Our teaching on sexual morality must therefore be positive, which is simply to say that we must put more emphasis on the beauty of sex than on the dangers and evils associated with it. In the attempt to educate people in responsible sexuality, accurate informa-

---

[36]This point was suggested by Brockman, *op. cit.*, p. 614.

tion, encouragement, advice and correction of mistakes play integral roles. But our teaching must also "be prepared to make allowances for human imperfection, precisely because...man is not a finished product but is very much 'in the making'." Thus the function of teaching might best be exercised by spending less time condemning the supposed excesses of the young generation and by bringing to bear on issues of sexual morality "the wisdom but not the prejudices of the past ages." The young generation, for the most part, is concerned with morality; young people are willing to listen, provided they are not talked down to; they both despise and despair of the hypocrisy of much of society. They can detect obscenity and they wish to avoid it, but they rightly refuse to locate that obscenity solely in the realm of sexual desire and activity, for they sense deeply the well of obscenity that springs from the oppression spawned by economic, political and racial injustices.[37]

With reference specifically to the issue of masturbation what kind of pastoral counsel is appropriate? Several observations are in order. To begin with, because of the unitive (love-giving) and procreative (life-giving) qualities and goals of the full richness of human sexuality, people must be encouraged to strive for growth in interpersonal and heterosexual sexuality. As human beings, all of us must keep in mind the question of whether or not we are making progress in developing mature and sensitive interpersonal relationships. For someone who is struggling with the matter of masturbation it is especially imperative that this issue be kept in proper perspective; people engaged in a conflict with masturbation can and should find comfort if they are advancing in moral responsibility in other areas of their lives. In keeping with this idea, Häring has commented that anyone experiencing difficulty with masturbation should not be discouraged "if, at the same time, he has developed the capacity to love others generously and commits himself to worthwhile causes for the common good."[38] Great

[37]W. Norman Pittenger, *Making Sexuality Human* (Phila.: Pilgrim Press, 1970), pp. 77-8.

[38]Bernard Häring, "Human Sexuality: The Sixth and Ninth Commandments," *Chicago Studies*, 13, 3 (Fall, 1974), 311.

sensitivity is revealed in the 1975 *Declaration on Certain Questions Concerning Sexual Ethics* when it speaks about the care that is necessary when trying to assess a person's overall culpability in any matter of sexual morality:

> It is true that in sins of the sexual order, in view of their kind and their causes, it more easily happens that free consent is not fully given; this is a fact which calls for caution in all judgment as to the subject's reponsibility. In this matter it is particularly opportune to recall the following words of Scripture: "Man looks at appearances but God looks at the heart"[1 Sam. 16:7]. However, although prudence is recommended in judging the subjective seriousness of a particular sinful act, it in no way follows that one can hold the view that in the sexual field mortal sins are not committed.[39]

Mortal sins, then, certainly are possible in the area of sexual expression, and even in the area of masturbation, but we must be extremely cautious when we counsel in these matters not to assume that the activity is so invested with self-choice or selfishness as to set the person at radical odds with God and neighbor.

The following example typifies the experience of many Catholics who are bothered by the incidence of masturbation in their lives:

> A young man has been struggling with a problem of masturbation for several years. He is convinced that he commits a mortal sin each time he indulges in the act. He goes to confession and is "wiped clean." Feeling whole again, he manages to avoid the practice for a week or two. But the old habit almost inevitably reasserts itself. He falls. Now the feelings of guilt, remorse, shame, self-depreciation, and profound discouragement come into play, mobilizing tension and anxiety. He has long been conditioned to release such tension through masturbation. He does so again, and the vicious circle is

[39]#10 of the *Declaration*.

complete. Masturbation produces guilt which produces anxiety which seeks release in further masturbation.[40]

To this description, it might be added that it frequently happens that once the person sees himself as having fallen back into sin, he will masturbate a number of times in close succession. Given this usual pattern of response to incidents or habits of masturbation, it seems appropriate that a priest or counselor should do nothing that will only aggravate the person's sense of shame. Rather, what the individual needs first, is to become convinced that change and growth are possible; then he or she must be encouraged and supported in the development of a lifestyle more in conformity with the image of self that serves as their ideal. Pastorally, then, it would be wrong to try to convince a person that masturbation involves no moral responsibility on his or her part. This approach would probably increase anxiety rather than relieve guilt, for "it implies a force beyond control and destroys motivation to overcome the habit. Almost no one wants to be told that he is not responsible for his actions... If there is no responsibility, there is no subjective possibility of control."[41]

To acknowledge, however, that individuals are largely responsible for their lives and activities, is not to suggest that, with regard to people struggling with masturbation, a pastor or counselor should concentrate on the number and frequency of their masturbatory actions. A much more helpful approach, I believe, and one that is more likely to be effective for change, is to instruct the person how to make an examination of his or her general lifestyle and behavior patterns. In this way the person may better come to identify those situations or circumstances in his or her life which always, or almost always, lead to masturbation. Furthermore, the individual must then face the very real possibility that he or she is unconsciously or semi-consciously involved in "setting up" the scene for masturbation. Once a person appreciates the causal connection between

---

[40]O'Neil and Donovan, *op. cit.*, p. 115.

[41]*Ibid.*, pp. 116, 110.

certain elements in his or her life-routine and the incidents of masturbation, and is then willing to alter that routine, an important step is taken toward eliminating or avoiding the kind of situation which, up until that time, has almost always proven to set the stage for masturbation.[42]

If there is a basic truth in the idea that it is one's pattern of behavior, more than any particular act in itself, which both determines and manifests a person's moral status before God, then it is also this life-pattern which should be not only the primary object of one's moral attention, but also the focus of one's moral energy. If, indeed, masturbation does reflect a person's refusal to meet the challenge to growth in sexual integrity, or if it serves as either an obstacle or alternative to the development of mature, morally sound and humanly fulfilling interpersonal relationships, then clearly masturbation confronts the individual with the necessity of making a fundamental moral option: "a serious determination to grow out of the habit [of masturbation] will indicate one fundamental option; a decision to make no serious effort to break it will indicate another."[43] And what ultimately concerns or interests God is precisely a person's fundamental option, so that if someone is and remains seriously involved in a struggle to move away from masturbation, this is far more significant in the eyes of God than any isolated or periodic lapses; once again, we need to be reminded that "God does not see as man sees; man looks at appearances but God looks at the heart" (1 Sam. 16:7). In this context, I would offer the judgment that people who make proper use of the sacrament of reconciliation, or honestly seek the help of a spiritual director or the advice of a counselor, are giving evidence of their good will and sincere desire for continued spiritual and moral growth. This fundamental option on their part should bring them the peace, strength and added confidence of knowing that God is with them as they carry on their struggle.

Within the last fifteen years two official Roman Catholic documents have presented the view that masturbation is

---

[42]*Ibid.*, pp. 114-15.

[43]Dedek, *op. cit.*, p. 65.

indicative of a person's immaturity, or symptomatic of other, more profound, problems and difficulties that "provoke sexual tension which the individual seeks to resolve by recourse to such behavior." Priests, pastors and counselors are advised, accordingly, to attend "more to the causes than to the direct repression of the phenomenon;" instead of overdramatizing the fact of masturbation, educators should undramatize it.[44] There should be no recourse to fear-tactics, threats, or physical or spiritual intimidation which "could encourage the formation of obsessions and compromise the possibility of a balanced sexual attitude, making [a person] turn further in on himself instead of opening himself to others."[45] Rather, people struggling with masturbation need encouragement to become involved in works of justice and charity; in addition, they should be reminded of the assistance available to them through recourse to prayer and the sacraments.[46] With reference to the role of the sacraments in the life of a Catholic who is exercising the fundamental option of trying honestly to move beyond the practice of masturbation, I find interesting the pastoral reflections offered in *Human Sexuality. New Directions in American Catholic Thought*:

> Persons seriously struggling with the task of integrating their sexuality, especially adolescents, should be encouraged to receive the eucharist at every opportunity even though occasional incidents of masturbation may occur. The presumption should be that such persons have not sinned gravely and consequently have not lost their right to receive the sacraments. The regular celebration of the sacrament of reconciliation and the wise counsel of a prudent confessor can provide additional support in the struggle toward integration.... Immediate confession after each act of masturbation ought not to be

---

[44]See the two documents drawn up by the Sacred Congregation for Catholic Education: *Educational Guidance in Human Love. Outlines for Sex Education*, (1983) nos. 99-100 and *A Guide to Formation in Priestly Celibacy*, (1974) no. 63.

[45]*A Guide to Formation in Priestly Celibacy*, no. 63.

[46]*Educational Guidance in Human Love*, no. 100.

encouraged, though periodic discussion of one's progress in this area can prove helpful to the counselee or penitent.[47]

There is one final issue I would like to address in this chapter. During a classroom discussion several years ago one of the male students asked me what was the best way to handle sexual frustration and how could such frustration be avoided or at least minimized. As he continued to speak, it became clear that what he really wanted to know was how to cope with sexual temptations and with the conscious desire and felt-need for genital pleasure. In his situation as a resident of a co-ed dormitory, he was beginning to doubt that he could ever maintain the Christian ideals of sexual morality. With some additions and emendations here included, the following suggestions reflect my initial response to the student's query:

1. The first thing a person should do is to remember that a lot more is involved than simply the urge for physical sexual pleasure. We have to be reminded of the psycho-social dynamics which underlie the persistent and consciously experienced physiological urges. In light of these dynamics, it is worth repeating a point made earlier in this book, namely, that one of the most helpful ways of fulfilling our physical sexual needs is to reduce those needs by defocusing sexuality from the genitals and concentrating on the development of a more diffused sexuality. In other words, we have to enhance our appreciation of the affective dimension of human sexuality and try to grow in sensitivity and tenderness.

2. Once our affective sexuality is developed more fully, the next challenge is to translate our affection for another into appropriate physical expressions; what kinds of physical sexual demonstrations are honest reflections of the love between two people, and at the same time manageable for both partners? This is where mistakes can often occur. It is imperative that we avoid the attitude that the only way to learn is through mistakes; nonetheless, I do think honest mistakes are possible. The way to test their honesty is to learn from them and not

repeat them. Honest mistakes, too, fill us with regret. In this, they distinguish themselves from rationalizations.

3. In trying to limit sexual temptation and the sense of frustration that often accompanies it, we will be greatly helped if we are prudent in choosing our reading materials and our forms and places of entertainment. Basically, we have to keep in mind what kind of person we want to be; then we must truthfully analyze what are our "occasions of sin," that is, where, when and with whom are we most likely to betray our ideals and settle for being less than we are called to be and really want to be. Once we identify our proven "trouble spots," we put ourselves on the line to see how sincere we are in trying to avoid them in the future.

This point is especially crucial since in human beings sexual behavior cannot be adequately or accurately described as the expression simply of a "sex drive." The urge and need for sex are not a part of us in just the same way as the urge and need for food and drink are. Rather, our sexual tendencies depend for their arousal upon external stimuli to a far greater degree than is true of hunger or thirst.[48] Donald Goergen elaborates upon this idea: "The important factor in human sexual arousal is that of an external stimulus, especially that arising from another person or partner. Sexual behavior seems not to occur in the absence of such stimuli although in human beings these stimuli can be symbolic."[49] To say, of course, that the external stimuli which play such a crucial part in human sexual arousal need only be symbolic means that they can and often do present themselves to us only through the powers of human memory, imagination and fantasizing. It is for this reason that we need to develop prudence, care and discipline in deciding upon our recreation, entertainment and reading.

Important as it is that we try to maintain some kind of monitoring of our mental "in-take" if we wish to avoid unnecessary turmoil in the struggle for sexual integrity, it is also

---

[48]Frank A. Beach, "Characteristics of Masculine 'Sex Drive,'" *Nebraska Symposium on Motivation*, ed. by M. R. Jones, vol. 4 (Lincoln: University of Nebraska Press, 1956), p. 5 as quoted in Goergen, *op. cit.*, p. 74.

[49]Goergen, *op. cit.*, p. 74.

wise to remember that thoughts are distinct from actions, and the desire is not always father to the deed. Michael Cavanagh, a Catholic psychologist, has offered some interesting and helpful observations about a "sexual domino" theory "which holds that if a person allows himself a sexual idea, this will automatically cause sexual feelings, which will, in turn, automatically lead to sexual activity." Unfortunately, what happens in the lives of many people, is that this sexual-domino myth takes on the power of a self-fulfilling prophecy; in other words, once these people "give in" to a sexual thought, their movement toward sexual feelings and activity is anticipated and precipitated "because they feel they have no control over it." Cavanagh suggests that the situation becomes further aggravated by the fact that there are still many people who even regard just having sexual thoughts and feelings as wrong and improper, unless one is married and is thinking about his or her spouse.

This kind of attitude results in nothing good, for either it misleads people into trying to become asexual by stifling or expunging all sexual ideas and feelings or, as is more likely, it encourages people to adopt what Cavanagh calls the "neurotic gambler's" credo:

> "If you are going to lose, you might as well lose big." Some people feel that as long as they committed a sin by "entertaining" a sexual idea, they might as well "go for broke" and "entertain" sexual feelings and indulge in sexual activity. Hence, these people end up participating in sexual behavior as much by default as by choice.[50]

Being properly advised, as we should be, of the errors and dangers connected with the sexual-domino myth and the "neurotic gambler's" credo, it nonetheless continues to make eminent sense that we ought calmly to regulate, as far as possible, those external stimuli which can prove so unsettling to our efforts at continued growth as Christians.

[50]Cavanagh's ideas are presented by Kevin H. Axe, "Sex and the Married Catholic," *U.S. Catholic*, 41, 11 (November, 1976), 6-11 at 11.

4. We will be immensely helped in our struggle for moral and spiritual maturity if we can develop friendships with people who understand, appreciate and share our values and Christian ideals.

5. In addition, one of the best things we can do for ourselves is to seek out a good, competent advisor or director who deserves our trust and enables us to be, not only comfortable, but also totally open and honest.

6. Finally, as Christians we will find that our moral and spiritual growth is immeasurably nourished and enlivened if we are faithful to prayer and if we draw frequently upon the strength of God's love and life as offered to us in a special way in the sacraments.

The reader deserves to hear what one student's reaction was to my response: "Father, I know your suggestions would work for me, but I'm really not sure that I'll follow them. Sexual temptation, it seems, is something I love to hate."

IX

Abortion: A Vipers' Tangle
for Morality

In reflecting on the issue of abortion it will be helpful if we group our thoughts around the following points: (1) some introductory clarifications; (2) the issue of when human life begins; (3) the question of when, if ever, fetal human life may be taken; (4) the debate over public policy on abortion; and (5) concluding remarks.

I. Introductory Clarifications

In addition to being a social, legal, medical and moral issue, abortion is also an emotional one. The stance that people take on this matter rests on premises, assumptions and feelings that are often unconscious but which are, nonetheless, largely determinative of the point-of-view adopted. In coming to grips with the reality of abortion, therefore, our constant efforts must be to think clearly and forcefully, but also dispassionately, to defuse the emotional overtones of the issue, and to uncover some fundamental principles. We are approaching the question of abortion as members of the Judeo-Christian tradition who recall and appreciate the truth that we have inherited the basic charge of Christ that we are to love one another even as we first have been loved. Our respect for the sacredness of human life is in a real sense an outgrowth and application of this radical command of Christ, because loving someone implies a willingness to promote the other's total welfare as a human being, and life is among the most basic human goods; it is also the condition of possibility for receiving all other human goods.

In practice, our basic respect for the sanctity of human life means that the burden of proof falls upon anyone who would take human life, whatever its form. Human life enjoys a presumption of value such that we are constrained not to kill, and we are released from this imperative only in exceptional instances. Moreover, it is the exceptional instance that must be proven, not the basic freedom or inviolability of human life from attack. It should be noted that this protection afforded human life by our Christian tradition is the same value that is preserved and reflected in the just-war theory which stands as "an initial presumption against the moral validity of particular wars."[1]

To say, of course, that human life is basically inviolable does not mean that the Christian tradition views human life as an absolute value which may never be violated. Thus, for example, as just indicated, mainline Christianity has traditionally allowed for the possible moral permissibility of war and the killing it entails; Christians, moreover, have traditionally affirmed the legitimacy of capital punishment (although in recent years the American Catholic bishops have spoken out against this practice); we still acknowledge the right of self-defense against an unjust aggressor, even to the point of inflicting death if necessary; we protect a person's freedom to die without having extraordinary medical means forced upon him which only prolong the dying process. These examples illustrate the fact that human life, while sacred and basically inviolable, need not and should not be protected or prolonged at any and all costs. Neither does our Christian tradition maintain simply that *innocent* human life is utterly inviolable; rather, what we have consistently argued is that innocent human life is inviolable

---

[1] In the development of these introductory remarks I have relied on Richard A. McCormick, S.J., "Abortion: Aspects of the Moral Question," *America*, 117 (1967), 716-19 at 716-17.

from *direct* suppression, but may at times be taken *indirectly*. The distinction between direct and indirect killing has long been regarded as crucial and, as we shall see, plays an important role in Roman Catholic thinking concerning abortion.

In an attempt to clarify what is at stake in discussing abortion and, at the same time, in order to allow reason, not emotion, to reign, I must suggest immediately that nothing can be gained by insisting from the start that abortion is murder. To equate, simply, immediately and automatically, abortion with murder is to confuse two levels of reality. In other words, "murder" is by definition a morally-charged word; it is used to describe an act which is inherently filled with disvalue; "murder" means malicious, unwarranted or unjust killing, taking human life with evil intent; by virtue of its in-built negative moral charge, the act of murder may never be turned to as an end in itself or as a means to another end. In contrast to the word "murder" with its unavoidable or built-in "moral content," "abortion" is definable simply in physical, non-moral terms: expelling, or causing the expulsion of, a presently-living fetus from the womb prior to its viability. This description of abortion contains no moral content; the word "abortion" by definition has no moral charge, positive or negative.[2]

To equate, therefore, the *physical* act of abortion immediately or automatically with the *immoral* act of murder or unjust killing is not to start a discussion, but to close it. For the very statement, "abortion is murder," embodies certain assumptions or presuppositions; two definite conclusions or judgments have already been reached, namely, that in aborting a fetus a *human* life has been taken, and that this human life has been taken unjustly. For purposes of furthering understanding of one's position on any matter, it is best not to start with one's conclusions, but rather to explore and expose one's premises. I suggest, therefore, that in initiating a discussion of abortion, it is more helpful and more accurate to say that abortion does indeed entail killing. But then it must be determined (1) whether

[2]See John G. Milhaven, "Moral Absolutes and Thomas Aquinas," in *Absolutes in Moral Theology?*, ed. Charles E. Curran (Washington: Corpus Books, 1968), pp. 155-56.

abortion involves the killing of human life and (2) whether the killing of this human life, if the embryo or fetus be such, is justified or unjust. Abortion is murder only if we are dealing with *human* life and that life is taken *unjustly*, that is, without a proportionate reason. Stating the matter this way clearly shows the critical importance of the two questions that we now must address: when does human life begin, and when, if ever, is fetal human life justly taken?

II. The Start of Human Life

Many different theories have been put forth regarding the time at which human life begins. Reasons have been offered for identifying the start of human life with each of the following events: the time of conception or fertilization, the time of uterine implantation of the ovum, the time of segmentation when the ovum is truly individualized so that twinning is no longer possible, the appearance of brain waves in the fetus, the time of fetal viability, the time of birth, the time when a child begins to respond to the process of socialization. Three of these theories (those identifying the start of human life with (1) fertilization, (2) with segmentation or (3) with the appearance of brain waves) seem more deserving of comment than the others. Before looking at these three major theories, however, it should be noted that although the Roman Catholic Church acknowledges the impossibility of deciding the theoretical question as to when human life begins, she nonetheless maintains that in practice we must act as though human life were present from the moment of fertilization. Her reason for insisting upon this practice is that when we are faced with a doubt of fact (that is, when does human life begin), we must follow the safer course of action — and it simply is safer to regard human life as beginning at fertilization rather than at some later time in the process of embryonic or fetal development.[3] Let us now look more closely at some of the arguments used to identify the time when human life begins.

a) *Fertilization*: Those who maintain that human life is present from the moment of fertilization do so because they claim, and rightly so, that from that moment on there is a new genetic package present which is certainly not a part of any species other than the human one, and which is different, moreover, from the genetic make-up of either of the parents; thus, there is no way that the newly fertilized ovum can be regarded as simply a tumor of the mother. For precisely this reason, arguments advocating a woman's right to have an abortion on the basis of that woman's right to privacy or on the basis of her right to do with her body as she pleases ring terribly hollow; they simply assume, even many weeks and months after fertilization, that no other life besides the mother's is present and involved.

---

[3]Charles E. Curran, *New Perspectives in Moral Theology* (Notre Dame: Fides Publishers Inc., 1974), p. 173. It should be noted that in her provocative and enlightening article, "The Tradition of Probabilism and the Moral Status of the Early Embryo," *Theological Studies*, 45, 1 (March, 1984), 3-33, Carol A. Tauer has made a strong case in arguing that the question of when the embryo receives the human or rational soul and thus must be considered truly human, in the sense of being a human person, involves not a "doubt of fact," as the official teaching of the Catholic Church maintains, but rather a "doubt of law." From an analysis of the examples used in the tradition of moral teaching to illustrate what is meant by "doubts of fact," Tauer shows that all such doubts "appear to involve empirically verifiable states of affairs." (p. 25) But the question of when the embryo receives a human soul is precisely "*not* a factual matter, since *in principle* it cannot be ascertained." (p. 24) The Church has herself admitted the non-verifiability of the human soul's presence in the newly fertilized egg: "It suffices that this presence of the soul be probable (*and one can never prove the contrary*)." See Sacred Congregation for the Doctrine of the Faith, *Declaration on Abortion*, (Washington, D.C.: U.S. Catholic Conference, 1975), 6. Tauer argues that the time of human ensoulment is a metaphysical question and, as such, involves a theoretical doubt that is more closely related to "doubts of law" than to "doubts of fact." This opens the door to an alternate moral response: since we are not dealing with a "doubt of fact," we are not required morally to follow the safer course of action; rather, in the face of a "doubt of law," we may follow what is a solidly probable opinion or theory. As we will see in our treatment of the issue later in this chapter, there are solid reasons for suggesting that human ensoulment and thus the beginning of human personhood in the fetus does not occur at fertilizaton, but at a later point in embryonic development.

At the same time, however, it must be said that simply because the just-fertilized ovum is clearly a genetically human organism, a human ovum, different from that of any other species, this fact in itself does not demand the conclusion that a human *person* exists from the moment of conception on. As a human organism, the newly fertilized ovum certainly has the potential or power of developing into a human person; but it cannot be said that simply possessing this potential for personhood immediately bestows on the fertilized ovum the title of person, for then every cell of the human organism in its early development as zygote, morula and blastula would have to be regarded as a human person since each cell possesses such potential for personhood; in other words, all the cells of the early-developing organism are totipotent; they have a pluri-potentiality such that each one, if separated early enough from the others, might develop into a human being.[4] Those who maintain that both human life and human personhood begin at the time of fertilization are exponents of the theory of immediate animation and immediate hominization or humanization. The two following theories advocate immediate animation but mediate or delayed hominization; this means that they posit some interval of time between the appearance of a genetically human organism (at fertilization) and the appearance of a human person.

b) *The Developmental Theory:* This theory attests to the belief that some development of the fetus needs to occur before this human organism is assigned the title of "person." There are two ways in which this theory regarding the beginning of personal human life is expounded: one way is quite ancient and is simply the application of some basic philosophical ideas; the other way is much more recent and rests upon the employment of contemporary technological advances. We will look first at the more ancient rationale for maintaining that the appearance of personal human life is not coincidental with fertilization of the human ovum.

[4]See Joseph F. Donceel, S. J., "Immediate Animation and Delayed Hominization," *Theological Studies,* 31 (1970), 76-105 at 96-98.

Both Aristotle and Thomas Aquinas held the theory of delayed or mediate hominization.[5] They maintained that although there is immediate animation at the time of conception, this animation or life is explained by the presence first of a nutritive or vegetative soul and then later by the presence of a sensitive or sentient soul. For both Aristotle and Thomas, all living things have souls; a soul (*anima*) is simply a living being's principle or source of vitality. Thus, with reference to the newly fertilized ovum which is clearly genetically human, we may speak of it as having first a plant soul (the embryo's nutritive or vegetative life-force); later, an animal soul evolves which explains and directs the developing organism's nutritive and sentient powers. These life-forces are understood to be material souls which successively guide the development of the embryo through its early days, weeks and months.

Aristotle and Thomas had a very specific reason for maintaining that the appearance of personal human life is delayed in the process of embryonic development. The reason was that they subscribed to the philosophical theory of hylomorphism—a theory which states that all physical creatures are composed of two principles of being, namely matter (*hylē*) and form (*morphē*), which are strictly complementary. For Thomas, a being's form, also known more fully as its substantial form, is identified with that being's soul if, in fact, the being is a living one. Thus, the traditional Thomistic teaching is that the human soul, which is spiritual, serves also as the substantial form of a human person. In saying that the spiritual soul is the substantial form of a person we mean "that it is that which makes the human organism into a human person." It must be remembered, however, that since, according to the theory of hylomorphism, matter and form are strictly complementary, it follows that precisely because the human spiritual soul serves also as the human substantial form, this

[5]The explanation of the traditional Thomistic view of delayed hominization in the following paragraphs is derived from Joseph F. Donceel, S. J., "Why Is Abortion Wrong?," *America*, 133 (1975), 65-67. See also Donceel's "Catholic Politicians and Abortion" *America*, 152, 4 (Feb. 2, 1985), 81-3.

soul can come into existence only "in a complex, highly organized body [matter]." Quite simply, then, Thomas' theory comes to this: the human soul or substantial form does not exist until the physical organism of the fetus is developed sufficiently enough so as to receive and support it; and until the human soul is present in the fetus, the fetus is not a human person.

Perhaps the full significance of hylomorphism can be better appreciated if it is contrasted with another major theory called dualism, which has also been used to explain the relationship between the human soul and body. Both Plato and Descartes maintained that the soul and the human body were two quite distinct, independent and separable beings, related to each other in the way, say, that a driver (the soul) is related to his car (the body). The driver may exist before the car and may even be involved in making the car which he will eventually drive. The reality is quite otherwise for the theory of hylomorphism; the human soul does not exist before the body; rather the "soul is to the body somewhat as the shape of a statue is to this statue," or we might say that the soul is "like the shape of a building as it exists in the finished building."[6]

With this understanding of the theory of hylomorphism and its explanation of the relationship existing between the human soul and body, Joseph Donceel can maintain that "the spiritual soul may be infused only in a body possessed of the main human organs;" included here would be the senses, heart, lungs, central nervous system, and the brain, especially the cortex; or it might be said simply that the human soul, because it is also the human substantial form, is found only in a material body endowed with those organs which constitute the necessary, even if not the sufficient, condition for the later appearance of the peculiarly human spiritual activities of thinking and willing. It should be noted, of course, that Thomas does not regard the human soul as a product of gradual evolution; rather, it is created by God and is infused by him into the developing human organism once that organism is sufficiently disposed to receive it — a time-period variously estimated by Aristotle and

---

[6]*Ibid.;* see also Donceel's "Immediate Animation," 83.

Thomas at between 40 and 80 days.[7] (This is a remarkable
estimate in light of what we now know about the stages of fetal
development: after six weeks (42 days) all of the internal organs
are present; after twelve weeks (84 days) the brain structure is
complete.)[8]

It must be mentioned here that opponents of the Thomistic
theory of delayed hominization argue that Thomas himself
would have abandoned his idea of the delayed creation and
infusion of the human spiritual soul if he had had the advantage
of our advanced biological knowledge. In other words, it is
suggested that the newly fertilized human ovum, as we view it

---

[7]Donceel's explanation of Thomistic hylomorphism's impact on the theory of
mediate hominization is worth recounting at some length:

    Hylomorphism cannot admit that the fertilized ovum ... is animated by an
intellectual, human soul. Soul [form] and matter are strictly complementary;
as the soul stands higher in the hierarchy of beings, the matter which receives
it, which is determined by it, must be more highly organized ... To each
specific degree of organization there corresponds a soul. The early embryo
possesses a rudimentary organization, which allows it to perform the operations of nutrition and growth. To such an organization corresponds a
vegetative soul...

    The processes of nutrition and growth render the embryo more complex,
more highly organized. Sense organs and a rudimentary nervous system
emerge. When this complexity has reached a certain stage, a threshold is
reached, a sudden ontological shift occurs. The vegetative soul is replaced by a
sensitive soul. The embryo is no longer a mere plant, it is a sentient organism,
endowed with an animal soul. Thomas uses old-fashioned language to explain
this transition . . . . He says that the generation of one soul *is* the corruption of
the other. Teilhard would have said: a threshhold has been reached, that is, a
sudden, radical change, after a long process of transition. And he uses the
example of water which, on being heated, increases gradually in temperature,
until suddenly the water becomes vapor... The appearance of vapor *is* the
disappearance of the water. Thomas would have said: the generation of one is
the corruption of the other.

    Animated by a sensitive soul, the embryo continues to develop.... Man's
higher, spiritual faculties have no organs of their own, since they are
immaterial, intrinsically independent of matter. But they need, as necessary
conditions of their activity, the cooperation of the highest sense powers,
imagination, memory, what the Scholastics call the "cogitative power." Its
activity presupposes that the brain be fully developed, that the cortex be ready.
Only then is the stage set for another ontological shift; matter now is highly
enough organized to receive the highest substantial form, the spiritual, human
soul, created by God.

[The above is from "Immediate Animation," *Theological Studies*, 31 (1970), 82-83.]

[8]Andre E. Hellegers, "Fetal Development," *Theological Studies*, 31, 1 (1970), 3-9.

today through our knowledge of DNA and RNA, would eminently satisfy Thomas' stipulation that an organism must be sufficiently organized and disposed for the reception of a human spiritual soul. Thus it is said that were Thomas living today, he would opt for immediate rather than for mediate hominization, which is to say simply that he would maintain that the human soul, and hence a human person, is present from the moment of conception.[9]

The modern version of this developmental theory claims that personal human life begins at the time when fetal brain wave activity is present as detectable through the use of an electroencephalogram (EEG); such brain-wave detections are possible from about eight weeks on in the gestation process, and they coincide roughly with the change in nomenclature from embryo to fetus in reference to the developing organism. Those who maintain that the origin of personal life coincides with the detection of brain-wave activity do so because of a claimed parallel with the reasoning that is employed when the question of human death is raised. There is a strong movement today to identify human death with brain death or the entrance of a person into an irreversible coma. One of the ways in which human death or brain death is confirmed is through the use of the EEG; if two readings of 10-20 minutes duration are taken 24 hours apart and no brain waves are recorded in either reading, then it may be judged that irreversible loss of brain waves has occurred; in such circumstances we may regard human life as having ended and the person may be declared dead.

It is essential to realize, however, that the use of the EEG to confirm death necessarily presupposes the presence of the usual clinical signs of death. In other words, the standard criteria for death are as follows: a person shows no spontaneous movement, no response to painful stimuli, no spontaneous breathing, no reflexes, and has fixed and dilated pupils. Moreover, the validity of both the clinical signs of death and the confirmatory data of a flat EEG requires verification of the exclusion of two

---

[9]Joseph T. Mangan, S. J., "The Wonder of Myself: Ethical-Theological Aspects of Direct Abortion," *Theological Studies*, 31, 1 (1970), 125-48 at 129-30.

conditions: the person must not have been subject to hypothermia (body temperature below 90° F) or involved in the recent use of central nervous system depressants like barbiturates.[10] As these criteria make clear, the declaration that personal life has ended is made neither arbitrarily nor facilely.

With this analysis as background, it must be pointed out that the argument put forth by the proponents of the view that personal life begins with the detectable appearance of brain waves is specious. We cannot say simply that just as personal human life ends with the detectable disappearance of brain waves, so also does personal human life begin with the detectable appearance of brain wave activity. As we have seen, the critical factor of human death is the *irreversible* loss of brain waves, not merely their absence or disappearance; thus, in the first two months of fetal development, brain waves may indeed not be present and they may remain undetectable for a while after they begin, but one thing is certain: during this period, fetal brain waves cannot be said to be irreversibly lost; in fact, there is every expectation of their eventual appearance; therefore, to regard a fetus as devoid of personal human status during the entire first two months of its gestation seems certainly to fly in the face of the criteria that are used to determine the presence or absence of personal human existence at the other end of the life cycle. This denial of the fetus's personal human existence until the appearance of brain waves is especially unwarranted when it is recalled that in trying to determine whether death has occurred, the testing for brain waves through the use of an EEG is required only when the application of the normal clinical criteria for death leaves some question or doubt regarding the "alive-or-dead" status of an individual. Such doubt, of course, does not arise with regard to a young embryo whose heart is pumping at 3-4 weeks, and who acts reflexively upon stimulation.

c) *The Time of Segmentation:* The third theory that I want to consider regarding the beginning of personal human life claims that such life is initiated at the time of segmentation; this means

---

[10]Kenneth Vaux , *Biomedical Ethics. Morality for the New Medicine* (New York: Harper & Row, 1974), pp. 102-04.

that personal life can be said to begin at that time when it is finally established or irreversibly settled how many organisms will be developing in a specific pregnancy. In other words, will there be one, two or more embryos? Personal human life can be said to be present only when that point in cellular division and multiplication has been reached such that twinning, tripleting and so on are no longer possible and thus the developing organism's individuality is established and guaranteed.

The conservative estimate regarding the length of time during which twinning may occur is 7 or 8 days, the time period roughly corresponding to the time needed for implantation of the fertilized ovum in the uterus. More liberally, it is estimated that twinning can occur up until 14-21 days after fertilization. In either interpretation, however, we see that the time needed for the establishment of individuality, and hence for the appearance of personal human life according to this theory, is a maximum of three weeks, a period of time considerably less than that suggested either by Aquinas using his theory of hylomorphism or by the modern developmental theory with its recourse to the appearance of fetal brain waves as a criterion for human life.

The rationale for saying that a human person is not present until individuality is established is articulated as follows: every person is an individual; speaking philosophically, this means that every person is indivisible and thus cannot be divided from self; one human being cannot in and of itself become two or more; a newly fertilized ovum, however, retains for some period of time the capacity to be divided from itself; when that capacity is activated, twinning occurs; so long as this power to divide into two separate organisms remains in the developing zygote, it is not an individualized being and thus is not a person. To maintain otherwise would be to claim that one person can become two or more persons, or that one individual can become two or more individuals. As just indicated above, however, such an occurrence would violate the philosophical definition of individual, namely, that which is indivisible in itself. One writer sums up the situation this way: "If the fecundated ovum can split into two beings which turn out to be two persons, it is difficult to admit that at first it [the fecundated ovum] was itself a person, hence fully human."[11]

Donceel, himself, presents the case against immediate hominization in clear terms: "Identical twins ... start life as one ovum, fecundated by one spermatozoon. For the proponents of immediate hominization, this fecundated ovum is one human person. Very early in pregnancy this ovum splits into two (or more) parts, each of which develops into an adult. This fact is difficult to reconcile with immediate hominization. A human person does not split into two or more human persons."[12] Further support for claiming that personal human life is not present until individuality is established may be garnered from the fact that some scientists estimate that anywhere from one-third to one-half of the number of ova that are fertilized never become implanted in the uterus but rather are expelled from the uterus during the woman's next menstrual cycle.[13] These fecundated ova that do not implant are sloughed off just as unfertilized ova are, but in light of the fact that ovulation occurs about 14 days before the start of the menstrual period, this sloughing-off occurs before the time that individuality would be reached. Can we really claim that such sloughed-off fertilized ova are personal human beings with immortal souls and eternal destinies? Would this not constitute an extravagant or prodigal waste of human life?[14]

[11]Donceel, "Immediate Animation," 99; he is here quoting P. Schoonenberg, S.J., *God's World in the Making* (Pittsburgh, 1974), p. 50.

[12]*Ibid.*, 98.

[13]See the information provided by James J. Diamond, M.D., "Abortion, Animation, and Biological Hominization," *Theological Studies*, 36 (1975), 305-24 at 311, n. 12. The article offers provocative data on the biological support which lends credence to the theory of mediate hominization. See also Bernard Häring, "New Dimensions of Responsible Parenthood," Theological Studies, 37(1976), 120-32; in n. 11 (p. 124) and n. 21 (p. 129), the author refers to other studies highlighting the high incidence of spontaneous loss of fertilized ova; confer Henri Leridon, *Human Fertility: The Basic Components* (Chicago: University of Chicago Press, 1977), p. 81.

[14]It should be pointed out that if the Roman Catholic Church were to be perfectly consistent in following out the implications of maintaining immediate hominization, it should call for conditional baptism over a married woman's menstrual flow on the chance that if she has been having intercourse regularly, a fecundated ovum (a human person) might have been sloughed off. Fortunately, the Church is not perfectly consistent on this issue and no conditional baptism is suggested or needed. See Donceel, "Immediate Animation," 99-100 and especially n. 77.

Any number of outstanding Christian theologians now support this particular version of mediate hominization, namely, that personal human life, as opposed to vegetative and sentient human life, begins some 14-21 days after fertilization at the time when twinning is no longer possible and thus the individuality of the developing embryo is assured.[15] This view is also reflective of the ancient definition of the human person put forth by Boethius: a person is "an individual substance possessing rational nature." In other words, no human person can be said to exist until an *individual* substance is present; thus in the first two or three weeks following fertilization, the primary point at issue is not whether the developing organism is of a rational nature, but rather whether it is truly an individualized substance.

There is substance to the view that it is the establishment of individuality at 14-21 days which sufficiently predisposes the developing organism for the reception of the human rational soul. Thus exception must be taken to Thomas Aquinas who did not think that the physical organism was sufficiently ready to receive the human soul until between 40 days (for males) and 80 days (for females) after fertilization. But questionable as well, is the view that a genetically human ovum, immediately upon fertilization, is adequately disposed to be infused with a human soul.

The idea that personal life begins at the establishment of individuality might be supported by some parallel scientific information. It seems fairly well determined now that a fertilized ovum up until sometime after its implantation is guided solely by the *maternal* RNA (ribonucleic acid), that is, by the genetic material present in the ovum alone prior to fertilization; during this time, then, the sperm apparently does not play a part in ordering the vital activity of the developing organism (the conceptus or fertilized egg). It is only sometime

[15]See, for example, Paul Ramsey, "The Morality of Abortion," in *Life or Death: Ethics and Options*, ed. Daniel Labby (Seattle: Univ. of Washington Press, 1968), pp. 64-9; Bernard Häring, "New Dimensions," 126-27; Charles E. Curran, *Transition and Tradition in Moral Theology* (Notre Dame: Univ. of Notre Dame Press, 1979), p. 212. This also is the opinion cautiously held by Richard A. McCormick, S. J., "Notes on Moral Theology," *Theological Studies*, 39 (1978), 127-28.

after implantation is completed that the genetic capital of the new organism is wholly activated, with the result that the conceptus begins to be directed by its own RNA.[16] It seems, then, that this transfer to the RNA of the conceptus itself coincides roughly with the time at which individuality is thought to be established, that is, some 14-21 days after fertilization. From at least this time on, therefore, I would maintain that we must fully acknowledge the fetus as a human person—an individual substance in possession of a rational nature by virtue of the spiritual soul that has been infused by God.

TREATING VICTIMS OF RAPE

To suggest that personal human life begins some 14-21 days after fertilization has a serious practical implication. While it is true that for two to three weeks following fertilization a woman does not know if she is pregnant, a woman certainly knows if and when she has been the victim of rape or has been subjected to incestuous intercourse. Thus the claim that personal life begins with the establishment of individuality would seem to allow a reasonable period of time for a woman to take appropriate action after having been subjected to felonious intercourse.

Regarding the treatment of rape victims, it is acknowledged first of all that the chances of conception after rape are statistically quite low; this is due to the fact that the traumatic circumstances of rape evoke such an emotionally upsetting response from women that physiologically their vaginal secretions become highly spermicidal so that an insufficient number of sperm survive for migration through the uterus to the Fallopian tubes for possible fertilization of any ovum which might be present. Despite the relatively low incidence of pregnancy following upon rape, the Roman Catholic Church nonetheless acknowledges that a victim of rape, since she is in no way responsible for any pregnancy that could result, has both the right and the duty to avoid or prevent it. It is for this reason that if any medical intervention at all is to occur, the Church requires that it be sought by the woman rather soon after the attack.

[16]Diamond, "Abortion, Animation," 310-11.

The standard ethical guidance that Roman Catholic moralists handed down in reference to rape victims is seen in this statement from a 1955 textbook in Medical Ethics:

> It has been said that an innocent victim of unjust aggression may eject or destroy the semen *provided it is done before conception takes place. But once conception has taken place nothing may be done.*
>
> . . . .
>
> The application of this principle obviously involves an estimate on the probable time at which conception takes place. It is possible that conception will occur within a quarter of an hour after intercourse, but it is also possible that it will not take place for some hours. Generous estimates hold that even in ordinary cases, conception may not take place for ten hours. It is *possible, but not probable*, that conception would take place even one or two days after intercourse.
>
> For this reason, then, the victim of a criminal attack might use all necessary means to eject or destroy the semen up to ten hours after the offense took place. This is certainly a generous estimate and provides a moral solution to the problem.
>
> In most instances, one might well say that if a victim of a criminal attack did nothing for ten hours, the unfortunate consequences would be largely the product of her own negligence or ignorance.[17]

In response to this stance I must observe that given the traumatizing effect which rape has upon its victim, along with the fear, confusion, shock and shame that accompany the experience, the Church's expectation and requirement that a woman act so quickly in seeking medical treatment might appear too restrictive. The reason for the Church's position, however, is simply that for her the only acceptable form of intervention is one that is contraceptive, but non-abortive. The Church claims that in the instance of rape it is permissible to prevent fertilization; however, once fertilization has occurred, human life is present and must not be

[17]Charles J. McFadden, O.S.A., *Medical Ethics* (Philadelphia: F.A. Davis Company, 1955, 3rd ed.), pp. 175-76.

violated by recourse to any abortive techniques. It might be noted, however, that if it can be reasonably held that personal human life does not begin until individuality is established, then it might be argued that a woman who has been raped has a two to three week period during which she might morally seek medical treatment to terminate any pregnancy that might have resulted from the attack.

Traditionally, certain medical procedures like a vaginal douche or a D and C (dilation and curettage of the uterus which involves scraping the lining or endometrium of the uterus) have been recommended by the Church for rape victims, but Catholic teaching requires that these procedures be initiated within a specified period of time following the sexual attack; as we have seen, usually the outside time-limit is 10-12 hours. The rationale behind both the type of intervention and the establishment of a time-limit is that the action can only be intended as a contraceptive technique; in other words, the intention and hope are to flush out from the vagina or scrape from the uterus any sperm that are present so as to prevent fertilization of an ovum. Supporters of the moral permissibility of a D and C in these circumstances realize that such an intervention would make it impossible for a fertilized ovum to implant in the uterus if in fact fertilization should occur. They argue, however, that the intention and purpose of the D and C are only to eliminate the sperm and thereby prevent fertilization of an ovum (a contraceptive intervention), rather than to prevent implantation of an ovum that might already have been, or might still be, fertilized (an abortive technique). With this understanding, so long as the D and C takes place soon enough after the rape, it can be justified by the principle of double effect.

Some comments are in order regarding the use of the douche and the D and C for rape victims.[18] In light of what we know today concerning the mobility of sperm, namely, that sperm can enter the Fallopian tubes in 5-30 minutes after intercourse, we would have to judge that normally vaginal douching after rape will be largely ineffective in preventing fertilization since the

[18]In what follows I am relying on Benedict M. Ashley, O.P. and Kevin D. O'Rourke, O.P., *Health Care Ethics. A Theological Analysis* (St. Louis: The Catholic Hospital Association, 1978), pp. 292-97.

significant sperm will have probably already migrated from the vagina before medical intervention is undertaken. Likewise, because of the sperm's mobility, I do not have much honest hope in the contraceptive effectiveness of a D and C. The sperm that will effect fertilization of an ovum is probably already in the Fallopian tubes and thus not the sperm that would be scraped from the uterus in a D and C. Thus any effectiveness of a D and C probably lies not in its contraceptive capacity but in its abortion-causing power; once even a couple of hours have passed since intercourse, I think a D and C would have to be judged primarily as having the effect of preventing the uterine implantation of any ovum that might already be fertilized or could become such shortly; in this sense, the D and C is an abortifacient (an abortion-causing agent); ". . . curettage of the endometrium after rape to prevent implantation of a possible embryo is morally equivalent to abortion."[19]

The official Roman Catholic teaching regarding the treatment of rape victims may be summarized this way: it is morally permissible, and even appropriate, to attempt to prevent conception from occurring in such instances; so long as there is a reasonable doubt that conception has occurred, properly indicated medical procedures may be initiated to forestall conception, but nothing may be done once that point in time has been reached when it may reasonably be expected that fertilization has already occurred, if indeed it is going to occur at all. The Church adopts this position because in her eyes from the moment of conception a new person is present whose life we are fully bound to respect and protect.

Something must be said now about the procedure which is used quite frequently today when treating victims of rape. The usual practice involves the use of various kinds of postcoital estrogens, one of which is the dangerous diethylstilbestrol (DES). These synthetic hormones are administered either orally or by injection; in order to prevent pregnancy, this treatment should be started as soon as possible after rape, "preferably within 24 hours

---

[19]See #24 of the "Ethical and Religious Directives for Catholic Health Facilities" which were issued by the U.S. Bishops in September, 1971. The "Directives" appear in John F. Dedek's *Contemporary Medical Ethics* (New York: Sheed and Ward, Inc., 1975), pp. 206-14.

but no later than 72 hours, and should be continued for 5 consecutive days."[20]

Catholic moralists have been cautious in their moral evaluation of this form of treatment because there has been some question regarding the exact nature of its mode of operation; sometimes it has been argued that these estrogens act contraceptively by preventing or suppressing ovulation; here, the line of reasoning is as follows: "if the woman who has been raped is at a point in her cycle when ovulation is imminent and the risk of conception high, DES will act as an antiovulatory agent and render fertilization impossible because the sperm will have died by the [next] time a fertilizable ovum is available."[21] It must be noted, however, that in recent years evidence has been accumulating to indicate that these hormones do not act only contraceptively by preventing ovulation; rather, their function can also be abortifacient, that is, the hormones render the endometrium of the uterus hostile to implantation with the result that if an ovum should be fertilized, it will simply be sloughed off at the time of the woman's next menstruation.[22]

To whatever extent it is established that DES and similar hormones do act mainly as abortifacients, the Roman Catholic Church can not approve of their use in the treatment of rape victims. The Church would have to prohibit the use of these hormones precisely because of her belief that personal life begins at fertilization of the ovum.[23] Some Catholic theologians, however, have given more or less cautious support to the use of these

[20]Richard P. Blye, "The Use of Estrogens as Postcoital Contraceptive Agents," *American Journal of Obstetrics-Gynecology*, 116 (1973), 1044-50 at 1049.

[21]Ashley and O'Rourke, *op. cit.*, p. 295.

[22]For the view that DES acts contraceptively see Donald McCarthy, "Medication to Prevent Pregnancy After Rape," *Linacre Quarterly*, 44 (1977), 210-22; for a refutation of this view and a presentation of the facts indicating that DES acts as an abortifacient see William Lynch, "Comments on 'Medication to Prevent Pregnancy After Rape'," *Ibid.*, 223-28. Consult the following note.

[23]In August, 1980 the Catholic bishops of Pennsylvania issued "Guidelines for the Treatment of Rape Victims in Catholic Hospitals." Regarding DES, the bishops continue to maintain that its use "is permissible only to prevent ovulation."

In 1985 the Bishops' Conference of England and Wales approved a report dealing with the appropriate moral treatment of rape victims. Prepared by a Joint Committee on Bioethical Issues of the Bishops' Conferences of Scotland, Ireland, and England and Wales, the report focused on the question of using so-called "morning after" pills to

hormones in the treatment of rape cases. The reason why theologians like Curran, Häring and McCormick take this stance is because of their adherence to the view that during the first 14-21 days following fertilization, individuality remains to be established and thus the human organism which is developing, while it surely constitutes a real potential for personhood, is nonetheless not yet a human person. Representative of the more cautious approval of postcoital hormonal treatment for rape victims is this comment by McCormick: "I would suggest tentatively that there is sufficient doubt about the claims of nascent life at this stage [7-21 days following fertilization] to say that the use of interceptors (which prevent implantation) in emergency treatment of rape cases is not clearly and certainly wrong."[24]

It should be mentioned again that in order for the hormone treatment to be effective, it must be initiated, at the outside limit,

treat women who have been raped. These pills, like DES, contain estrogen or estrogen-compounds in large doses. According to "responsible scientific opinion," the effect of large doses of estrogen or of estrogen/progestogen combinations "varies according to the stage in the menstrual cycle at which they are administered."

Three stages can, in fact, be distinguished. (1) If the intervention occurs *prior to ovulation,* the estrogen will render the woman's cycle anovular, that is, ovulation will not take place and, hence, fertilization will be impossible. (2) If the estrogen is administered *just before ovulation* is to occur, it will not prevent ovulation, but it may prohibit conception or fertilization "either (a) by immobilizing sperm in the genital tract or (b) by preventing those physiological changes in the sperm which are necessary for fertilization or (c) by affecting the cells surrounding the ovum during the ovum's own process of preparation." (3) If administered *after ovulation* has occurred, the estrogen's only effect, if it has any, will be abortifacient. The abortion will be due to "(a) alteration in the environment of the Fallopian tube, (b) inhibition of implantation by creation of a hostile environment in the endometrium and/or (c) hormonal effects producing shedding of the endometrium and loss of the implanted or un-implanted embryo."

In light of this information, the bishops conclude: "Catholics may seek and administer *hormonal* postcoital contraception after insemination by sexual assault, provided (i) that there are no grounds for judging that ovulation preceded or will coincide with the administration of postcoital contraception, and (ii) that the postcoital contraception is administered urgently, within about a day, after the assault." [For the text of this report, see *Origins,* 15, 39 (March 13, 1986), 633, 635-38; also see *Origins,* 16, 13 (September 11, 1986), 237-38.]

[24]McCormick, "Notes on Moral Theology," *Theological Studies,* 39 (1978), 125-28 at 128. Speaking in more general terms and not with specific reference to treating victims of rape, Häring says: "To disturb or to interrupt the life process during this phase [between fertilization of the ovum and its implantation and final individualization] is, in my eyes, not an indifferent matter. But it seems to me that it does not have the same gravity or malice as the abortion of an individualized embryo, that is, of the embryo after successful implantation or specifically at a time when twinning is no longer possible." See Häring, "New Dimensions," 127-28.

within 72 hours following the attack. This raises the question as to whether some other forms of intervention, such as a D and C or the RU-486 pill, might morally be employed if a rape victim seeks help, let us say, 7-14 days following the attack. While such interventions would indeed disrupt or prevent any implantation that might be in progress, some moralists would consider them to be interventions which thwart only the *potential* for human personhood; within this time-frame, therefore, the actions would not constitute a deprivation of an actual person's right to life.

Let me briefly summarize this matter of the origin of personal human life and its implications for the treatment of rape victims. As indicated earlier, there seem to be sufficient philosophical and biological reasons for maintaining that in the three weeks following fertilization there exists only the potential for human personhood rather than an actual human individual. In certain circumstances, moreover, some moralists believe there can be a proportionate or sufficient reason to intervene against this developing life during these first three weeks. For example, in the case of incest or after a forced rape (but not after statutory rape), intervention by means of some postcoital hormone treatment or, if necessary, by a D and C would be permissible prior to the time of segmentation or the establishment of human individuality; once this time-period has elapsed, however, intervention would be considered morally wrong since the fetus now exists as person.

It ought to be clear, moreover, that not every reason is sufficient to warrant intervention prior to segmentation. Thus, as indicated earlier in our discussion of contraception, the regular use of the I.U.D. and RU-486 or other so-called "morning after" pills cannot be condoned, for these methods of birth-control or birth-limitation (these are not methods of contraception because their mode of operation is rather to prevent implantation, not fertilization) indicate too great a complacency or satisfaction in regularly thwarting the potential for personhood. The same concern, namely, their frequent functioning as abortifacients, explains the moral difficulty with the conventional so-called "oral contraceptives" as well; in other words, to allow for the possible fertilization of an ovum every month and then to acquiesce in effecting its sloughing-off by whatsoever means—"oral contraceptives," I.U.D.'s, RU-486 or "morning after" pills—is unwarranted and highly irresponsible. The situation of the rape victim is quite otherwise, however.

Rape is a traumatic experience. A woman needs time to respond to the event with freedom and prudence, and this might very often mean that she will require more time than the Catholic Church is willing to allow in order for her to seek and receive proper medical attention. A woman would seem entitled to more than 10 to 12, or even 24, hours of grace; she is also entitled to the most effective means to prevent pregnancy following upon rape; finally, some moralists suggest that she is also entitled to prevent or interrupt the implantation of an ovum whose fertilization resulted from rape; but she is not entitled to deprive the fetus as person of its right to life. Thus any intervention must come within three weeks of the attack, before the individuality and personhood of the fetus are established. As an exceptional instance, rape requires and deserves an exceptional and extreme response. Thus it is said by some that following upon incidents of rape or incest, the potential for personal human existence, which is present if fertilization has occurred, may be thwarted by medical intervention, but only during the first three weeks following the attack. It should be noted, finally, that in a great many instances, perhaps even most, such medical interventions will not even be frustrative of any potential for human personhood since conception and pregnancy will not have occurred.

III. When May Human Life Be Taken?

As already indicated, once the claim is made that personal life begins somewhere between 14 and 21 days after fertilization, it does not follow that, prior to that time, the life of the developing organism, which bears the potential for human personhood, can or should be arbitrarily or complacently thwarted. Similarly, however, it does not immediately follow that once personal human life is present in the fetus after the first two to three weeks of development, no abortive action whatsoever may be taken with moral justification. For it sometimes happens that the life of the fetus comes into conflict with the life of the mother or with some other value of comparable significance, in which case some moral solution to the dilemma must be sought.

When such conflicts of life versus life, or life versus some other comparable value, arise involving human life *outside* the womb, solutions can sometimes be reached by means of using the category of the unjust aggressor. Roman Catholic tradition maintains that a person designated as an unjust aggressor may be repulsed by the degree of force that is necessary, even to the point of inflicting death, however, in order to protect one's own life or the life of an innocent third party. In addition, if necessary, such deadly force may be used to safeguard other values which are considered to be proportionate to life itself. Such action, moreover, may be taken against both formal and material aggression; this means that one may respond in the same way both against a person who is causing harm consciously and freely and thus is morally responsible for the action (a formal aggressor), as well as against a person who is mentally deranged or of diminished capacity due to the influence of drugs or alcohol, in which case there is little or no subjective guilt or moral responsibility (a material aggressor).

It should be clearly understood, however, that Catholic teaching has not allowed the category of unjust aggressor, formal or material, to be used in conflict-situations involving fetal life. But this is not to say that Catholic teaching prohibits all abortions. Rather, where life-conflicts do arise between a fetus and a mother, or when complex human situations develop where both good and evil are intertwined, Catholic theologians have traditionally employed the distinction between the direct and indirect effects of a contemplated action. Using this distinction, the Catholic Church has maintained the position that direct abortion is always wrong, whereas indirect abortion may be permitted for a sufficient reason. In order to appreciate the difference between direct and indirect abortions, some explanation must be given of the principle of double effect which traditionally has provided the basis for making the distinction between what are called the direct and indirect results or effects of our actions.[25]

THE PRINCIPLE OF DOUBLE EFFECT

The principle of double effect is brought into play whenever we are considering the performance of an action which is seen to have two rather simultaneous effects or results, one of which is perceived as good and is the one which we sincerely desire and intend to achieve, while the other is bad or evil and is not the object of our desire or intention, but is merely to be tolerated or permitted. This bad or evil effect is such, in fact, that we would rather that it not occur if only that were possible. The diagram below may help to illustrate what is involved in the application of the double-effect principle:

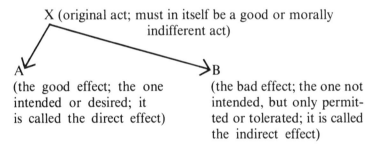

X (original act; must in itself be a good or morally indifferent act)

A
(the good effect; the one intended or desired; it is called the direct effect)

B
(the bad effect; the one not intended, but only permitted or tolerated; it is called the indirect effect)

The moral question which the principle of double effect is meant to answer is whether or not some contemplated action may be performed when it is clearly foreseen that some evil will inevitably result from the posited act. The principle of double effect claims that the proposed act may be performed provided four conditions are met: (1) the original or proposed action must not in itself be evil; it must be a good or morally indifferent

[25]In the following explanation, development and critique of the principle of double effect, I am greatly indebted to the work of Charles E. Curran, especially as it appears in his book, *Ongoing Revision: Studies in Moral Theology* (Notre Dame: Fides Publishers, Inc., 1975), pp. 173-209. Also see Timothy E. O'Connell, *Principles for a Catholic Morality* (New York: Seabury Press, 1978), pp. 170-73.

act; (2) the motive or intention behind the performance of the original act must be the attainment of the good effect; the bad effect must not be intended; it is merely tolerated or permitted; (3) the good effect (A) must not be achieved as a result of the bad effect (B); in other words, the bad effect must not be the means to, or cause of, the good effect; the good effect must truly be caused by the original act (X); (4) there must be a sufficient or proportionate reason for performing the proposed act (X) in the first place, and thus for permitting the evil effect to occur. It should be noted, finally, that the intended effect (A) is viewed as the direct effect, while the permitted effect (B) is regarded as the indirect effect.

In order to see how the principle of double effect has been applied in the past, we may employ an example which raises the moral question of proper military conduct during war when a proposed offensive action is seen as certain to bring death to a number of the civilian or non-combatant population. The specific question centers on the moral permissibility of bombing a highly efficient weapons-manufacturing plant which is located in the heart of a heavily populated urban area; it is inevitable that a bombing strike on the plant will result in the deaths of a large number of civilians, many of whom (children and the elderly) have nothing to do with the military or the defense industry. Morally, may such a bombing strike be initiated?

The traditional moral response has been in the affirmative so long as the four conditions of the principle of double effect are perceived as being verified: (1) the act of bombing (X) is not regarded as in itself always or necessarily evil; (2) the intention behind the act of bombing must be to curtail or destroy the plant's ability to produce weapons; this is the anticipated good effect (A); the bad effect (B) is the death of civilians which is in no way desired or intended; (3) both the destruction or incapacitation of the defense plant and the death of the civilians result from the bombing; the death of the civilians is not what causes or results in the plant's cessation of operations; (4) assuming that the planners of the bombing attack are involved in a just war which they wish to bring to an equitable end, and assuming, too, that the defense plant, because of its efficiency, is a valid military target which cannot be struck in any other way (that is, by internal sabotage), there is a sufficient reason to initiate the bombing raid (*non-nuclear*, of course), even though innocent civilians will be killed.

The destruction of the plant is called the direct or intended effect of the act of bombing, while the deaths of the local civilians are regarded as the act's indirect, permitted or tolerated effect. The civilians are, in other words, said to have been killed *indirectly*. As we indicated earlier in this chapter, our moral tradition has insisted only that innocent human life may not be taken *directly*; but while it may never be directly suppressed, innocent human life may be taken *indirectly*, if there is a sufficient or proportionate reason for doing so.

DIRECT VERSUS INDIRECT ABORTION

We are now in a position to see how the principle of double effect has been brought to bear upon the Roman Catholic Church's stance on abortion: the Church prohibits all direct abortions, but she allows for indirect abortions under certain conditions. To put it another way, the Church says that there must be no direct or intended abortions, but she leaves room for indirect or "permitted" or "tolerated" abortions. The usually-cited examples of indirect abortions are those which occur in the removal of a cancerous uterus from a pregnant woman, or in the removal of a Fallopian tube containing an ectopic pregnancy. Let us look at each of these procedures.

If a woman who is three or four months pregnant is discovered to have cancer of the uterus, it is morally permissible for her to undergo a hysterectomy, which means that the uterus, the pathologically affected organ, is removed from the woman's body, necessarily resulting in the death of the fetus. The rationale given for the morality of this procedure follows the stipulations of the principle of double effect: (1) a hysterectomy is a morally indifferent act; it is not evil in itself; (2) the intention here is to save the pregnant woman's life by excising a cancerous organ from her body before the cancer spreads; this is the desired good effect, so the uterus containing both the malignant tumor and the fetus may be removed; (3) it is not the fetus's death (the permitted bad effect) which causes the woman's life and health to be preserved (the good effect); rather, both the good and bad effects result from the initial act of performing the hysterectomy; (4) the proportionate or sufficient reason for performing the hysterectomy and for tolerating the fetus's inevitable death is the preservation of the woman's life. In this situation, the fetus is said to be killed indirectly and the abortion is referred to as an indirect abortion. We can well imagine, of course, that were the woman much further along in her pregnancy so that the fetus was very close to the time of viability, she might decide to postpone the hysterectomy until after the fetus is safely delivered, but such a decision is not one that she is under moral obligation to make.

When dealing with an ectopic or "out-of-place" pregnancy, the moral analysis follows the pattern established in the previous examples. One notices immediately, however, that in the case of an ectopic pregnancy where an embryo begins to develop, for example, in one of the Fallopian tubes, the cause of the "pathology" and of the medical concern for action is the presence of the embryo itself. The embryo is growing where it ought not to be, and where there is practically no chance of its survival. Moreover, it constitutes a serious threat to the life and health of the mother since, if it remains in the Fallopian tube, it will very likely result in a tubal rupture and severe hemorrhaging.

Initially, moral theologians maintained that no action against an ectopic or tubal pregnancy could be taken until after the tube itself had in fact ruptured; however, once the tube ruptured, it could be regarded as a pathological organ and thus could be removed even though it contained an embryo or fetus. More recently, theological opinion has come to maintain that it is not necessary to wait until a rupture has occurred before removing the Fallopian tube; rather, the tube may be considered infected and therefore pathological even before the rupture occurs, and hence it may be removed. It must be understood that in either instance, that is, before or after a rupture has occurred, the medical procedure that is morally prescribed calls for the excision or removal of that portion of the Fallopian tube containing the embryo; the two ends of the tube are then tied off. In either case, the resulting death of the embryo is seen as an indirect killing and the abortion is regarded as indirect and thereby morally acceptable. All of the stipulations for the use of the principle of double effect have been fulfilled: a non-evil act (the removal of a pathological organ) has been performed with the good intention of saving a woman's life (the proportionate reason); the bad effect (the fetus's death) of the original action was not intended and was not the means used to bring about the good effect.

A question has been raised, however, concerning the moral permissibility of an alternate procedure in the face of a tubal pregnancy. Suppose it were possible simply to remove the embryo from inside the tube without removing any portion of the tube itself, thereby preserving the full extent of the woman's child-bearing capacity since she would retain two Fallopian tubes instead of only one.[26] Laser surgery is one technique that might be used today in order to remove a fetus from within a Fallopian tube where it is developing ectopically. Even assuming that this procedure is medically advisable and would not result in the formation of scar tissue within the tube, thereby increasing the likelihood that a subsequent pregnancy might also be ectopic, such a technique would not be viewed as morally acceptable by the Catholic Church for in this case the death of the fetus would be seen as a direct killing and the abortion would be regarded as direct.

In introducing this discussion of when human life may be taken, I made the point that the Catholic Church allows for an indirect abortion when a sufficient or proportionate reason, such as, for example, saving the mother's life, requires it. It should be noted, however, that it would be wrong to conclude that the Catholic Church is hereby granting approval for what are often referred to as "therapeutic abortions," for, as John Connery points out:

> The abortion in the cases allowed is not really the *therapy*. The therapy is the removal of some diseased organ (e.g., a cancerous uterus). It would seem more accurate to limit the term

[26]Curran, *Absolutes in Moral Theology?*, pp. 112-13.

"therapeutic abortion" to those cases in which the abortion is the therapy. It is not quite true, then, to say that the Church allows some therapeutic abortions. What it has allowed are abortions incidental to other therapy .... Catholic theologians have traditionally allowed the removal of the cancerous (pregnant) uterus, and the pathological (pregnant) fallopian tube; they have not allowed abortion to solve a heart problem or craniotomy to solve a delivery problem threatening the life of the mother.[27]

What Connery does here is to identify an indirect abortion as one which is incidental to other therapy needed by the woman; as incidental, the abortion is seen as not intended, and thus it is permitted. Anytime, however, that an abortion itself (in order to cope with a woman's heart problem), or the destruction of the fetus (as in a craniotomy at the time of delivery), constitutes the suggested or proposed therapy, the abortion is seen as being intended and is morally prohibited. In Connery's words: "If it was the removal of the fetus itself that solved the mother's problem, it was considered intentional and a violation of the precept not to kill. If, however, the means of saving the mother's life was not the removal of the fetus but the removal of a diseased organ, the removal of the fetus was not considered intentional, hence forbidden, killing, but the unavoidable result of a perfectly legitimate procedure."[28]

Connery goes on to assure us that there is a long moral tradition, especially among Jesuit theologians, which claims that a "mother need not forgo life-saving treatment to preserve the life of the fetus." Thus, when the mother's life is at stake, her obligation to safeguard the life of the fetus ceases and she may undergo treatment deemed necessary to preserve her own life. The tradition maintains, however, — and this is crucial — that although the obligation to preserve the fetus's life ceases in this life-threatening situation for the mother, she remains under the

[27]John R. Connery, S.J., "Abortion and the Duty to Preserve Life," *Theological Studies*, 40, 2 (June, 1979), 318-33 at 320.

[28]*Ibid.*, 322.

obligation not to kill the fetus. It is for this reason that Catholic moral tradition has ruled out as a legitimate form of life-saving treatment or therapy any "induced abortion or treatment aimed at abortion [aimed, that is, at the killing of the fetus]." In traditional morality, then, the obligation not to kill the fetus and the obligation to preserve the fetus's life are clearly distinct, and only the second of these obligations can cease to exist under certain extreme circumstances.[29]

In the current official teaching of the Catholic Church, the duty not to kill the fetus translates into the stance that there is to be no direct or intentional killing of the fetus, and this prohibition is expressed in the Church's total banning of direct abortions. At the same time, the Church's acknowledgment that a woman does not have an absolute obligation to preserve the life of a fetus is expressed in the teaching that indirect, incidental or non-intentional abortions are permissible, given a sufficient or proportionate reason. An indirect abortion is one where the death of the fetus is a necessary, inevitable, and thus foreseen, side-effect of an otherwise non-abortive medical procedure; in other words, the fetal death occurs as a result of an action that is not designed or intended to rid the woman's body of the fetus. Thus a pregnant woman judged to be in serious need of life-saving surgery (on her heart, stomach, etc.) or of some kind of drug- or chemo-therapy is not morally obliged to forgo such medical interventions, even though recourse to them clearly poses a serious danger to the health and/or life of her fetus.

I wish to point out that an interesting alignment of ideas and terms has formed in the Church's official teaching regarding abortion: direct or "therapy-in-themselves" abortions are called intentional abortions and these are immoral; indirect or incidental abortions are regarded as non-intentional abortions and these are morally permissible. In the first type of abortions, the killing of the fetus is said to be direct, intended and, hence, immoral, while in the second type of abortions, the fetus's death is seen as indirect, unintended and, therefore, moral. But the

[29]*Ibid.*, 329.

question must be asked: how exactly is it being decided or determined what one's real intention is with respect to the fetus's death; what is the critical and, seemingly, only reference point which distinguishes between direct/ intentional abortions and those which are indirect/ non-intentional? The official line of reasoning of the Catholic Church, in effect, seems to come down to this: a direct abortion is one that is intentional or intended, and one's intention is revealed by looking at what is the sole and immediate object of the physical act or medical procedure. Thus, the object or aim of one's direct intention is identified or equated with whatever is the immediate object of some single or isolated physical action. Indeed, the *Directives of the Catholic Hospital Association* refer to direct killing as a procedure "whose sole immediate effect" is the death of a human being (n. 12).

The situation, then, is this: if the fetus itself is somehow "lethally touched" by being removed or by being hormonally induced to abort, then its death is seen as intended and direct, and this is morally reprehensible, whereas if the medical intervention "touches" and removes a diseased organ containing the fetus, the removal of the fetus is seen as non-intentional and indirect, and hence is permissible. Thus, as we saw earlier, the Church says that when confronted with a tubal pregnancy, a Fallopian tube containing a fetus may be removed, but it would be morally prohibited to attempt to remove only the fetus and thereby leave the tube intact in the hope of fully preserving the woman's life-bearing capacity.

Many moralists today have difficulty in accepting the stance of the Church on this point. They do not think that the Church's presentation necessarily reflects the proper order of things or the true motivation of people. It is not at all clear, in other words, that a woman and a physician must invariably be any more intending the impending death of a fetus by removing it from the Fallopian tube than they would be if they removed the tube with the fetus inside. Rather, the argument may be made that in either procedure the real and only intention is not the death of the fetus, but the preservation of the mother's life, and if this can be achieved in a way that contributes to the woman's life-bearing capacity, so much the better.

MORAL "PHYSICALISM"

I think it is fair to say that the growing dissatisfaction among Christian ethicists, both Catholic and Protestant, with the official distinction that has been drawn between direct and indirect abortion arises from the fact that this distinction in practice reflects a world-view referred to as "physicalism." We have seen this world-view operating in the Church's descriptive analysis of direct killing and direct abortion, but it needs more explicit attention, explanation and evaluation. Stating the case most simply, many contemporary theologians are uneasy with the distinction made between direct and indirect abortions because the differentiation is made to rest solely or primarily upon the physical structure of some action, "and does not give enough importance to the complexity and multiple relationships involved in human actions."[30]

What "physicalism" basically does is to identify the human act, and hence the moral act, with only the physical structure of the act itself. In other words, "physicalism" says that when it comes to weighing or evaluating the morality of an action, we should look only at the physical structure of that act; we can and must prescind from the context in which the act occurs and from any circumstances surrounding the act. Critics of this view are quick to point out that this is not the approach usually adopted, even by traditional Church theologians. As Charles Curran reminds us: "In the vast majority of cases, moral theology has always distinguished between the physical structure of the action and the morality of the action. The moral act of murder differs from the physical act of killing. The physical act of taking another's property does not always involve the moral act of stealing."[31]

Along the same line, traditional moral theology has no difficulty agreeing with the statement of Cornelius J. van der Poel: "The same material act of shooting a person to death may be an act of justice [as in capital punishment], it may be

[30]Curran, *Ongoing Revision*, p. 150.

[31]Charles E. Curran, *Themes in Fundamental Moral Theology* (Notre Dame: University of Notre Dame Press, 1977), p. 43.

self-defense, or it may be plain murder — the same material act and effect, but three different *human* acts."[32] And, hence, we must add, there are three different *moral* acts. The intention or aim behind the act of shooting and killing a person cannot be determined apart from a consideration of the context and circumstances surrounding the act itself. Moreover, only when we know the intention, aim or end of the act considered in its full and proper context, can we adequately evaluate the act from the perspective of morality. We simply cannot weigh an act morally until we know what the human meaning of the act is. The aim, goal or intention of an action is never said to justify an action, but the goal, aim or intention does specify the human meaning of an action, and the goal or intention cannot itself be identified in isolation from the context of the action. The action which is performed as a means to an end shares in the human meaning and hence the moral propriety or impropriety of the end itself. As van der Poel duly notes, however, none of this is meant to imply "that *any* reason is proportionate and acceptable for *any* means. There must be a due proportion between the means and the end."[33]

We ought not, therefore, try to evaluate an action morally simply on the basis of the physical structure of that act. We recognize that at times the act of shooting a person to death is the moral evil of murder (when the act occurs, say, for reasons of greed or revenge); at other times, however, such a shooting embodies not a *moral* evil, but rather the *premoral* or *physical* evil of taking human life for what is regarded as a proportionate or sufficient reason like self-defense or social justice. If one and the same physical act of shooting a person to death is open to a range of moral evaluations, why, it is asked, might not the physically direct act of abortion also be open to the same range of possibilities, so that sometimes it does in fact embody the human and moral evil of murder while at other times it does

[32]Cornelius J. van der Poel, "The Principle of Double Effect," in Curran (ed.), *Absolutes in Moral Theology?*, pp. 186-210 at 204-205.

[33]*Ibid.*, p. 205.

not, even though, materially or in terms of its physical structure, the act remains exactly the same?[34]

In summary, according to many moralists, it is simply too facile to say that a person's intention is clearly embodied in an action's direct effect; likewise, it seems too undiscerning to claim that an action's moral value or disvalue is to be identified or equated with the sole immediate object of the physical act alone. Thus, the act of shooting a person to death in self-defense has been justified in two different ways: some moralists say that the killing is indirect because the intention behind the act is not to kill the person but rather to save or defend myself or another; other moralists would maintain that the killing is indeed direct or intended but, nevertheless, justified, because of the presence of a proportionate reason. Why, then, cannot the same analysis be made of abortion? Could not a fetus be killed as the immediate object of some physical procedure without, however, its death being intended, or could not the fetus's death be intended in some instances where a proportionate reason prevails? Or can it be persuasively argued that the moral innocence of the fetus precludes such possibilities when in fact our moral tradition maintains, as we have seen, that even a material aggressor — one who bears no moral responsibility or guilt—may be killed when necessary?

It should be said that the moral rationale for allowing self-defense against even a material aggessor is that such a person, even though not responsible for it, is nonetheless involved in an objectively wrong action which should be prevented. However, in the case of a pregnancy which may be threatening a woman's life, the Church claims that the fetus itself is doing nothing wrong; it is not doing anything more than it should be doing, namely, being a fetus. Theologians like Charles Curran and Paul Ramsey see the situation differently. They believe that it is not in the very nature of fetuses to pose a life-threatening

---

[34]See Curran's *Absolutes?*, p. 113, with reference to W. van der Marck, O.P., *Love and Fertility* (London: Sheed and Ward, 1965), pp. 59-60.

danger to the women who bear them and, therefore, when such danger is encountered, it is a form of material aggression.[35]

The point which many Catholic moralists would urge today is simply that moral determinations or evaluations ought not to depend solely on a consideration of the immediate effect of a particular physical act. In the words of van der Poel, "the physical structure of the act is merely a pre-moral consideration, and not in itself determinant of morality."[36] The example used by both van der Poel and Curran to illustrate this point centers on the question of the morality of organ transplantations when living donors are involved. Some moralists initially argued against the morality of such procedures because they involve direct mutilation, which is to say, that healthy organs are deliberately and directly removed from a living person's body; such direct mutilation has always been considered immoral since, on the basis of the so-called principle of totality, the only surgical procedures permitted were those required for the physical well-being of the patient.

In time, of course, organ transplantation received moral approval by a combination of rationales; on the one hand, the principle of totality was expanded in this context to include not only a person's physical well-being, but also his or her spiritual and human well-being so that a live donor could indeed be said to be personally enhanced or benefited by the organ-offering; on the other hand, the whole procedure is undertaken in recognition of another's desperate need and the call to meet that need out of love. There is no denying the fact, however, that excising a person's healthy organ involves in itself what has been called a direct mutilation, that is, the sole immediate effect of the physical action is bodily mutilation; this fact does not change, even though the healthy organ is then given to someone in dire need. The point to be made, then, is that "the physical structure of the act of excising cannot be the ultimate determinant of morality. The physical excision of the organ is a

[35]Charles E. Curran, *Politics, Medicine, and Christian Ethics* (Philadelphia: Fortress Press, 1973), pp. 124-25; 127-28; also see Curran's *Transition and Tradition*, pp. 220-24.

[36]van der Poel, *Absolutes?*, p. 194.

part of the total human action of transplantation."[37] Now if the physical acts of surgically excising a human organ, or of shooting a person to death, or of taking someone else's property, cannot be morally evaluated until the human meaning of these acts is first discerned, why, then, cannot the same caution be exercised in presenting a moral analysis of the physical act of abortion?

THE PRINCIPLE OF PROPORTIONALITY AND BEYOND

Theological dissatisfaction with the "physicalism" reflected in the traditional differentiation between direct and indirect abortions has led a number of Christian theologians to conclude that this distinction alone can no longer serve as the key to deciding which abortions are morally permissible and which are not. Instead, such moral evaluations should be made with reference to the so-called principle of proportionality. We must ask, in other words, if there are any reasons which would be proportionate or sufficient enough to justify an abortion, whether physically direct or not. If an abortion were seen as justified in certain circumstances, namely, those constituting a proportionate or sufficient reason for the abortion, the action would still be regarded as a physical or premoral evil (taking human life), but it would not embody the moral evil of an act of murder (deliberate, unjustified killing of a human being).

In general, it has been argued by moralists like McCormick and Curran that human life should only be taken when doing so constitutes, all things considered, the lesser of two evils. McCormick notes that in fact all of the traditional exceptions (e.g., self-defense, just war, capital punishment, indirect killing) to the general prohibition against taking human life are "formulations and concretizations of what is viewed in the situation as the lesser human evil."[38] Now in order for the

---

[37]*Ibid.*, also Curran, *Absolutes?*, p. 113.

[38]Richard A. McCormick, S.J., "Notes on Moral Theology: Abortion Dossier," *Theological Studies*, 35 (1974), 312-59 at 354.

taking of a human life to qualify as a lesser evil, that life must itself be jeopardizing another human life or some other value comparable to human life and, hence, life's moral equivalent.

When Charles Curran discusses the question of when abortion might be justified in a conflict situation, that is, where the value of fetal life conflicts with one or more other values, he does so against the backdrop of the traditional teaching of moral theology which "justified the killing of an unjust aggressor as a last resort in defense of one's life, bodily integrity, [or] spiritual goods 'of greater value than life or integrity' such as the use of reason or conservation of reputation in very important matters;" such killing might also be warranted in order to preserve "material goods of great value" so that, for example, one might kill a person who is about to destroy one's only source of livelihood (one's place of business). While Curran admits that our moral tradition may in fact have been too liberal in seeing all these values as comparable to life and, hence, as life's "moral equivalents," his own conclusion regarding abortion is to say that indeed abortion "could be justified to save the life of the mother or to avert very grave psychological or physical harm to the mother with the realization that this must truly be grave harm that will perdure over some time and not just a temporary depression."[39] Curran believes, in addition, that in extreme situations, which are rare, "other values of a socio-economic nature" can justify recourse to abortion.[40]

There are undeniable dangers and difficulties involved in assessing abortion's morality through the employment of the principle of proportionality and the determination of which values do indeed exist as the "moral equivalents" of human life. Subjectivism, personal rationalization, cultural relativism and societal prejudices may easily enter into the process of moral evaluation in such a way that other values are so highly touted that the value of fetal human life is underestimated; the result is that the fetus's right to life is effectively undermined and unjustifiably denied. To acknowledge, however, that there are

[39]Curran, *New Perspectives*, p. 191.
[40]Curran, *Politics, Medicine*, p. 131.

dangers in the methodology associated with the use of proportionality is not to argue that this approach must be judged inherently deficient; but the dangers surely do suggest the need for caution, prudence, honesty and hard reasoning when trying to resolve a conflict of values, especially when one of these values is the human life of someone who cannot speak or act on his own behalf.

Curran sees as morally permissible more exceptions to the general prohibition of abortion than seem warranted. And one must wonder if the list of situations in which he foresees the possibility of abortion as a moral action would be shortened were he to put more emphasis on the fact that in our Christian tradition human life is not to be taken lightly or unnecessarily, but only as a last resort. While one might agree that the distinction between direct and indirect abortion serves inadequately in the decision-making process about abortion's morality, he might also maintain that the use of the principle of proportionality should be further qualified or circumscribed. Thus, in an attempt to introduce more guidelines that might facilitate cautious, honest, prudent and hard-reasoned decisions regarding abortion, the principle of proportionality might well be inserted into the context of the criteria usually delineated in an effort to determine the justice of recourse to war. It perhaps seems extreme to link the actions of war and abortion, but both do, after all, involve acts of violence; in abortion, as in war, people are violated, and it is imperative that this not occur casually, indiscriminately, and without justification.

Over the centuries, theologians have proposed that in order for a war, and the violence it necessarily involves, to be considered justified, each one of the following stipulations or criteria must be verified: (1) the war must be declared by a competent, legitimate authority, (2) for a just cause (e.g., national defense), (3) with the right intention (e.g., for preservation of human rights, not for reasons of greed, hatred or vengeance), (4) as a last resort, (5) with reasonable hope of success, and (6) only after evaluating that the evil surely to be perpetrated by the war will be less than the good one hopes to accomplish by the recourse to war. I do not want to get into an overly extensive application of these criteria to the issue of abortion, but it is necessary to indicate in some detail how they might shed some light on this complex question. Together, the second and sixth criteria embody the matter of proportionality: is there a sufficient reason or cause that would justify the violent act of killing a fetus; in other words, when, if ever, would killing a fetus be the lesser evil, a physical, premoral or non-moral evil? I should add here that I do not see the fifth criterion as pertinent to the abortion issue. With this said, let us look at some of the criteria and see what questions and suggestions they might provide for establishing a moral frame of reference with respect to decisions about abortion.

Competent Authority: When we ask the question who should be seen as possessing the competent and legitimate *moral* authority to permit an abortion, we do so knowing full well that as of 1973, the Supreme Court (*Roe v. Wade*, and *Doe v. Bolton*) has given expansive *legal* permission for abortion to any pregnant woman and her physician. In terms of the usual trimester divisions during the time of gestation, the Court's ruling is reflected in the following determinations: during the first trimester of pregnancy, a time when abortion is judged safer than childbirth, no state may enact laws prohibiting abortions, so that the decision to abort is left entirely to a woman's choice or desire and her physician's medical compliance; in the second trimester, states may establish laws only to ensure that medically safe abortion procedures occur; thus regulations may be proposed concerning where abortions are performed and the types of procedures used; finally, in the third trimester, when the fetus is considered viable, a state's interest in protecting fetal life can be judged compelling enough to permit the state to prohibit abortions "except when necessary to preserve the life or health of the mother." Consideration for the "health" of the mother, moreover, is meant to include both her physical and emotional well-being; abortion could well be legally permitted, therefore, on the basis of such "hardships" as "the stigma of unwed motherhood," and "the distress, for all concerned, associated with the unwanted child."[41] Thus, the effect of the Supreme Court's decision, in practice, has been to allow for "abortion on demand."

In a 1976 decision (*Danforth v. Planned Parenthood of Missouri*), the Supreme Court went further and declared, among other things, that during the first trimester "a state *may not* constitutionally require the consent of a spouse to an abortion," nor may a state require the consent of a minor's parent or parents to an abortion during this period.[42] In 1981, however, the Court did uphold the constitutionality of a Utah law requiring that, before performing an abortion on an unmarried girl under 18 who is living with and dependent on her family, a doctor must inform the girl's parents; the physician does not, however, need the parents' permission to perform the abortion, although the same physician would need parental consent to perform a surgical procedure like removing the girl's tonsils. As an *America* editorial points out, both the Utah law and the Court's decision are quite narrow: "The law does not reach an emancipated minor, and the Court's decision left open the possibility that the law could not be applied to a dependent minor who can prove to a court that she is sufficiently mature."[43]

In none of the Court's declarations, as is obvious, is much made of the fetus and its human rights. More, it seems, by fiat than by reason, argumentation or demonstration, the Court in *Roe v. Wade* asserted that "the word 'person,' as used in the Fourteenth Amendment, does not include the unborn." Moreover, after offering the view that the judiciary "is not in a position to speculate as to the answer" to the question when life begins, the majority opinion concludes that this difficult question need not be resolved by the Court. "For all practical

[41]"Abortion: The New Ruling," *The Hastings Center Report*, 3, 2 (April, 1973), 4-7; also George J. Annas, "Roe v. Wade Reaffirmed," *The Hastings Center Report*, 13, 4 (August, 1983), 21-22.

[42]George J. Annas, "Abortion and the Supreme Court: Round Two," *The Hastings Center Report*, 6, 5 (October, 1976), 15-17 at 15.

[43]*America*, 144, 14 (April, 11, 1981), 290.

purposes," however, as Daniel Callahan has observed, the Justices (7-2) did resolve this difficult question for "they say, by perfectly plain implication, that life does not begin during the first two trimesters."[44]

We must assume that in expressing its doubt about the time when "life" begins, the Court's real skepticism concerns "human" life and, more specifically, "personal" life, for, as we have seen earlier, there is "life" from the moment of conception. On this point, whatever the situation may have been in 1973, it seems accurate to say that today there is an identifiable consensus arising either from ordinary common sense or from intelligent reflection — or from both — that the fetus is indeed human and personal life from at least the early weeks following fertilization, if not from the moment of conception. Thus, in today's debate over the fetal deaths resulting from abortions, the major point at issue is not whether human beings are being killed, but rather whether these human beings are being killed justifiably or without justification. And it is this question which taunts the minds and sensitivities of a broad spectrum of people, believers as well as non-believers; thus, it is a question posed directly neither by divine revelation nor by any particular religious dogma or tradition. Should we expect, therefore, a definitive answer to the question from God or theology?

The Supreme Court's stand, being what it is, allows the Court to restrict, in great measure, consideration of the question of fetal rights or the rights of persons. However, for people who recognize the fetus as a person from quite early on in the pregnancy and who maintain that from the time of conception there is in the fetus unquestionable and valuable potential for personhood, the judgment seems inescapable that the interests of the fetus, far from being recognized, have in fact been betrayed by the Court. Such people, too, must probably view the Court's legal determinations regarding the status of the fetus as misinformed, and its recommendations permitting abortions as at least misdirected, if not irresponsible. The Court's rather wholesale bestowal of freedom to abort upon the

[44] *The Hastings Center Report*, 3, 2 (April, 1973), 7.

woman must be challenged for its failure in large measure to regard the fetus's distinct existence and real presence as a being with rights. In recognition of its existence and presence, the fetus deserves an advocate; it seems inadequate, therefore, both legally and morally, to establish the woman alone as the competent and legitimate authority in the decision to abort. Someone must formally represent the fetus's cause, and a serious case might also be made to the effect that the person responsible for the pregnancy, that is, the woman's husband or the child's father, has a right to be consulted before an abortion is performed.[45]

Just Cause: What circumstances might morally justify recourse to abortion? In response to this question, various people have suggested that abortion might be a moral option in any of the following situations: if a pregnancy has resulted from forced rape or incest, or if the pregnancy is posing a threat to either the life or the physical, psychological or emotional health of the woman; the option for abortion might also be exercised, some say, when there is evidence that the developing fetus is defective and will be born with a variety of physical or mental handicaps; finally, socio-economic pressures are often cited as warrants for abortion.

Before commenting on these circumstances which have been proposed as justifications for abortion, some insight into the reality of the abortion scene today might be derived from a statistical analysis of the characteristics of the women obtaining abortions. In 1983, the January/February issue of *Family Planning Perspectives*, which is published by the Alan Guttmacher Institute, the research arm of Planned Parenthood, analyzed the 1,553,890 abortions which were reported in 1980. The women obtaining abortions were young (65% under 25; 32% were teenagers); they were unmarried (79% — up from 75% in 1976); they were white (70% — up from 67% in 1976); they were well-educated (14% were college graduates and 38%, age 20 and over, had some college); 33% had had one or more previous

---

[45]Eugene Kennedy illustrates the fallacy of the view that abortion is an issue between only a woman and her doctor in *What A Modern Catholic Believes About Sex and Marriage* (Chicago: The Thomas More Press, 1975), pp. 107-11.

abortions — up from 20% in 1976; finally, 50% of these girls/women had no children.

I do not wish to canonize these statistics, but if they in any way reflect the truth of the American scene, it seems accurate to suggest that since for the most part the girls/women obtaining abortions are young, they are probably also generally healthy individuals who turn to abortion because their pregnancies simply are unintended and unwanted; since most rapes do not result in pregnancies, we must further conclude that the aborted pregnancies are unintended and unwanted even though they do not result from forced intercourse, except in the broad, but real, sense in which society, through its mass media, pressures all young people, men and women, into early sexual activity. Generally, then, the women who abort have willingly entered into sexual intercourse, knowing the risk of becoming pregnant even with the use of contraceptives; once pregnant, they conclude that they dare not, cannot or will not, bear the pain, social and emotional embarrassment, or economic inconvenience of supporting and nurturing the child, even, or at least, until birth. In light of the statistics presented here, then, it seems fair to say that were we legally to permit abortions only when rape or incest was the cause of the pregnancy, or when the pregnancy seriously threatened the woman's life or physical health, or when it was certain that the fetus was defective, we would be permitting precious few abortions. With this point made, let us look at these frequently-cited moral justifications for abortion.

Since we have already reflected on the question of treating victims of rape and incest, I am going to move directly to a consideration of the other reasons frequently put forth as moral justifications for abortion. Most often it is maintained that abortion should be judged morally acceptable when undertaken "to preserve a woman's life or physical health." I find this terminology itself too vague and all-encompassing. It is one thing to be confronted with a scenario where a woman is in imminent danger of dying because of a medical condition severely complicated or aggravated by pregnancy; it is another thing, however, to face a situation where a pregnancy, as it develops, will undoubtedly or probably require special attention and treatment because of some physical ailments suffered by the mother. In the latter instance, the pregnancy may indeed be said to pose a threat to the woman's life or physical health, but there is also the likelihood that this threat can be successfully met and overcome with adequate medical supervision and care.

Many physicians today would in fact urge the view that, given the proper care and treatment, a woman can be gotten through any pregnancy, barring traumatic and unexpected complications. While I am predisposed toward sympathy with this view, honesty demands admission of the fact that it entails a major proviso — given proper care and treatment — and one that cannot always be met. Good care costs, and it costs dearly, so that, in truth, not all women have equal access to the quality of health services that may be required in a complicated pregnancy or in a pregnancy that creates new strains upon a chronic health problem. Thus not every pregnant woman who is afflicted, for example, with a severe heart problem or with deteriorating kidneys may be able to respond positively to a physician's judgment that she has a good chance of carrying to term provided that she spends the last two months of her pregnancy in the hospital or with complete bed-rest.

As much as some of these women may be inclined to want to follow their doctors' advice and recommendation for getting through the pregnancy in such circumstances, they simply may not be able to, either because of their financial situation or because they have no one to care for their other children. In circumstances such as these, or in others like them, women may honestly feel trapped, with no other viable option or alternative but to turn to abortion. Their personal or subjective assessment of their situation may or may not be accurate, but at the very least their predicament suggests that the question of abortion should be seen as more than a private, personal decision which may have to be faced by a woman or a single family; abortion is a more complex issue, a matter of social morality; as such, it raises other questions, not the least of which is why our society does not make good health care more easily accessible to everyone. We will have occasion to return to this perception of abortion as a social moral issue later; for now, however, I want to consider the question of abortion as a moral response in the situation where a woman's life is in imminent danger.

As we saw earlier, the Catholic Church is morally opposed to all direct abortions, including so-called therapeutic abortions in which the act of abortion itself is intended as the prescribed therapy for some medical problem afflicting the mother. According to this teaching, there may well be situations where it is morally necessary to allow both mother and child to die rather than perform a direct abortion. The teaching has been popularly summarized in the expression: "Better two deaths than one murder." We might judge today that with adequate and proper prenatal care, such tragic situations need rarely arise, and this is probably true. Recourse to a craniotomy, for example, could and should, I think, be avoided by a physician's being aware early in a woman's pregnancy of the possibility that a Caesarean section may be medically indicated. It would be naive, however, to think that all such moral dilemmas arising from severe conflict situations can be foreseen and circumvented. At times, as Bernard Haring and others have suggested, it may be that recourse to a physically direct abortion to save a mother from imminent death constitutes the most moral response to a tragic situation. Consider the following case that was reported to Häring by a gynecologist:

> I was once called upon to perform an operation on a woman in the fourth month of pregnancy, to remove a benign uterine tumour. On the womb, there were numerous very thin and fragile varicose veins which bled profusely, and attempts to suture them only aggravated the bleeding. Therefore, in order to save the woman from bleeding to death, I opened the womb and removed the fetus. Thereupon the uterus contracted, the bleeding ceased, and the woman's life was saved. I was proud of what I had achieved, since the uterus of this woman, who was still childless, was undamaged and she could bear other children. But I had to find out later from a noted moralist that although I had indeed acted in good faith, what I had done was, in his eyes, *objectively* wrong. I would have been allowed to remove the bleeding uterus with the fetus itself, he said, but was not permitted to interrupt the pregnancy while leaving the womb intact. He informed me that my intervention constituted

an immoral termination of pregnancy, even though the purpose was to save the mother, whereas the other way would have been a lawful direct intention . . . and action to save life, as in the case of a cancerous uterus. For him, preservation of the woman's fertility . . . played no decisive role.[46]

In his reaction to this conflict situation, Häring's line of reasoning differs significantly from that of the moralist mentioned in the case. As Häring views the scene, three options presented themselves to the gynecologist: to do nothing would result in the death of both mother and fetus—a clearly irresponsible decision; to perform a hysterectomy would save the mother's life, the fetus would be killed indirectly, but the woman would be rendered sterile and thus have to remain childless; finally, the doctor could open the uterus and remove the fetus, thus performing a direct abortion; in this way, the mother's life is saved and her fertility is preserved. According to Häring, in acting as he did, the doctor accepted "the only chance to protect and serve life which Divine Providence has left to him. He saves the life of the mother while he does not truly deprive the fetus of its right to live since it could not possibly survive in the event of the doctor's failure to save the mother's life. Moreover, the preservation of the mother's fertility is an additional service to life."[47]

The crux of this analysis lies in what Häring perceives as the real malice of abortion. For him, the evil of abortion exists in the fact that it constitutes "an attack on the right of the fetus to live." Attacking the fetus's right to live is what makes abortion immoral. But as we have just seen in the case presented, the doctor did not attack the fetus's right to live; it was rather the woman's unfortunate medical condition which robbed the fetus of its right to live. The doctor simply recognized that given the mother's medical condition, the fetus's death was inevitable; the only question was whether the fetus's death was to be direct or indirect. The doctor did not, moreover, make the decision to

---

[46]Bernard Häring, *Medical Ethics* (Notre Dame: Fides Publishers, 1973), p. 108.

[47]*Ibid.*, p. 109.

save the mother rather than the fetus; nor did the doctor assign more value to the mother's life than to the fetus's; the doctor saved the only life which could be saved in the circumstances, and thus did not choose between the mother and fetus. Lest there be any confusion on this point, it should be said that just as the Catholic tradition has argued against directly killing the fetus to save the mother, so also has it maintained that it is wrong to directly kill the mother in order to save the fetus. Where death is threatening both mother and fetus but both have a chance of being saved, the Church sees it as morally wrong to give either mother or fetus preferential treatment by deciding to kill the other: "Better two deaths than one murder," says the traditional teaching.

What some theologians are pleading, however, is that in cases like the one described here and in others where a woman in imminent danger of dying is carrying a fetus which is not yet viable, a direct abortion presents itself as a moral response in a final attempt to save the only life which can be saved, namely, the mother's, rather than allow two deaths to occur. In such circumstances, it is suggested, the act of intervention against the fetus, while surely being the physical act of abortion, does not embody the moral malice of abortion, and thus is not murder; such an act does not rob the fetus of its right to live, since the fetus must die even if no intervention occurs and the mother also dies.

With reference to the case presented to Häring, one final important point should be made. The only reason the "noted moralist" mentioned in the case could offer the advice he did, namely, to remove the whole uterus with the fetus inside (an indirect abortion), was because the bleeding uterus, given its condition, could be considered a pathological organ which warranted surgical removal just as a cancerous uterus would. If, however, the woman's life had been in the same degree of danger due to a heart problem or kidney problem which was being complicated and aggravated by the pregnancy, the "noted moralist" could not have advised either the hysterectomy or any direct, intentional, physical act of abortion even as a final recourse in the attempt to save the woman's life, because for him the physical act of abortion is also always weighted with the moral malice of murder, an attack on the fetus's right to live.

But there may be some new nuances emerging in the traditional Church teaching that both a fetus and mother must be allowed to die rather than have recourse to a direct abortion. Richard McCormick has proposed that the substance of the classical Christian position on the question of when human life may be taken can be formulated as follows: "Human life as a basic gift and good ... may be taken only when doing so is the only life-saving and life-serving alternative, or only when doing so is, all things considered (not just numbers), the lesser evil. "[48] This would mean that with respect to determining the morality of taking the life of a fetus, the ultimate question is not whether the proposed intervention would constitute a direct or an indirect abortion, but rather whether or not taking the fetus's life is truly the lesser evil and is in fact the only life-saving and life-serving option remaining.

McCormick takes note, as well, of what seems to be some hierarchical support for a more nuanced approach to what he calls "those very rare and desperate conflict instances (where both mother and child will die if abortion is not performed)." He quotes from a statement of the Catholic bishops of Belgium: "The moral principle which ought to govern the intervention can be formulated as follows: Since two lives are at stake, one will, while doing everything possible to save both, attempt to save one rather than to allow two to perish."[49] A comparable sentiment seems to be embodied in a statement by the Catholic bishops of Germany: "In irresolvable conflict situations where the decision is between losing both mother and child and losing just one, the medical conscience-decision is to be respected."[50]

Given the rather ambiguous and obscure formulation of these episcopal views, it is not easy to know exactly the full implications of their intended significance, but at least this

[48]McCormick, S.J., "Abortion: A Changing Morality and Policy?," *Catholic Mind*, LXXVII, 1336 (October, 1979), 42-59 at 48.

[49]*Ibid.*, 50, quoting "Déclaration des évêques belges sur l'avortement," *Documentation Catholique*, 70 (1973), 432-38 at 434.

[50]"Schwangerschaftsabbruch: Kirche und Gewissen,"*Orientierung*, 42 (1978), 66-9, as quoted in McCormick, "Notes on Moral Theology," *Theological Studies*, 40 (1979), 67-9, n. 27 where McCormick is citing an article by Karl-Heinz Weger.

much might be said: if one is to find in these statements any basis for suggesting that an abortion might be performed in a last-effort attempt to save a mother's life rather than allow both mother and fetus to die, great caution must be counseled. Indeed, in such situations, the judgment must first be verified that given its lack of development, the fetus cannot presently be saved; therefore, it is not a question of choosing one life over another or of giving preferential treatment to the mother; it is rather an attempt to save the only life which can be saved; when this is done, the act of abortion would seem not to be an attack on the fetus's right to life; nor would the act appear to bear the moral malice of murder.

Turning now to the issue of the moral permissibility of abortion in response to the emotional and psychological turmoil which pregnancy stirs up in some women, it must be said at first that a more basic question has long been debated, namely, whether or not there are criteria which can be consistently and validly applied in such a way that it becomes clear to mental-health experts that in a particular case abortion is medically advisable. As far back as 1969, a study reported by the *Group for the Advancement of Psychiatry* concluded that in terms of the kinds of conditions which could consistently be identified as indications for advising abortion, the following might be mentioned: (1) when previous pregnancies had repeatedly brought on post-partum psychotic reactions; (2) when the woman had been previously lobotomized; (3) when a woman is a clear-cut schizophrenic or is in the midst of an acute schizophrenic episode; (4) when the woman has a serious and recurrent affective disorder; (5) and finally, when a woman manifests profound suicidal or homicidal tendencies.[51]

The report is quick to note, however, that these kinds of conditions are rarely encountered among women seeking abortions. Rather, the conditions these women do manifest are much more ambiguous and thus less useful as indications for advising abortion. One may find in these women: (1) mild

[51]"Right to Abortion: A Psychiatric View," prepared by a Committee on Psychiatry and Law, *Group for the Advancement of Psychiatry*, VII, 75 (October, 1969), 203-27 at 214-15.

suicidal fantasizing or gestures, (2) symptoms of mild neurosis, (3) emotional or intellectual immaturity which would make child-rearing and motherhood quite difficult, and (4) psychological hardship arising from a broad range of socio-economic factors. Quite apart from the recognized difficulty of applying this latter set of criteria consistently, the report remarks that the suggestion of using any criterion from either set as a valid indication for abortion is open to dispute because a basic issue remains unresolved: "will the abortion and *its* effects be more traumatic than pregnancy, childbirth and forced motherhood?"[52]

This last question is by no means an idle one. Some studies have indicated that while the immediate effect of abortion upon the woman is relief and an ability to cope with life again, within several months the woman's situation can be quite different; she may be experiencing strong guilt feelings, acute depression, inability to work, and an immature dependence upon family or parents. There is, moreover, a strong possibility that these psychological and emotional repercussions of abortion may only be aggravated by the long-term physical effects that are now being attributed to abortion. One study, for example, concludes that "a previous abortion increases the chances of a later perinatal death by 50%;" also, "there may be a 40% increase in premature births," and "a fourfold increase in pelvic inflammation and menstrual disorders;" finally, "2% to 5% of those who have abortions may subsequently be sterile."[53]

Even if a woman's long-term psychological trauma following upon an abortion could in fact be shown to be less than the trauma associated with continued pregnancy, childbirth and child-rearing or placement of the child for adoption, I am not persuaded that a woman has the moral right to obtain an abortion as a way of avoiding what for her will be an admittedly emotionally painful, and perhaps embarrassing, experience. There must be, I think, other, less drastic, ways in which to respond to a woman's anxiety and fears in the face of an

[52]*Ibid.*

[53]I am quoting an article by the editor and staff of *The Month*, "A New Catholic Strategy on Abortion," *The Month*, Second New Series, 6, 5 (May, 1973), 163-71 at 168-69; the article refers to two studies, one in California, the other in London.

unintended, unwanted, and hence troublesome, pregnancy.

I would like to consider one final situation. What should be said of the idea that abortion might be regarded as a moral option when it is discovered that a woman is carrying a defective fetus? The proposed rationales for aborting fetuses afflicted with a variety of diseases involving mental and physical handicaps are themselves numerous and diverse. Sometimes the stated intention is simply to spare the child-to-be-born the pain, suffering and frustration associated with the reduced quality of life that is projected; sometimes the prospective parents express the honest fear that they would not be able to witness the anguish endured by their afflicted child, and the prospect of their own suffering haunts them; in some instances, parents say that they do not want to burden their other children by having a handicapped child at home, while in other cases families say that they can neither afford the financial burden of placing the handicapped child in a private hospital, nor can they stand to think of their child being confined to a public or state-run institution. Thus finding themselves confronted with the painful news that their child will be handicapped in one way or another, many people, with or without justification, feel trapped and then, sadly and half-heartedly, turn to abortion which presents itself as the most readily available resolution of their doubts and confusion.

While I can only imagine the sense of disappointment and helplessness which such people must experience, I do not think that abortion is a moral option available to them. But is there a possible exception to this view? In the event that it is clearly determined that the developing fetus is so seriously deformed as to be lacking even the biological or physical substratum needed for any expression of truly human and personal life, an intervention to terminate the pregnancy might not be regarded as an action bearing the full moral malice of abortion. Such a situation would exist in the case of a fetus which is anencephalic (showing no brain development past the time when it should be in evidence). When this occurs, Häring suggests that intervention might be a moral response, "since our concern is not just for biological life but for *human* life." Häring proposes that the situation here is analogous to that which exists after we are confronted with confirmation of human brain death. In other words, once a human being living outside the womb suffers irreversible brain death and there is no further hope or expectation for real personal communication or relationship, personal human life may be considered to have ended and life-supports may be withdrawn. Similarly, says Häring, when it is confirmed that there is no hope for the appearance or development of a fetus's brain, the fetus may be seen as devoid of personal human life and action to separate the fetus from its organic life-supports might be viewed as moral.[54]

It happens at times, of course, that seriously deformed fetuses will abort spontaneously. It also happens that false diagnoses are made concerning a fetus's condition, and even when a diagnosis of a disorder is accurate, it is not possible to know how severely the disease will affect the child-to-be-born. Knowing these things, though, probably affords little consolation or comfort to people who must battle many uncertainties about the kind of life awaiting their child and themselves as they struggle with the prospect of abortion after being told that the fetus is afflicted with a serious disorder. Such people often need and want help, not to run away from their difficult situation, but to cope with it successfully and responsibly. These people require reassurance that the truth lies elsewhere than in the conclusion that abortion is the best recourse because it is the only realistic one.

Last Resort: What I wish to suggest here is that no matter which of the proposed "justifying causes" for abortion one takes into consideration, and regardless of the judgment one makes concerning the inherent value or validity of any cause's claim to justify an abortion, the suasive force — whatever its degree —of that "justifying cause" finds itself enhanced, for reasons external to itself, when abortion appears as a woman's only or last resort. Thus, if we are serious in our belief that no human life should be taken except when doing so is the only life-saving and life-serving option available, or when doing so truly is the lesser evil, then whether we are talking about abortion to save a mother's life or health, or abortion of a defective fetus, or

[54]Häring, *Medical Ethics*, pp. 110-11 and nn. 44, 45.

abortion in the face of serious economic strain, it is imperative that as a society we must do more in the way of providing viable options or alternatives to abortion, thereby ensuring that women need not have recourse to the very abortions which they may not really want. Moreover, not only must viable and realistic options exist, they must also be known about and readily available. Too many women and families turn to abortion thinking it is their only or last resort when it really is not, or when, at least, it does not have to be.

There are, of course, organizations like *Birthright International* and *Alternatives to Abortion, Inc.* which for a number of years have been prepared to refer women to available medical, psychological and legal resources in local communities, and to arrange for financial aid, maternity homes or whatever other help may be required in order to support a woman's desire not to have an abortion. And yet a gap still seems to exist between pregnant women in need and the kind of assistance which would free these women from the conviction that abortion is their best or their only course of action, however undesirable they may find it. Either this is the situation which prevails today, or there must be many women for whom the lives of their unborn childen count for little or nothing when the preservation of these lives would admittedly necessitate some struggle, inconvenience or a change of career plans, even if temporary. I dread to say that it is callousness or self-interest rather than desperation which rules in the decision made by women to abort; and every attempt must be made to deprive these women of the grounds for their desperation.

Over a decade ago, the editors and staff of the British journal, *The Month*, in consultation with physicians and theologians, prepared a marvelous essay entitled "A New Catholic Strategy on Abortion" in which they maintained that "the main practical aim of Catholic policy ought to be to make abortion as unnecessary as possible."[55] The article points out that a woman's request for abortion is never a simple matter; it always derives from a conflict situation, and thus a woman needs to be

[55] *The Month*, 169.

informed of all the options available to her for a resolution of the conflict. The writers go on to suggest that "the more we oppose abortion, the more we ought to show compassion towards those who seek it. Not the abstract compassion of pious sentiments, but the practical compassion which issues in action."[56]

In addressing the issue of practical compassion, the authors first refer to the results of a study published in Geneva which showed that "the real motivation behind the request for an abortion is rarely the health, physical or psychological, of the mother-to-be. The reasons are much more frequently social and economic." If this is indeed the case, then clearly any society, if it chooses to do so, can "so modify the social and economic conditions that the motivations [for abortion] would no longer apply." Putting the matter most bluntly, the writers lay down the admonition: "if social and economic motivations predominate among those who at present seek an abortion, society should treat these requests as a *symptom of its own sickness*, and not just as an individual problem to be resolved in individual cases."[57]

Were I to express this viewpoint in terms of its moral overtones for the Catholic community, I would have to conclude that if we insist on the overall immorality of abortion, then any failure of energy on our part in trying to ensure that abortion is rendered truly unnecessary (because other viable options have been made readily available), means that we cannot escape a share of the moral blame for the fetal deaths that occur. Given the Catholic Church's strong conviction that abortion is morally repugnant, the Church must do all it can to facilitate and encourage a woman's decision to preserve the life of her fetus. In no other way will the Church avoid the appearance and the reality of self-righteous hypocrisy. The practical compassion reflected in the pastoral letter written by the bishop of the diocese of Shrewsbury, England cannot be

[56] *Ibid.*, 167.
[57] *Ibid.*, 169.

praised enough; it should, moreover, establish a pattern of response for every diocese:

> We recognise that, for one reason or another, a pregnancy can cause a problem, distress, shame, despair to some mothers. Perhaps, in our concern to uphold the sanctity of life, we have failed to show sufficient practical concern for the mother-to-be who feels herself to be in an intolerable situation. That is all over.
>
> The Diocese of Shrewsbury publicly declares its solemn guarantee. It is this: Any mother-to-be, Catholic or non-Catholic, is guaranteed immediate and practical help, confidentially and at no expense to herself, if, faced with the dilemma of an unwanted pregnancy, she is prepared to allow the baby to be born and not aborted. This help includes, if she wishes, the care for her baby after birth. All the resources of the diocese are placed behind this pledge.[58]

Let me conclude this discussion of the possible justifications for abortion. In my opinion, there can be no moral justification for an abortion undertaken for social and economic considerations. When such considerations do in fact serve as a woman's reason for seeking an abortion, it is possible that the woman has not clearly understood the values at stake in her decision and thus has honestly misjudged her responsibilities; it is also possible that the woman knows full well what she is contemplating and nevertheless decides upon abortion as the course of action least burdensome to her in terms of time, energy, money and inconvenience. Finally, it is possible that a pregnant woman may honestly feel trapped by her socio-economic situation so that she turns in desperation to abortion; to the extent that her reaction reflects the reality of the situation — she has no other realistic option — society must bear some moral

---

[58] *Ibid.*, 169-70; this pledge was made on April 10, 1972. In a speech delivered on October 15, 1984, the Cardinal Archbishop of New York, John J. O'Connor, pledged that his Archdiocese would offer free and confidential care for "every single or married woman facing an unplanned pregnancy...whatever [her] religious affiliation."

burden for the abortion. Obviously, however, in this matter, as in any other, the existence, locus and degree of moral responsibility and guilt are not easily assessed or determined by external observers; I conclude only that abortions performed for socio-economic reasons are inappropriate and objectively wrong; but there may well be moral blame for these abortions, and that blame may belong to society as well as to any individual woman.

With regard to women who have been raped or been victimized by incestuous intercourse, I would suggest that they may and should seek medical treatment as soon as possible after the attack, but in contrast to the Catholic Church's traditional stance which prohibits treatment after several hours have passed, some theologians believe medical intervention should be allowed for a period up to three weeks at which time, should fertilization have occurred as a result of the attack, the individuality of the ovum would be established and personhood conferred. They say, however, that intervention from this point on would be morally unjustified.

Finally, some moralists suggest that in addition to those abortions identified traditionally as indirect, other so-called direct abortions may be morally justifiable in instances where a woman's life is in very clear and present danger due to a complicated pregnancy or one that is aggravating some other medical problem affecting her. But intended here are interventions which are judged medically necessary during the time preceding viability so that if the mother were to die, so too would the nonviable fetus she is carrying. It is suggested, therefore, that killing the fetus in these circumstances is a lesser evil than allowing both the mother and fetus to die. Of course, medical honesty and great caution must be exercised lest the danger or threat to the woman's life be overestimated and the decision to abort be premature or precipitate, and thus irresponsible. Once a fetus is viable, every effort should be made to preserve the lives of both the mother and the fetus, without prejudice, however, to the mother's right to receive the care and treatment judged appropriate and necessary for her specific medical problem even though such treatment may clearly endanger the life of the fetus.

A final observation is offered. Because any decision to abort, even in order to preserve the life of the mother, is a terribly hard, unfortunate and tragic one, and because they are not convinced that the heroic courage needed to maintain a pregnancy that is honestly judged life-threatening can be morally required of a woman, some moralists propose an admittedly extreme alternative to abortion, namely, sterilization. Speaking generally, these moralists suggest that in some instances a woman's voluntary decision to undergo sterilization may be an acceptable way to avoid having to face the prospect of seeking an undesired abortion during a subsequent pregnancy that would prove to be seriously dangerous.

Thus, it is said, a woman might morally request a sterilization in any of the following situations: (1) if it is medically indicated that a future pregnancy will be seriously problematic because the woman has a weakened and scarred uterus resulting from previous Caesarean sections; now the medical judgment is that another pregnancy will result in spontaneous abortion and severe hemorrhaging by the woman; (2) if a future pregnancy is judged as likely to pose a serious threat to the woman's life because she has a weakened heart or deteriorating kidneys; (3) or if a future pregnancy is ill-advised because it would expose the developing fetus itself to an increased risk of serious deformity because the woman must stay on medication to control either some chronic physical problem or an ongoing emotional or psychological instability; similarly, any future pregnancy might be counter-indicated if it is discovered that both prospective parents are carriers of a serious genetic disorder.

The long-standing and present teaching of the Catholic Church regarding sterilization is that such a procedure is permitted only for strictly therapeutic reasons, but not for contraceptive purposes. In other words, a woman's uterus or ovaries may be removed if they are themselves cancerous; likewise, the female or male gonads (ovaries and testes), although not cancerous themselves, might be removed or subjected to radiation in an effort to avoid or inhibit the spread or metastasis of certain forms of cancer. The Church rejects, however, any sterilization which clearly intends the suppression of fertility (contraception, whether temporary or permanent), either as an end in itself or as a means to another end, such as, for example, wanting to avoid the strain of a future pregnancy, given a woman's chronic cardiac or renal disease. Thus, with reference to the situations listed in the previous paragraph, the Church recognizes the morality of sterilization only in the instance involving the weakened and scarred uterus. The rationale used by the Church in this case is that, given its present condition, the uterus itself can now be regarded as a pathological organ since human organs must be understood in terms of their functions; in other words, since the primary function of the uterus is to carry a fetus or sustain a pregnancy, and since this uterus is now judged incapable of doing so, the uterus may therefore be viewed as a "functionally dangerously pathological organ." As such, the uterus may be removed (hysterectomy) or it may simply be left in place but "isolated" by means of tubal ligations.[59]

What some suggest, however, is that in the other situations presented above, a woman's decision to undergo sterilization in order to avoid the possibility of later yielding to the temptation to abort need not embody the moral malice which the Catholic Church usually associates with contraceptive sterilization. Indeed, moralist John Mahoney has argued that the sterilization which is condemned by the Church should be understood as any direct attack on a woman's ability to procreate in "the full sense of the term." And precisely in the full sense of the term, "procreation," which the Church sees as a basic purpose of sexuality and marriage, must mean not only the power of human conception, but also "the total process including conception, nidation, gestation and parturition culminating in the birth of a live child in human society."[60] Thus

[59]See Thomas J. O'Donnell, S.J., *Medicine and Christian Morality* (New York: Alba House, 1976), pp. 132-34.

[60]John Mahoney, *The Clergy Review*, 55 (1970), 180-93 at 189-90; also see *Theological Studies*, 31 (1970), 507-08, and Corrine Bayley and Richard McCormick, S.J., "Sterilization: The Dilemma of Catholic Hospitals," *America*, 143 (1980), 222-25.

sterilization is morally wrong when it intentionally and directly robs or deprives a woman of the power to conceive and carry a child, as well as to give birth to and educate that child.

But in reference to the situations presented above, it is being suggested that the woman has already lost the capacity to procreate in this full sense, or has had this capacity seriously diminished, and that, therefore, the force of the Church's moral objection against contraceptive sterilization is not suasive here. Moreover, sterilization in the situations described might be viewed as both life-saving and life-serving, and as an action which is clearly the lesser evil, given the life-threatening or life-damaging danger to either the woman or the fetus or to both which a future pregnancy would pose. Accordingly, there might seem to be simply more moral sense in the decision to allow sterilization in these circumstances than to insist that a woman either abstain completely from sexual intercourse or risk facing a future pregnancy when there is every likelihood that during this pregnancy the woman may well find herself inclined to the judgment that abortion is a lesser evil than the other alternatives confronting her. This position, of course, neither entails nor intends any moral support for the view that sterilization may be encouraged or sought as a way to escape sexual responsibility; nor does it in any way wish to nurture an irresponsible contraceptive mentality which is shaped simply by considerations of expediency and personal convenience, and thus refuses thoroughly to be held accountable for the actions it inspires.

IV. Abortion, Law and Public Policy

Daniel Maguire has made the observation that "abortion is always tragic, but the tragedy of abortion is not always immoral."[61] I agree with this sentiment, but I am also compelled to the view that in the vast majority of instances, the abortions being performed are indeed immoral as well as tragic.

[61]Daniel C. Maguire, "Abortion: A Question of Catholic Honesty," *The Christian Century,* 100, 26 (Sept. 14 -21, 1983), 805.

This judgment seems inescapable in light of the fact that conservative estimates indicate that at least 80% of the abortions being performed involve healthy women and healthy fetuses.

The judgment that abortions are generally immoral means that I view the deaths of the fetuses involved as objectively unjustified. The abortions being performed constitute, it seems to me, an instance of social injustice which is of gigantic proportions. The question thus necessarily arises as to the appropriate response in the face of such injustice. It seems utterly inadequate for people who believe that the rights of fetuses today are largely denied or ignored to say simply that they are personally opposed to abortion but that they can or will take no action to protect fetuses and guarantee their rights in the public, political or legal forums. But my disagreement with this stance does not mean that I am certain how best to safeguard the lives and rights of fetuses from unjust attack in our society. What I would like to offer here, however, are some thoughts which might serve as a general background against which to view this question, even if its answer remains open to debate.

To begin with, we see an undeniable nobility and truth in the sentiment that "one of the marks of a civilized society is the protection it affords to the poor, the defenseless, the unfortunate, those who cannot protect themselves."[62] And when a civilized society freely professes its belief in the God of the Judeo-Christian tradition, then its concern and care for those who are threatened, forgotten or abused, whether they be in the dawn of life, the twilight of life or the shadows of life, properly express fulfillment of a sacred obligation. With reference specifically to abortion and the protection of those in the dawn of life, the point at issue is whether this sacred obligation can best and most effectively be met through directly restrictive measures like the enactment of laws prohibiting all or most abortions, or

[62]Testimony of Victor G. Rosenblum, Hearings Before the Subcommittee on the Constitution of the Senate Judiciary Committee, U.S. Senate, 97th Congress, (Nov. 16, 1981); quoted by Mary C. Segers, "Can Congress Settle the Abortion Issue?," *The Hastings Center Report,* 12, 3 (June, 1982), 20-28 at 27, 28, n. 42.

in a more indirect manner by trying to change public opinion in such a way that it will respond more sensitively to the lives and values which have been put under siege in our current situation.

There are arguments on both sides of this issue. In support of more restrictive laws on abortion, one line of reasoning suggests that surely people who view fetuses as human beings have a right, even a duty, to work for laws that will win fetuses protection from deliberate personal injury, violence and oppression. It is simply a matter of good logic, common sense and social justice that these people should seek legal protection for fetuses individually and as a group, in exactly the same way and with the same conviction that they support laws to guarantee protection for the lives and rights of abused children and battered wives. Furthermore, in response to the counter-argument that in our pluralistic society there is not a sufficient public consensus at present which could succeed in sustaining any reversal of, or significant retrenchments on, the Supreme Court's abortion rulings, the observation by Rep. Henry J. Hyde, a Catholic congressman from Illinois, is well taken: "The duty of one who regards abortion as wrong is not to bemoan the absence of consensus against abortion, but to help lead the effort to achieve one." We must remember, he added, that "no consensus was demanded before adopting the Civil Rights Act of 1964 . . . proponents helped create a consensus by advocacy and example and by understanding that the law itself can be an excellent teacher."[63]

On this point, we should not forget, moreover, that the battle for consensus over civil rights had to be fought and eventually won against some people who still thought and felt — honestly, if they are to be believed — that black people were not fully human and therefore did not hold title to personal rights and those of full citizenship. But by means of the civil rights legislation that was passed, our nation declared that this view regarding black people, however sincere its adherents, should no longer simply be allowed to wreak its havoc, at least, not

[63]Rep. Hyde in a speech at Notre Dame, Sept. 24, 1984; quoted in *America*, 151, 9 (October 6, 1984), 176.

with impunity. Is the time perhaps not long past when we can continue simply to acquiesce to those lingering views which maintain either that a fetus is not a human person — at least from within two to three weeks following conception — or that the fetus, although truly human, does not deserve, and need not be accorded, the same respect and protection granted human life outside the womb?

On the other side of the issue, people who resist any attempt to restrict legalized abortions argue that they do so because they see a clear distinction between laws and morality. They express a deeply-felt and widely-shared conviction that not everything deemed "immoral" or "sinful" should be rendered "criminal" or "illegal." This is true and, therefore, although there are large and varying segments of our society which view divorce, adultery, gambling and consumption of alcoholic beverages as immoral, few would seriously consider it desirable, advisable, or even possible, to prohibit any of these activities simply by having them declared illegal and criminal. And yet, while none of these activities is in fact completely outlawed, there are legal regulations or implications surrounding most, if not all, of them. These regulations, moreover, seem designed to reflect the realization that people simply cannot engage in activities like these with impunity or total abandon, for such actions can bring hurt to those who engage in them and to others as well. Thus, for example, laws establish minimum-age requirements for legal gambling, those considered to be minors are forbidden to buy or use alcohol, and it is a crime for anyone to drive while under the influence of alcohol. Clearly, the right of self-expression is not absolute, and it certainly ceases when its exercise would deny or infringe upon the rights of others.

Another dimension of the opposition to curtailing abortions by constitutional amendment or by more restrictive legislation is linked to the fact that such political maneuvers are regarded as an "authoritarian shortcut to consensus and uniformity." Thus, the prohibition of abortions represents to some people "a despairing effort to compel those whom one cannot convince."[64]

---

[64]Maguire, *art. cit.*, 806.

In recognition of the pluralistic character of America, Mario
M. Cuomo, the Catholic governor of New York, recently called
his fellow Catholics to caution against any recourse to heavy-
handed and desperate legal restrictions on abortions: "The hard
truth is that abortion isn't a failure of government. No agency
or department of government forces women to have abortions,
but abortion goes on. Catholics, the statistics show, support the
right to abortion in equal proportion to the rest of the
population." This seems to put Catholics, the hierarchy and
others, in the position, said Cuomo, "of asking the government
to make criminal what we believe to be sinful because we
ourselves can't stop committing the sin. The failure here is not
Caesar's. This failure is our failure, the failure of the entire
People of God."[65]

Governor Cuomo went on to outline in a most helpful way
the point of controversy centering on the relationship between
one's moral convictions with respect to abortion and one's
subsequent political and social responsibilities in this regard. In
his heart and conscience, said Cuomo, he is in full agreement
with, and fully accepts, the official Catholic position on
abortion; but does this mean he must insist that everyone else
accept it? As a public official must he try to have the Church's
view and his imposed on others: "By law? By denying you
Medicaid funding? By a constitutional amendment? If so,
which one? Would that be the best way to avoid abortions or to
prevent them?" In trying to answer this question, the governor
first made note of the fact that with respect to the interplay
between our human and religious values and our public policy,
"there is no inflexible moral principle which determines what
our *political* conduct should be." Even the American bishops
do not insist that in our pluralistic society all of our human and
Christian values must be encased as the law of the land, and so
they "abide" the present civil laws, for example, regarding
divorce and the funding of contraceptive programs.[66]

---

[65]Governor Cuomo's remarks were made in a speech at the University of Notre
Dame on September 13, 1984; quoted by Charles M. Whelan, S.J., "Religious Belief
and Public Morality," *America*, 151, 8 (September 29, 1984), 159-63 at 161.

[66]*Ibid.*, 160.

The bishops act differently, however, when it comes to abortion, and this is understandable because abortion is unlike any of these other issues; it is literally a question of life and death. Cuomo fully admits the seriousness of the abortion issue, but he nonetheless maintains that, as Catholics, "while we owe our bishops' words respectful attention and careful consideration, the question whether to engage the political system in a struggle to have it adopt certain articles of our belief as part of public morality is not a matter of doctrine. It is a matter of prudential political judgment." I personally think that Governor Cuomo errs in seeing opposition to abortion as an expression or article, simply or even primarily, of religious belief; but this, I suggest, does not blunt the point of his remark that prudential political judgments must be made about any attempt to have one's values, however they are grounded, embodied as part of our public morality, for such an attempt may so fundamentally divide Americans "that it threatens our ability to function as a pluralistic community."[67] One sees, moreover, an example of political realism reflected in the very decision of the American bishops to support the Hatch Amendment once they realized that given today's social and political climate, there is no way for them to win an absolute ban on abortion. Thus although the bishops may regard abortion with almost total moral repugnance, they have come to judge that the best chance they have at present for winning fetuses some justice is to back Senator Hatch's constitutional amendment which "would leave discretion in Congress and the state legislatures as to which abortions, if any, to forbid or fund."[68]

In lending their support to the Hatch Amendment, the bishops are exercising a "prudential political judgment," which they have every right to do, but they can claim no special inspiration, no infallible insight, which brought them to their decision that this is the only, the best or the correct way to guarantee that fetal lives will be protected. Nor can the bishops require that Catholics or others agree with this decision of theirs

---

[67] *Ibid.*

[68] *Ibid.*, 161; the phraseology here is Fr. Whelan's, not Cuomo's.

on political strategies. And this, it seems, is the point that Governor Cuomo wishes to stress: he and many other people equally abhor the injustice being perpetrated against fetal life, but on the identification of practical strategies for achieving justice for fetuses, they part company from those seeking constitutional amendments, total banning of abortion or refusal of Medicaid funding for abortions. The rejection of these strategies has been variously argued: it is pointless to pass a law if there is no will to enforce it; or the law itself may be unenforceable or ineffective, and it may simply engender broader contempt or disrespect for law.

At this time I surely do not know what strategies would prove most successful in regaining recognition and protection of a fetus's fundamental right to life, but it does seem to me that all the people of good will who sincerely disagree in their analysis of the relative strengths and weaknesses of the various proposed strategies might advance in their search for justice were they to heed the plea of Oliver Cromwell: "I beseech you in the bowels of Christ, think it possible you may be mistaken." The pathway to truth may be circuitous, but an open mind, one that is free of prejudices, not values, serves as a fine guide.

There is, of course, no mistaking the moral challenge surrounding the issue of abortion. People who personally oppose abortion do so because they see it as an act of violence, an attack on a fetus's right to life, which is unjustified in all or most instances. Those who maintain this view but who, nonetheless, remain unconvinced about the prudence or ultimate effectiveness of the politico-legal strategies already suggested for gaining protection for fetuses, have the moral responsibility to search out, propose and support alternative strategies. Both justice and logical consistency require no less. There is a gap in the morality and logic of the statement: "I am personally opposed to abortion but I'm 'pro-choice' on the issue." I maintain that the attitude reflected in such a statement leaves something to be desired both morally and logically because opposition to abortion would seem necessarily to imply one's recognition of the values at stake: human lives are being taken, often squandered. Every human life ended unjustifiably constitutes a moral tragedy, and thus any opposition to abortion must involve some attempt to end or reduce the unjustified killing of fetuses. The question is how best to accomplish this, but the answer, as we have seen, is not beyond legitimate dispute.

My own inclination is to support those who argue that there is a need for tighter legal restrictions against abortion, but before going into any details regarding the nature of these restrictions, it might be helpful to ponder John Courtney Murray's observations on the nature and purpose of criminal law. The remarks date from 1960 and are rooted in St. Thomas Aquinas' understanding of law:

> The moral aspirations of law are minimal. Law seeks to establish and maintain only that minimum of actualized morality that is necessary for the healthy functioning of the social order.... It enforces only what is minimally acceptable, and in this sense socially necessary.... Therefore the law, mindful of its nature, is required to be tolerant of many evils that morality condemns.[69]

Within the context of this understanding of law, Murray then asks the following pertinent questions: "Is it prudent to undertake the enforcement of this or that [moral] stand, in view of the possibility of harmful effects in other areas of social life? Is the instrumentality of coercive law a good means for the eradication of this or that social vice? And, since a means is not a good means if it fails to work in most cases, what are the lessons of experience in the matter?"[70]

Father Murray's questions still stand tall, and they are not easily avoided by the people today who maintain that abortions should be legally curtailed; at the same time, however, many of these people are deeply convinced that the values denied by the mass recourse to abortion are of such fundamental significance that the force of the law must be employed in an effort to

[69]John C. Murray, S.J., *We Hold These Truths: Catholic Reflections on the American Proposition* (New York: Sheed and Ward, 1960), p. 166. See also Aquinas' *Summa Theologica*, I-II, Q.96, a. 2 and a. 3.

[70]*Ibid.*, pp. 166-67.

counteract the injustices being perpetrated. I share this conviction, but I do not know how the needed legislation should be formulated so as to have the desired effect of minimizing the number of unjustified fetal killings. This determination, it seems to me, requires legal expertise and sharp political analysis, for a law is no more noble than its ability to be implemented or enforced allows it to be.

This is the sentiment embodied in Richard McCormick's statement that law must look "not merely to the good, but to the good that is possible and feasible in a particular society at a particular time." And yet, this is not the whole story, for a system of laws should do more than merely mirror a society's present values and moral achievements; it should also challenge that society to become its better moral self. As McCormick puts it, the law, "while taking account of the possible and feasible at a particular time, must do so without simply settling for it. Simple accommodation to cultural 'realities' not only forfeits altogether the educative function of law, but also could leave an enormous number of people without legal protection."[71]

It is, of course, precisely the situation that fetuses have gone largely without legal protection since 1973 when the Supreme Court in a use of "raw judicial power" made its *Roe v. Wade* and *Doe v. Bolton* rulings which imposed the Court's "own poorly researched and shabbily reasoned moral values as the basis for the law of the land."[72] But any serious effort to correct by legislation the wrong done to fetuses would require, according to McCormick, that the law must "contain provisions that attack the problems that tempt to abortion;" judged by that criterion, "our mistake as a nation and that of many countries has been just that: to leave relatively untouched the societal conditions and circumstances that lead to abortion, and to legislate permissively, usually on the basis of transparently fragile slogans created by a variety of pressure groups."[73]

[71]Richard A. McCormick, S.J., "Moral Notes," *Theological Studies*, 35 (1974), 356.

[72]*Ibid.*, 358; also see McCormick, *Catholic Mind*, 52.

[73]*Ibid.*, 357.

Thus McCormick believes that abortion must be given more attention in the public forum because "to settle for the *status quo* is to settle for societal sickness."[74] As of 1979, McCormick has argued that Congress ought to take the initiative for new abortion legislation, since Congress is the place "where all of us, through our representatives, have a chance to share in the democratic process." In its attempt to formulate "a feasible protective law" for fetuses, Congress might well be guided, says McCormick, by the notion "that many people would agree that abortion is legally acceptable if the alternative is tragedy, unacceptable if the alternative is mere inconvenience."[75]

Concretely, Congress might then prohibit abortion except in the following circumstances: if the mother's life is at stake, if "there is a serious threat to her physical health and to the length of her life," or "if the pregnancy is due to rape or incest;" finally, with great hesitation because of the necessary ambiguity surrounding this stipulation, McCormick suggests that the law might permit abortion in situations where "fetal deformity is of such magnitude that life-supporting efforts would not be considered obligatory after birth." McCormick is quick to emphasize that he does not view these legal exceptions to the prohibition of abortion as morally right. Rather, he is listing these exceptions for two reasons: in recognition of the current situation in which many people maintain "that continuing the pregnancy in such circumstances is heroic and should not be mandated by law;" in addition, McCormick judges that "among the evils associated with any law, these seem to represent the lesser evil."[76]

A few comments on McCormick's proposal are in order. First, in light of his earlier warnings against a law's "simple accommodation to cultural 'realities'," we might indeed wonder if his listing of exceptions to a proposed law's general prohibition of abortion sufficiently urges the desired and needed "educative function of law." Secondly, I imagine that

[74]*Ibid.*, 359.
[75]McCormick, *Catholic Mind*, 52-3.
[76]*Ibid.*, 53.

McCormick himself would insist that any congressional legislation on abortion ought to include provisions designed to
curtail those societal wrongs, economic injustices and sexual
oppressions that in so many ways contribute to a woman's
decision to seek an abortion. Only in this way, I think, can we
move toward some kind of guarantee that the legal exemptions
allowing abortions under the specified circumstances will not
be invoked precipitously or prematurely. In other words, as I
would maintain, even the abortions which would be legally
permitted should be considered within the broader context of
the requirement that they constitute a "last resort." Finally,
however inadequately the proposed legislation may reflect my
own moral judgments about abortion, it must be evaluated in
terms of its intended effectiveness in protecting fetal life from
unjustified attack. I am of the opinion that the suggested bill,
assuming it can and would be implemented and enforced,
would signal a significant victory for fetuses by regaining for
them the respect and care which they deserve. I say this because
the abortions that are sought for the reasons and in the
circumstances identified by McCormick as suitable for legal
exemptions from the general prohibition of abortion do in fact
make up only a small fraction of all the abortions performed.
Thus, were only these legal abortions to occur, the lives of the
great majority of fetuses would be spared.

Others may argue, however, that fetuses will be helped little
by this or any such legislative fiat; to the extent that this may be
so, then I would urge, as I indicated earlier, the moral
imperative that other approaches to the problem be taken.
Surely, this is no time to suggest or settle for mere symbolic
gestures on behalf of fetuses. Everyone, including people in
public office, who is personally opposed to abortion must act
on the conviction that the injustice being inflicted upon fetuses
ought not to go unchallenged any longer. But it remains an
open question how best to secure real protection for fetuses.
This point was acknowledged recently in a statement issued by
Bishop James W. Malone, president of the United States
Catholic Conference, in the name of that group's administrative
board: "On questions such as these [prevention of nuclear war
and opposition to abortion], we realize that citizens and public

officials may agree with our moral arguments while disagreeing with us and among themselves on the most effective legal and policy remedies."[77]

In recognizing and publicly admitting this distinction between moral convictions and decisions of public policy, the bishops have taken a long-awaited step, and one that may spark the consciences of people claiming personal opposition to abortion to realize that, while there may be a variety of legal or political strategies for limiting abortions, any "pro-choice" stance on this issue is far too cavalier and far too insensitive to the need of fetuses for protection. At the very least, it seems, a way must be found to enlighten and sensitize public opinion to the human outrage that is being perpetrated by "abortion on demand," especially since this demand arises not so much out of necessity, but out of a desire for personal convenience.

Our society needs to be shaken out of its apparent delusion that the freedom of self-expression and the right to privacy are absolute; that the right of one person ends where the right of another begins, is a hard but necessary lesson to learn. Still, it would be wise for us to remember that resistance to "hard sayings" is not always selfish or deliberate. There is a world of difference between people who argue that, in principle, women have a right to abort at will, and the pregnant woman who desperately values the new life within her but who simply cannot find the interior strength and courage, which even she may desire, to see her child born.

I suggest that, in the long run, the lives of fetuses will not be saved or served by written laws alone. At most, perhaps, we may hope that laws more humane than those presently operating may serve as effective stop-gaps against the killing of fetuses until such time as our society is re-created with a new and more compassionate heart. The signs of a spiritually renewed and morally sensitive nation will be many: surely, a fetus's right to life will be cherished, but beyond this we will witness a society "where the right to life doesn't end at the moment of birth; where an infant isn't helped into a world that

[77]Bishop Malone's statement was given on October 13, 1984.

doesn't care if it's fed properly, housed decently, educated adequately; where the blind or retarded child isn't condemned to exist rather than empowered to live."[78]

In short, a society which is anxious to respond in a consistent manner to the Spirit of God, who wants what is best for his people, will take seriously the now-famous challenge laid down by Cardinal Joseph Bernardin that Christians and all people of good will must weave a "seamless garment" in their moral support for the values affecting human life. As a loving heart employs the hands of justice, so a society that favors life will resist the proliferation of nuclear arms, and it will find an alternative to capital punishment; it will spend itself, finally, in the effort to overcome the evils of racism, religious bigotry and the obvious political, economic or sexual oppressions that deny its citizens the liberty of body, mind and spirit which they own as the people of God.

V. Conclusion

As a society, we can take no pride in the fact that it is now estimated that each year approximately twenty-six percent of all pregnancies in America are being deliberately aborted. And something is terribly wrong in a nation in which abortion has become the most frequently performed surgical procedure. In the presence of such realities, I can only urge once again that any abortion which constitutes an unjustified attack upon the human life of a fetus must be morally resisted. At the same time, however, I appreciate the claim that sometimes the physical act of abortion does not bear the moral malice or evil usually associated with that action. And yet, the point which is most deserving of our emphasis in the forum of public discussion is that abortion ought to be seen for what it really is: a matter of human life and death. As such, the facts regarding abortion must be kept distinct from any romanticizing over the rights of

[78]Governor Cuomo's speech, *America*, 162.

sexual freedom or the liberties of a sexual revolution. Abortion is not a matter simply of sexuality, and it is not a form of contraception. Moreover, any clear exposition of abortion ought quickly to disentangle itself from the issues of women's rights and the right to privacy.

As a matter of life and death, abortion deserves a discussion that is carried on in the context of our deepest and richest Christian sensibilities. As Christians, we know that God has called us to labor in the creation of a world that struggles to be ever mindful of the dignity of human life and the respect which is its right. This is a labor which we are privileged to undertake and empowered to continue because we have been gifted with the Spirit of Christ who is the power and authority of God. Moreover, in and through Christ, God has offered us a share in his own power and authority over life and our earth, but in no way is our dominion complete or absolute. This means that we can and must expect that suffering will be a part of our human existence. Yet, if the truth be told, the prospect of suffering still has the power to confuse and mystify us, and perhaps nowhere than in the face of suffering are we more likely to be overpowered by our capacity for rationalization.

But at this point there is a valuable lesson to be learned from the life of Christ: suffering, and even death, can be accepted out of love; good can result from the voluntary surrender of power and the use of authority in the service of others. There is no reason, then, for Christians to be confined to the view that suffering is absurd, an evil to be avoided and resisted, no matter what the price. It is in the knowledge that suffering can be redemptive and can serve life, that women may find the strength to face the pain, anxiety and fear which must surely come with an unintended and unwanted pregnancy; from this same knowledge may also spring a woman's decision to face the risks of a difficult pregnancy rather than resort to abortion. But this is a knowledge that indeed astounds and confounds the wisdom of the world.

A Selected Bibliography

Chapter I
Morality and the Spirit of Christian Living

Abbott, Walter, S.J. (ed.). *The Documents of Vatican II.* New York: America Press, 1966.

Braaten, Carl E. *Eschatology and Ethics. Essays on the Theology and Ethics of the Kingdom of God.* Minneapolis: Augsburg Publishing House, 1974.

Cox, Harvey. *On Not Leaving It to the Snake.* New York: Macmillan Paperbacks, 1969.

Curran, Charles E. *A New Look at Christian Morality.* Notre Dame: Fides Publishers, 1968.

Evely, Louis. *Our Prayer. A New Approach to Everyday Prayer.* Garden City, N.Y.: Doubleday Image Books, 1974.

Gaffney, James. *Moral Questions.* New York: Paulist Press, 1974.

Gallagher, John, C.S.B. *The Basis for Christian Ethics.* New York: Paulist Press, 1985.

Genovesi, Vincent J., S.J. "Christian Poverty: Sign of Faith and Redemptive Force," *The Way*, Supplement 32 (1977), 78-82.

_____. *Expectant Creativity. The Action of Hope in Christian Ethics.* Lanham, Md.: University Press of America, 1982.

Gleason, Robert W., S.J. *Grace.* New York: Sheed & Ward, 1962.

Hanigan, James P. *As I Have Loved You. The Challenge of Christian Ethics.* New York: Paulist Press, 1986.

Häring, Bernard. *Morality Is For Persons. The Ethics of Christian Personalism.* New York: Farrar, Straus and Giroux, 1971.

Jonsen, Albert R. *Christian Decision and Action.* New York: The Bruce Publishing Co., 1970.

Keane, Philip S., S.S. *Christian Ethics and Imagination. A Theological Inquiry.* New York: Paulist Press, 1984.

Lewis, C.S. *The Four Loves.* New York: Harcourt Brace Jovanovich, Inc., 1960.

Luijpen, William A., O.S.A. *Existential Phenomenology.* Pittsburgh: Duquesne University Press, 1963.

Lyonnet, Stanislas, S.J. "St. Paul: Liberty and Law," in C. Luke Salm, F.S.C. (ed.), *Readings in Biblical Morality.* Englewood Cliffs, New Jersey: Prentice-Hall, Inc. 1967, pp. 61-83.

Milhaven, John G. *Toward a New Catholic Morality.* Garden City, N.Y.: Doubleday, 1970.

O'Connell, Timothy E. *Principles for a Catholic Morality.* New York: The Seabury Press, 1978.

Regan, George M., C.M. *New Trends in Moral Theology.* New York: Newman Press, 1971.

Rush, Vincent E. *The Responsible Christian. A Popular Guide for Moral Decision Making According to Classical Tradition.* Chicago: Loyola University Press, 1984.

Stevens, Edward. *Making Moral Decisions.* New York: Paulist Press, 1981 (rev. ed.).

_____. *The Morals Game.* New York: Paulist Press, 1974.

Watkin, Dom Aelred. *The Enemies of Love*. New York: Paulist Press, 1965

Chapter II
The Authority of the Magisterium and Individual Conscience

American Catholic Bishops, *Human Life in Our Day*. A Pastoral Letter. Washington, D.C.: United States Catholic Conference, 1968.

Dulles, Avery, S.J. *A Church to Believe In. Discipleship and the Dynamics of Freedom*. New York: The Crossroad Publ. Co., 1982.

Glaser, John W. "Conscience and Superego: A Key Distinction," *Theological Studies*, 32 (1971), 30-47.

Komonchak, Joseph A. "Ordinary Papal Magisterium and Religious Assent," in Charles E. Curran (ed.), *Contraception: Authority and Dissent*. New York: Herder & Herder, 1969, pp. 101-126.

Maguire, Daniel C. "Moral Absolutes and the Magisterium," in Charles E. Curran (ed.), *Absolutes in Moral Theology?* Washington, D.C.: Corpus Books, 1968, pp. 57-107.

McCormick, Richard A., S.J. "Authority and Morality," *America*, 142 (1980), 169-171.

_____. "Personal Conscience," *Chicago Studies*, 13 (1974), 241-252.

O'Connell, Timothy E. "Conscience," in *Principles for a Catholic Morality*. New York: The Seabury Press, 1978, pp. 83-97.

Sullivan, Francis A., S.J. *Magisterium. Teaching Authority in the Catholic Church*. New York: Paulist Press, 1983.

Chapter III
Human Sinfulness

Curran, Charles E. *Contemporary Problems in Moral Theology.* Notre Dame: Fides Publishers, 1970.

Glaser, John W. "Transition between Grace and Sin: Fresh Perspectives," *Theological Studies*, 29 (1968), 260-274.

Gula, Richard M., S.S. *To Walk Together Again. The Sacrament of Reconciliation.* New York: Paulist Press, 1984.

Häring, Bernard. *Sin in the Secular Age.* Garden City, N.Y.: Doubleday, 1974.

Maly, Eugene H. *Sin: Biblical Perspectives.* Dayton: Pflaum/Standards, 1973.

O'Donnell, John, S.J. "The Need to Confess," *America*, 144 (1981), 252-253.

Chapters IV & V
Morality and Human Sexuality

Bird, Joseph and Lois *The Freedom of Sexual Love.* Garden City, N.Y.: Doubleday Image, 1967.

Cahill, Lisa Sowle. *Between the Sexes. Foundations for a Christian Ethics of Sexuality.* Phila.: Fortress Press & New York: Paulist Press, 1985.

_____. "Teleology, Utilitarianism, and Christian Ethics," *Theological Studies*, 42 (1981), 601-629.

Dedek, John F. *Contemporary Sexual Morality.* Kansas City: Sheed Andrews and McMeel, 1971.

_____. "Premarital Sex: The Theological Argument from Peter Lombard to Durand," *Theological Studies*, 41 (1980), 643-667.

Fromm, Erich. *The Art of Loving.* New York: Bantam Books, 1963.

Goergen, Donald, O.P. *The Sexual Celibate.* New York: The Seabury Press, 1974.

Greeley, Andrew. *Sexual Intimacy.* Chicago: The Thomas More Association, 1973.

Hanigan, James P. *What Are They Saying About Sexual Morality?* New York: Paulist Press, 1982.

Häring, Bernard. *Free and Faithful in Christ.* Vol. 2 *The Truth Will Set You Free.* New York: The Seabury Press, 1979.

Hettlinger, Richard. *Sex Isn't That Simple. The New Sexuality on Campus.* New York: Seabury Press, 1974.

Keane, Philip S., S.S. *Sexual Morality. A Catholic Perspective.* New York: Paulist Press, 1977.

Kennedy, Eugene C. *The New Sexuality. Myths, Fables and Hang-Ups.* Garden City, N.Y.: Doubleday, 1972.

Kenny, Gregory (with Edward Wakin). "Sex and the Young Catholic," *U.S. Catholic/Jubilee,* XXXVI, 10 and 11 (1971), 7-13; 7-13.

Kosnik, Anthony *et. al. Human Sexuality. New Directions in American Catholic Thought.* New York: Paulist Press, 1977.

Liebard, Odile M. *Official Catholic Teachings.* Vol. 4 *Love and Sexuality.* Wilmington, North Carolina: McGrath Publ. Co., 1978.

McCormick, Richard A., S.J. *Health and Medicine in the Catholic Tradition.* New York: Crossroad, 1984.

Nelson, James B. *Embodiment. An Approach to Sexuality and Christian Theology.* Minneapolis: Augsburg Publishing House, 1978.

Pittenger, W. Norman. *Making Sexuality Human.* Philadelphia: Pilgrim Press, 1970.

Ramsey, Paul. "A Christian Approach to the Question of Sexual Relations Outside of Marriage," *The Journal of Religion,* 45 (1965), 100-118.

Sacred Congregation for the Doctrine of the Faith. *Declaration on Certain Questions Concerning Sexual Ethics*, 1975. Text can be found in Anthony Kosnik *et. al.*, *Human Sexuality*. New York: Paulist Press, 1977, pp. 299-316.

Chapter VI
Contraception and Marital Sexuality

Axe, Kevin H. "Sex and the Married Catholic," *U.S. Catholic*, 41 (1976), 6-11.

Benecke, Mary Beth. "Rhythm: Ideal and Reality," *America*, 137 (1977), 240-241.

Burtchaell, James T. "'Human Life' and Human Love," in Paul T. Jersild and Dale A. Johnson (eds.), *Moral Issues and Christian Response*. New York: Holt, Rinehart and Winston, Inc., 1971, pp. 139-147.

_____. (ed.). *Marriage Among Christians. A Curious Tradition*. Notre Dame: Ave Maria Press, 1977.

Farrelly, John, O.S.B. "The Principle of the Family Good," *Theological Studies*, 31 (1970), 262-274.

Ford, John C., S.J., and Grisez, Germain. "Contraception and the Infallibility of the Ordinary Magisterium," *Theological Studies*, 39 (1978), 258-312.

Hallett, Garth L., S.J. "Contraception and Prescriptive Infallibility," *Theological Studies*, 43 (1982), 629-650.

Hilgers, Thomas W., M.D. "The Ovulation Method: Ten Years of Research," *The Linacre Quarterly*, 45 (1978), 383-387.

Komonchak, Joseph A. "'Humanae Vitae' and Its Reception: Ecclesiological Reflections," *Theological Studies*, 39 (1978), 221-257.

Martinez, Elise B. "The Ovulation Method of Family Planning," *America*, 144 (1981), 277-279.

Noonan, John T., Jr. *Contraception: A History of Its Treatment by the Catholic Theologians and Canonists.* New York: Mentor-Omega Books, 1967.

_____. "Contraception and the Council," *Commonweal*, 83 (1966), 657-662.

Örsy, Ladislas, S.J. "Faith, Sacrament, Contract, and Christian Marriage: Disputed Questions," *Theological Studies*, 43 (1982), 379-398.

Quinn, Archbishop John R. "New Context for Contraception Teaching," *Origins: N.C. Documentary Service*, 10 (1980), 263-267.

Wright, John H., S.J. "An End to the Birth Control Controversy?," *America*, 144 (1981), 175-178.

_____. "The Birth Control Controversy, Continued," *America*, 145 (1981), 66-68.

Chapter VII
Homosexuality

American Catholic Bishops. *Principles to Guide Confessors in Questions of Homosexuality.* Washington, D.C.: United States Catholic Conference, 1973.

Barnhouse, Ruth T. "Homosexuality," *Anglican Theological Review,* 58 (1976), 107-34.

Bell, Alan P. and Weinberg, Martin S. *Homosexualities. A Study of Diversity Among Men and Women.* New York: Simon and Shuster, 1978.

Bell, Alan P., Weinberg, Martin S., and Hammersmith, Sue Kiefer. *Sexual Preference: Its Development in Men and Women.* Bloomington: Indiana Univ. Press, 1981.

Catholic Social Welfare Commission (a working Committee of the Catholic Bishops of England and Wales). *An Introduction to the Pastoral Care of Homosexual People.* Mt. Rainier, Md.: New Ways Ministry, 1981.

Curran, Charles E. "Dialogue with the Homophile Movement: The Morality of Homosexuality," in *Catholic Moral Theology in Dialogue*. Notre Dame: Fides Publishers, 1972, pp. 184-219.

_____. "Moral Theology and Homosexuality," in *Critical Concerns in Moral Theology*. Notre Dame: University of Notre Dame Press, 1984, pp. 73-98.

_____. "Moral Theology, Psychiatry and Homosexuality," in *Transition and Tradition in Moral Theology*. Notre Dame: Univ. of Notre Dame Press, pp. 59-80.

Furnish, Victor P. *The Moral Teaching of Paul*. Nashville: Abingdon, 1979.

Gallagher, John (ed.). *Homosexuality and the Magisterium. Documents from the Vatican and the U.S. Bishops, 1975-1985*. Mt. Rainier, Md.: New Ways Ministry, 1986.

Harvey, John F., O.S.F.S. "An In-Depth Review of *Homosexuality and the Christian Way of Life*," *The Linacre Quarterly*, 50 (1983), 122-143.

_____. "Homosexuality," *New Catholic Encyclopedia*. New York: McGraw Hill, 1967, Vol. 7, pp. 116-119.

_____. "The Controversy Concerning the Psychology and Morality of Homosexuality," *The American Ecclesiastical Review*, 167 (1973), 602-629.

Hays, Richard B. "Relations Natural and Unnatural: A Response to John Boswell's Exegesis of Romans 1," *The Journal of Religious Ethics,* 14, 1 (Spring, 1986), 184-215.

Kraft, William F. "Homosexuality and Religious Life," *Review for Religious*, 40 (1981), 370-381.

Malloy, Edward A. *Homosexuality and the Christian Way of Life*. Lanham, Md.: University Press of America, 1981.

McNeill, John J., S.J. *The Church and the Homosexual*. Kansas City: Sheed Andrews and McMeel, 1976.

Nugent, Robert (ed.). *A Challenge to Love. Gay and Lesbian Catholics in the Church*. New York: Crossroad Publ. Co., 1983.

Scanzoni, Letha and Mollenkott, Virginia Ramey. *Is the Homosexual My Neighbor? Another Christian View.* New York: Harper & Row, 1978.

Scroggs, Robin. *The New Testament and Homosexuality.* Philadelphia: Fortress Press, 1983.

Vacek, Edward C., S.J. "A Christian Homosexuality," *Commnonweal,* CVII (1981), 681-684.

Woods, Richard. *Another Kind of Love.* Garden City, N.Y.: Doubleday Image, 1978

Chapter VIII
Masturbation

Brockman, Norbert C., S.M. "Contemporary Attitudes on the Morality of Masturbation," *The American Ecclesiastical Review,* 166 (1972), 597-614

Häring, Bernard. "Human Sexuality: The Sixth and Ninth Commandments," *Chicago Studies,* 13 (1974), 301-312.

Tyrrell, Bernard J., S.J. *"The Sexual Celibate* and Masturbation," *Review for Religious,* 35 (1976), 399-408.

Chapter IX
Abortion

American Catholic Bishops. *Ethical and Religious Directives for Catholic Health Facilities.* Washington, D.C.: U.S. Catholic Conference, 1971.

Connery, John R., S.J. "Abortion and the Duty to Preserve Life," *Theological Studies,* 40 (1979), 318-333.

Curran, Charles E. "Abortion: Its Legal and Moral Aspects in Catholic Theology," in *New Perspectives in Moral Theology.* Notre Dame: Fides Publishers, 1974, pp. 163-193.

Diamond, James J., M.D. "Abortion, Animation, and Biological Hominization," *Theological Studies*, 36 (1975), 305-324.

Donceel, Joseph F., S.J. "Catholic Politicians and Abortion," *America*, 152 (1985), 81-83.

_____. "Immediate Animation and Delayed Hominization," *Theological Studies*, 31 (1970), 76-105.

_____. "Why Is Abortion Wrong?," *America*, 133 (1975), 65-67.

Häring, Bernard. *Medical Ethics*. Notre Dame: Fides Publishers, 1973.

_____. "New Dimensions of Responsible Parenthood," *Theological Studies*, 37 (1976), 120-132.

Hellegers, Andre E. "Fetal Development," *Theological Studies*, 31 (1970), 3-9.

Mangan, Joseph T., S.J. "The Wonder of Myself: Ethical-Theological Aspects of Direct Abortion," *Theological Studies*, 31 (1970), 125-148.

McCormick, Richard A., S.J. "Abortion: A Changing Morality and Policy?," *Catholic Mind*, LXXVII (1979), 42-59.

_____. "Abortion: Aspects of the Moral Question," *America*, 117 (1967), 716-719.

_____. *"Notes on Moral Theology: Abortion Dossier,"* *Theological Studies*, 35 (1974), 312-359.

O'Donnell, Thomas J., S.J. *Medicine and Christian Morality*. New York: Alba House, 1976.

Sacred Congregation for the Doctrine of the Faith. *Declaration on Abortion*. Washington, D.C.: U.S. Catholic Conference, 1975.

Tauer, Carol A. "The Tradition of Probabilism and the Moral Status of the Early Embryo," *Theological Studies*, 45 (1984), 3-33.

Whelan, Charles M., S.J. "Religious Belief and Public Morality," *America*, 151 (1984), 159-163.

Index of Names and Authors

Annas, George J., 367nn. 41, 42
Aquinas, St. Thomas, 63-64, 67, 78n, 93,
    94, 122, 125-126, 136, 168-170,
    276-277, 334-337, 339, 341, 393
Aristotle, 136, 334-335
Ashley, Benedict M., 232n. 45, 344n. 18,
    346n 21
Augustine of Hippo, 57, 135, 190
Axe, Kevin H., 145-146, 326n

Bailey, D. Sherwin, 265n. 38
Barnhouse, Ruth T., 280-282
Baum, Gregory, 284n
Bayley, Corrine, 385n. 60
Beach, Frank A., 325n. 48
Bell, Alan P., 258n. 26, 260, 292-293
Benecke, Mary Beth, 232n. 47
Bernardin, Cardinal Joseph L., 398
Billings, John and Evelyn, 229
Bird, Joseph and Lois, 242n. 60
Bleistein, R., 315n. 31
Blye, Richard P., 346n. 20
Böckle, Franz, 110
Boethius, 341
Braaten, Carl, 48n
Breuning, Klaus, 148n. 27, 315n. 31
Brockman, Norbert C., 309-310, 318n
Burtchaell, James T., 156, 160, 208-210

Cahill, Lisa Sowle, 180n, 261, 265n. 39,
    284-286
Callahan ,Daniel, 368
Carey, Art, 152n
Cavanagh, John R., 209n. 23
Cavanagh, Michael, 326
Chirico, Peter, 82n. 10
Connery, John R., 355-357

Cox, Harvey, 46n, 149-150
Cromwell, Oliver, 392
Cuomo, Gov. Mario M., 390-392, 398n
Curran, Charles E., 25n, 58n, 76n, 86,
    111nn, 115n. 15, 123, 137-139, 176,
    209n. 23, 274, 289-290, 291n, 297n.
    88, 314-315, 332n, 341n, 351n,
    355n, 359, 361, 362, 363-365
Czerny, Michael, 35n. 14

Davis, Charles, 124n. 23
Dedek, John F., 154, 168n.9, 170, 307n.
    16, 308n. 17, 309n. 19, 314-315,
    322n. 43, 345n. 19
Dewart, Leslie, 71n. 38
Diamond, James J., 340n. 13, 342n
Donceed, Joseph F., 333n, 334n, 335,
    340
Donovan, Michael A., 300n, 321nn
Dulles, Avery, 78n, 82, 84

Evely, Louis, 27n. 1, 54n

Farrelly, John, 217n. 35
Fitzmyer, Joseph A., 115
Ford, John C., 235-237
Freud, Sigmund, 94, 96, 256, 303
Fromm, Erich, 151, 153
Furnish, Victor P., 263-265, 270n. 272n

Gaffney, James, 27, 37-38, 154-155, 160
Gallagher, John, 251n. 14
Glaser, John W., 95-96, 111n. 9, 113n
Gleason, Robert, 57n
Goergen, Donald, 143n. 13, 144, 147-
    148, 167, 304-307, 325
Goldbrunner, Josef, 133
Greeley, Andrew, 135n. 145

410

Index of Subjects